Broken

Sandi Gamble

First published in Australia by Ambitions Publishing
Copyright © Sandi Gamble 2013

The right of Sandi Gamble to be identified as the author of this work has been asserted in accordance with the *Copyright, Designs and Patents Act 1988*.

All rights reserved. No part of this publication may be reproduced, stored in a retrieval system, or transmitted in any form or by any means, electronic, mechanical, photocopying, recording or otherwise, without the prior written permission of the publisher.

Copyedited by Wendy Millgate (www.wendyandwords.com)
Cover photograph by Sanja Gjenero
Book cover design and typesetting by BookCoverCafe.com

Cataloguing-in-Publication entry:
A catalogue record for this book is available from the National Library of Australia.

Cataloguing-in-Publication entry:
Broken / Sandi Gamble
362.76092

Broken: An Extraordinary Story of Survival by One of Australia's Forgotten Children
Gamble, Sandi

ISBN: 978-0-9922846-6-4 (pbk)
ISBN: 978-0-9922846-2-6 (e-bk)

*To my beloved husband Shaun, my hero,
my strength, and my rock. Without you in my life
I would not have made it. I could not do any of the
things that I do without your support.
You truly are the man of my dreams.
You have made all my cherished wishes come true,
and I thank you from the very depths
of my heart and soul.
When I first met you, I knew you were the one
I had been looking for my whole life—
and I've been grateful every day since.*

"The most beautiful people we have known are those
who have known defeat, known suffering, known
struggle, known loss, and have found their way out
of the depths. These persons have an appreciation,
sensitivity, and an understanding of life that
fills them with compassion, gentleness,
and a deep loving concern.
Beautiful people do not just happen."

Elizabeth Kubler Ross

Acknowledgements

To Mom. Even though my life as a child living with you was hell at times, I don't regret a minute of it. It was during the tough times that I learned the most about you—your hurts, your deepest emotions, and … your courage. In the end, what you left me with was the courage and determination to fight for what I believe to be right and to do it with dignity, and to keep moving forward in life, no matter what the odds and how little you have to work with. For that fighting spirit, I can only thank you, Mom. I miss you.

To my husband Shaun, I cannot thank you enough for your devotion, love, understanding, patience, and perseverance without which I would not have been able to complete my story. Thank you for the endless cuddles and the continual supply of tissues. I am grateful that you are in my life.

To my children, thanks for sticking in there with me through the tough times and the good times. I know your life has been bumpy because you did not come with a care tag on your bums. But after you know my story, I think you will understand me more and maybe understand the reasons why. I love you all—you are my world.

To Wendy my editor, well, what can I say? What a road we have travelled together. I thank the day that you agreed to take me on and work with me. Your patience is beyond extraordinary; your nature is nothing short of beautiful. I know I could not have done this without you. You have been the solid foundation that has allowed me to express myself in ways I never thought possible. As I have stated to you many times over, even if I never sell a copy of this book, I must thank you in particular for being instrumental in making me face the demons that lived within me. The cost was worth the therapy. Without your constant "where are your feelings?" I would never have been able to reach down within me and pull them to the surface so they could heal. Thank you. A new me has emerged, and I have you in part to thank for that.

To Anthony Puttee and Penny Springthorpe at Book Cover Cafe for project management, graphic design and typesetting. Thank you both for your patience and great work in helping me get my manuscript to the publishing stage. I couldn't have done it without you.

To my Divas, my sisters. Thank you very much for your continual support and love and virtual smacks in the head when needed. Your belief kept me going. You are all very much an ingrained part of my life and will forever hold a very special place in my heart, especially you, the only Mother of the Sisterhood.

To my "Soul Essence" sisters from around the world. You have kept me grounded. When I have needed refuge from the storm of life, you have always been there for me. Thank you.

My "Why"

"It has been said, *time heals all wounds*. I do not agree.
The wounds remain. In time, the mind, protecting its
sanity, covers them with scar tissue and the
pain lessens. But it is never gone."
Rose Kennedy

I HAVE BEEN WRITING my book now for well over twenty years. I first started the day my father died. I was so angry with him that my anger spread out like bacteria all over the pages, until finally I had downloaded it from my mind and my psyche. The disk that stored my first attempt was destroyed when our house flooded. They say everything happens for a reason.

This is my second attempt, written from a different place and for a different purpose. Who am I?

Well, for many years I struggled with that question until about four years ago when I learned that I was, for lack of better words, a *Forgotten Australian*. This title belongs to half a million children raised in institutions, orphanages, and foster care in Australia throughout the last century. That also includes about 7,000 child migrants from England.

Forgotten Australians like me are children who survived the physical and emotional abuse, atrocities, horrors, and sexual abuse within children's homes in Australia during the 1900s. These institutions were run by the government and private entities such as religious organizations and other not-for-profit associations. But Forgotten Australians are mostly a generation of misunderstood adults bearing scars that nobody can truly understand or see. It's amazing how a human being can be made to feel so insignificant by the actions and words of others.

I remember the day, the moment, I first realized with a shock that I was a Forgotten Australian. It was the 16th of November, 2009, and the Prime Minister of the day, the Hon. Mr. Kevin Rudd MP, was giving a formal apology to Forgotten Australians at Parliament House.

I was at work and had just gone on a coffee break. Standing in the kitchen after having made myself a lovely cup of tea, I heard Mr. Rudd's words coming from the television in the lunch room. He spoke about children who were kept in homes and orphanages in the early parts of the last century, up to and including the 1970s. My mind and heart immediately registered that he was talking about *me*.

I nearly dropped my cup and tears fell unexpectedly down my face as I stood, mesmerized, listening to him apologize for the abuse that we had suffered and were forced to endure all those years ago. I looked around the tea room, afraid that someone would see me crying and realize that I too had been kept in an orphanage the same as those who were seated in front of Mr. Rudd. In fact, I was to discover that some of my dearest friends from the convent were actually there. Fear swept over my body, but still I stood fixated on that screen, taking in every word that Mr. Rudd said. Flashbacks of abuse inflicted upon me came in waves; it's funny how your memories can be triggered by something so simple.

Until that moment, it had never actually dawned on me that I had been abused as a child. I knew that my childhood had not been a bed of roses and that not all kids had experienced the kind of life that I had, but I guess I just wanted to keep my head in the sand a little longer. But no more—at that very moment the floodgates opened.

In fact, my emotions from this day spiraled inwards and downwards, to a deep, deep, dark crypt within me that was far from empty. Emotions, memories, and pain from my life resurfaced, one by one, screaming at me to deal with them. My head was definitely coming out of the sand. But I couldn't deal with it all—I didn't know how to.

You have to remember that I hadn't even thought I had been abused—I couldn't recognize it. How does one go from having their head in the sand to siphoning through all of the events in their life to find inner peace? I knew what had happened to me was wrong, but it had been so deeply buried that

I had figured it was safer to leave it, where it had always been and not deal with it. I had no idea that the longer it remained buried the more it would fester, until finally it would overwhelm me and take me to the pits of hell.

You are going to read my story and wonder how the hell I didn't know that I was an abused child. Did I abuse my own children in the same way because of my ignorance? No, all of my children were loved and protected within an inch of their lives, as much as I had control over, anyway. My failing as a parent was wrapping my children in so much cotton wool I stifled their growth. So, my subconscious mind knew I was abused, but admitting that to myself was something else.

I contacted my doctor as once again I felt myself falling into a deep depression, something I have suffered with my whole life. My doctor put me onto another course of anti-depressants and referred me to a counselor. I had seen numerous counselors, psychologists, and psychiatrists in my past, but to no avail. None of them had been able to help me. They may have been able to; but I never went back after the first appointment. I found talking about myself in any real depth confronting, so I usually clammed up and the sessions would never go anywhere. I knew there was a reason why I was depressed, but I put it down to everyday stresses like children, work, and finances. I thought I was just a "non-coper"—a bit soft and foolish. But this time, I finally knew there was more to it

It was when one of my convent friends caught up with me, through social media, that everything started to fall into place. She gave me the name of an organization, CLAN (Care Leavers Australia Network), and advised me that they could help me to work through how I was feeling. I went home and didn't contact them for a while; I procrastinated. However, she called me one night and told me that CLAN was celebrating their tenth anniversary in Sydney that weekend and asked if I would like to attend. I did. I became a member of CLAN.

It dawned on me at one point during that weekend why I had always felt like the square peg trying to fit into the round hole. Except for a very few in my life, not many people had time for me, often passing me over as a fool or just someone to gossip about, or ridicule. I never shared tales of my daily life with those around me, preferring not to join in most times while they complained about their lot in life. You see, I had nothing to complain about. I finally had the man of my dreams, a beautiful home, and brilliant children. I appreciated these things more than anything else in my life, as best as I could do, anyway.

But there was clearly still something wrong, and I couldn't put my finger on it.

I had always felt that I lacked in social skills because I just wasn't like the other women around me. You know the type that has the penchant for gossip, for wanting to belong, for feeling that they have to be someone else to be accepted. You see them heading to the toilet at night clubs in pairs. Yes, that sort of female. Well, I was never one of those. It seems I was taught a very different range of social skills, like being grateful for the small things because at least you have something, and to work hard and not complain as that's just the way it is. Not to want anything because chances are you will not get it. And lastly to respect my elders regardless of how they treat you in return.

My parenting skills ... Well, they've always been raw, sometimes tough, and at times incorrect—but never abusive. My sons remember me as a great parent; my daughter sees me as an ogre. I was a person who yelled a lot, but I was never belittling. It was my way of coping, and all I knew how to be. I had no good role models to guide me. My people of influence had taught me significantly different things to the norm.

And my relationship skills! ... Hmmm, let's just say Shaun my husband took on a lot when he asked me to marry him. Thank heavens he is a patient and loving man.

So, back to the weekend in Sydney...

It was busy, with guest speakers, counselors, and CLAN members. For the first time in my life, I walked into a room with over one hundred people in attendance and I felt I *belonged.*

I was home.

Tears immediately welled up along the rims of my eyes. I tried to blink them away as I looked around at those who still to this day sleep on the streets, live in poor conditions, and have extremely poor physical and mental health. It didn't matter where they came from; every single person in that room was emotionally the same. We were systemized, dependent, and cynical. None of us really knew who *we* were, though being recognized as a group—"Forgotten Australians"—was finally going to help shed some light on who we were, on understanding ourselves, with the help of professionals who had been made available to do just that. In so doing, we would have the comfort of knowing for the first time in our lives that we were not alone. It felt good to be around like-minded people for once. I finally felt understood, accepted.

The Royal Commission into Sexual Abuse that has just been announced in Australia may help to highlight this forgotten generation, and, with this new awareness, put the onus back on to those who were responsible for the often long and lasting abuses that occurred in institutionalized care and its endless after-effects for the victims, us.

CLAN have been instrumental in their lobbying of the Australian Government for the recognition of Forgotten Australians and continue to lobby for compensation and recognition of other crimes against children.

I was able to walk away from that week-end and say to my husband that I could finally forgive myself—and that was big. I realized that for many of my actions right up until that weekend, I did not have only myself to blame. I was not solely responsible; my actions were the result of ingrained patterns and damage from an abusive and systemized childhood/adulthood. This is something that nobody could ever understand unless they had lived through it.

One piece of excellent advice that was offered that weekend was to go home and start writing. *Write about all your hurts, all your memories. Put them down on paper. Express your thoughts unhindered, and let the process be healthy and cathartic.* Sadly, some people who shared in my life did not like that I was able to finally take stock of my situation and let my healing begin, in baby steps. They didn't really want to know and so walked away. It's a shame really because a new better me has emerged.

Nevertheless, that sounded good to me, and that is where this second attempt at writing my story started. To say I have struggled to write about my life is an understatement. It has been painful, emotional, and one of the hardest things I have ever had to do. As I read back over my story for editing purposes, even I find it hard to believe that I survived as well as I did. I began to see my own resilience and maturity—my strengths. After years of self-accusation, writing my story has allowed me to heal and forgive firstly myself, and then others. I now have an inner peace that has always escaped me. Everybody should feel worthy of this type of peace. I have no malice or hatred towards anyone who has been in my life. If they had or have issues with me, that is their journey and is not for me to worry about. I have lived mine and made peace with it.

Nobody can understand the torment and anguish that a Forgotten Australian goes through on a daily basis, except another Forgotten Australian. One member of my family said to me, "But you weren't forgotten." I had two sets of grandparents and numerous aunties and uncles, one uncle who had even offered to take me. But there I was in an orphanage, deprived of all the normal daily requirements that a young child needs—love, care, and understanding. I wonder how that family member may have coped if it was them placed in that orphanage instead of me?

I have pondered why I would want to write about my life, share my story with everyone, and put myself out there to be possibly ridiculed and scrutinized—the thought undeniably sickens me. In fact, when I think about it, there are skeletons in my closet that some may think should never see the light of day. However, I just hope that my story might help save someone else out there who thinks that they've had enough. I hope that I can keep one child from having a life similar to my own by allowing adults to have a glimpse at what I went through—because it was adults who turned a blind eye to what was happening to me. If only one of them came forward and questioned what was happening, my life may have been an awful lot different. I don't claim to have had the worst life, far from it. There are others out there who have had it much worse.

I have learnt a lot of lessons along the way while writing my journey. A few years ago I learnt that not everybody sees things the same. In fact, even more recently, I have been shocked to learn that two people can travel the exact path and at the end of that path they can see an entirely different story to the other, based on their perception of events. Isn't it a wondrous world that we can have different points of view?

So this story is about *my* life, as it happened to me, as I saw it. Some names have had to be changed for legal reasons and to respect those who do not wish to be identified, although to soften the words or modify the content would, to me, feel like I was lying—something that I can't in good conscience do. That would make this a book of fiction, and it is definitely not fiction. This book is therefore extremely explicit in places, and I make no apologies for the content. This is my life I'm writing about, and for me it was a full-on, multi-sensory, explicit experience.

The first thing you need to know is that my birth name was Beverley Forster. At some point in my journey, to symbolize a new beginning, I changed my name to Sandi. In fact, it was the day I divorced my first husband. I simply could not bear his name for another minute.

Yeah, I had it tough, but so did a lot of people in my age group. I know of at least 500,000 others who will either relate to my story as they have experienced similar, or the same, themselves. I am not the only child who has ever been left behind or forgotten about; I am one of many. However, I am now willing to become a voice for those who are incapable of speaking out, who are no longer able, or who have chosen not to speak out because of their undeserved shame. There is often a stigma attached to having lived a life the same as the one you are about to read, although there shouldn't be. We were not responsible for what happened to us—we were children.

Never would I have believed that events from my childhood would impact so heavily on my adult life. Never would I have believed that the demons of my mother and father would stay with me for so long. Sadly, as the case will be for so many children who grow up these days, their lives will be torn apart by deceit, innuendo, adult insecurities, and society's laws. It is a shame that, unless the cycles are broken, these children will probably pass those same insecurities along to the next generation, and so on. I hope that through reading my book, some who have been through a similar life as mine will be able to deal with their long-held insecurities and pain, to heal, and hopefully not pass down as much trauma to the next generation…

The purpose of this book is not to instill a victim mentality in those of you who have been on a similar path to mine—it is to empower you. I want to share my story with those of you who just might be going through something similar to me, or have gone through it, so you too can believe there is a way to break out of the darkness, a way to free yourself from the ingrained patterns. A way to find who you truly are, to break the bonds of the past, and to start afresh. You can actually win. Yes, you may have to look back, painfully, like I did, but when you do, please know that the game of life is winnable and there is still good in the world. Hopefully, my book will show you that. There truly is good—believe it! You just have to have faith in yourself and keep putting yourself out there, to experience what life offers. The tough lessons I've learned through often horrible circumstances of life haven't stopped me from still giving of myself, and it doesn't have to for you either.

One of my favorite verses simply says:

"You are not responsible for the negative programming you picked up in childhood. However, as an adult you are one hundred percent responsible for fixing it." Ken Keys Jnr

The title of my book is *Broken*. But by the end of the book, you will know that I took responsibility for *fixing* myself and entering *life* again as a new me, solid in my identity.

LIFE! Enjoy the beauty, experience the magic, and drink it in. Remember you are loveable and deserve love!

I present to you, the story of Beverley Forster…

> *"A child's life is like a piece of paper on which every passer-by leaves a mark."*
> Chinese proverb

Prologue

"Bev, was it really all *that* bad?" my elderly, beloved aunt is asking me while I'm visiting her in Melbourne. The topic of my childhood has come up. *Did she see the Prime Minister on television apologizing to Forgotten Australians? Did she realize that I was one, and what that meant?*

I have only just found out myself through the TV during my morning tea at work that I was a Forgotten Australian. It explained a lot, and since then I'm starting to remember a hell of a lot. It's all starting to come out, like sores from a deep, deep wound. But right now I say nothing about all that to her. I just scream so loud inside my own head that I am surprised she doesn't hear it: IF YOU ONLY KNEW! I'm feeling ANGRY, but I don't show it. I know better.

Can I say, "Nah, not so bad, Aunty. All in a day's work. I'm an Aussie—I can take the knocks. Let's see, my childhood … hmmmmm. Sexual assault and abuse, emotional abuse, physical abuse, being abandoned and kicked out, torment and torture, hunger (jeez I was hungry), poverty, neglect, slave labor (for the redemption of my sins) … and oh, yes, the suicide attempts … and then after all that, the guilt trips, feeling like shit, disease and illness…"?

Nah, say nothing. I don't like hurting people's feelings, never have. And I don't want her to feel guilty. How can I tell her that her sister, my mother, had treated me so disgracefully, that I am lucky I even survived my childhood? No, I can't tell my aunty the whole story—I would be too embarrassed and she would be upset beyond words. So I just nod and brush the comment aside.

"So, how have you been, Aunty?"

What's the use of dredging up the past? I think that some things are best left buried when it comes to your elders. They've got to be respected, and no respectful woman would want to hear all that!

I am to find out later that that particular aunty is the one who actually paid for me to be in that orphanage all those years ago, separating me from the only life I had known and the only family I had. I don't know who suggested that I be put there though. Funny that … In an orphanage when somewhere out there I had two parents, grandparents, and family that cared and might have taken me. You see, when I was admitted to the convent I had the title of "boarder", but that title did not protect me. I was a number not a person. Just another troublemaker the nuns had to supposedly "care" for. *Was my aunt hoping that it wasn't that bad to ease her conscience?*

Back home, things are stirring inside me. *Stuff it! I'm going to tell how bad it really was!* I pull out the manuscript that I had begun writing three years earlier. My manuscript that shares the secrets—family secrets that the family didn't even know about! The secrets of the Catholic orphanage as well. I suppose I should have some form of gratitude for the care my aunty believed I was receiving in that place, but I can't find it in my heart to be thankful at all for the experiences—it was at times brutal and overall de-humanizing. I suppose she wasn't to know, as we were not allowed to tell! But guess what? *I'm gonna tell!* Thank you, Prime Minister Rudd, for helping me to realize who I am and that I have a voice.

1
Daddy's Little Girl

> "Attention, this is a public service announcement. Allan Forster, you are now the father of a brand new little girl. Both wife and daughter are doing well … Now back to the race …"

LIKE SO MANY OTHERS, I was born during the baby boomer years, in Sydney, Australia—in 1956 to be exact. I don't know if it was a sunny day or a rainy day. My mother went into labor and my father dropped her at the Crown Street Maternity Hospital on his way to the horse races at Rosehill Racecourse, as one's father did back then. No, oh sorry! I "thought" that was the way it normally was. In fact, he often recalled that I was born on the second leg of the daily double, as my birth was announced over the loud speaker at the races just after the winner was announced—solely for my father's information as a public service announcement.

"Attention, this is a public service announcement. Allan Forster, you are now the father of a brand new little girl. Both wife and daughter are doing well … Now back to the race …"

And no, he didn't win the double that day. He was a compulsive gambler, who would eventually take my family to ruin. My father Allan, to his favor, was a warm, charismatic, optimistic, and funny man. To his detriment he had *Post-Traumatic Stress Disorder* (PTSD) and everything that comes along with it. Plus he was a womanizer.

His PTSD was caused by many years at war with the Japanese in the Pacific, where he served as a gunnery sailor on HMAS *Australia*, affectionately called *The Aussie*. He saw and experienced many things during those years that would make even the most hardened of war veterans troubled. Like on the twenty-first of March, 1944, when a Japanese kamikaze hit his ship, engulfing the bridge above him in flames and killing his favorite captain, Captain Emile Dechaineux. I'm not sure if Dad liked to drink before the war, but I know that he drank after it. They didn't recognize PTSD back then. When the men were to return home from the war, families were told that they had been through an awful lot and it was better not to talk to them about it.

I was born at 4 p.m. on a Saturday in October, a Libran baby to a beautiful mother, Joy—Mom. Joy came from a medium-sized family who were then living in the suburbs of Melbourne. Her father's side originally came from the Ballarat area in Victoria before moving on to the Mallee region, an area of farming families. On her mother's side, it was Castlemaine, Victoria, after her family had emigrated from Ireland. Joy had a limited education because she left school early to assist her family financially.

The wars and the following post-war depression saw my grandmother struggle to raise her children. She had limited funds due to the early and untimely death of my grandfather. The gasses used in World War I, where he served as a soldier, contributed to his death later on in life. There is always a rhyme and reason for people's emotions, feelings, and actions, and perhaps this explains my grandmother's. She did it tough both during the war and after; she was made from real tough stuff.

Mom worked as a weaver in a weaving mill, looking after eight looms at any given time. She worked long and hard even after she met my father. She also joined the Women's Land Army to assist with the war effort, working on farms and so on—work traditionally reserved for the men who were away serving in the war.

She never complained about her lot as a youngster. It was something she did because she had to, and she always said they were the good times. The only regret she ever expressed to me was the fact that she never got to finish school, so she could not write well.

My mother was the second youngest of a family of four—three girls and one boy. She was a strong swimmer, one of her only leisure activities, and was a villain on a motor bike. She once won a small trophy for her swimming efforts, which she treasured until the day she died. She also won the attention of the local police on her motorbike on occasion, much to my grandfather's dismay, as he was one of the local constabulary after the war.

I can see my own need for acceptance in her. I was not afforded the tenderness I craved from my grandmother, neither was my mother. I was my mother's daughter.

It appeared to all that Joy and Allan were terribly in love when I was born. Or were they? They had met, fallen in love, and married some thirteen years before. They were not young when they married, not by the standards set in those days. They were both in their early twenties, and Mom was four years older than Dad. They married during the war, and shortly afterwards Dad was deployed to the Pacific to fight the Japanese. Not long after that my sister Robyn was born.

A couple of years later, and shortly before Dad's discharge from the Navy, my older brother Daniel was born—another post-war baby conceived on furlough. With him they had their perfect pigeon pair, as a boy and girl were often called. Mom and Dad were delighted and proud that they had a son and a daughter, the perfect family.

They wanted for nothing else but a home of their own. When the war was over and Dad returned, they set up their first home together in Melbourne, not far from Mom's parents.

My brother Daniel's life was anything but perfect, and because he is older than me he was able to relate to much more. But my sister Robyn, being the eldest, remembers much better than both of us—well, she remembers what happened while she lived with us. There is much she missed after she left home at seventeen. Robyn often talks about the wonderful life that she had as a young child, something I can't relate to at all. My brother has shared few memories with me about anything in his life. Let's just say that the years I remember with him, were not kind to him.

I know remarkably little about my father's family. I understand from various sources, including my mother, that they were from "good stock", meaning that they were paying passengers of the First Fleet, not convicts. From what I know, I have no English convict relations on either side of my family. They were a Parramatta family of some wealth and owned a fairly large portion of land along the old Great Western Highway—if you lived there these days you'd be more lovingly known as a "Westy", and I know that would be quite distasteful to my grandfather, who once corrected one of my letters, sending it back to me to point out that they were not a bunch of "yous" in Sydney—he marked it 6/10 for effort.

Dad was the youngest in a family of eight children—five boys and three girls. He was the baby and his brothers and sisters doted on him. He had a caring and loving mother and father—Grandma and Grandpop—who remained married their entire lives. They celebrated their fiftieth wedding anniversary shortly before they both died. Dad was a carpenter by trade and then when the war came to the shores of Australia, he joined the Royal Australian Navy as a carpenter. He went on to become a gunner on HMAS *Australia*.

My recollection of this time is non-existent because I had not been born yet. I don't know what happened to make my mother want to go to Sydney in New South Wales and live with my father's family. I think that Dad needed to readjust to civilian life and could find work easier at home in Sydney, which he did. He eventually set up a small carpentry business with his brothers. It was known as Forster Brothers Builders. It wouldn't be such a struggle for Mom and Dad because Dad had an established network of family and friends in Sydney. Still, it was exciting for Mom as she had never been outside of Victoria. She went to many places … but only in her dreams. I was later to cultivate the same wanderlust as my mom.

But something was amiss.

I can only assume that my father may have missed the closeness of his family circle; maybe my mother wanted to experience some of that closeness also. Maybe it was a way to escape from her situation. From what I remember later in my life, my mother's family was quite distant and judgmental towards her. For whatever reason, my parents finally left Melbourne and moved to Sydney, where they built a house and lived happily … until I was born. You thought I was going to say 'ever after'. Yeah right … not likely!

As Dad was a carpenter, it stood to reason that he would build his own home. It was situated just a short distance from his parents' house in a suburb called Westmead. Apparently, Mom was an excellent homemaker.

My sister Robyn has spoken of the beautiful home that Mom kept, and the beautiful home-cooked meals that were prepared every night. By all accounts her home was exceptionally well-kept, like a page out of a Home Beautiful magazine, without the luxuries. Her children were well looked after, with beautiful manners.

Robyn also speaks of Mom's delight as she tended her children, home, and garden. Mom became an avid gardener and had a vegetable garden to die for. Her garden beds were the envy of the area. In her spare time, she embroidered doilies, did rug making, and knitted. Robyn recalls Mom knitting jumpers and cardigans for her dolls that matched those she had knitted for Robyn. I never personally saw Mom embroider, but I saw the results and I was always astounded. Her stitching was that neat and precise, you could never tell which side was the front and which was the back.

By all accounts it seems that at this time in her life, Mom tended to her family and her husband; she was the doting wife and mother she was expected to be. I wish that I had known that mother. The one I grew up with was a distinctly different woman to the one my sister speaks of. I'm sure that she was in there somewhere; it seems that both time and life were extremely cruel to her.

Much later on in my life, on the day Mom died, the twenty-fourth of May, 1997, I found out that I was conceived in a boat shed in Woy Woy, NSW, while the family were there on holidays. Due to my date of birth, I would consider my conception to be near or on the Australia Day long weekend … As you'll find out later in the story, another Australia Day long week-end was going to be very significant in my life—the weekend that I would almost die, at age twenty-three.

But for now, back to that boat shed in Woy Woy...

The family often travelled to Woy Woy, one of my father's favorite getaway spots. It is now a sprawling suburban jungle. They stayed in a boat shed at night and lived on the beach during the day. There was fishing to be had and happy family times to be shared by the camp fire.

On or near the Australia Day long weekend in 1956, the family once again headed off for a short family vacation to the boat shed. My sister clearly remembers one particular night during that holiday, as embarrassing as it was. While all the children lay up in the loft, they listened to a new life being conceived below. It was me! I'm not sure why she is so sure this is the night I was conceived; however, the dates match and it's a lovely story—one of the few I have about my early days. I was lovingly accepted by both parents as a mistake from an obvious night of passion.

Mom suffered through a long and complicated pregnancy with me as she fell ill in the very early stages. She was not young and the doctor gave her two choices: go home and go to bed, and you should give birth to a healthy baby, or, go home and do the house work and the baby will terminate in a matter of days. Even though my life has been anything but perfect, I am so glad that my mother cared enough to go home and rest. My grandmother travelled to Sydney to help her through this period, and eventually I made my entry into this world.

There are pieces of my life still missing that do not seem to correlate with anything else, such as the distrust and dislike that my aunts and uncles, on my father's side of the family, had for my mother. And why my sister tells me not to listen to what they say because it is "not true". Why is it not true when it sounds so much like the mother who brought me up? What happened that made my mom change? What I do know is that the beginning of my story was the end of my mother and father's story.

Something went terribly wrong while Mom and Dad lived in Sydney. I have heard biased stories that my mother had a drinking problem, and that she would cause arguments on family occasions at Grandma and Grandpop's house so that she could be the center of attention. I was also told that Grandma and Grandpop didn't like her uncouth conduct. This seemed particularly strange to me at the time.

The main thing I remember about my mother, through all of her ups and downs, was that she was a lady. She disliked swearing in any shape or form, and, as nasty as I ever saw her get, she never used foul language, well maybe once, but once only. My mother was always able to convey her message in a way that was far worse than her using swear words. She would drop the tone of her voice, grit her teeth, and speak with such authority—and sometimes venom—it was actually scary. A trait my daughter tells me that I have inherited. The statement about my mother was made to me in all earnest by another loving aunt. I am sure that I will never know the truth now; but, really, does it actually matter?

On the other hand, I have heard from Mom's side of the family that my Dad's parents treated Mom terribly. They made her feel unwelcomed because she was an outsider. They didn't trust her and never offered her any assistance. To my knowledge, they were also extremely good people, and this certainly sounds like a normal mother-in-law–daughter-in-law, relationship. I never actually knew them personally, so I cannot attest to this being the case either. More recently I found out that my father gambled our home away, which rings more true to me than anything else I have been told. Hence, the move back to Melbourne. Truly though, it doesn't matter what happened, does it? This was the beginning of the end, and my family's demise was imminent. Do I need to know the truth that is my mother's story? No, as it is not mine to bear the burden of! I do know the truth about my part in it, and that is what I have to come to terms with.

As you read my story, you will see how my childhood reached into and affected my adult years. I often sit and wonder if my mother ever held me in her arms and looked into my eyes, touched my fair skin, or ruffled her fingers through my golden crown of curls. Like I have done to my own children. Did she ever whisper, "I love you" before placing me in my crib to sleep? Did she sing to me if I felt sad or hurt myself? … I don't remember a single time when I was comforted, until once, much later in life when any parent's compassion would have gone into automatic.

2
Childhood Antics

"To me, my sister Robyn was my mother. Dressed up in Robyn's petticoat and shoes, I was her. All little girls want to be just like their mother."

My uncle Merv, my father's brother, told me that I was about six months old when my father and mother packed up and went back to Melbourne, my mother's hometown—back to the safety and security of her own family, perhaps? He remembers coming out into his front yard and finding me bundled in my travelling bassinet under the letterbox, not a parent in sight. As I said earlier, my father was a character and this was his way of having a joke with his brother who adored me. He had thought they had left me behind for him and didn't mind at all. Uncle Merv would offer to take me and raise me as his own later on when things got really hard for my mother—no joke. Instead, I was sent to an orphanage.

When we moved back to Victoria, Dad found work as a carpenter at the Broadmeadows Army Camp. We actually lived on Camp Road, Broadmeadows, 301 to be exact, and the old house still stands there today. It was just up from the army camp. My first real recollections were from about the age of three. My sister was almost sixteen and my brother was around thirteen. We had three pets: Tiny who was our kelpie cross bitzer dog (bitzer means that he had no particular breed); Ginger-bum our Persian cat (he loved to laze around in the sun and often found me chasing after him with the scissors to trim his fur); and then there was Jimmy the canary. My mother loved the way that canary would sing. He was a later addition.

CHILDHOOD ANTICS

Most weekends were brilliant at our house. It was always bustling with some kind of event or party. The Defense Force was quite large at that time, mostly full of young men doing their country and parents proud. The war in Korea had been raging since 1952 and there was no end in sight. Our house was always full, mostly with the boys that my sister had gone to school with who had joined the Navy, Army, or Air Force. On weekends they would naturally migrate to our place, bringing with them their homeless buddies from other states who had nowhere else to go—they were made welcome. At our place, they found a home away from home, a place to forget their problems for just a little while. They were the basis for the festivities that occurred regularly at our house on weekends. After many of these unplanned Friday and Saturday night parties, I remember I would wake in the morning and tip toe from my bedroom, stepping over a layer of bodies on the lounge room floor, on my way to the kitchen to get something to eat.

For a while this was tremendous fun. I was usually the center of attention, which I grew to realize I was extraordinarily talented at gaining. I still attract the same kind of attention today with my quick wit, facetiousness, and self-effacing naivety. I would squeal with delight as I was spun around by one of the boys to music like *Rock Around the Clock* by Bill Hayley. To a three year old it was tremendous fun to have playmates. I didn't know anyone else who was my age at the time.

This driving need for attention, for love, would put me into many unfortunate situations in my life.

This is the time where my love of music was formed. Music was later to become my only friend, my escape, a place where I could find solace, happiness, and sorrow depending on my mood. It became my way of putting up mental markers, reminders of episodes in my life that will haunt me forever—music that represents each event in my life. It is not often that I will hear a song, even the most modern of music, that does not generate a memory. I was barely without music as a child. As I got older, I had a portable transistor radio, which is similar to today's iPod but without the technology and a little bit larger. My transistor radio was almost always glued to my ear, in every waking moment, and at night was placed under my pillow. I usually fell asleep to the sound of music—3XY Melbourne radio station was the best. As I go through my story, I will share a song here and there with you, which was connected to that time in my life. If you listen to those songs you just might hear my emotions entwined in them.

Being the baby, I was the apple of everyone's eye, or, if you were one of my sister's boyfriends, I could also be a thorn in your side—it depended on which side of the coin that you were on at the time with my sister. The boys almost all wanted to date my sister—she was incredible and a remarkably beautiful looking girl. So what better way to get in her good books than to treat her younger sister wonderfully? I was stuck to her like glue anyway because she babysat me most of the time. So if you wanted my sister, you would have to put up with me. Therefore, they all had a lot of time for me.

I have to say, I have fantastic memories from that time in my life. It was fun. I still love each and every memory dearly. I have them tucked away safely in a memory locker, somewhere inside my heart from where I can replay them any time I want to. It was a happy time in my life that clearly left an impression. And those who left these impressions on my soul wore a *uniform*, and men wearing uniforms would play a large part in my life as an adult.

I was also quite the little entrepreneur back then; in fact, extraordinarily advanced for my three years, I was capable of extortion and on a good day could extract up to two bob or twenty pence (twenty cents) for threatening to dob these boys in for snuggling on the couch with my sister while she was babysitting me.* Usually though, it was thruppence (three pence, equal to about three cents)—cheapskates—but it still bought a whole brown paper bag full of lollies and got rid of me for at least half an hour while I walked to the store to get them. Yes, I did walk the streets at three and four years of age; it was accepted back then. My dad, who was fiercely protective of my sister, would not have been extremely pleased at all that she'd been left alone with a boy, and they knew it.

My sister was left alone to babysit me when Mom wasn't there. Mom worked to help make ends meet as we were a relatively poor family. I only ever remember my sister being the one who tended to all my needs back

---

* Dob: Australian slang meaning to 'inform on somebody'. Hence, dobber, a tell-tale.

then, not my mother. Robyn was the one who dressed, fed, and looked after me. I have very limited memories of my mother being there at all. All in all, my sister nurtured me. She would sit me on the table and plaster Curly Pet in my hair, encouraging my already messy mop of unruly curls to become even more unmanageable. She was the one who tied the ribbons in my pigtails and who fed me breakfast. She struggled to keep my older brother under control. Daniel was a little bit on the wild side, not too wild, because our father was pretty hard on him. I can remember Daniel getting the belt; he had it rough being the only son.

My favorite time of the week was Friday night. Dad would come home with a bag of lollies behind his back for each of us and he wouldn't give them to us until we told him our preferred football team—The Bombers. Funnily enough, I still barrack for that team today, but I don't get a bag of lollies now. A penny went a long way back then, and my favorite lollies were always the liquorice ones, with the brightly colored layers of confectionary in between the liquorice—yellow, pink, and green.

Friday night was always "fish 'n chips night"—remnants of Mom's Catholic upbringing. For Dad it was an excuse just to have them—he loved potatoes of any variety. His belief was that a woman could not peel a potato properly and should not be let near a potato, for fear of butchering and wasting it. He stated that we wasted so much of the potato that it was a crime. I think he was right. He said chips could be made out of the peels left over by women after they finished peeling a spud. This line of thought came from the long hours he spent on the deck of the *Aussie*, helping the cook peel the spuds for dinner. Food was scarce back then, especially at sea, and he could peel a potato to within an inch of its life. The remnants of the peel would be no thicker than a slither; he amazed me with his skill and it was always done with a sharp knife.

Yes, that time in my life was perfect. I was always the curious, pesky little sister, and I had an insatiable appetite for my sister's belongings, cultivated by the fact that we shared the same bedroom—nothing was sacred. It was not easy for her to hide anything from me. You often saw a little girl with brown, curly, unruly hair tromping down Camp Road in her sister's multi-layered, multi-colored netting can-can petticoat, which was usually reserved to be worn under her sister's sixties style, rock 'n roll dresses. Also, I would wear and carefully clomp along in my sister's best black Paton leather high heels—clomp, clomp, clomp. Oh, she wanted to hurt me so bad when she found me in them; she was never pleased by it at all. It wasn't good for her shoes either. But I felt pretty; I was a ballerina, a princess, my sister, or some other fictional character that made me happy that day! It was my love and admiration for the leading female role in my life that made me want to be just as beautiful as she was. I was always a beautiful little girl in Robyn's petticoat and shoes. I felt safe and loved. Yes, I idolized her. To me, my sister, Robyn was my mother. All little girls want to be just like their mother.

My brother, Daniel or Danny as I would call him, was in many ways my biggest hero and champion, but he was also my tormentor and torturer. For obvious reasons I was my sister's biggest curse, so perhaps what I am about to describe to you could have been called pay-back via my brother. Daniel would chase me down the road, tormenting me with the feet, claws intact, that my mother had cut off the fresh chook to be used for the roast that night. They always had a smattering of blood where they had been cut from the chook—pale, wrinkly, nasty looking things with long, sharp claws on them. If he caught me, he would put those horrible claws on my shoulders. They scared me to death, and I would run screaming all the way around the block. You know that ear-piercing, shrill scream that can only come from the very depths of a little girl's lungs. Well, I had that down pat. My brother knew it and our neighbors knew it too. Still, to this day, I panic if I am chased. My heart will quicken and I will have a flashback to that time in my life.

Bloody brothers.

My husband plays on it often, since he is a jokester just like my dad was.

I know that Daniel loved me to death, but besides the dead chook leg torture, he also used me in his Evil Knievel experiments, such as the time he built his new billy cart. He told me to jump in and proceeded to push me, running as fast as he could, down the hill towards the nearest T-intersection. I was squealing with delight at the top of my lungs, but then the billy cart got away from him and, as it did, he realized he hadn't built in any brakes. Just before leaving the footpath, luckily it hit a bump in the concrete and flipped over, throwing its contents, me, onto the nature strip before it spewed out onto the road in pieces.

Hunting was quite an acceptable pastime back in the day. Early one morning, on my father's return from one such trip, a piercing scream came from my sister's bed. My father had placed a tiny joey into the bottom of her bed. I had never seen her move so fast. Another time it was a dead snake beside her bed. That same morning, a tiny baby bunny was placed into the end of mine. Dad had felt sorry for the poor creatures, so he brought them home to look after them.

Dad kept a friend's 303 rifle on top of the cupboard in his bedroom; Johnny was in the Citizens Military Forces (CMF) and didn't trust keeping it at his own home because of his brothers. It was never secured safely, but there was a cardinal rule in our house that nobody was to touch it—ever. One night when Mom and Dad had gone out and left us at home alone with Robyn, a battle of the siblings took place. Daniel retrieved the gun from Mom and Dad's room and brought it into the lounge room. He pointed it at my sister Robyn, who grabbed me, pulling me in front of her. He threatened to shoot her if she didn't change the channel on the television.

She retorted, "No."

So he fired the weapon.

The kickback from the shot put him firmly on his butt on the floor and the bullet went through the ceiling. If it hadn't, I would not be here to tell my story. I can remember screaming a lot, as was my sister. My brother took off because he knew he was in trouble, and all I could think was, *Gee that's a big hole*. Needless to say, Daniel was not in Dad's good books when he got home.

Guns were never kept in our home again after that.

Daniel also had lots of fun things in his bedroom, but I didn't dare go there as he had warned me that there were chooks' feet in there and that they would get me if I went in. I was terribly naive as a child, and not much has changed. If he didn't have chooks feet in his room, all wrinkly and lifeless with their claws still intact, it was bound to be the live yabbies that my father tormented me with. A yabby is like a miniature version of a crayfish, dark brown in color, and is often found living in fresh water streams, rivers and dams in and around Australia. When removed from the water, they will crawl around as they try to escape their captor. Their shell-strong claws will clink on hard surfaces, making horribly scary sounds when there are multitudes of them; I remember them well.

My father often went out with the boys, yabbying, and would return home with bucket loads. Yabbies are edible once boiled, and to a poor family like us they were a treat. On one trip, he came home just before my bedtime and put a bucketful of them on the floor in the kitchen while he prepared a large pot of water to cook them on the stove.

I curiously snuck forward to see what was in the bucket. I didn't like the look of them as they clambered over each other—they scared me. They had claws on their front legs that were still moving, pinching together—click-clack, click-clack. My father tried to convince me to come closer, telling me that they wouldn't hurt me. But I backed off, feeling a little overwhelmed by it all. As I did so, he moved to grab the pot lid from the sink and kicked the bucket of yabbies, spilling them out onto the floor in all directions. I remember being surrounded by these horrible creatures as they snapped their claws at my bare feet and chased me across the kitchen floor. Just to add insult to injury, I slipped on the linoleum floor in my hurry to escape and landed on my bum in the middle of them all. I screamed and clambered for the door. My experience was only made worse by my brother Daniel picking up one of the offenders and chasing after me with it. I hid in my bedroom for the rest of the night and would not come out until all the yabbies had gone.

I was a bugger of a child and usually got into things I shouldn't be into (except dead chooks and yabbies!). One day I went to my new friend's house around the corner. She had found a block of her mother's chocolate and offered me some. I knew what chocolate was and loved it. We often got freckles or small chocolates buddies in our bag of lollies on a Friday night. Mmmm ... We gobbled that whole bar of chocolate right down, half each. Well, I had severe pains in the stomach when I went home that caused me to soil my pants. My father smacked me on the leg and then placed me on the toilet to finish what

I had started. I sat there for what seemed an eternity as the contents of my stomach emptied into the bowl. The pain racked my little body and I was bent over, crying. Dad demanded to know what I had eaten while I had been at my friend's house.

I kept saying, "Nothing."

I knew if I told him about the chocolate that I would get into serious trouble. Eventually, because of his persistence and annoyance, and because he pulled his belt off his pants and slapped it together in front of me, I told him we had found a bar of chocolate and had eaten it. He put me in the car and took me back to my friend's house. When he knocked on the door, he was greeted by my friend's mother. They spoke for a little while and then laughed together.

When Dad got back into the car, he said, "Well, that will teach you to eat Laxettes."

My little friend was also sick. I didn't know what Laxettes were, but I didn't want to eat them again. He told me that my illness was punishment enough, so there was no belt that night. We always knew when Dad removed his belt or went and got the belt, we were in trouble. Thank God that was not going to happen tonight. I felt so sick and, anyway, I spent most of the remainder of the night on the toilet.

One day Robyn spent hours putting my hair into rags then curling my hair into the latest Shirley Temple hair style. I had that kind of hair. She tied a pretty yellow ribbon in my hair and then dressed me in a lemon, striped dress that had buttons down the front of it. It had lace on either side of the row of buttons that complemented the dress nicely. She completed the outfit with a pretty lemon, angora cardigan, which my mother had knitted. I had on a pair of white anklet socks and a brand new pair of black patent leather shoes. I can remember Robyn was so excited and was pleased that she had done a particularly excellent job of dressing me that day. Before I knew it, I was the center of attention, the place I loved to be. Mom wanted to take pictures of me, so they sat me on top of her camphor wood box in the lounge room and she clicked away with her old Box Brownie camera. She loved that thing.

That was the day of my sister's sixteenth birthday, and even though the day really should have been about my sister, she wanted me to look pretty also—and I did. I felt very pretty. Even today I can think back to that moment and remember how I felt so special, so loved, and so safe—perhaps the only time in my childhood. Every time I hear the song *Sixteen Candles* by The Crests and *Happy Birthday Sweet Sixteen* by Neil Sedaka, I still think of that day and feel good.

Little did I know that my sister had more pressing issues to deal with. She had to tell Dad and Mom that she was pregnant. This in itself was a surprise to both of my parents. At a later stage they demanded that Robyn marry the boy, George, who had fathered her child, and subsequently arranged a wedding in the Melbourne Registry Office. I don't remember anything of my sister's pregnancy. I know that she lived with us as we still shared the same bedroom. When the baby was born and brought home from the hospital, I had to move into my brother's room.

I was jealous of the baby and when my father reached for her and said, "Oh, isn't she beautiful? Grandpop's little peanut," that was the last straw. I was Daddy's little peanut, not the new baby.

When all the adults were sitting in the lounge room and the baby had been put down for a nap, I snuck in to take a closer look at the new little intruder (who I was to eventually come to love more than life itself—but not yet). I couldn't quite see her over the side of the bassinet, so I pulled it forward to try and see her better. The bassinet and the contents tumbled out onto the floor in front of me. The baby started to scream and, well, the rest is history. My Dad belted me for the very first time, telling me that I was a jealous little so-and-so and that I would be staying in my room for an awful long time. I hadn't meant to overturn the baby onto the floor, but everyone believed I had tipped her over intentionally because I was jealous.

I had many adventures when we lived at Broadmeadows. Once I followed Daniel when he had been given permission to go to the visiting circus and I wasn't allowed to go with him. He knew I was following him, so he deliberately lost me. Knowing I was going to get into trouble for leaving the house at night when I had been told not to, I didn't dare go back home. Instead, I hid under the local primary school, which I had recently started attending.

It wasn't long before there were red and blue flashing lights everywhere and heavy smoke choking me. Someone had set fire to the school—right above me! Just my luck. I came out from under the school and the police took me into custody.

They asked me who I was and I told them my name. They then asked me why I was there, and I replied that I had run away to go to Nanna's. They were astounded as I then proceeded to give them a detailed explanation of how to get to Nanna's, considering she lived in Heidelberg, which was a tremendously long way from Broadmeadows. I told them that you "go up Ding Dong Street, past the hopital and over the peddepbian crossing, then to Motor Mower Road." This translated to travelling up Bell Street, past Preston and Northcote Community Hospital (PANCH), stopping for the pedestrians on the pedestrian crossing, and then continuing to McEwan Road in Heidelberg. If you got that far you were nearly at my grandmother's house.

They shook their heads in disbelief, took me back to the station, and gave me a bag of lollies. I had the run of the police station until my father came barreling through the door. I could tell he was relieved to see me, and so I smiled at him. I was sitting on the policeman's desk with a police hat on my head. Dad removed the hat, thanked the police officers for their time, and told them it would not happen again.

He bundled me into the ute† and drove. On the way home he looked as though he was going to bust a vein in his head, but he didn't say a word. When we got home, Dad told me to go to my room and that I was going to get a hiding. I went crying into my room and told Daniel that Dad was going to belt me. I crawled under my bed as far as I could into the corner, to hide from Dad. Daniel told me that I should get under his bed and he would go out and tell Dad that I was under my bed. I crawled out from under my bed, but when Daniel left the room I climbed back under again as I figured

---

† Ute: Australian slang for utility truck.

that he would do one of his usual tricks and squeal to get me into trouble. I heard Dad entering the room and I heard Daniel tell him that I was under my bed, just like he had promised. DOH! Dad pulled me out by the feet and I received five good ones to the bare bum. It smarted and tears poured out of my eyes. But I never ran away again, not from Dad anyway.

3

The Confrontation

"I had been so sure that he would hold me and tell me that everything was alright; that I was still his little girl ... I was so wrong."

I SPENT MORE TIME WITH my father than I did with my mother in my childhood. Often I went to work with Dad during holidays and weekends. Our time together was magic. Dad would let me bang nails into pieces of wood, which made me feel so smart. He would often say, as he ruffled his fingers through the top of my curls, "I'll make a carpenter of you one day."

He met a man named Don, who invited Mom and Dad to come to his house to have a few drinks with his wife Dixie and himself. This became a regular occurrence. Daniel and I had terrific fun playing with Don and Dixie's children, and when we were all together, mischief was not far away. I was closest to one of the younger children, Harry, who was almost my age.

The card nights usually involved copious amounts of alcohol for the adults, and more often than not if we went there with our parents, Daniel and I usually woke up there the next morning. I was scared of Dixie, though. She growled a lot and didn't treat us very politely when our parents weren't around. After a while, if she felt that I did something wrong, she would punish me by shutting me in a wardrobe in Harry's room for what seemed like a couple of hours at a time. It was quite upsetting, but I was too afraid to come out until I was allowed to.

Another time she locked me in the bathroom and wouldn't feed me when she fed the other children. She would tell me my mom was too lazy to look after me and that's why I was there. I felt like I was being singled out because I was my father's favorite.

I told my dad, who was always the one that came and picked us up, but he didn't seem to believe me. Regardless, I loved going to the camp as it was so much fun with the other kids. Life was pretty relaxed. We built sleds made from tin and rope and spent all day sliding down the hills of dead grass and prickles at the back of the army camp. As long as we were home by dark, no one cared what we did. We sometimes put stones on the railroad tracks and waited for the heavily-laden freight carriages to pass by. Then we ran to pick up all the dust off the track that once had been a rock. Life was an adventure when we were there—a dangerous, uncontrolled, adventure!

Soon, though, Daniel stopped coming to the camp and just Dad and I went. I didn't know why Mom no longer came with us, but I would harp on at him so that I could play with my friends, my only friends, and finally he would let me go. We often went to see Dixie during the day, even when Don wasn't home. Months passed and my parents were starting to lead quite separate lives. Dad was always at the army camp with Dixie, drinking, and Mom was either at work or at home, drinking.

When we were at the army camp, I was always told to go outside and play with the rest of the kids, which I happily complied with. It was against the rules for us children to go back inside after we had been told to go outside to play.

One day, Harry forgot something that we wanted to play with in his bedroom, and so together we snuck in the back door of the hut and into his room. He quickly searched for what he wanted, and then we heard Dixie's and Dad's footsteps coming down the hallway. We both scurried into his wardrobe and stayed there as still and quiet as church mice, both of us not wanting to get into trouble. My heart was beating hard against my chest wall, and then I noticed that the door to the wardrobe was slightly ajar. I was sure that they would be able to hear my heart beating. If we got caught I would not be allowed to return again, so we pulled clothing across in front of us, attempting to hide our little bodies. We could see Dixie enter the room and look around, and my father immediately enter behind her. It was so quiet you could hear a pin drop.

THE CONFRONTATION

"See, I told you that they were playing outside," my father said, and then he pulled Dixie close to him and kissed her on the lips. He told her not to be silly and then they left the room.

Harry and I knew what we had seen, but neither of us said a word about it as we climbed out of the wardrobe. We quickly and quietly grabbed what we had come for and snuck back outside.

I was only five years old, but I knew what I had seen my father do was wrong. By his reaction, Harry did too.

We didn't say a word about it to the other kids. We just continued to play—Harry and I were as thick as thieves. It was that very same night that we realized it was dark and we hadn't been called in yet. When we went to the front door, it was locked. So we went to another door and knocked as loud as we dared.

Dixie yelled out from inside the hut, "Give us five minutes."

So we sat on the step and waited and the other children started to gather around. Next moment the door opened and we were told to go inside.

Don came home and was asked to go and get fish and chips for dinner. So we all piled in the back of his ute and went to the fish and chip shop. When we got back to the army camp, Dad had gone home without me. Dixie told me I would be spending the night there. I was looking forward to spending more time with the other kids.

Harry and I played until it was time to go to bed, then we were top and tailed in the one single bed in his room. Even after the lights went off, we still continued to tell stories and laugh and giggle about silly things that made no sense to anyone but little children. We finally fell asleep.

The next morning we were summoned to the breakfast table where a bowl of porridge was waiting. All the children quickly gobbled down their breakfast. I tasted one spoonful of the lumpy, dry, and not terribly well cooked bowl of oats and wouldn't touch anymore. It wasn't the same as I was used to at home and I didn't like it. Okay, so I was probably acting like a spoilt child, but you get used to certain things and Mom's porridge was the best. That, I do remember. At home it was sweet and creamy and never had lumps.

I was ordered to eat it or go hungry and go to Harry's room. One of the older girls leaned across and told me that her mother didn't like me, so she had put poison in it. My mind immediately raced to my Golden Book story of Sleeping Beauty and I imagined Dixie to be the wicked witch—I actually wasn't far wrong. Dixie had no tolerance for me even in the future.

Again, Dixie yelled for me to eat my porridge, and with that I yelled back, "No! It's not as nice as my mom's." And with that I crossed my arms and threw myself back down into the chair, with a disgruntled pout on my face.

"You had better get used to it," she said.

I yelled back, "No, I saw you and Daddy yesterday and you're gonna get into a lot of trouble by my mother when I tell her."

Well, I was sent to Harry's room and told to stay there until my father arrived. I felt real hate for her as I stomped off up the hallway!

A few hours later, Dad turned up and I thought that he would come and hug me and let me know that everything was going to be alright—that we would never see her again. Instead, he stayed out in the living room with Dixie. I could hear them talking. As much as I strained my ears, I couldn't hear what they were saying as the door was closed.

Dad came to Harry's bedroom door, opened it, and scolded me for being naughty. He told me that I was not allowed to talk to adults the way that I had, and, because I had been so rude, I would never be allowed to go to the army camp with him again. I was also to get the strap when I got home. I felt sad as I sat in the car with Dad that morning. I had been so sure that he would hold me and tell me that everything was alright; that I was still his little girl … Isn't that what Daddies are supposed to do? I was so wrong.

As we drove out of the army camp that day, I looked over my shoulder to see Harry playing in the playground and knew it would be the last time I would see him as my dad was always true to his word. I started to cry as I waved shyly from the car. Harry was my best friend; Harry was my only friend except for my dog, Tiny. I wasn't allowed to play with my other little friend around the corner anymore because of the "chocolate" eating episode.

Later that day at home, I heard Mom and Dad yelling at each other from the kitchen. Mom was quite loud. I couldn't help but think that it was my fault, because of what I had told Dixie. Dad was so mad at me for causing trouble at the camp, I didn't think it was a good idea to tell Mom what I had seen Dad doing. If I hadn't been so naughty at Dixie's house then maybe everything would be okay. The yelling and arguments were to become commonplace after that, and it was something that I would not get used to.

One day not so long after, I came home from playing and saw Mom crying on the backdoor step. I went and sat beside her and put my hand on her knee. As I looked up I could see the tears falling from her eyes. I innocently asked, "Are you okay, Mommy?"

She looked at me and said that she was just a little sad and tried quite hard to hide her tears from me. I knew that she was crying because of Daddy's new friend.

"Is it because of Daddy's new friend?" I asked.

Mom's eyes looked straight at mine. She glared at me and asked what I meant by "Daddy's new friend". I told her that I had seen Daddy kissing Dixie in Harry's room. Mom didn't ask me any questions. Tears rolled freely down her cheeks and she sobbed into her hands. I just sat there quietly with her, patting her on the knee with my little hand. I didn't know what else to do; what I could do to make her feel better. Our family dog Tiny sat quietly next to her also. I put my arm around her back to try and comfort her in my own childlike way. I felt like I was a bad child. *If I hadn't told Dixie what I had seen, Dad and Mom wouldn't have had the fight and now Mom wouldn't be upset.*

It was about this time that our family life started to change. Mom started to drink alcohol more frequently and Dad spent more and more time at the army camp, at Dixie and Don's house without Mom, Daniel, or me. Life was changing too fast and I was not coping with it emotionally. My dad was barely around; my mom just around—there, but not. When they were together, they just yelled at each other, and this usually ended up with Mom throwing things—plates and any other items she could get—with Dad begging her to stop.

My sister was trying to cope with a new baby, trying to raise her younger sister, and trying to control her little brother, who started to act out as teenagers do in these circumstances. He was older and what was happening around him was too much for him to handle while going through puberty, and all that comes with it, at the same time.

Shortly after that, we moved from Camp Road to Southern Road in West Heidelberg. Things were looking up. The house was beautiful and relatively new. It was right next door to my nanna's house and three doors down from my sister's new home, where George and Robyn had finally decided to start their lives together as a family. What a bonus.

When the real estate agent showed my parents the electric stove for the first time, I was amazed! I had never seen one before. The spiral turned bright red, and then he turned the knob the other way and it went back to black. As they moved to the next room, I stayed behind, and just as my dad yelled out from the other room, "Beverley, don't touch!" it was too late. I had touched the coils to see if they were still hot and burnt my hand. Extremely painful circular, red welts immediately appeared on my palm.

Both of my parents yelled at me while I was crying, as parents do when they are scared themselves because their child is hurt. They ordered me to go to Nanna, who lived next door, so that she could tend to my hand. Yes, Nanna was next door! How close we were all going to be living: Nanna next door, Robyn three doors away, and best of all, we were a long way away from the wicked witch at the army camp.

In my little mind, everything was going to be wonderful again … once I got over my burnt hand. But even though life did continue for us, sadly, it would never be the same. Such is change, and such is life! My life was about to drop into the pits of hell, from where it seemed I may never again surface.

4
Changes

"There'll be no bloody Christmas this year!"

L IFE AT SOUTHERN ROAD was quiet to begin with. There were no friends to play with because we didn't know anyone. Every day I wandered up and down the street, hoping that another child might just come out and play. There had to be children living near me; but they never did come out. My brother wasn't around very often; he had made new friends at school and generally hung out with them.

My sister had a baby of her own to take care of and didn't want me dropping in out of the blue as often as I had been. Dad was spending more time at work and Mom also worked to help pay the bills. So I usually amused myself when no one else was around by reading my Golden Books and playing games made for one in the lounge room.

I didn't have a lot of toys; in fact, I don't remember any! There must have been some, though. I developed a vivid imagination and could dream up the best of scenarios. I could transform my lounge room into a jungle and play stepping stones, using my books as the stones. I would spread my Golden Books out all over the floor and jump from one to the other, afraid that the crocodiles would jump up and eat me. I would spend a lot of time in the backyard, consoled by the only true and loyal friend in my life, my dog Tiny.

Tiny was a Kelpie cross Fox Terrier. He was black all over and had little brown eyebrows above his eyes. He was a wonderful dog, loyal and faithful. He never threatened anyone and was always around to catch a ball or run in the yard with me. If I ventured to the street, he would stay by my side. When I started school, Tiny would accompany me to the school gate, and he would be there when the bell rang to go home. He was wonderful. Anyone could come into our yard and he wouldn't even growl, but if anyone tried to pick something up from our yard and remove it, well, that was a different story. He would bail them up until they replaced the item. Then he would allow them to walk away. He knew his territory and how far he could go with each person. He did, however, have two problems, the postman and the pan man.

A funny thing happened when we lived in Broadmeadows before the move to West Heidelberg. This was back in the days when everyone had a dunny and you had a weekly collection of sanitary pans (poo pans).[*] The dunny can man would come on his run to remove the old pan, to be emptied and replaced with a cleaned one. Mom was always extremely careful to tie Tiny up on pan days, and on this particular day, she thought she had ...

The dunny can man arrived with the new pan. He pulled out the old one, clamped the lid down, hoisted it up on his shoulder, and walked out of the outhouse ... to be greeted by Tiny, baring his teeth nastily and not looking particularly happy. The man yelled out for my mom to come and help. While he waited, he hopped around, trying to avoid Tiny's warning nips at his ankles. His biggest mistake was trying to negotiate his way past Tiny to the gate so that he could escape from the backyard while he had the pan on his shoulder. He got right near the gate when Tiny nipped him sharply, and he promptly dropped the pan. The lid came off and the dunny can man and Tiny were both covered in poo. Mom and Dad were used to paying for the mailman's pants, but this was something quite different.

Tiny was in the doghouse after this. Poor Tiny. He was just protecting the poo pan. All the guy had to do was put the poo pan down.

---

[*] Dunny is Australian slang for an outside toilet/outhouse.

Everything in my life happened so quickly once we moved to Heidelberg. In fact, I can't remember at all what interaction I had, if any, with Mom at this time. I just remember their arguments. Mom and Dad drank a lot more, and their arguments became more frequent and more abusive. Dad was very non-physical during these arguments and would raise his voice, but he never raised his hand, that I saw. For that I am grateful. On the other hand, my mother often broke plates on the floor and on the walls, behind my father's head. She had a terribly fierce temper.

I saw less and less of my brother as he amused himself elsewhere. I would run up to my sister's house to say hello, but more often than not she would not be at home, so I would go to my grandmother's, who would also be out, or too busy to keep me around. Again, I would return to my own empty house and my faithful friend, Tiny.

I finally befriended Bevan. Bevan was a young boy with cerebral palsy. He would slowly wheel himself up and down the street in his wheelchair. He lived next door to my grandmother, on the other side. Bevan's mother was lovely and opened her house and her heart to me. To this day I am grateful for her love and kindness.

Every day, at approximately the same time, I would go to Bevan's house to play games and read books with him. Through a child's eyes he was so lucky; he had so many things to amuse him. We would talk and play for a few hours, and then I would have to go home. I had no idea that Bevan was disabled at that time. It never occurred to me. The fact that he had to sit in a chair with wheels did not make him disabled in my books; through my eyes he was as normal as me. Being with Bevan was a reprieve from being at home alone all day. I enjoyed my time at his house—it was a lot of fun. Bevan had toys and games like I had never seen before, and he willingly allowed me to play with them while he sat and watched with amusement, always smiling. I think that he was my very first real friend, aside from the children at the army camp.

My brother and I kept up our shenanigans at Southern Road; he would be the tormentor and I would be the victim. I didn't know how much I would miss that when we no longer had each other.

We had a tradition. I would go into his room and unintentionally break something of his, and he, in turn, would go on a seek-and-find mission to locate my one and only doll and deliberately pull an arm or its head off. I guess that is how we let each other know that we still cared about one another.

My father had a rule that boys never hit girls. So when my father was washing up in the kitchen and could see into the backyard, I'd deliberately hit or kick my brother and scream while running away. My father would then look up and discover Daniel hitting me back. Daniel, in turn, would get into quite a bit of trouble for hitting me. I wasn't big enough to get him back for hurting my doll myself; he was thirteen by now and had grown a lot taller than me.

But besides these scenarios of ours, I always knew that Daniel was my older, protective brother, and I always felt safe when he was around. Unfortunately, I didn't realize that by doing this to him, I was adding to Daniel's unhappiness about his relationship with our dad and his own insecurities. I was too young to realize that he believed that his father's love was waning, and that was to play a significant role in my brother's future.

If I thought life was moving fast up until this point, from hereon in everything zoomed so fast that it left me spinning and unsure of what was going to happen next.

One night just before Christmas, we were sitting in the kitchen eating dinner. After a few minutes, Mom and Dad started to fight. Mom picked up her glass of beer and threw it across the table, and the beer landed all over my dad. He didn't react; instead, he just sat there and stared at her sadly. We sat there quietly and tried to continue eating. Mom jumped up off the chair and grabbed the beer bottle that was sitting on the bench in the kitchen where Dad had placed it, anger spread across her face. She did not look normal; her face was contorted.

My dad yelled for us to go to our rooms immediately. The tone of his voice told us that something was wrong and not to argue back. I turned as I was leaving the kitchen to see my mother throw the beer bottle right at my father's head, narrowly missing him and Daniel in the process. The bottle neck embedded itself into the dining room wall beside Dad's head.

For nearly an hour after that, I lay on my bed crying. I was extremely scared. I could feel my heart hammering within my chest while I listened to my mother and father arguing with each other. Back and forth their accusations flew, Mom yelling as loud as she possibly could, the sound of glass smashing and more yelling. I didn't understand why they were doing it. What's more, I felt somehow responsible for it all.

Is it because of me? I wondered, between gulps of air.

Eventually, my father pleaded for my mother to stop. When all was quiet, I left my bedroom and headed to the kitchen. Dad was cleaning up the smashed dishes that were scattered everywhere—over the floor, on the bench, and over the kitchen table. Nothing in the cupboard survived Mom's tirade that night.

I had never seen my parents like this, and I was scared. There are a range of feelings that a child will get when they witness this kind of anger and hatred. And I experienced them all …

First, I felt an awful sense of helplessness, like I was suspended in mid-air with nothing to grasp onto and I might fall at any minute into a bottomless pit. It was like being alone in the dark and not being able to find your way home.

Then came the fear—I felt very unsafe, in the place where I should have felt safest, my home. Also, I feared that I would lose one of my parents, or both.

And then came the guilt … *This must be my fault … Maybe it would be better if I wasn't around. Did I do something wrong? Maybe if I'd picked up my books when I'd been told to? IT MUST BE MY FAULT!*

I had all those thoughts swirling around in my head, churning my stomach and making me feel like it was hard to breathe. Silent panic! I crept back towards the kitchen, wanting Daddy to reassure me that everything was alright. But instead he growled at me for coming out. I just couldn't help screaming as I ran back towards my room, crying. But I took a detour instead into my brother's room.

Daniel sat on the floor in the corner of his room and motioned for me to come to him, into the arms of my "Danny". I sensed the fear permeating from my brother; he too must have felt helpless. And that beer bottle could have hit him. We sat there together until very late in the night, with my head lying on his chest and his arms wrapped around me, keeping me, his "bubbalouie", safe in his cocoon.

I felt safe with Danny.

I still remember the quiet sniffles from the tears that he fought back. He was a boy and boys don't cry. We heard Dad leave the house, get in his car, and drive away. Daniel put me to bed and then went back to his room. Mom went into the lounge room with her beer and, as she had on many occasions, she started to play her music until the late hours. I can remember hearing the song *Are You Lonesome Tonight* by Elvis Presley as I lay in my dark room. I cried for a very long time until I finally drifted off to sleep.

∽

This was an event to be repeated many times over before things finally began to settle down a bit, in the weeks leading up to Christmas. But things were simmering under the surface. I wasn't aware at that time that my father was still seeing Dixie at the army camp and he was gambling heavily, spending all of the household money on his own interests. One night he even asked my mother for her wedding ring so that he could hock it to get more money for gambling. He also had the gumption to bring Dixie to our new house, our home, and apparently promised her that one day she would have the same.

I guess I can understand Mom's tirades to some extent.

As Christmas approached, there were no incidents as Dad wasn't around terribly much. Mom, she cried a lot. But, as little girls do, I began to dream of a happy Christmas and that things would go back to "normal".

We went with Dad to pick out a pine tree for Christmas, which Dad propped up in a nail tin filled with old bricks in the corner of the living room, as he did every year. Daniel and I spent a couple of hours decorating it.

I loved Christmas; it was such a magical time. There were never many presents as most of the money went on gambling. Nanna's Christmas tree and decorations would already be up, and there were always lots of presents under her tree. My sister Robyn also had her Christmas tree and decorations up. I loved going to their places, so I could hang around the tree like children do, trying to figure out what presents were there for me. I couldn't wait to see what I was going to get from Santa Claus for Christmas; I had been a really good girl. I jumped around the lounge room to the Christmas carols playing on the stereo while Daniel and I worked together to put beautiful colored balls and tinsel all over the tree. It looked pretty and we had done such a good job. Expectation and the joy of Christmas were singing in our hearts. We were hoping to have a happy Christmas, when we would all be together as a family again. Without the fights and the booze and the disruption of "a third party".

But our joy and laughter was to be short-lived. It soon stopped when we heard Mom and Dad arguing in the kitchen—again. My heart sunk, and I can only imagine my brother's did also. I began to feel anxious and frightened, remembering what happened not so long ago. Yep, Mom and Dad were drinking. It seemed that alcohol was a burden on our household, with the same old problems resurfacing every time they drank, and every time they drank, they fought. Their arguing got louder, rougher, and more disturbing! Daniel and I sat together in the dimly-lit lounge room, nervously waiting for our parents to come in so that we could turn on the Christmas lights and put the star on top of the tree. It was a family tradition that we all had to be there together as a family. Surely, if we did that, everything would be okay…

Dad burst into the lounge room, his face contorted with anger. He grabbed the tree violently from the tin. "There'll be no bloody Christmas this year!"

With that, he took the tree and threw it out into the backyard—decorations and all—then left the house in his car—again. I looked at my brother, and he at me. I saw tears welling in the base of Daniel's eyes. He quickly wiped them off and stomped to his room. I tried to follow him in, but he sat up against the door so that I couldn't get to him. So I sat on the other side of the door and waited.

There were no presents that year except for the couple that we got from our grandmother next door. Every year it was a tradition that we went to Nanna's house on Christmas Eve where we would gather as a family and pass out our gifts to each other. I really miss that tradition. Sadly it died with my grandmother and I have never been able to resurrect it within my own family as they all have their own agendas. It is something that I do miss terribly; it was the only time I felt part of a family.

Every time I hear the song, *The First of May* by the Bee Gees, I am instantly transported back to this time in my life and to that exact day. I always get choked with the tears.

It doesn't help that my brother's birthday is also the first of May. Even though we still love each other, Daniel and I have been distant for so long now that it will be difficult to get all the lost years back—but we are trying.

Yep, it is undeniably my brother's and my song.

Dad didn't come home for a couple of days, so he wasn't there for Christmas that year. We spent it alone with Mom and each other at our grandmother's house. That was the last time that we would have had the chance to spend Christmas together as a family. He did come home again after a few days, and once again life went on and all seemed well. Mom and Dad still didn't laugh and talk like they had in the past, but my daddy was there at least. I had missed him.

Shortly after Christmas, I was to start at my new school. Mom and Dad had disagreed over my schooling. Mom wanted me to go to the Catholic school down the road; Dad wanted me to go to the state school. He told my mother he didn't want "God botherers" looking after his kids, even though my mother had compromised with my father all those years ago when she agreed to marry him in the Church of England, as long as her children were raised Catholic. My father had his own religion; he said it was the Church of Turkey. I wasn't sure where that was, but it sounded intriguing.

The new school year started and now I was all "growed up". I would be in Grade One. Mom seemed particularly happy. She made my brother and I stand in the backyard and took a dozen pictures with her old Brownie camera before we were allowed to leave for school that day—the state school. My father had won the argument.

On my first day of school, Dad saw me off at the front door, handing me a brown paper bag with my school lunch in it. My brother delivered me to school that day and continued to do so for a little while until I knew my own way there. Tiny would also follow along. Finally, Tiny would take me to school and re-join me at the school gate to go home when the bell went.

I was so happy on my first day of school; I made a fantastic new friend named Vicky Barnett. She lived a few blocks away from me, and after school on my very first day, Mom, who had stayed home for the day, let me go to her house to play. What a treat! I hadn't had a friend for so long, except for Bevan. But he couldn't actually really talk to me; he would just sit and laugh at me. After that day, Vicky and I became inseparable. We played before school, during school, and after school, always together, never leaving each other's side.

Meanwhile, Mom and Dad were still arguing and drinking—or should I say "drinking then arguing". Dad continued to gamble and there was no money coming into the house, other than the money that Mom was making from her job. Most of that went to pay the bills that my father was racking up, for his tools of trade and materials that he never paid for and his gambling habit.

Each day after school, I would come home, check in with my brother if he was there, change into my play clothes, and go to Vicky's house and play. One night I came home from Vicky's house only to be told to go and sit in the lounge room with my brother until I was called out to the kitchen. Mom and Dad were sitting at the kitchen table, looking pretty grim. I did as I was told. I asked Daniel if he knew what was happening. He didn't but said that he would tell me when he knew. We sat there together for the longest time, and then Mom called out Daniel's name. Daniel was with them for about five minutes.

He came out and told me that Mom and Dad were playing a game and now it was my turn to go in and see them. As I walked toward the door he said, "Mom and Dad are playing a driving game. Tell them that you want to go in Mom's car," and with that I did.

I sat at the table like a big girl. Mom and Dad had set up a make-believe intersection made out of matches. They were not aware that I already knew their game and I was going to pick Mom's car. My eyes quickly scoured the table, assessing the situation. I noticed the usual glass of beer sat in front of them both, and I assumed that I should do what my brother said and not hurt my mother lest they start fighting again.

They had a match sitting at the intersection on one side of the table and another match sitting at the opposite intersection. They explained to me that one of the matches was my mom's car and the other one was my dad's. Now, to me that was just silly because my mom didn't even drive. Of course I wanted to get in Mom's car, because at six years of age it was a novelty; maybe even at fourteen for my brother … unless my brother knew the bigger meaning of the game …?

I chose Mom's car. Daniel had too. With that one small choice both Daniel and I set the direction for our futures in concrete. What a way to decide who gets the kids! Looking back now—and retrospect is a marvelous thing—I can honestly say that neither path would have been perfect for us. But try telling that to a child whose world is being turned upside down and inside out; whose soul is being ripped out inch by inch as each minute of the day ticks on, as those who are supposed to love her most are the ones tearing her heart apart. I never had a fantastic life as a child. That decision, however, was probably a lot better for me than I could have ever been aware of at the time. I still now shudder when I think of the consequences if I had chosen the other car.

I cannot say the same for my brother. I can say that his life changed that night; his whole world collapsed. And he has never fully recovered. Never!

5

Runaway

"Something truly significant was taken from my life; something I needed to have there for eternity."

THE VERY NEXT DAY when I arrived home from school, my father was on the sidewalk packing things into his ute. Dixie was sitting in the front seat of the car! I asked, in quite an angry voice, "What are you doing, Daddy?" He told me to go inside and stay with Daniel.

Again I asked, "What are you doing, Daddy?" with my hands on my hips and the attitude of one angry young girl. He told me he was going away.

"Can I come too?"

He answered, 'No, you can't. You chose to stay with your mother." I didn't understand what he was telling me, but his voice was terribly cold. I started to get upset, whining at him, and begging him not to run away. He told me to go to my brother. With that, my father got in his ute and just drove off, leaving me standing there on the sidewalk, screaming his name over and over. "Daddy, Daddy, Daddy." I ran to the corner, chasing after him and the car.

He didn't stop.

He didn't look back.

He didn't say goodbye.

He just left.

I ran into the house to Daniel—my Danny—and couldn't find him. *Runaway* by Del Shannon reverberated throughout the house from the stereo in the lounge room. I ran around the house, calling out for my brother, but he didn't answer me. Eventually, I heard sobs coming from under the kitchen table. I crawled under there to be with Daniel, but he pushed me off and told me to go to my room. He was so upset; I'd never seen him like this before. He was much older than me, so he knew what had happened. His eyes were wide, red, and swollen from crying. I wasn't to know it then, but he had begged Dad not to go, just like me, and was told to mind his own business. None of it made sense to me. I just knew that I should be upset too, so I started to cry. My brother was hurting and I couldn't make him better. Something was very wrong. I was sure Danny would tell me later.

This episode was to have a profound, long-lasting effect on both my brother's life and mine. Our father had left us. He had separated from my mother. In his wake, he had left us with no food, penniless, and with mountains of outstanding debts and unpaid rent. He had left us to go away with Dixie, the mother of five or so children. Were we not worthy of his love anymore? Obviously not. We were rejected. He never came home again; instead he was now a father to her children.

Later that night when Mom returned home from work, I remember the family—my grandmother, my aunty, my sister—gathering around her, telling her what she should be doing. I watched from a distance as my mother's face went from grey to white while they all talked 'at' her. No one held her and told her it was going to be okay or that she would be able to get through all of this with their help. I don't think they thought to do that. They may have hugged her, but I never saw it. It has always been a long-standing attitude in my family: Don't complain or dwell on it, just get over it and get on with it. But considerations were a little different this time as my mother had been left alone with two children and a mountain of debt. Mom didn't get a lot of money and her life was collapsing around her. In her precarious position she could not see that she was taking Daniel and me down with her.

Nobody other than me would understand the reasons why my mother had been so bitter towards my father for all those months. As I grew older, my mother, in her drunken states, would openly share with me, her daughter, vivid recounts of different things that happened between her, my father and Dixie. Every night she would communicate these things, over and over, to her seven-, eight-, nine-, ten- then eleven-year-old daughter …

Then it continued ... twelve, thirteen, fourteen, fifteen, and sixteen years old ... Night after night after night, until one or two or even three o'clock in the morning. Until, as you will find out later in my story, enough was enough.

Mom didn't cope remarkably well after Dad left. Debt collectors came to the door and many times she would be reduced to tears. She just couldn't pay them. They were sent to collect bills that were my father's that he had left unpaid, for fuel, tools, hardware. Anything he could put on tab he did, so that he had more money for alcohol, gambling, and Dixie, instead of for his family. He just walked out and left us to cope with it all. I truly do not know what he was thinking. God only knows what else he had spent it on. Not us! We never had a lot of food either, so we just coped with what we had.

Sometimes Mom made arrangements to pay off the bills by selling what she could. But we only had a small amount of stuff left. Dad had taken most of the things that were worth anything with him. Nine times out of ten, when the debt collectors came knocking at the door, she would just let them in to take whatever they wanted to try and cover the debts.

Mom fell deeper into depression with every day that passed; but this seemed to go unnoticed by those around her. Every night I would lie in bed and listen to my mother in the lounge room playing *Are You Lonesome Tonight?* on the stereo. Over and over again! It was my mom, Elvis Presley, and a bottle of beer. This was her nightly ritual. I would hear her crying and sobbing. I was so small I couldn't do anything to help her. My brother and I witnessed this time and time again. I loved her in the only way I knew how to.

I missed my daddy, and I didn't know when he was going to come home again. But I always hoped it would be soon. I wish I had been older. I could have held her and assured her everything was going to be alright. But it wasn't alright. It would never be alright again.

Like me, I suppose through music she could express her sadness and gain a lot of solace. (Or is it that I am like her?) As an adult I listened to that Elvis song and I could feel her desperation, her cry for help.

It left me in tears and made me feel sad that my mother was tormented enough by the words to take the action she would ultimately take. She knew that Dad wasn't going to come back and the only option in her mind was to "bring the curtain down".

Some people drift through life and have such an easy time that they could never truly understand pain on this scale. Others are exceptionally good actors and can pretend that they are not hurting, or that they have nothing wrong in their lives. Their facades stop real feelings from entering and hurting them. Keeping up appearances for the good of whatever is their main priority. Then there are those who have no dramas in their lives, so they make up dramas to get attention. Finally, there are others who just do not recover when something like this does happen. Well, my mother was in the latter category. She was never good at hiding things; she coped the best way she knew how to, but in the end it would all beat her.

Debt collectors continued to knock at the door. At first our landlord was remarkably understanding, but his understanding could only go so far. Then he started to pressure Mom for the outstanding rent. It wasn't his fault.

One night my brother said, "I know a way that we can help Mom. Do you want to help me?"

Always willing to be my brother's sidekick, or shadow, I said, "Yeah."

The next morning we got up in the early hours and dressed quickly and quietly. We probably wouldn't have woken Mom anyway, as she slept soundly after drinking. Daniel had lain awake and waited for the milkman to go past. Clip, clop, clip, clop went the horses hooves slowly up the street—the only sound in the early hours of the morning. The rattle and clink of the empty glass bottles also gave him away. We snuck out of the house and ran after the milkman, stealthily collecting all the milk he was leaving on the doorsteps of our neighbors.

When we couldn't hold anymore, we went home and put it under the house and went back for more. The idea was that when Mom needed a bottle of milk we could save her money and just grab one from our secret hiding place. By sunrise, we had about twenty to thirty bottles of milk!

We were so proud of ourselves until a couple of days later when my grandmother came to visit. As she walked up the back steps, she smelt a terribly bad, curdled milk aroma drifting out from under the house. The milk had soured because it wasn't in the fridge and the stench was downright dreadful. Mom told us off in front of Nanna for stealing the milk, but when Nanna went home, she told us that she was really pleased that we had tried to help her, though we were not to do it again—because stealing was a terrible thing. If we'd been caught, we would have gotten into a lot of trouble.

Next, Mom was to receive another blow; we all were.

Approximately three or four weeks after Dad left, a man came to the door holding Mom's beloved cat, Fluffy Bums, in his arms. He had hit Fluffy on the road with his car and Fluffy was dead. Mom was shaking as she gingerly gathered Fluffy Bums into her arms. We had a little funeral for him in the backyard. Mom's tears fell freely.

Fluffy was the very first death I ever experienced as a child. I was very sad that Fluffy had died, but was also reassured by the fact that he had gone to God and now he was in heaven. I wasn't sure what heaven was, but it sounded nice. I reached up and tried to take Mom's hand, but she pulled away from me. That was my first experience of real rejection. I just wanted some love and reassurance. I had lost a fair bit in the last few weeks: my daddy, my cat Fluffy … and now, it seemed by the withdrawn hand, my mother.

I was always Daddy's little girl, so Mom saw a lot of Dad in me, I suppose. Many times she would take that out on me. This was something I needed to get used to, but I wasn't to know that at the time.

Mom was just not coping with everything, and trying to support two children was starting to be financially above her means. In those days there were no social security benefits to help separated parents. We are so lucky these days. Back then there was a payment you could obtain from the local court house if you were deemed poor enough. It was about one pound fifty pence, paid monthly. That's about forty dollars by today's standards.

I guess it was with a heavy heart that one day my mother approached my grandmother and asked if she could take Daniel. As he was older, he probably ate more and had other things that he needed for school and so on. I do not condone what my mother did, giving up her son, but I do not judge her either. From my own personal experiences later on in life, I know where she was at, mentally and financially. People who are desperate do desperate things. She was desperate.

That night after school, Daniel and I went up to Nanna's house with Mom. Daniel was told that he was going to be living with Nanna from that night. I can't even begin to comprehend what my brother must have been thinking at that moment. Nanna took Daniel and showed him what would become his bedroom—the back verandah where there was a single bed set up. Other than a fly screen, the verandah was totally exposed to the elements. There was a single chest of drawers for Daniel to store his belongings, which he then was told to go and collect from our house. He didn't come home again, only to visit.

I don't blame Nanna for this. It was the best she could do under the circumstances. She already had a houseful, and trying to find just one more bit of space in her small house would have been trying. It was either that or they probably would have sent Daniel off to a boys' home.

As we stood there together on the back patio looking at the bed, I slipped my hand into Danny's and he held my hand tight. The wind rustled through the fly screen straight onto us. This is where my lovely brother had to live now. I was devastated.

To this day that patio has never been built in. There is just plastic in the place of the fly screen that was once was there. Eventually, they built a bungalow for my uncle and moved my brother into my uncle's old room. But that was to be a while down the track. Until then, he would live on the verandah, exposed to the elements.

A few days after Daniel moved in with Nanna, I left school at the normal time; Tiny was waiting at the gate for me as usual. Daniel had moved onto high school by this stage, so he was not there. As my friend Vicky and I walked the two blocks home to my house that afternoon, a car pulled up beside us. We ignored pleas for help in getting directions, even though stranger danger was not an issue back then.

Next thing, they said they had a puppy in the car and we both ran over to see. As I got closer to the window, the driver had jumped out of the car and proceeded to grab me by the arm. He started to pull me towards the car. When I started to scream, Tiny didn't hesitate! He jumped up and ripped the man's arm to bits. The man released me to free himself from Tiny, and Vicky and I started to run towards my house. I turned to see him kick Tiny and heard Tiny yelp. I screamed for Tiny to come, so he ran quickly behind me. He had done his job and was so proud of himself.

Once safely inside my house, Vicky and I showed Tiny how extremely proud of him we were by giving him lots of pats and love and telling him he was a good boy. I told Mom about what had happened and she warned me that if that was ever to happen again, to get the number plate of the car. That bit of advice was going to come in handy further down the track.

Two days later, I woke to get ready for school and heard Tiny whimpering in the backyard. I went to see if he was alright and was terrified by what I saw. Tiny's flesh was bleeding over much of his upper body. He was very sick, but still he limped toward me, to be loved, accepted, and patted. But I screamed and ran away because the sight of him like that frightened the hell out of me. I will never forgive myself that I couldn't return the love and the bravery that he had shown to me when I had needed him the most.

Mom heard my screams from the backyard and ran outside. She saw Tiny and just collapsed on the ground in front of him. She couldn't be consoled. Mom had told me in later years that someone had thrown acid over the fence, all over him, and it had eaten him away. I can only assume it was the men in the car, from the attempted kidnapping. No one else had a reason to hurt him. My brother recently told me that Tiny had mange. Nevertheless, we couldn't afford a vet, so Mom had to call the police to come and shoot him.

I will never forget the sound of the bullet as it left the gun, heading for Tiny's head. I was at Nanna's house, but it echoed through her house. I froze, tears pouring down my face. My best friend was lying dead in the backyard, and there was nothing I could do to change it, or to make him better. He was gone. My Tiny was gone and I was upset beyond words.

I would not even know how to begin or where to start in putting onto this page how I felt. There are just absolutely no words that I could use to describe the pain that I experienced when I lost my friend that day. Fifty years later and I still become upset when I think about him, and I think about Tiny often.

We buried Tiny next to Fluffy Bum in the backyard. My friend was handed over to the angels, but he didn't deserve to die that way. I hoped whoever did that to him experience the same suffering that he knew; I still feel like that today.

Of all the things that had happened to me up to that point, and for many years to come, none had such a major impact on me as what happened that day. Something truly significant was taken from my life, something I needed to have there for eternity. My solid, stoic embodiment of love and acceptance, no questions asked, come what may, yes, come what may—my faithful little friend, Tiny. It is so hard to write about him, even now, without crying. These last few paragraphs about Tiny actually took three months to finally write, as the tears and pain hidden deep within my soul from that day, when no comfort was given to me, seeped out onto the pages.

Many an afternoon, I had sat in the backyard and told Tiny all about my problems, my fears, my hopes, and my dreams. He had always sat quietly and listened to me—and now I was alone. He had wanted me around when no one else did. Now I had no one. My mother didn't seem to have a lot of time for me; she was too caught up in her own hell. My brother was gone and my sister had her own life and problems. Nanna didn't want me hanging around much either, so I would sit by Tiny's graveside and still talk to him. It was somewhat comforting. As I look back now, I feel sad for that little girl, that all she had to talk to was her poor, dead dog.

As if fate plotted to drag my mother down to new depths in her hell, the very next morning after Tiny's burial, our canary Jimmy was found dead in the bottom of his cage. I think that tipped the scales for Mom. It was the straw that broke the camel's back … or Mom's at least.

As Vicky and I walked home from school that day we could see in the distance a small crowd gathered outside my house. I crossed the road and joined them… and that's when I saw the ambulance there.

"Don't go in, love. Just wait," someone said. So I stood quietly and did what I was told. The next moment a stretcher was pushed out of the front door towards the ambulance by two men in white uniforms. There was a body on the stretcher, covered by a white sheet. The woman I was standing next to gasped, "Oh my God, she's dead!" There were whispers in the crowd that my father had left and my mother had committed suicide because she couldn't cope.

I didn't know what suicide was, but I saw my sister and grandmother walk out immediately after the stretcher, so I ran to them and asked, "What's wrong with Mommy?"

Robyn just said to me, "Go up to Nanna's place, *now*."

There was a late night vigil at Nanna's that night, with Nanna, my aunty and my sister all talking in the lounge room about the events of the day. My mother had attempted suicide and was not out of the woods. If she had not been found when she was, she would have succeeded. She had overdosed on a large number of sleeping tablets and alcohol. They had pumped her stomach and now it was all up to Mom—if she wanted to come back to us or not. A man who had been my mother's boyfriend before she met my father was by her side at the hospital. Uncle Geoff was a constant figure in Mom's life. Uncle Geoff had been Mom's first love. They had spent many hours together as teenagers riding motorbikes, and generally having fun. He was about to propose to Mom when she met and fell head over heels in love with my dad.

Uncle Geoff held Mom's hand, talked to her, and tried to coax her out of her coma. He supported her continuously throughout the extremely long event, and it was not just overnight. It was well over twenty-four hours before Mom became conscious enough to realize that she hadn't died.

Uncle Geoff was a burly, short man who drove semi-trailers interstate for a living. He loved my mother with all his heart, and I think he did so till the day he died. He was there to try and pick up the pieces that were left. Every hour or so, he would call Nanna to inform her on Mom's progress. I didn't know whether my mom was ever going to come home again, and no one bothered to explain to me what had happened. Why would they? I was only a child. From the way they were all talking, it seemed like she wouldn't be coming home, ever.

I went to bed that night thinking that my mother was dead and that I was all alone now. *What will happen to me?* Everyone, every single person who had ever comforted me and given me love and understanding was gone from my life. I was alone. Not only had my mother lost my father, Danny, Fluffy Bums, Tiny, and Jimmy, but I had too. And now, as far as I knew, I had also lost her.

Even though I lacked love and compassion from my mother, don't think for one moment that it was all doom and gloom. There were happy times that I had spent with her; those moments in time were the very thread that kept me longing for the mother that was now lying in a hospital somewhere, nearly dead. Thinking that I had lost her forever was incomprehensible. She was the familiar—this was the ultimate abandonment.

I stayed at Nanna's house that night and heard them discussing my future. Would I end up out on the verandah with Daniel now? In a way, I hoped so; at least we could be together again. I missed my brother. I also heard them express how selfish my mother was for doing this. As I remember this, I find it hard to comprehend that they didn't know that when someone is at the point where she is willing to take her own life, it's because she has reached a point of no return. She has crossed over mentally to a place where suicide makes sense, and in that state there is no right or wrong, there are no selfish actions. There is only that final surrender to the only obvious option for her to find peace and clarity! My mother's life since Dad had left had been a compounding roll-on of events, which had pushed her beyond the threshold of normal mentality. And me?

I just wanted my mommy to come home to me.

I wanted my daddy back too!

I wanted Daniel.

I wanted Tiny, Fluffy Bums, and Jimmy.

I wanted my safe, little life back, the one that someone stole away from me.

No, life was never going to be the same again. Ever!

This period would also establish a precedent for my young adult life. My mother and role model showed me the way to escape, or more to the point, how to run away from the problems that you should stand and face. When things got too difficult to keep going, thoughts of suicide often clouded my judgment. There is a song from Kelly Clarkson, called *Because of You*. Every time I hear this song now, it reminds me that I have to be so much stronger than my mother was, for the rest of my life. It would be so easy to give in sometimes to the clouded thinking that still haunts me to this day. Death could seem such a sweet relief from the anguish inside my head.

6

P.S. Bubby, I Love You

"I danced around the kitchen like I'd never danced before."

WELL, MOM DIDN'T come home from the hospital. In fact, I didn't see her again for a long time. She did recover but was sent away to take a break, or went away herself; I don't know the real reason.

She had suffered a nervous breakdown. The day she attempted suicide, she had received another bill in the mail for Dad. This bill was from a motel in Queensland in my father's and her names. Quite a hefty bill too. Obviously, my father and Dixie had a lot of fun at our little family's expense. While we were struggling to get from one day to the next with the very basic of essentials, such as food, he was living it up next to the beach with his new family on holidays. Then they had the audacity to leave and not pay the motel bill. In the corner was stamped "Honeymoon package".

I still feel extremely bitter towards them both when I think of this, and I find it extremely difficult to move on from it. I have a dear brother, who was probably conceived as a result of this holiday, and while I would never wish him gone, I do wish it could have been any other way but that.

Back at home, my sister packed up her family and took over the rental on Mom and Dad's house. Mom had been asked to leave before her attempted suicide because she could not pay the rent and the back rent. The house was slightly larger than the one Robyn had and she intended to look after me as well until Mom was well enough to return.

Over the following months, a lot of things happened. Robyn was expecting to give birth to another child and George and she were trying to stabilize a rocky relationship. Both of them were still very young also, and now they had the added hassle and expense of a child who was not even theirs, just a little pest sent to make their lives a misery. This is not how my sister made me feel, but it was definitely how my brother-in-law did.

A lot of this period in my life has been forgotten. There are certain events that stand out, but mostly it was just daily grind. My grandmother took me away from the public school that my father had placed me in and marched me off to the Catholic school, St Pius X in West Heidelberg. I didn't want to go. Leaving there meant I now could no longer play with my best friend Vicky at school. No one listened to my pleas, and with that I was enrolled at St Pius X. I must admit, though, I excelled at school, so it was probably a good move even though it didn't seem like it at the time.

I didn't make friends easily at St Pius X and would spend hours alone in the playground. Children tormented me because some knew of my mother's attempted suicide, and, being Catholic, they called her the devil and me too. I was told that I would go to hell for what she had done, and that certainly frightened me because the school had taught me that hell was an unpleasant place where you burned in pain forever—as if I didn't have enough to cope with.

I was not the prim and proper private school girl. I suited public school much better. You possibly could categorize me better with the tag "St Trinian's" with my tomboy attitude, pre-loved hand-me-downs, crumpled clothing, and mop of curls. I just didn't fit. Still, even with all that was happening around me, I surpassed everyone and was the top of the class each year. I loved learning. I yearned for it; knowledge was my outlet. I had a particular aptitude for history and excelled in it. Later in life I would find out that I had a higher than average IQ.

My sister's life was anything but easy, with her baby now growing and another on the way. Robyn did what she had to, to maintain a beautiful home and try to appease her husband and also look after a forgotten sister. Quite a big ask for one so young. George, on the other hand, didn't seem to like me much, or just didn't like me being around. At times he treated me despicably, mostly when my sister was not in ears' reach. If she had heard some of the things he had said to me, another fight would have ensued. So I just tried to blend into the background as best I could. But still he would have a go at me whenever he could.

One night Robyn dished up lamb chops for dinner. I was never one to pick at food; normally it was all gobbled up within minutes and that night had been no different. George had other ideas for me that night. I have never been able to eat animal fat. As a child, Mom and Dad would always cut the fat off the meat for me. This night the plate was put in front of me and I cut the fat from the chop and ate everything on the plate except for the fat. George was in quite a bad mood that night and told me that I could not leave the table until the fat had been eaten. He growled at me for ages until I cut off a piece of fat and put it into my mouth. I sat with the fat in my mouth only chewing it when he looked at me. I sat there like that for several hours.

My sister was really upset with George for forcing the issue, but he reminded her that he was the one paying for the food and her ungrateful little brat of a sister would not only respect that, but from now on would eat everything on her plate. He tried to force me to swallow the fat and every time I tried, I dry reached until eventually I was ordered to bed. I never ate one morsel of the fat and ended up spitting it into the rubbish bin.

Christmas time was another occasion I remember clearly. I had been sent to bed at the same time as the baby. I laid there wondering what might be under the Christmas tree for me from Santa Claus the next morning. In reality I never got a lot at Christmas, or at any other time of the year, but I knew that Santa Claus was always extremely generous to Carol my niece. Or at least he had been the year before. So I hoped that he might see his way clear to be nice to me this year because I had been extra good.

My bedroom was actually the hallway between the front of the house and the bathroom and toilet, and George had to walk through it to get to the toilet. It hadn't always been my room. Carol now slept where I once had because it was closer to the main bedroom. The back room, where Daniel had once slept, was empty; I'm not sure why I wasn't allowed to sleep in there.

That Christmas Eve, I couldn't sleep because I was so excited. Robyn had placed a Santa sack on the end of my bed and told me that if I had been really good, Santa might leave me something. I had never had a Santa sack before.

On his way back, George stopped and asked in his usual gruff voice, "What are you so happy about?"

I told him that I couldn't wait to see what Santa Claus was going to leave for me that night.

In a cold and abrasive tone, George turned and said to me, "Nothing, Santa Claus is dead."

I immediately started crying for my dad, and quick as a whip he turned to me as he was exiting the room and said, "So is your dad."

I remember I stopped crying and just stared at him for the longest time. Then he left and shut the door behind him. No one could hear my crying; no one was coming to comfort me and to tell me it was going to be alright.

My sister's life was not easy with George. The relationship was abusive. I can't remember alcohol being involved, but I do remember the bashing my sister received just before she was about to give birth to my niece, Kerry. They had fought and it got loud. Neither of them realized that I had seen all of this before in this house; frightening memories were stirring within me.

Robyn told George that she was going out and proceeded to the front door with her bag. George chased her up the short hallway and grabbed her arm. He flung her around and threw her to the floor where she slid seven or so meters down the hallway, landing flat with her back smashed up against the wall.

I ran to help her. I wanted to kill him, but I could see the fear in her eyes. She told me to get the egg from the stove that she had been cooking for me and to run as fast as I possibly could to get my nanna from next door—I didn't need to be told twice ….

I grabbed the spoon from beside the stove and quickly fished out my hardboiled egg. I wrapped it in a tea towel and ran out the back door, across the yard, and up the road to Nanna's house. Tears streaming down my cheeks, I rang the doorbell.

Nanna answered the door with a gruff, "What do you want?"

I told her what had happened.

I was told to wait in the lounge room and I watched as my nanna walked into the kitchen and grabbed a pot. With pot in hand, she headed out the front door and down to Robyn's. What follows is hearsay, but from what I know Nanna hit George over the head with the pot and told him to get out of the house. It was quite cold that night and he was skimpily dressed for May in Melbourne.

Later the next day, Robyn's waters broke and an ambulance was called. She was taken off to the hospital to deliver my beautiful new niece, Kerry. George apparently caught quite a terrible cold and had a sore head. I don't ever remember them having another physical fight after that, at least not while I was around. But George continued to subject me to a lot of mental games.

Meanwhile, I was growing up. I flitted between our house and Nanna's, and I was able to play with my best friend Vicky after school on occasion and often would visit Bevan's house. Because the walk between the Catholic school and home was much longer, and I had to take a different route, I even managed to pick up a new friend along the way who I was able to spend some time with. Her name was Joy, the same as my mother ...

Yes, my mother. How was she? Where was she and when was she coming home?

I can remember on occasion Nanna would stop and say, "Your mother wrote us a letter." She never did say how Mom was, where she was or when she was going to come home—just that she had written. Because of that, every day I would check the mailbox, just in case Mom wrote me a letter. None ever came ... but life went on. I was now becoming used to living my life without my mom around.

Still, one day I asked Nanna if I could write a letter to Mom. She said yes and gave me a pencil and some paper. I remember that I asked Mom how her holiday was going and where she was. I also told her that I missed her and loved her and wished she would come home to me. I talked about my new school and friends, and how life was with Robyn and George. I remember putting three kisses on the bottom of the letter ... *XXX*

A couple of weeks later, while visiting Nanna's house, I was handed a folded-up piece of paper. On it Mom had written:

My darling Bev,
I got your letter. It's nice here in Redcliffe. I can sit and look at the beach. It's nice and relaxing. Yes, I am feeling better now. I have some good news for you. I am coming home. I will see you soon.
Love Mom
P.S. Bubby, I love you.

Yes, underneath she had written *P.S. Bubby, I love you!!*
I danced around the kitchen like I'd never danced before. I even gave Nanna a lovely, big hug. Of course, Nanna pulled away as she was not used to such shows of affection. She was from a different era when things were more formal and dignified. I told her that my mommy was coming home. I went running down to Robyn's and told her that Mom was coming home. I tried to show her the letter, but she told me she knew. I don't know how long it would be until she was to come home, but it didn't matter. All I knew was she was coming, and everything was going to be alright.

But ... with Mom's arrival, what semblance of a near normal life I was living, again was about to disappear like a sink hole. Life was to regress in a downward spiral from that day forward. I was to plunge into total despair, as slowly but surely Mom dragged me down into the very pits of hell where she now existed.

7

On the Road Again

*"I was not used to not being fed;
it was something I would learn to get used to."*

It was hard to settle down again when Mom came home. We lived with Robyn and George for a little while, and I don't think Mom was still quite emotionally or mentally well, even though she put on a brave face. She was still drinking and because of that everyone was telling her how to live her life. She managed to get a job working in a weaving mill. The money helped out for the day-to-day things that we needed.

I figured out a way for me to make money too. I had seen my brother do this for extra pocket money, so that he could get his bits and bobs for chemistry and other good things he tinkered with. He is the only person I know who can blow up a shed by mixing items from a chemistry set.

By knocking on neighbor's doors and collecting their old newspapers on weekends, I was able to sell them to the fish and chip shop owner to wrap his chips in and to the butcher to wrap his meat.

The butcher used to tease me. Every time I walked into the butchers shop hauling my jeep full of newspapers, he would always ask if I had been throwing pebbles into the dunny can—because I have freckles. I didn't find that particularly funny and would always just roll my eyes. He was a good customer though, so I put up with his jokes.

I would take Nanna's shopping jeep every Saturday and walk the streets. I knew the houses to go into and finally learnt the houses I shouldn't go into.

At the start, the little bit of money I earned from doing this I gave to Mom to mind for me.

But one day when I was walking home, I saw a Barbie doll in the window of the newsagents. I can remember standing there staring at her for the longest time. Barbie dolls were new to Australia and all my friends had one. I knew not to ask for one because it was just too much money.

One day, though, I got brave enough to go in and ask how much she cost. The shop owner told me that I could put her on lay-by and pay her off. I didn't quite understand that, but every week when I collected my newspapers, I would give him half of the profit and the other half to Mom. It took me forever to pay the doll off, but I did. She was mine and I loved her. I paid for her all by myself. We became inseparable; she became my best friend since Tiny. Yep, I talked to Barbie.

The final straw for Mom came when I received my school report. At the end of the year in Grade Three, I was awarded a Principal's Award at school assembly for being the top academic student in my class. I couldn't wait to show my newly-returned mother; how proud she would be of me. Finally, I knew someone would be there for me, to share my important achievement with. I was proud of myself. I knew that I had worked hard and had done a good job, under some pretty extreme circumstances.

I ran home at the end of the school day and paced around the front door, waiting for Mom to come home from work. And when she did, I quickly pounced on her and handed my school report and the Principal's Award to her. I had the biggest smile on my face. She grabbed my hands and we danced around in circles on the spot. She was thrilled.

I can never, ever remember seeing Mom looking like that, either before that day or afterwards. Her face was soft and the light curl that her hair naturally settled into fell down onto her face. She looked down and smiled at me and then … she bent down and hugged me!

"I'm sooooo proud of you, Bev, and Nanna will be too. Come on, let's go show her."

This is one of the few times I remember my mother hugging me, and I remember feeling delighted about that, maybe even more than the award. With the presentation and my report in her hand, we headed off to Nanna's house next door. I skipped merrily along behind Mom. It was a hot December day and Nanna and Aunty Beatrice, as usual, were seated out on the front verandah, taking in the warmth at the end of the day.

Mom reached out her hand and gave Nanna the report and Principal's Award.

I waited for Nanna to tell me how proud she was, but it never came. She looked at me and grunted the words, "Good work," and handed the report to my Aunty.

My Aunty said to me, "I suppose you think you're really smart now."

I nodded my head in wholehearted agreement with a smile still spread across my face. At that moment little Bevan from next door was wheeling himself past the front gate.

Aunty Beatrice yelled to Bevan, "Bevan, come here," gesturing for him to come to her. As Bevan wheeled himself up the driveway, Aunty Beatrice turned to me and said, "I bet Bevan is smarter than you."

"Hang on ..." Mom objected.

But my aunty ignored her and asked me, "How high is Mount Kosciusko, Bev?"

I had no idea. I hadn't learned that yet.

She looked at me and then looked at Bevan. "Bevan, how high is Mount Kosciusko?"

Bevan responded, "7,310 feet."

She turned to me and said, "See, told you Bevan is smarter than you."

My mother eyeballed my aunty for the longest period of time and snatched the report from her hands. She grabbed me by the arm and said, "Come on, Bev, we're leaving. We won't stay where we are not wanted."

For the first time in my life I felt my mother's pain. In fact, I felt just like her—uncared for, rejected, and not worthy of love or pride. It's strange how we let other people destroy us, our self-esteem, our self-worth; but we do it, even as children. I had only just turned eight at the time, and I can't even begin to imagine how my mother coped if she had been brought up like that her entire life, or didn't cope, as was the case. I have no idea what my aunty hoped to achieve by the demonstration; however, it was a turning point for all of us.

As we walked quickly back to Robyn's house, Mom turned to me and said firmly, "We're leaving."

And with that, in the following few days, we were gone.

※

Mom was not really one for speaking her mind openly, so when she felt stressed she would often hold it in and then let it out all at once. Living in close confines with my sister and also her family took its toll. She had suffered so much stress from my father leaving, to the point of attempting suicide, yet she still felt misunderstood and rejected by her family also.

Now, they may not have even been aware that she felt this way, but it was enough to cause her to take action. It would be one of the many things she discussed with me at length later in my life, during Mom's more loose-lipped moments under the effects of alcohol.

We didn't go too far—three blocks away, in fact. "Just far enough away to make sure that they're not watching us all the time," Mom had said. "What I do is my business not theirs."

We moved into a bungalow behind a house in Porter Road. It had an extremely small kitchenette and just one bedroom. We had the double bed that Mom and Dad had shared as their marital bed, and not much else. There was a wardrobe with our clothing, some odds and ends that allowed Mom to keep her sanity, and a pot or two to cook with.

Life was vastly different now. School was further for me to walk to, but I still went every day. I didn't have my little nieces around to keep me company, but I made sure to drop in on them every day on my way home from school, when Robyn was at home. I would follow her around like a bad smell until I was told it was time for me to go home.

About three days after moving in, I came home from school and the kitchen area was a mess. We had nowhere to store anything, there were no cupboards. I was quite a resourceful little girl, and on the way home from school the next day, I passed the back of a green grocer's shop where there were about four or five unused wooden fruit cases just laying around.

I quickly got changed and went back to the fruit shop and asked if I could have the crates. The green grocer was only too happy to give them to me when I told him that I wanted to make some kitchen shelves out of them. So I went and got the boxes and brought them home, one at a time. I stacked them up against the wall, one on top of the other on their sides, to create more shelf space. Then I put what kitchen stuff we had into them—sugar, tea, and so on. I then put one of Mom's old table cloths over the front of the crates to cover up how awful they looked. I was immensely proud of myself for what I had done, so I sat and waited for Mom to come home from work so that I could show her.

It was about 11 p.m. that night when the light flicked on and Mom walked slowly in the door of the bungalow. I rubbed the sleep from my eyes, which were still sore from crying while I had pondered where my mom was. I forgot that I hadn't eaten and I rushed to show her what I had done. I was very proud of myself. My stomach was rumbling from hunger. I was not used to not being fed; it was something I would learn to get used to.

She was immensely proud of my resourcefulness, but told me that I needed to put myself to bed.

I told her that I hadn't had dinner yet, and she said, "It's too late now. Tomorrow night you need to make sure you eat earlier."

I tried to find something easy to eat, but Mom shuffled me off to bed.

This began a pattern, one which would only get worse as time went on. I think my mother felt isolated and was craving human contact with others her own age, perhaps believing they understood and accepted her. She had found a pub to go to after work where she could forget who she was for just a little while and attract the attention of a possible partner. The only problem was she forgot me too. She may have come home, but now she was never truly there.

The next night I scavenged around the house until I found something that would make my hunger pangs go away. Eventually, I fell asleep only to be woken up by my mother sneaking in the door at an unusually late hour of the night, again reeking of beer—a smell I still can't bear today. I was so happy to see her after spending all those hours alone; I buzzed around her until I was finally told to go back to bed.

The next morning when I woke, I saw my mother leaving to go to work. It was somewhere around 5.30 a.m. I got up and got ready for school. I dressed myself, brushed my hair and teeth, then had some cereal for breakfast. We didn't have anything there for lunch, so I went to school without any.

That night, again, was the same as the others. I foraged for food until eventually exhaustion overtook me and I fell asleep. Again, in the very late hours of the night, my mother came home. Again she reeked of alcohol, but this time she put herself to bed and just left me in the kitchenette. She didn't even know I was there. She walked around like a zombie and within minutes of her lying on the bed, she was asleep.

I just sat quietly in the kitchenette and listened to the radio, until finally I also could fall asleep again, which was a while as all I could think of was my hunger.

This became my life. Every day of the week, Mom left at 5.30 a.m. and didn't return until 11 p.m. or so. Sometimes she would be responsive; other times she didn't know I was there. I coped the best I knew how to and foraged for whatever food I could get. I was hungry, I was alone, and I was just surviving. I knew not to say anything to my sister or grandmother. My mother warned me that if I did, I would be taken away. When Mom had been taken away, the experience hadn't been so delightful and I missed her too much. So I just shut up.

One night I was sitting in the kitchenette under the dim light, trying to do my homework, when my brother knocked on the door. It was about half past five in the evening. It was the middle of winter and it was dark and cold. Daniel had come to see Mom quickly on his way home to Nanna's from his friend's house. I told Daniel that Mom was late, so he waited for a while for Mom to come home. He left soon after as he didn't want to be late for dinner. Nanna always had dinner on the table at six o'clock sharp.

A couple of nights later, Daniel came again, and after waiting for a while, he asked me what time Mom usually got home. I started to cry and told him everything. He gave me a real big cuddle and said, "Don't worry, sis, I'll take care of you."

With that he put me on the bar of his bike, which was parked outside the flat, and dinked me down to Nanna's house. I knew he couldn't tell Nanna I was there and I had begged him not to. He said he wouldn't, but that I had to eat something. He made me hide in Nanna's backyard and saved me some scraps off his plate, which he snuck out to me in the yard after dinner. I hadn't had a decent meal for a while.

This became a ritual, but not every night. Daniel would come and get me and bring food to me in the backyard, and then he would dink me back home on his bike. That is until one night Nanna became suspicious and followed him outside. She must have wondered what he was up to.

I got into an awful lot of trouble, as did Daniel. Nanna said that Daniel wasn't to feed me anymore; that it was up to my mother to do that. I didn't realize it then, but I believe my Nanna was angry because my mother had moved away from the family.

With that Daniel never came to get me again. He did visit on occasion and sometimes was able to share little bits of food he had with him. I think he was scared that Nanna would throw him out on the street, so he didn't want to cross her. She was a very strict woman who wasn't to be messed around with.

After this happened, my mother was confronted by my grandmother. She came home and told me that we were moving again, this time further away. I found out that the people who owned the house in front of our bungalow had also told Mom that if she didn't begin to take proper care of me, the police would become involved.

And with that, we packed up and moved to Fairfield. Now it was too far for my brother to ride and too far for our family to interfere. It was also too far for me to retain any semblance of the life I had put together for myself in Heidelberg.

I was enrolled into another Catholic school, St Anthony's, where only "good Christian children" attended. Here I was starting again, trying to find new friends and invariably gaining new tormentors. You know the ones; they call you names and poke fun at you because you're dressed shabbier than they are, or your hair might not be as clean as theirs or even brushed on most days. The fact that they had lunch and I didn't was another teasing point. There was no compassion when they saw me pulling scrunched up lunch bags out of the bin because I was hungry enough to eat their leftovers. Apparently, unlike me, these "good Christian children" were "nice" children.

This is where I got my very first nickname, rag doll. The song by Frankie Valli and The Four Seasons, *Rag Doll*, was probably hugely responsible for that nickname. As well as the fact that I always looked ragged in my un-ironed uniform and unpolished school shoes.

My father would have been very disappointed to see the state of my shoes as he was very particular about school shoes being highly shined and clean.

8
The Loss of Innocence

*"I saw a shadow and the door handle started to turn.
I had never been so frightened of anything
in my whole life."*

LIFE CHANGED, AGAIN. We moved further away still, into a bungalow at the back of another family's home—this time an Italian family. Mom kept up the same behavior. She found a new place to drink, and so again I was left for hours on end, often with no food in the house whatsoever. This went on day after day after day. Mom would stumble through the door at around eleven o'clock every night, often too drunk to care if I had been fed, washed, or otherwise.

The only day I ever spent with my mother when she had not been drinking was Sundays. I loved Sundays. Mom would run around the house and clean what had to be cleaned and do the washing. She would shop for food on Saturday mornings before she went to the pub, so we always had a roast dinner on Sundays. We lived on the remnants of that roast for the following week. Sometimes, on a Saturday afternoon, Mom would take me to the pub with her when she had finished her shopping.

Mom's time away from the house became much more frequent; so much so that once when she didn't come home for two days, I went to look for her. I figured she would be at the hotel where she had taken me on Saturdays. It was around 9.45 p.m. on a week night and I had walked the three miles from Fairfield to Northcote by myself. I turned onto High Street and continued until I came to the pub. It was quite frightening for me as I had never really ventured out at night and every shadow made me jump. When I walked in, I saw her sitting with a bunch of people. Unlike Saturdays, they didn't give me a drink of raspberry lemonade or chips, just scowling looks. There they were, a band of lonely old men, working extremely hard to be in my mother's bed that night. I looked at each in turn, taking in the wrinkles, slurred speech, and unsteady steps as they headed to the bar to get two or three more glasses of beer before closing time, calling out to each other about how many they should get. These were the days when all pubs closed at 10 p.m.

My mother looked up from her beer and said, "What are you doing here?"

I grabbed her arm. "Come home, Mommy. I'm hungry."

Everything happened so fast.

Mom jumped from her seat and smacked me so hard across the face that I fell back against a table and the wall, hitting my head against the chair and my face against the corner of the table.

The proprietor ejected her that night and banned her from ever coming back. He told her how lucky she was that he didn't call the police on her and have me taken away. So many people were to threaten Mom with the police because of her treatment of me; yet none of them would ever carry out their threats.

Mom staggered all the way home with me holding her hand. It was a long walk. I was lectured on how bad I was to have done what I did and told that I was never do it again "or else". And I didn't. I would never take that walk again. Even if she never came home, I would not go to the pub to find her. It was obvious I had done something terribly wrong. My face ached with pain where the table had caught me before the wall met my head.

The next day I had a black eye and had to lie to my teacher about how I got it. I knew I was going to hell for that lie because she was a nun. It also became clear to me that I had become somewhat of a burden to my mother, so I learned to cope better by myself. I figured that if I learned to take better care of myself and took that responsibility off her shoulders, she would love me more. Luckily, I was smart and intelligent and self-preservation kicked in. I learned that if I hung around the back door of the Italian family's home at the right times in the evening, I would get an invitation to dinner, where there would be lots of food. They were lovely to me, except for their little girl Mariella. She always said nasty things to me in Italian, calling me a *bruto* and telling me that she was *bella*. I figured out what that meant. I hate that word with a passion—bella, bella, bella. It makes me want to poke somebody in the eye with a ball point pen! (Okay, so that's my street kid defense showing through. We're supposed to mellow with age, right? I must have missed the mellowing part of the maturity cycle.)

Life wasn't all bad in Fairfield. I met some boys and we would often go to the local creek and catch tadpoles in the puddles. I was such a tomboy and often came home from school covered in mud. I would wear the same uniform to school the next day, which was probably another reason for my not being liked.

The same boys also showed me where the local swimming pool was. I wanted to go to the pool on Saturday afternoons when Mom went to the pub, as she no longer took me with her. For that I needed to scratch together enough money for my entrance fee. I could no longer walk the streets collecting newspapers because I had nothing to carry them in since moving away from my grandmother. I knew I was stealing from my mother, and I knew how much we needed the money for food, but I scrounged just a five cent piece here and a ten cent piece there. I never took more than I needed, just enough for my two bob entry and an ice block. I figured it couldn't hurt too much; it was such a small amount. I sure did enjoy those afternoons at the pool.

One day I came home from school and again sat and waited for Mom to come home. We didn't have a television at this point. The only time I got to watch a television was if we went to my sister's or my grandmother's, which was a rare treat in those days. We only went to Robyn's if she needed a babysitter and to Nanna's sometimes on my school holidays, though mostly now just at Christmas.

I sat and listened to the radio and studiously did my homework. For all that I was going through I tried quite hard to keep up with my schoolwork.

I never missed a day of school. By six o'clock my stomach was ready to crawl up and eat my head, so I hung around the back door of the warm Italian family, hoping for an invite to dinner. I was not to know but they had decided not to look after me anymore, and they intended to kick my mother out of the bungalow as soon as possible. They had seen enough, just like everybody else.

When I didn't get invited in to eat, I went in search for whatever food I could find in our cupboards. We didn't have a refrigerator at that time and there was only one egg—nothing else. So I grabbed a pot and boiled the egg as I had seen my sister do when I had lived with her. When I had cooked it for an unusually long time, I cracked the shell open and ate it with a small spoon.

Within minutes, I started to feel ill and my stomach ached so much that it bent me over with severe, stabbing pain. Minutes later I could not stop throwing up. I put myself to bed but still the vomit kept coming. We only had the one bed, a double, and I was to share that bed with my mother until I was sixteen.

By the time my mother came home at 11 p.m., I had vomited so much that I had fallen asleep from exhaustion and dehydration. Mom just climbed into bed beside me. The next morning she woke up and found herself amongst all the vomit from the night before. She realized immediately that I was terribly sick, so she took the day off work and dressed me to get me to the doctors.

On the way out of the yard, the father of the Italian family tried to stop her to talk, but she pointed out how sick I was and told him firmly that she needed to get me to the hospital. He moved away and let her through. His battle would be fought at a different time.

It took several days, but eventually I recovered from my bout of food poisoning. Mom had long since returned to work and her long nights away. I'm not sure if the father of the house spoke to her; all I know is that we stayed for a few months longer in Fairfield.

It was during this time that Mom brought a guy home from the pub and introduced him to me as "Uncle Graham". She seemed to be quite taken with him and he was very good to me. Uncle Graham had a car and he would take us on trips on the weekends, to the bush or to the beach. He would buy me ice-creams and drinks, and he often came around with the odd toy or a new dress for me. He was a lovely-natured man, very tall and dark in complexion, with extremely dark hair. It was easy to like him; I could understand why Mom was so smitten with him. He wanted to teach her to drive, and I remember the comedy of errors that became Mom's driving lessons until he finally gave up and just drove her around so she couldn't destroy his car any further.

A few weeks after he entered our lives, he took us to Doncaster to introduce us to his family. When we walked into their house, my mouth dropped in awe. There were large sculptures adorning every mantle, bench, and table in the home. Large mirrors and paintings on the walls gave off an air of luxury and wealth that was far beyond anything I had ever imagined.

We were directed to sit on the leather lounge suite. I had removed my shoes at the door, so I could feel the plush carpet beneath my feet. Everybody was well-dressed and polite, and before long another girl my age, Mary, was asked to take me to her room where we could play without disturbing the adults.

Another Italian family! They accepted my mother and I with loving energy; it was such a large, extended family. From then on I loved going over to their place. It was always so happy and so much fun. Food was plentiful and if I wanted anything, I only had to ask. Graham's mother was always pushing food into my hand and I gladly accepted every morsel.

Mary's grandfather seemed so friendly and gentle, just like Graham. He always gave me twenty cents to buy lollies with. I was so taken with this family. I felt a sense of love that I had never experienced before, a sense of acceptance, and, of course, a sense of not wanting for anything. It was a little girl's dream!

School holidays were fast approaching and Mary asked her parents if they would let me stay for the two weeks, so she would have someone to play with. It was decided. I packed a few things into a string shopping bag and waited for Graham to pick me up after work. He arrived on time and took both my mother and I over to his parents' house to drop me off for my holiday.

Later that night, his parents left the house and Mary's grandfather was left in charge of us. She called him "Nonno". He let us get away with anything that we wanted and told us to dress up for him. It was fun.

We dressed up as dancers and frolicked around the lounge room in front of him. He seemed to take delight in every second. Then he told us it was time for us to take our baths and get ready for bed. We did! When we had settled down in the bedroom and turned the light off, Mary climbed into my bed. We pulled the sheets up over our heads, turned on a torch, and read her story books. We could hear her grandfather moving around in the lounge room.

"I need to tell you a secret," Mary whispered conspiratorially but with an edge of urgency to her voice.

"What is it?" My ears pricked up. I'd never been trusted with a secret before from my friends and it felt really good—except I could already sense some fear in her voice.

"Nonno comes into my bedroom and does things to me when Mommy and Daddy are not here."

"What kinds of things?" I was starting to feel a little nervous.

"He gets in my bed and touches me … down there. I don't like him doing it—it hurts—but he scares me. He told me that I would get in trouble if I tell."

Well, I became terribly scared too. I couldn't really understand what she was talking about—I was only eight years old—but something in her voice told me that it was going to happen tonight and that she didn't want it to.

After Mary returned to her bed, I laid there for what seemed like an eternity and stared at the light that was coming from the crack under the door. I didn't say a word. I was wound up with fear and my stomach was feeling sick. Then I saw a shadow and the door handle started to turn; I had never been so frightened of anything in my whole life. I took a deep breath in and lay as still as I possibly could, pretending to be asleep.

I heard Mary's grandfather whisper something to her in Italian, so I couldn't understand what he was saying. I did recognize the word "bella" and I knew that translated to beautiful—yep, that's another reason why I *hate* that word.

I heard the squeak of the springs under her mattress as he got into bed with her. I felt confused. He stayed there for what seemed like an eternity while I lay there with my heart beating hard in my chest. I didn't know how he was hurting her; all I knew was that she was scared of him and didn't like it when he did this. I felt as scared as a rat caught in a trap.

The squeak from the springs told me he had left her bed. I could see him moving quietly towards me ... I was frozen in terror.

Mary's grandfather, who had only a while ago been laughing at us dancing, gently pulled the sheets back and climbed into bed with me. I was shocked to feel his naked body. Immediately, he started to feel my little under-developed breasts. It was dark and I couldn't see anything, but every sense in my body was switched on! I felt sick.

"No," I said, pulling away from him.

Mary then whispered softly, "Please don't stop him or he said he will hurt me." Later I would find out that I was not his only other victim. Mary told me that many of her other friends had also been violated by him.

He moved his hand under my pajamas to my genitals and started to rub—it hurt. He then starting rubbing even harder and pulled at my hands to put them on his penis. Each time I pulled my hands away from that hard "thing" to try to hide my crotch area with them he shushed me away and became more forceful, until he was smacking my hands out of the way. Finally, he won and inserted his fingers into my vagina. I figured this was what Mary meant when she said he sometimes "hurt" her.

In the end, all I could do was to give in and stop struggling. He was just too big for me to stop, and too scary. It didn't matter if I screamed or made a fuss, there was nobody in the house to help me. The fight in me was gone. I lay there silently crying, just like Mary. I was scared for Mary and frightened that she would be hurt, and even more so I was frightened for myself.

I could not sleep for such a long time after he crept from the room for fear that he would return, and because of the burning in my vagina. I lay awake for such a long time after he left, watching his shadow pace backwards and forwards in the dim light coming from the crack under the bedroom door. It was like he was unsure whether he wanted to come back in. I had never been assaulted in this manner before and I was left feeling very confused as to what had just happened to me. All I knew for a fact was that if I told anybody what had happened, he would hurt Mary and he would hurt her badly. That was enough to retain my silence and, in his mind, my permission.

The next day the mongrel was still not finished with me. As Mary and I played in the yard, in full view of the kitchen window, he called me into the front seat of the car where he was sitting, fixing the steering wheel. I didn't dare disobey him for fear that he would come back again that night. Mary disappeared. I'm not sure if she went inside; she suddenly just wasn't there anymore.

After I got in the car, his hand went straight between my legs and he rubbed my clitoral area under my pants, pushing my legs further and further apart while he relieved himself with his other hand. The whole time he was in full view of the kitchen window. Looking back, it appears that he got excited by doing it in the open and not being caught—he seemed to thrive on risk.

I had never seen a penis before, let alone an engorged one, and I was horrified when the white stuff came out of the end of it. I knew better than to scream, but when he finished with me and himself, he let me out of the car and I ran into the house to the safety of the lounge room where the family had gathered. I knew he would not come in there after me. I started crying.

"I want to go home! I want to go home!" I told them quite forcefully through my tears. I was so insistent that they had Graham collect Mom and bring her to the house.

Mom was extremely upset with me for causing so many problems for Graham's family. She berated me in front of them and told me that I couldn't always have what I wanted. And with that Graham took her home, leaving me there. I was so frightened. I don't think Graham's mother wanted me there anymore either because I had been so naughty by demanding to go home. She looked at me more like a problem child now. Nothing more was said on the subject though, and Mary and I were told we had to play outside and away from the house.

We went back out to the yard and sat in the furthermost corner, as far away from the house as possible, where I cried. I told Mary what her grandfather had done to me and that I wanted to go home. She told me that her grandfather often "hurt" her in the car and that I was lucky that he hadn't "hurt" me. I didn't understand. In my mind he had already hurt me. How could he hurt me more? I had never encountered anything to do with sex or sexuality before this trip to Graham's parents' home. I had no idea what Mary was referring to.

"What do you mean?" I asked, shaking.

I was soon to find out …

※

Because I didn't tell on the grandfather, he took this as his signal that he was free to do whatever he wanted to me, as there was no risk I would expose him. But the only thing that was keeping me quiet was that I knew he would "hurt" my friend if I said anything. I was his for the taking, and at every opportunity while I stayed there, he did take what he wanted.

There were several more instances of babysitting by him before the end of the school holidays, and each time he took more liberties with my tiny body. He performed oral sex on me and further penetration of my vagina using his fingers.

I was sickened by his advances but allowed them because of the fear that he engendered in me. I avoided him at every turn; however, when we were playing in the yard or left in his care at night it was impossible. Most children were sent outside during the day when I was a child and you could guarantee that he would choose to be in his car at that exact time. I felt trapped. There was nowhere to hide from him.

Then one day when his family were in the kitchen preparing the evening meal, and the car and him were in full view again, he called me to the car and again I quickly obeyed; I was very frightened of him. He straddled me across his lap, facing me away from him so he couldn't see my face. He brought one arm across my midriff, and, as he lifted me, he pulled my underpants to the side with his other. I felt his engorged penis push up as hard as he could make it go into my vagina. Then he used the arm that he held me secure with across the midriff to push me down onto him even further. I put my hands over my mouth to cover my muffled screams—I didn't want to cause another scene. I knew I would get into so much trouble if they had to call Mom again.

As he pushed me up and down on him, I thought I was dying. Tears streamed down my face from the pain, and then just as I thought I could take no more, he pushed harder—and I died just a little more as I felt myself tearing in two. But still I didn't scream out for help. This was to set a pattern in my life, a cycle of abuse from many others and self-preservation at any cost.

All the time he was doing this he told me that if I didn't let him do it, Mary would pay for it.

"I will hurt her too, you know," he said.

He spoke in broken English, but it was abundantly clear what he would do to Mary if I made a sound or stopped him. Mary had already warned me that he had said this to her. I didn't want this for her. I didn't want him to hurt my friend; so I obeyed. I stayed straddled across his lap, with my hands over my mouth, staring at the cross on the rosary beads hanging from the rear-view mirror as it swayed gently backwards and forwards in front of me. I wondered if Jesus could see me, and if he could whether I was now going to hell. This is where I learned to disconnect during abuse, being mesmerized by a swaying crucifix.

Eventually, the grandfather's breathing became labored and with each thrust up he started to moan. Then he stopped. I felt wet, sticky liquid between my legs ... and then he quickly threw me off onto the seat. He discarded me like a piece of trash. He passed me an old oily rag, which he told me to wipe between my legs to clean myself up. When I saw the blood on the cloth I panicked and didn't know what to do. He opened the door to the car and told me to get out.

I learned that day that not all love is good. When I told Mary what had happened, she told me she knew and confirmed that that was the "hurting" her grandfather did to her.

That was my last day at Mary's house, and fortunately we never went back there again. If my mother had ever told me that I was going back there again, I would have run away. I never pushed my mother to let me see Mary again, and I never told her what the grandfather had done to me either.

THE LOSS OF INNOCENCE

I just retreated into a little make-believe world where I was safe, loved, and fed; everything was beautiful there. In this world I would crawl up onto my dad's knee every night and talk to him about everything, while he would sit patiently and listen to me. I told him about all the things that were happening to me. I imagined him as a beautiful angel up in heaven. Sometimes I would go out into the yard and look up at the night sky and try to figure out which star my father was. I still do that today. I thought he was dead because George had told me he was.

~

Images of this time and many other days have haunted my dreams for decades, and still do. Sleep is not always respite from these memories; neither are my waking moments. They are simply never far away from me. I just keep them in the dark recesses of my mind, where, until recently they have mostly stayed concealed and secure. I have come to a place in my life where I have been able to bring them to the surface now and deal with them. For years I have been scared of the monsters in my bed.

We didn't see Graham for a long time after that. He just stopped coming around. It was as if he sensed there was something wrong on the car journey from his parents' house to mine. He was very quiet. Mom accused me of being so naughty while staying at his parents' house that he no longer wanted to know us.

It wasn't long after that that I heard the Italian father from the main house yelling at my mother in the yard. He told her that she was an unfit mother and that if she didn't take better care of me, he would call the police and I would be taken away. They raised their voices at each other and he ended his argument with the words, which he almost spat out in disgust, "Get out. You have one week, you drunken puttana!" (Puttana is Italian for whore or prostitute.) I didn't know that at the time, but my mother was anything but one of those.

Later on that week, just before we moved, I was walking home from school when I saw these cute little yellow birds in the window of the pet shop. I stood there for the longest time, just staring at them. I then asked the guy at the counter if I could hold one. He took one out of the cage and gave it to me. When he put that little yellow bird into my hands, I just wanted to take it home.

Each day on my way home from school, I would stop and just stare at these cute little birds. Then the man who owned the store asked me if I would be allowed to have one.

I replied enthusiastically, "Yes."

So, he opened the cage and gave me one to hold while he went to find a small box to put it in. I ran all the way home with the little bird in the box. All I could hear was "Cheep, cheep, cheep." I was so excited when Mom came home. I showed her my new friend.

She was annoyed to begin with, but then she asked me, "What are you going to call him?"

"Chirpy," I answered.

So Chirpy was his name, and now my home was Chirpy's home. Chirpy became a very significant participant in my life over the following two years. He would be my friend, my confidant, my all. By the way, Chirpy was a chook!

On that Saturday morning, as the last box was carried out to the moving van, I placed Chirpy in his box. Then I climbed up into the back of the truck and sat on the little box seat that the removalists had left for me to sit on. With Chirpy safely in his box on my knee, they pulled up the back of the van and locked it in place. I could still see out over the tail gate. Then off we went, along the road to new adventures and what I hoped would be new beginnings, with no evil grandfathers.

9
GROOMED

"I needed and wanted reassurance, the security of love ... I felt deep down that this was all wrong ... but who could I tell that would care?"

THE SIXTIES WERE certainly turbulent times. It was the dawning of the Age of Aquarius. Teenagers were givin' it to the man, women were burning their bras, the first issue of the pill took place, new electric Pope refrigerators were being delivered to homes, putting the iceman out of business, man first flew into space, and then Neil Armstrong walked on the moon.

There were young men being conscripted and sent to war, and louts with long hair, jeans, flares, and pencil legs, swaying and smoking to the Beatles, Rolling Stones, and the Who. They were fun times, and they say if you can remember the sixties, you weren't really there. Well, I wasn't quite old enough to "not be there" in the drug sense, but I really remember this time very well, sometimes too well.

You see, on another note it was also a particularly dark period in Australian history because not everything was dealt with appropriately. Terrible things were covered up or not considered crucial enough to be spoken about, like the abuse of children and women—they actually seemed unimportant. For me the sixties were a period of contrasts: the light and fun of the music and friends, and then there was the darkness ...

My first real memory of living at 448 St. George's Road in Thornbury was playing in the front yard, not long after moving there. Two young girls walked past the front gate, Josephine and Lyn. They were much older than I was, but still they stopped and talked to me for quite some time. They asked me if I wanted to come and hang out with them. Josephine was a teenager, about thirteen, and Lyn would have been around twelve. I was a friendly nine-year-old child who was now much wiser than her years. Nevertheless, I was accepted easily into their fold. We had a particular connection, and pretty soon I found myself following them everywhere. I think it was a connection of like-minded souls—children whose parents didn't care enough about them to worry. Latchkey kids. It was at this time that I started occasionally wagging school; it was much more fun hanging out with them.

Often we went to boys' houses during the day, while their parents were at work, and played "Spin the Bottle". Josephine was like my guardian and never let any of the boys touch me. She had no idea of what I had been through at that point. But I saw the attention that Josephine and Lyn got from the boys and I wanted it too. Josephine showed me how she wore her mother's bras and filled them with socks; soon I was doing the same. I was a nine-year-old girl, walking around with a D-cup bra. I smile at the recollection of how stupid that must have looked. It didn't matter back then. I was accepted and it felt so good to belong, and hey, it was the sixties, so why not? While others were burning their bra, I was trying to expand my mother's with hankies and socks.

We lived in a half-house; we had a kitchenette, one bedroom, a bathroom, and an outside toilet. In the backyard we also had a bungalow, which came as part of the package. Mom decided to let one of her male friends from the local pub live in the bungalow as the rent he paid her helped to purchase essential items like alcohol, and it paid for a gambling habit she had now acquired. His name was Ernie, "Uncle Ernie".

We had a few bits of furniture: a two-seater dining room table, a small refrigerator, a double bed, a stereo HMV (His Masters Voice), and a small, black and white television that we had inherited from my sister. There was also one old, green lounge chair with wooden arms. This is where Mom would sit on a Sunday afternoon and watch the weekend 'yippee' movie as she would call it, or Westerns such as Wyatt Earp and High Noon, and then the Sunday wrestling after we had eaten our roast lunch. I loved Sundays and will always remember them with affection. It was the only time I got to spend with my mother. I would lie on the floor in front of her, glued to the television set, watching Chief Billy White Wolf—a fairly famous wrestler—toss other men around the ring. He was my favorite.

Days passed and I continued to wag school, and Josephine and Lyn came to my place and we hung out. If Mom had any concerns, she never showed it. She still came home at 11 p.m. every night. Something had changed, though. Now she started to continue her drinking at home until the early hours of the morning: one, two, even three o'clock. Most nights she called me out into the kitchen after I had put myself to bed to talk to me about the "old times" and how much of a bastard my father was.

I learnt many family secrets this way. I didn't like these talks and somehow I would eventually manage to wiggle my way out of them and go back to bed. As I got older, this started to happen more frequently and I was getting back to bed later and later.

Josephine came around one day and told me that the Master's Apprentices were going to be the guest band at the YMCA dance in Thornbury that Saturday night. She asked if I would be allowed to go with her, if I wanted to go. I was totally over the moon for Jimmy Keays, the lead singer. The age limit was thirteen. She told me not to worry; she would make sure I passed to get in.

I asked Mom if I could go and she agreed and gave me the entrance fee. We told her the shorter version, not including the age limit. Josephine dressed me in her baby doll swimmers, which looked just like a go-go dress, and stuffed the bra full of socks and hankies. She put a small amount of make-up on me and, voila, I looked great! Well, at least in a child's eyes anyway. I passed for thirteen, and after that if anyone ever asked my age, I told them I was thirteen. After that night, it was common knowledge that I was that age, and I was also known as *Duncan's Apprentice*—Duncan being Josephine's last name.

I was in love with the Master's Apprentices and sat as close as I could to the stage so that I could take in every part of them. When they sat down for a rest, I snuck around the back of their chairs and attempted to remove a strand of hair out of Jim Keay's head; instead it was Molly Meldrum's hair (if I'd known how scarce Molly Meldrum's hair would be in the future, I would have kept that strand for him). All I will say on that matter is he was NOT happy and used some real colorful expletives to express that to me. I ran off laughing and continued to have a fantastic night, even though I was a little sad that I didn't get Jim's strand of hair. I didn't dare try it again, but Josephine somehow managed to.

The dance at the YMCA continued to be the highlight of my life. Every month a different band played, and every month after that until I was eleven I attended, even if the crowd that I went with changed. Eventually, Josephine outgrew me as Lyn already had. I was too young to keep up with them. They were in their mid-teens and didn't want a child hanging around them. I missed their friendship, but eventually I moved on and found another group to hang with—a boy named Ricky and his sister Kylie, more my own age. It wasn't long before Ricky and I became boyfriend and girlfriend; we went everywhere together. We had some stolen kisses in the back lanes of Thornbury with the purity that you would expect from kids our age. The only thing was that I was an extremely grown up ten year old by then; I had had experiences far beyond my years. But I kept that knowledge to myself.

Sometimes I was sent to stay with Nanna for school holidays. When I went to her house, I was more of a nuisance factor. I found it boring, not being able to be my own person, not being able to go out and run the streets when I wanted. I was used to a certain way of life now, a wilder kind of life, and every time I was at Nanna's I had to revert to someone I wasn't.

I had a terrible resentment towards my cousin Anne. Anne lived with her mother, who was my Aunty Beatrice, at Nanna's house. She was protected, loved, fed, and had everything a teenage girl wanted. She had good looks, a fabulous body, grace and modesty, private schooling and, well, everything I didn't have. Most of all, she had my grandmother's affection. Nanna would say to me that if I was only half the girl that Anne was, I might be able to make something of myself one day. Lovely!

I envied Anne so much. None of this of course was her fault; just different things had happened that encouraged me to form that opinion, and the adults in our lives did not help to promote any other type of relationship between us. Anne was much older than me, so she lived in a different reality, one of a teenager. I would be given some of her hand-me-downs to save money. Not all of them mind you, not the really good stuff. Don't get me wrong; her hand-me-downs were exceptionally good, but I hardly ever got anything new that was only mine, except this one time.

On one of these trips to Nanna's house, my sister bought me some new clothes. We were shuffled into the backyard together for photos: my brother, Anne, and me. I was so happy to have something new for once. I think my grin went from one ear to the other. Finally, I had something that was mine, all mine and not anyone else's. I will always be grateful to my sister for doing that.

Every night at Nanna's I would sit between her legs on the floor in the lounge room and have my hair brushed. She was not a gentle person when it came to brushing. On one particular night I can remember the hairbrush crashing into the back of my head and Nanna stating with such disdain, "The dirty little bugger has got nits." She demanded that I go directly to Anne's room. I had been sleeping in Anne's bed while she was off somewhere.

My Aunty was up in arms, saying she didn't want me near any of Anne's things in case I gave Anne nits. I can remember sitting on the bed in Anne's room with a smile on my face. I finally had something that Anne didn't have. I was so happy. I had nits.

The next day I was taken up the road to a lady named "Aunty" Pearl who was a hairdresser. She cut off all my hair and doused me with kerosene. They would continue to smother me in kerosene every day for the following week. I stunk. It stung my eyes and I was scared I would catch on fire when people smoked around me. They truly did not know any better back then. That was just the way nit treatments were done back in those days. I was ordered to stay away from "the little bastards" that gave me nits or we would have to do it all again. Mom copped a mouthful from Nanna for sending me there with nits. It seemed to be the way; every time we went to Nanna's, Mom was the target.

Once I returned home to Thornbury and the school holidays were over, life resumed as always. Again, I gladly hung out with Ricky and Kylie, nits and all. I loved these guys, especially Ricky who had now started to hold my hand whenever we walked the streets together. We had a ball, often going to the storm water drains near the golf course in Thornbury and sneaking over the fence. We would walk for miles in those drains, not knowing the real dangers of doing so. When I grew up, a young child would later be killed in those same drains from storm water that was released during a rain storm. How lucky we had been. I must have lived down in those drains for almost a year.

We hung out down there, just talking, playing, and living. At night, though, Kylie's parents would make sure that they were safely bathed, fed, and tucked away for the evening. I would return to the loneliness of the half a house where we lived and wait to hear Mom's footsteps come up the garden path. Her footsteps were unique. She walked heavily, and later on in my life they would actually save me by bringing me out of a comatose state.

Instead, on this particular night I heard Ernie come home. It was about 8 p.m. He popped his head in the back door and asked, "Is your mom home yet?"

I am sure he would have known because he was usually with her at the pub until closing time.

"No."

"Have you eaten yet? I have some leftover chips you can have. But you'll have to come to the bungalow and get them."

Wow! Chips! Food! I merrily skipped along behind him and it wasn't long before we were eating hot chips from the packet. He turned on his television and we sat for a while and watched a show.

"Hey, Bev, have you ever been to Luna Park?"

"No," I replied.

"That settles it then. I'll ask your mom if I can take you. It's lots of fun."

After about an hour, he sent me back to the house where I sat and watched the television until Mom came home.

When Mom arrived home that night, about 10 p.m., she brought Graham in with her. Graham hadn't been to our place in a long time. She immediately told me to go to bed and I complied willingly. I lay in bed for the longest time, listening to them laughing and whispering, and then I slowly fell off to sleep.

When I woke the next morning, Graham was laying in the bed beside me, his arm over my waist and his hand down my pants and his fingers on my genitals. My mother lay right beside him on the other side, asleep. I spun around towards him, nearly falling out of bed in the process. The look in his eyes was cold and calculating, just like the grandfather's—and, I realized, just like *his* father's. It told me that I shouldn't utter a single word.

I lay there frozen. He took my hand and placed it on his penis, which had grown fat and hard. I had learnt by now that when this happens, it is no use struggling. So I just surrendered, as I had with his father—I knew I wouldn't win.

He kept one hand over mine, rubbing his penis while he continued to keep his hand down my pants touching my genitals. He rubbed me harder and harder and it was hurting, but he didn't stop until he had orgasmed. Then he just stopped and rolled over to face my mother. What was it with this family? They were a pack of perverts and pedophiles.

He didn't visit every night, but when he did I knew what was going to happen.

First, he would get my mom into such a drunken state that she would fall into a deep sleep, and then he would take what he was really after—me. With her lying beside us in the bed, he would have penetrative sex with me from behind. It was as if his father had told him that I was there and able to have sex. He was a predator, and a particularly scary one at that.

Once I tried to call out "Mom" in a whimpering voice as he hurt me on entry.

His hand quickly covered my mouth and his cold stare met my eyes in warning as he leant up on his arm to look at me. Mom stirred in her sleep and mumbled something. He stopped, dead still, but when she settled down again he continued. He whispered in my ear that I was a fuck'n little bitch and that if my mom woke up, he would have to kill her.

After a couple of weeks, I was so afraid when he came around, I didn't know what to do. So on any nights that I was pre-warned of his arrival,

I would ask Mom if I could sleep at Kylie's house. I did this almost every time until he realized that I wasn't going to be there and he stopped coming around.

At the back of Kylie's house, in one of the many back laneways that are Thornbury, there was an old car seat up against the fence, near their back entrance and garage door. This is where I slept on the nights that he was coming. Rain, wind, and cold were far better than what waited for me at home.

※

At least I had someone kind in my life to look after me—Uncle Ernie. Every few nights after the first time that Uncle Ernie had fed me, he always brought home something for me to eat from the pub—a packet of chips, some hot chips or a Chiko roll. Then he started to bring me home a small bag of lollies to go with it. It was wonderful. We took our trip to Luna Park. What a fun day. Afterwards he let me run in the small waves along the shore at St Kilda beach. He bought me all types of little things that day: a doll on a stick with a pretty pink dress, a bag full of liquorice, and other assorted goodies.

Uncle Ernie started to become like a father to me, one that I needed so badly. I began to look up to him as someone with whom I'd always be safe. A relationship was forming between us, one that would be difficult to break. It had been several months now, and one night after we had eaten dinner in his bungalow, Uncle Ernie asked me to come and sit on his knee and tell him about my day. I happily did as he asked; I wasn't afraid of him at all. I had no reason to be. He had always been supportive and kind to me.

As I talked about my day he placed his hand on my knee, and while I talked, he stroked his hand up and down my leg. After I finished telling him about my day, he patted me on the head and told me that I had better go before my mother came home. So I went back to the main house and waited for Mom.

This was a ritual every night for the following few weeks: eat in the bungalow, sit on his knee, and tell him about my day. It felt so good and safe to be there with him, receiving the love and care of parents I had longed for.

He instilled a sense of love into me that I had not known until then. He was there to listen, and he seemed to care about me. He was the only one who had ever shown me any real attention or affection.

But ... after a few weeks, one night as I was sitting on Uncle Ernie's knee, his hand travelled gently from my leg up to my crotch. I stiffened, my faith instantly now betrayed! I knew what was coming. I had been here before. Graham's father, and Graham, had trained me well to be a lifeless and empty vessel for their sexual desire. He obviously became aware of my response because he stopped and sent me home. However, that wasn't enough to stop the deep need I had to be loved by someone, and the offerings of food also helped. The next time Uncle Ernie beckoned me to return to his bungalow, I once again followed him.

This regularly happened over and over, for many weeks. Deep down I knew it was wrong, even at that age, but I craved the security and love that I felt in his bungalow. I know now that he had groomed me to allow him access to my genital area, without fear that he was going to hurt me. He told me that in the future I should not wear underwear when I came down to see him, and I complied.

Every time after that, before I went to his bungalow, I would take my underwear off. He only had to put his hand on my leg and I knew to open them freely and grant him access. The natural progression to that was to allow him to give me oral sex. It took him weeks to convince me that it would feel nice and not horrible. He also told me that I could tell him if I wanted him to stop at any time, and he would do so.

After oral sex, he introduced me to his penis, as if it were a natural progression.

"Have you ever seen one of these before?"

I told him about Graham and his father, which seemed to please him.

"I'd like to show you how to have intercourse *without* pain ..." He pulled my head down to put his penis in my mouth.

"No," I said, as I pulled away, but he tried to push it into my mouth anyway. So I bit it.

He jumped away from the sudden attack and told me to get out.

He had not kept his promise to me that if I said no, he would stop.

I was such a confused little girl. I needed and wanted reassurance, and the security of love. Uncle Ernie gave me lots of little gifts and was always there when I needed someone to listen, someone to care. At the same time I felt deep down that this was wrong; it wasn't natural. But who could I tell that would care? At the same time, other adults had done this to me, so a part of me figured it was perhaps just a part of life. I had been used and discarded already in my life and couldn't see any issue with this happening again, as long as I was loved, protected, and fed. If I didn't go through with what he wanted, he would stop caring, he would stop giving me food, and everything would go back to the way it had been.

He told me the next night that he would move out and I would never see him again if I hurt him again. I didn't want that to happen. I knew Mom would ask questions because she needed the rent he gave her to survive. I believed he would tell her what I had been doing and she wouldn't understand, and so I just allowed him to have me. I couldn't see any other way out of it.

He did have me, often, nearly three to four times a week for nearly two years. I would lay there like a little piece of wood while he had his way.

They say that you go to your happy place, but I always stayed in the moment. I remember every single solitary second like it was only yesterday …. His breathing … His gross grunts … It all seemed surreal and strange at the same time.

I was frightened and quite alert always, as the window was often open. Sometimes I would silently scream swear words at him. I still remember the smell of alcohol on him, which would turn my stomach as I lay under him—to this day I cannot stand the stench of beer. Though, at the time, in a way I preferred it when he was drunk as he couldn't do much.

I accepted that it was normal and there was no way out. He was always gentle with me. He said that he would never hurt me, and he didn't, except just once, which I will share with you soon. He told me that once I became a woman that we would have to be more careful and use condoms so that I didn't get pregnant. I had no idea what he was talking about, so I just agreed. Somewhere in his sick mind he anticipated that this would last forever. He even spoke once of "when we are married".

But he was wrong; this was all terribly wrong. I now know he wasn't just a sicko; he was a pedophile of the worst kind. He lived in our house, taking advantage of a naive girl who was in moral danger. A child who had nobody that cared enough to worry about what was happening to her. Even Carmel, the daughter of the lady who owned the house, once asked me if my mother knew I was visiting that man so often but never said anything to Mom.

At one point Uncle Ernie suggested that it would be good if he could invite a couple of friends over who would also be really nice to me. I wasn't sure what he had in mind, but I agreed because I thought about the presents that I could get from them. That never happened, thankfully, because all of this was about to stop.

⁂

In Mom's drunken tirades, she often expressed that she was worried that I would start having sex and get myself into trouble. I didn't have time to have sex with anybody else, let alone get into trouble. I knew that she meant pregnant as Uncle Ernie had explained that to me when he told me about the condoms that he would use later on.

Love and sex. What did they mean? At that time it seemed to me that sex was all about love and caring … and getting what you wanted. And love was all about sex. If you wanted to be loved then you had to open your legs.

It wasn't long after that that I met a young teenage boy, Tony, who lived up the road. He was American and very tall for his sixteen years. He walked around in an army trench coat and black boots and had long locks of curly blond hair, which he sometimes pulled back into a pony tail. For months I had ogled him. He was the epitome of everything a young girl my age would lust after. It was the Beatles era and with his long hair, dress, mannerisms, speech, and gait, I found him appealing.

At first he took no notice of me. Then one day he stopped and asked me my name. At the time I was sitting in the lane on the bench at the back of Kylie's in the late afternoon, avoiding Graham. I was so overcome with joy when he spoke to me that I jumped around him like a little puppy that was being promised a stick.

He asked if I wanted to come back to his house and listen to some Beatles albums. Of course I did! Did he think I was crazy? Everyone wanted to go back to his place.

Now you have to remember, I was young and extremely exposed and vulnerable, and stranger danger, especially from a teenager, was not an issue back then.

His parents weren't home, so I followed him to his bedroom where he put the Abbey Road album by the Beatles on his record player. He pointed to his bed and told me to sit down. He took off his coat and his boots … and then I was surprised as he continued to remove his jeans and his underwear. I didn't know what I had expected, but this was not it. I sat on his bed staring wide eyed at his penis, which had now swollen to twice its size or more.

"Um, I had better go home. My mother wants me," I said as I quickly tried to dodge him while I ran to the door. It was locked, and he had the key and wouldn't let me out. I was trapped. I started to scream.

"It's no use screaming. Nobody is home and no one can hear you."

I ran to the window and tried to open it to climb out, but he grabbed me roughly from behind, smacked me across the face, and threw me onto the bed where he proceeded to rape me.

The little girl inside me was silently screaming but nobody was listening, except me. His penis was larger than anything that had come before it and hurt me so badly that I almost passed out from the pain. I couldn't look at him, so I kept my head turned to the wall while the song *Come Together* by the Beatles blared out from the record player beside us. I felt gutted, dirty, and worthless. I was shocked by what was happening; I had not expected that his innocent invitation would end up like this.

When he had finished with me, I lay there and cried for what seemed like an eternity. I just wanted to put my underpants on and go home, but he wouldn't give them to me.

"Stop being a sook. You asked for it."

I sat on his bed, wide eyed, and watched his every move while he ambled around his bedroom. He had still not unlocked the door so that I could make an escape. He then proceeded to rape me a further two times over the course of several hours.

When the ordeal was finally over, he grabbed me by the back of the neck, pushed me out of his bedroom and along the hallway to the front door, which he opened, and then he just threw me out of the house, literally. I landed on my knees on his verandah but quickly pulled myself up and ran out of his front gate and along the street towards home as fast as I could… trying to get as much distance as I could between him and me before he could get me again. I was very frightened.

I had no underwear on as I ran home sobbing. I had no soul left in my body. To me sex meant that when commanded, I opened my legs and men and boys took what they wanted. I was a broken and used girl, only eleven, damaged beyond my years.

It was a Saturday afternoon and Mom and Graham had gone to the pub by the time I returned, so I sat in the bath for a very long time until it got cold, hoping it would wash the memories away—I'm still waiting for that… After the bath I was still upset and needed to tell someone what had happened to me. I couldn't tell Mom, my friends, or anyone else for that matter. I knew I would be blamed for it somehow—everything was always my fault. But also some would blame Mom too—they always did … and I didn't want to be taken off her and put away somewhere. So I went to the only person who showed me any care—Uncle Ernie.

When I told him what happened, my heart was open in desperation to receive some care and comfort. But, strangely, Uncle Ernie seemed excited by my story. That familiar lump rose in his crotch and he pulled me towards him, groping at my small breasts underneath my jumper … This time he was rougher with me.

He also seemed agitated by the knowledge that someone else had taken me by force. It appeared that had been his secret desire all along, and with that I was once again on my back on his bed. He was on top of me, trying to hold me down while he roughly inserted his penis inside me.

I screamed at the top of my lungs. Not just because of the pain but at the injustice of it all. It just wasn't fair! Not again!

He placed his hand over my mouth. "Shut the fuck up or else."

The cocky outside the bungalow heard my scream and started to squawk loudly, "Margaret!" It did this every time it heard a noise.

Margaret lived in the other half of the house and I hoped that the cocky's squawk would bring her out and that would be my escape. But she didn't come.

I had never seen Uncle Ernie like this. Only hours before, I had been raped multiple times by another person and now Uncle Ernie had his penis inside me. Did he have no heart? He was desperate and angry. His breathing was extremely hard and agitated. He grunted at me and for the first time with Uncle Ernie I felt it was all so absolutely disgusting. I felt ashamed.

Over and over he said, "Take this, you little whore. You know you fuck'n want it. Don't ever let anyone touch you again unless I tell you so, do you understand? Fuck'n answer me! How does that feel, bitch? Better than the little boy's dick. It'd fuck'n want to be."

Why do they all think that *we want it*? It was the last thing I wanted.

It seemed like he was in a competition with no one.

I truly wish I had been one of those children that went to a safe place during these moments. I had no safe place. All I could do was stare into the face of the man who had told me he would never hurt me, and now he was. My confidence in him was totally gone. When he had climaxed, he casually lit up a cigarette and said, "Get out, you disgusting little whore." He had been like a dog marking his territory to make sure it stayed his. And I was then thrown out for the second time that day, like a piece of old, rotting meat.

I never, ever, went down to Uncle Ernie's bungalow again. The price to pay for some care and attention had become too great. The pain had been too much. I didn't care if he moved out; I never wanted to see him again. I didn't care if he told my mom, I wanted this to stop.

My spirit was broken. My body was broken. My heart was broken. I was later to find out that my body was really broken.

When he knocked on the door, I ignored him. If he came down when Mom was there, I went into the other room. I was eleven years old and it had finally clicked somewhere inside me that all of this was very wrong. After what Tony had done to me and then Uncle Ernie's reaction, the penny had dropped ... I got it ... Sex was just some kind of primal need that was desired more in some than others, and some would do anything to get it.

What my experiences to this point did was make me a target for more men who wished to pull the wool over my eyes and pretend to love me in exchange for sex. It was even like I had some sort of mark on my forehead—*child sex victim for the taking*. A lot of Mom's so-called pub "friends" also thought that they could have a shot at me too. Some tried, but none of them succeeded after Ernie … *because I wouldn't let them*. I was getting wiser. It didn't stop them trying though, even in the public toilet at the pub when they'd follow me in because I went in by myself. Another day on my way home in the dark, one of them waited in the laneway that I often used to walk to get to the back gate. But I knew how to dodge him.

I wasn't always going to be so savvy though in the future. Self-preservation habits and the need for the love I never had would kick in. This theme of sex in exchange for love, often at the hands of users and abusers I would attract, was to continue throughout my teens and adult years when I was also going to become very sexually promiscuous.

I've heard that sexually abused or raped children can often go in either of two directions regarding sex as they grow up: sexual promiscuity or sexual repression (even to the point of developing conditions like *vaginismus*—fear of intercourse). I was to follow the road of the former: sexual promiscuity. Some would call me a whore, but none understood the depth of the road that I had already travelled. Looking back, I know I was looking for that one person who was going to love me.

I always believed until recently that I was the guilty one who caused these men to do what they did. How many other children out there believe it is, or was, their fault? Thank God I now know differently—that knowledge has saved me. I must admit though, that even in sharing all the details of this story now, as an adult, the little girl in me is sometimes still afraid of being punished somehow for "telling". In fact, I have been told just recently that I shouldn't be telling my story. It seems some would just like to see it stay buried. What are they scared of?

10

Mislaid Innocence

"Malevolent love is better than no love, and so the blueprint for my future relationship behaviors was born."

MANY THINGS HAPPENED in my eleventh year. I was now hanging around with a new group of friends as Ricky and Kylie had moved away to Rosanna. I amused myself daily by roaming the streets and nightly by doing the same thing, roaming the streets. School was a thing of the past. Josephine and Lyn had taught me to wag school and I found it was unnecessary for what I needed in my life. I was too busy struggling to survive day to day. I continued to wear that label on my forehead "Yours for the taking". Many men and boys tried to take me, and many of them failed.

In this year alone I was subjected to three attempted abductions, each reported to the police. The first time a man slowed his car in the street, got out, and tried to grab me. My neighbors reported that to the police; the second one was similar. The third one made the front page of the Northcote newspaper as six young men were charged with attempted abduction and two counts of abduction of a minor.

I had been walking home to my girlfriend's house from the YMCA dance. Her name was Kerrie and we were with a group of the toughest kids known at that time—the Stoke Street Boys. Okay, well we may have been with their little brothers. But despite our numbers, this maroon Ford drove past us slowly. There was something about it that put my senses onto high alert immediately. It pulled around the corner into the darkness and off the main road, where it stopped. By this time I was street smart; I knew what they intended and I knew what I had to do.

Mom had always told me if someone grabbed me that I should kick the guy in the balls and then run. If they attempted to pull me into a car, I was to try and remember the number plate. I was armed with knowledge and ready when three male figures came out of the darkness. I screamed to Kerrie, "RUN!" … But it was too late. Two of them had grabbed her. The boys who had been with us were now nowhere to be seen; they had scattered in different directions. Gutless wonders. So much for being tough. One of the goons stayed in the car for a quick getaway but he was having problems with his car and was trying to keep the engine going.

The tallest and the oldest of the group ran at me. I stood there and quickly assessed the situation. I knew that if I ran away with my back to him, he could grab me and drag me the same as they had done with Kerrie. So I stood my ground!

He grabbed me from the front so I kicked him as hard as I could, fair square in the groin. Thanks Mom!

He dropped like a sack of spuds and writhed in pain on the ground. He was six foot one and I was four foot five. Round one over, I ran to the car, which they were not able to start, and I screamed for them to let Kerrie out. They refused and the car started with two of them sitting on her in the back seat where she lay screaming. I kicked the door of the car as it took off and made a mental note of the number plate—KEB577. Yes, forty plus years on, I still remember the plate. [Any reference to that number plate in the present time would be invalid, of course.]

I couldn't keep up with the car, so I ran behind it and screamed at the top of my lungs. You know … that piercing, blood-curdling scream that can come out of an adolescent girl's mouth. Yes, that one! The one I perfected in childhood.

That brought Kerrie's mother running out of her house. I know that God was with Kerrie that night because the car broke down again, this time right in front of her home. I ran up the street screaming to Kerrie's mother, "They have Kerrie in the car!"

Somehow she managed to extract Kerrie and they took off. This was reported to the police who were able to apprehend the four guys and arrest them. It would go to court when I was fourteen years old, and they would be incarcerated for their crimes, except for the youngest.

Yep, we lived in a great suburb!

※

Around this time I had fallen head over heels for one of the boys in the Stoke Street gang— puppy love. I seemed to be boy crazy. I met the Stoke Street kids when I changed to the Preston Swimming Pool that had recently been built; it was where they hung out. I easily fell in love with one. His name was Paul, and my other girlfriend, Carolyn, encouraged me to go out with him. This relationship was a gentle one, similar to my last relationship with Ricky. Little stolen kisses and time spent alone, talking, listening to records in his bungalow, but never anything more. All the time I thought of Ricky and the puppy love that we had experienced, the closeness I had felt with him. We had shared so many days and childhood memories together; I missed him.

I missed Danny, my brother, too.

On the twenty-eighth of April, 1969, Danny showed up at home dressed in his Army uniform. He looked so handsome and grown up. I was so excited to see him again. Daniel had joined the regular Army, rather than waiting for conscription. I was very proud of him, as I am sure Mom was. He had come to tell Mom that he was being shipped to Vietnam the next day and he was leaving Melbourne that night.

I don't know what the conversation was between Daniel and Mom that night, but there was a bit of huffing from Mom and I'm assuming a little anger. Once it was all said and done, Daniel said goodbye to Mom, threw his duffle bag over his shoulder and left. He had called a taxi to take him to the airport and it would be at the house soon, so he had to wait for it outside. I know Mom never rose to accompany him to the door. I can't remember if she hugged or kissed him goodbye either; that would have been unusual anyway. Mom was not a hugger, just like Nanna.

What I do know is that Daniel dragged me the length of the sideway to the front gate, wrapped around his leg like a koala, screaming at him not to go. I think it took all his strength to pry my grip from his leg so that he could get in the taxi and go. I stood on the sidewalk and watched him drive away from me, just like I had watched my father many years ago when he left. I know Daniel couldn't possibly know how I felt that night, but he took a part of me with him to Vietnam.

School holidays rolled around and my annual trip to Nanna's arrived. I was excited this time because Kylie and Ricky lived not far from Nanna's house. It was a good three to four kilometre walk, but I knew where they were, and as soon as I could get out the door by myself, I made a beeline for them. We had so much fun! We spent almost every day of the holidays together. I was out of Nanna's hair and she was out of mine.

The three of us roamed the streets, looked at the shops, and enjoyed exciting times together playing board games like Monopoly and Mousetrap. Ricky and I picked up where we had left off and held hands wherever we went. It was great. I loved being around them. They accepted me, we were the same, especially Ricky. I didn't think of Paul the whole time I was there. I knew I was destined to be with Ricky forever.

When it was nearing the end of my summer vacation, Kylie asked if I could sleep the night. She walked back to Nanna's with me while Ricky waited at the corner for us.

I asked Nanna if I could stay overnight with them and she said, "Yes."

I knew that if she knew Ricky was going to be there, she would not have given permission. I was so excited. It would be so much fun. Nanna had no idea that they were the "little bastards" who had given me nits. If she had, she never would've agreed.

This was the first semblance of normality I had experienced in a long time; not since the soul-destroying sleep-over at Mary's house. But that didn't enter my mind at all. This was going to be a normal childhood sleepover on school holidays—what a novelty. We made it back to their house on dusk. Kylie's mother had made dinner and we were told to go clean up before eating. I sat at their kitchen table and tucked into a homemade dinner, with a family, all sitting together. It was heaven. I tried to imagine what it would be like to do this every night, to sit as a family and eat. Kylie and Ricky were lucky.

After dinner, Kylie's mother had to go out, maybe to work, so she was not at home. When the dishes were done, Kylie, Ricky, and I sat on the floor in Kylie's bedroom playing Monopoly. When Kylie went out to get a glass of water, Ricky lent over and gave me a full-on kiss on the lips. It was our first real kiss, childish, pure, and beautiful. As fate would have it, at that exact moment his father walked in and caught us in the act. I didn't know what to do or where to look. I knew by his face we were in deep shit.

Ricky's father yelled at him. "Get out and go to your room! … And you," he said, looking straight at me and wagging his finger in my direction, "I'll deal with you later."

When Kylie came back, she asked what had happened. After I told her, she was worried that her father might take me back to Nanna's right there and then; so was I. If he told Nanna what he had caught me doing, well, just let's say the devil was scared of my grandmother. But he never came back in, and neither did Ricky. I felt terribly sorry that I couldn't spend my sleepover night of the holidays with Ricky. It had been so much fun until then. I was still worried when it was time for us to go to bed, but as Ricky's father hadn't told me to get dressed into my clothing, I figured I was safe and wouldn't be returning to Nanna's that night.

After lights out, Kylie and I lay in bed and chatted until both of us drifted off to sleep. It must have been around ten o'clock when I felt someone tug on my shoulder. I woke up and saw Ricky's father standing over me.

"Come with me, shhh, quiet. I don't want Kylie woken up."

I got out of bed and followed him down the hall, wondering why he would wake me from my sleep at this hour. I followed him into the back room of the house. When he opened the door, Ricky was standing there. I could tell by Ricky's eyes that he had been crying.

That's when I sensed we were in big trouble.

I half-expected to receive a belting from him, as on the odd occasion he had hit me before when they had lived in Thornbury, for playing up. I must admit he had always been a fair man, thus far, and heard us out before punishment—at times we certainly did deserve it. In a way, he was the closest thing I had known to a real father, punishments and all. I figured this time we had been pretty bad for kissing.

Then he told us to both to remove our pajamas … Ricky and I stood there frozen to the spot and just stared at him, in shock. Ricky's eyes were like a deer's that had been caught in headlights. I can't even imagine what mine were like. His Dad started to undo the belt on his pants and we both knew what that meant. So our pajamas were off—he didn't have to ask again. We stood there in front of him, both of us stripped to our underwear.

He had a thin bamboo stick in his hand and he pushed it towards me, hooking my underpants and saying, "Them too."

I glanced sideways, embarrassed at Ricky, and then back at him as tears welled up in my eyes. I knew what was going to happen—I was wiser than my years—and I didn't want Ricky to see it. In front of me was a man who I had respected, but now he was just another man with a penis, like the others, who was going to use my body for his pleasure.

You can't imagine my surprise when he told Ricky to take off his underwear too.

"If you want to behave like adults then you have to learn to do it the right way."

Once Ricky removed his underwear, I was told to fondle him. I hesitated, but the little whips I received across the bottoms of my legs forced me to comply. It wasn't long before Ricky responded to my touch, even though he was scared. I had experience in this from the years of sexual abuse I had already endured, and I think that his dad quickly picked up on that as I used my hand to make Ricky hard.

His father ordered me to lie on my back on the bed and to spread my legs wide. He whipped the insides of my knees with the cane to extend them further and further until I thought my hips would break. He ordered Ricky to lie on top of me and to put his penis in me. We tried to do as we were told. Ricky lay on top of me and pretended that his penis was in me, but he had no idea what to do. And so he just lay there.

"Come on, boy. Move backwards and forwards, in and out," Ricky was told over and over again that he was a fucking idiot if he didn't know how to fuck a girl. He was lashed with the cane across his back and buttocks every time he refused to enter me properly.

He started to cry and defiantly yelled, "No!"

I found some inner strength also and begged along with Ricky for this to stop. At this his father stood beside the bed looking down at me. He hesitated for a minute and then told Ricky to get off me.

"I'll show you how a real man does it!"

I cried and begged him not to touch me. I gathered the courage to make fists with my hands and I struck out at him. But he moved forcefully between my legs and entered me anyway. I stopped dead. I knew what to do ... Like the good little girl that I had been groomed to be, I lay there moving my hips to satisfy his desire. It was then he realized that he was not my first and his excitement took over. Tears rolled from my eyes, down the side of my face, filling my ears. Of all the times I had been raped, this was probably the worst of betrayals. I couldn't look at Ricky and he couldn't look at me. I felt his father leave my body before he ejaculated and then he ordered Ricky to get back on top of me.

In a very deep, low, threatening manner, he growled, "Now fuck her."

As cold as that!

So Ricky finally did what he was told. His father beat Ricky across the backside many more times with the cane, telling him to go faster and faster, yelling at him that he had to learn to satisfy a woman or he would never be a man. It actually was all over faster than it began, but still his father wasn't satisfied. I'm not sure what his father thought the stamina of a twelve-year-old boy would be, having his first sexual encounter, but we laid there rocking backwards and forwards for an awful long time until his father told him not to be greedy.

Again he pushed him off and entered me—violated me.

I was twelve years old.

Ricky stood silently beside the bed watching, tears slowly falling down his cheeks while he mouthed the word "Sorry" over and over.

When his father was finally finished and had ejaculated, then and only then did he pull his pants on and leave the room, without a word, a look, or an order...

Ricky stood there silently, still looking down at me, and I stayed there only for a moment longer before we both dashed for our clothes on the floor. I ran outside of the house, totally naked, to the toilet in the backyard, and I stayed in there for an hour or so crying.

I had company. Ricky sat on the ground on the other side of the door continuing to say "I'm sorry" over and over again through his tears.

We both stayed in the backyard until the lights went out. Only then were we brave enough to go back inside the house. All I wanted to do was to go back to Nanna's house, but it was so late. I knew she would just never understand. Somehow I would be blamed.

I finally climbed back into the bed in Kylie's room and lay there until the sun came up, keeping one eye firmly on the door.

The next morning we ate breakfast at the kitchen table as if nothing had ever happened. Everyone was chatting like one big, happy family, except Ricky and I, who were extremely withdrawn and quiet. Ricky's father took pleasure in poking fun at us for our solemn attitude. As soon as breakfast was completed and the dishes were washed, I left the house, went home to my grandmother's house, and never returned—ever.

Holidays were never the same after that. I found a new friend who lived up the road, but I missed Ricky and Kylie a lot, for a long time. In my adult years, I was to meet up with Ricky again. He was living in a gay relationship. I often wondered if the events of that night contributed to his choice of lifestyle, or if it was always that way and that is why I had felt so safe with him personally. I suspect it's a bit of both. I know that for myself the blueprint for my future relationship behaviors was firmly imprinted that night … Malevolent love was to be all I felt I deserved, and that's what I got.

11
Jingle Bells

"I twirled my finger around in circles on the table in front of the opened box. Why can't I keep it?"

CHRISTMAS—THAT SPECIAL time of the year that everyone looks forward to, right? No! Not me. Even now I have a hard time putting on a brave face. There isn't too much happiness for me in Christmas or birthdays or other notable events. Life has never been a celebration. Instead, it has been a constant trail of hurdles that I have had to jump over, or tunnels I have to crawl through, to continue to survive. I don't mean that to sound whiney. It's just I was never taught how to celebrate such events. My experience in childhood was that these special events mostly caused pain, and birthdays were a non-event. I never had one.

Christmas in our family was the same every year. The one constant was Christmas Eve at Nanna's house, where the family met and passed out their Christmas presents to each other. Then off we'd go home with our stash and wait for Santa to arrive that night and see what he left us on Christmas morning. That was the tradition.

The truth of the matter was that Mom worked hard and tried to do her best to pick out the best presents that she could afford for everybody. Often they would not match the level of others' presents. Mom and I would play

JINGLE BELLS

Christmas carols at home while we wrapped Christmas presents, ready for our long journey to Nanna's house. Mom would load all the presents into her shopping jeep and off we'd go on public transport. Every year, I remember Mom would tuck two bottles of beer into her jeep also. That did not take into account what she may have drunk before we left. It didn't matter if they hadn't seen the bottles; as soon as Mom walked in the door of Nanna's house, she was bombarded with accusations of boozing.

"You're not going to drink tonight are you, Joy?" Nanna would ask scornfully. "You're not going to cause trouble here tonight by getting drunk." It seemed that they were always onto her—because most of the time Mom did have bottles in the jeep!

The Christmas when I was twelve years old was a little different. At some point in the afternoon, my Aunty Beatrice took me into the kitchen alone and placed a small box on the table in front of her.

"Your father has sent you a Christmas present," she said, rather matter-of-factly.

"My father? ... My father? ..." I kept repeating this. No wonder my aunty thought I had mental issues, but she had no idea I had been told by my sister's husband, George, that my father was dead.

Now I wasn't really too sure how my father had managed to send this gift when he was dead! I was baffled, to be honest. I had not even assumed he was alive and that good ol' George had lied. She told me that Dad had sent me a watch. *How did he know?* My mom had asked me earlier that year what I would like for Christmas, and I told her, "I'd love to have a watch." When we went to do grocery shopping later that same morning, I showed her the exact watch that I wanted. It had a small, silver face and two thin, black elastic-looking bands that attached to the clip. They were made of soft leather. I really wanted that watch, but I had put it out of my mind because I knew I would never have it.

Unbeknown to me, Mom had put a watch on lay-by for me and had been paying it off—which my aunty explained to me in considerable detail. She told me that it was unfair of my father to send me only one present in years and assume that I should be allowed to keep it. And also, that if I did keep it, it would hurt my mother's feelings deeply. With that, she asked

115

me if I thought it should be returned to my father. I told her that I didn't know. I twirled my finger around in circles on the table in front of the closed box. *Why can't I keep it?* How is a small child supposed to take all of this information in: my father is still alive but I'm going to hurt my mother's feelings if I keep his present?

What about me?

What about my feelings?

Why would it hurt to keep both presents? I thought.

"Why can't I keep both presents, Aunty Beatrice?" I asked.

"Because he's given you the same present as your mother," she said in a slightly exasperated tone, as if she thought I was thick.

I asked if I could see it and she showed me. It was exactly the same watch that I had pointed out to my mother that day when we went shopping. My father had my taste in watches.

"But why can't I have both?" I pleaded.

"Your mother worked hard to provide for you and if you keep this, you should be ashamed of yourself for hurting your mother! You shouldn't be so ungrateful."

I really got the impression she thought I was a spoilt little brat. Some people have even said that to me, that I had everything my own way. I so wish that was the truth. I only ever got one thing that I asked for, which was a new pair of bathers. And they were quickly taken off me. No, I was far from a spoilt little brat. I just wonder how and why people could have seen me like that. The mind boggles at people's blindness. They see what they want to see.

The next thing Aunty Beatrice did was to push a piece of paper and a pencil in front of me and order me to write a short note to my father to tell him that I didn't want his gift.

I dutifully obeyed. I always knew when I was beat.

Later that night, we all sat around in the lounge room and presents were passed out. Eventually, I was passed the present that Mom had bought for me. I unwrapped it with such excitement. In the box was a lovely, shiny, new watch, but it wasn't the one I had pointed out to her. It had a small silver face with a thick, light brown leather band. I know disappointment came over my face, tinged with sadness because of the earlier events of the day. She told me the watch I had chosen was impractical. I thanked her for the present, but I know she felt my sadness. As much as I try to cover up my feelings, I always wear them on my face.

As with every other Christmas Eve, I also received my usual stash of lavender powder and bath salts and a coloring-in book or two. That was pretty much the extent of it. Later on that evening, Aunty Beatrice told Mom that Daniel had sent a Christmas tape from Vietnam. They got the tape recorder out to listen to it and we sat around, waiting to hear his voice, so far away. It must have been a surprise for Mom because it had been sent to Nanna's house. I was sad and had tears in my eyes as I watched my mother's expression. She breathed in every sentence that my brother spoke. If she had never told him how proud she was of him, I think seeing her face that night would have more than convinced him that she was. I wished my brother was there with us; I missed him. The adults then moved to the kitchen. It was my bedtime and I was sleeping on the couch in the lounge room.

I lay on the couch that night and cried myself to sleep, holding onto the little box with Mom's watch in it. Why would it have hurt to have kept both watches? I still do not know. I never heard from my father again as a child, although, many years later when I was an adult, I found him. I don't know what happened to the present, whether it was sent back to my father or not. It was never mentioned again. Not even Dad mentioned it years later when I finally met up with him.

As with most Christmas Eves, the night ended with Nanna and Mom having an argument over her drinking. I just wished she wouldn't drink for this one night. Everyone started on her. I just wanted to get up and leave. I lay on the couch listening to them ... If they only knew the half of it. But then I wonder if anything would have been changed—probably not.

I was soon heading for a much worse fate, and if they had known what my life was *really* like, with the sexual abuse, Mom's drinking and neglect, wagging school, and running the streets at night, I probably would have been fast-tracked to that fate anyway.

12
Blah Blah Blah

"Save me!"

D AY IN, DAY OUT, MY life continued. Grade 4 was fantastic ... Grade 5 I enjoyed ... Grade 6? What was Grade 6? Oh that's right. I think I attended the first day of that.

I can remember sitting mesmerized, staring at Sister Malachy most of the day attending to one of her favorite pastimes—holding her false teeth in her hands and picking out all the food from breakfast, then morning tea, then lunch, then afternoon tea. I would daydream the rest of the day away until I received a whack across my knuckles from the ruler in Sister Malachy's hand —her other favorite pastime.

I would let out a little scream as the pain brought me back to reality.

"Seven sevens are forty-nine." ... whack ... "You're not saying it properly!"

"Eight sevens are fifty-six." ... whack ...

"Louder!" she would yell.

I hate this nun and if she hits me again I'm going to hit her back, I thought to myself. *Violence is highly likely.*

Yep, lots of incentive to get out of bed when I'm tired and head off to a hard day at school—not! Contemplating moving out of bed each day was more than I could handle. My body was tired ... my mind was tired ... I was tired so, so tired ...

Why? Because of the night time routine with Mom.

Night times were always the same. Race home just before 10 p.m. from wherever I happened to find myself that night, turn on the television, and wait for the heavy footsteps up the sideway. In comes Mom.

"Hi Mom."

"Get me the bottle opener will you, Bev?"

"Okay," I respond. Back to television!

"You'd better get into bed, Bev."

So I do.

An hour later, "Bev, come here."

"Yes Mom." Up I get.

Blah, blah, blah!

Blah, blah, blah!

"Mom, I have to go back to bed. I have school tomorrow."

"Don't be rude; you'll listen to me if I'm talking to you," Mom rants. Blah, blah, blah … Your father is this, your father is that, this person is this, that person is that.

At 1 a.m. I say, "Mom, I really have to go back to bed. I have to go to school in the morning."

To which she responds, "Oh, okay, you'd better go to bed … Why are you up so late?"

And back to bed I'd go! Sleep would be just starting to overtake me again when from the kitchen I'd hear, "Beverley, come here. Why did you walk off when I was talking to you?"

"I don't know, Mom. I thought you had finished, so I went to bed."

Blah, blah, blah! "I don't know why you put your father on a bloody pedestal. It's me who feeds and clothes you, not him. He doesn't pay a cent."

"Yes, Mom. I won't in the future."

"You know he wanted to have sex in our bed with that woman—a threesome."

Why do I need to hear this?

But on and on and on it goes.

2 a.m. "Mom, I really have to get some sleep. I am so tired."

"You'd better pop into bed then."

"OK!"

"Beverley. Beverley, stop ignoring me. Get your bloody self out here; I want to talk to you."

"Mom, it's three o'clock in the morning." I whine, coming to the end of my patience.

"No it's not; you're a bloody little liar."

Blah, blah, blah.

And that is how my nights went. At 6 a.m. I would hear the latch on the door click and the heavy footsteps head back down the sideway of the house. I don't know when she slept.

Time to sleep!

Life was a ritual, a not-so-nice ritual, but at least it was familiar. I knew what would happen each day and each night, just like there was a book of rules for it. Sometimes it was quite late into the night, and at other times Mom would stop earlier. It depended on her mood.

Some days I would get up and try to go to school. I would put on my uniform and promptly go back to sleep. After I woke up, I would mostly just hang out at home or at the hump. I had been hanging out there now for a couple of years. The hump was an unusual place. A small bridge allowed trams from St George's Road in Thornbury to cross over the railway lines and continue to the tram lines in High Street. Underneath the tram lines was a gap of about 3 x 3 square meters, where we, the truants, could all fit in quite comfortably, out of the sight of the police. By now I was running with a bunch of kids, smoking, swearing, and quite simply doing whatever I wanted.

The hump is where I originally met sisters Kerry and Debra a year or so before. They also wagged school on a regular basis, and it wasn't long before we formed a real strong attachment to each other. I don't imagine a day went by when we didn't see each other. I had become very familiar with their family and had been more than welcomed into their home by their incredible angelic mother. Mrs. White took us all in. She had a heart as large as Australia and enough love to go around her own eleven children, plus all the strays that they brought home, and there were quite a few of us.

Everyone needs a Mrs. White to be there for them, understand them, help them, and feed them when they are hungry. My angel in heaven, rest in peace; I will always remember you.

One night Kerrie introduced me to "snow dropping". That is Australian urban slang for taking other people's clothes off their backyard clothes lines. Many people left clothes out overnight, and often we were able to pick up a bargain. It was wrong and naughty but quite exhilarating at the same time. We used the various back lanes in Thornbury to attack, lying low until the coast was clear. We would then scale the back fence, taking what we wanted, and hightail it out of there.

Mom never questioned where my new wardrobe had come from; I don't think she cared. She was never there anyway and she never bought anything new for me to wear, even when I was growing out of all my clothing and had stopped receiving Anne's hand-me-downs. Kerrie came from as poor a situation as me, with her family having so many children to contend with and not enough money to go around. It was inevitable that we would find each other on the streets and become the best of friends.

One night I failed to meet my curfew and 10 p.m. came and went. I had been quite taken with what we were doing and forgot to go home.

Mrs. White came out to Kerry's bedroom. "My God, you'd better go. Your mom will be home by now."

I took off, running all the way. I finally got to the house and snuck up the sideway. I thought that if I snuck in the window Mom might not notice that I hadn't been there. I tried both the windows in the sideway and they wouldn't open, so I figured I was going to have to face the music. I had never missed my curfew, so I wasn't sure what to expect.

I put the key in the door and went to open it, but as I pushed something was blocking the entrance, so I pushed harder. I was able to get my head in the door, half expecting to have it taken off with a cricket bat, but instead, there she was.

Mom lay sprawled on the floor and was blocking the door. She had wet herself and was shaking. Froth was coming out of her mouth.

I screamed and screamed while frantically pushing the door to enter. "Mom, are you okay? Muuum!" She didn't respond and I couldn't get to her.

I ran next door to Carmel. She came straight away. Her husband managed to push the door open and went inside, and Carmel and I followed. They both bent down to Mom on the floor and after checking if she was okay, they turned to each other and both said, "She's drunk." I often wonder if that was so, as my mother had some very serious medical conditions that would only be picked up later in life. Maybe something more sinister was at work that night.

Carmel's husband picked Mom up and helped Carmel take her into the bathroom. They were in there a long time while Carmel washed her. I was told to put myself to bed, which I did. But I couldn't sleep because I was worried that my mom might die, the same as last time, and that she would have to go away again for a very long time. I had never seen her collapse like that before. I couldn't lose Mom too. I would have no one.

Carmel helped Mom into our bed and then left. Mom was gone early the next morning as if nothing had happened. I wonder if she even knew.

If I had lost Mom then, I would have had no one but Chirpy. Remember my little yellow bird, Chirpy? Well, we still had Chirpy. It turned out that he was a rooster, with an attitude. We had built a makeshift pen for him, and every day I would take him for a walk up to the park on a strap that I had made. I always sat and talked to him whenever I was sad or just needed someone to talk to. He was my Tiny surrogate. I spent a fair bit of time with my chook. He even got fed some roast vegetables on Sundays when Mom cooked a roast. He was mine and he loved me. Often when I came home in the afternoon, I would call for him and he would come running straight to me.

New people moved into the other half of the house who made it clear they didn't particularly like Chirpy. They complained about him on occasion. One day I came up the sideway, just in time to see the man next door cut the head off a chook that he had tied to the line by its feet. At first it didn't register … The chook flapped and carried on for what seemed an eternity before it hung still, dead. Then I realized ….

"Noooo! Chirpy! What have you done?" I ran at the man, fists cuffed, and I hit him in every place I could as he held me back with one hand. I wanted to hurt him as bad as he had hurt Chirpy. I just broke down and ran inside where I sat in the corner, rocking backwards and forwards until Mom came home. She saw me there and looked at my tear-stained face, and for the first time in a long time, I saw her soften.

"What's wrong, Bev?" she asked gently. I told her what had happened.

She marched straight out to the neighbor's door, with me in tow, and demanded to know why they had done such a heartless thing. He told Mom that Chirpy had pecked at his wife and she was pregnant. Mom told them they did not have any right to do that, at which point they handed Chirpy to Mom, perfectly plucked and ready to roast. We went back home. I sat with Chirpy for a while until Mom told me to go to bed. She tucked him away in the refrigerator. And that was where I thought he would remain forever. But no!

Sunday came and Mom cooked a lovely roast lunch. Roast chook! That's right, roast Chirpy! I screamed at her when she went to cut him. I cried and cried until finally Mom agreed that Chirpy deserved to be buried. With that we walked up the backyard, dug a hole, and buried Chirpy, stuffing and all. I made a little make-shift cross out of twigs, which I placed on his grave. I sat with him often over the next few days, talking to him about my life and troubles. But it wasn't the same. He wasn't there to react like he used to, just like Tiny hadn't been.

I have a little black freckle on the crease of my right arm and often when I had held Chirpy in my arms, he would peck at it. Not to hurt me, but I expect to try and eat it.

Needless to say, after that I became more restless and more of a problem. Now, as well as being a difficult child, I had an attitude. Not because I wanted one, but life was tough and I needed one. Without an attitude I would never have survived. I was street smart and a latchkey kid. However, underneath I was still just an innocent young girl screaming out at the top of her lungs, "Save me!"

Christmas came and went and another new school year began—Year 7, Corpus Christi. This was the senior girls' section of St Mary's, the primary school I had attended ... or not. Needless to say, I passed my Year 6 exam. It seems skipping that year didn't hurt me much in the learning stakes. Mom purchased all new school uniforms for me and made me promise that I would attend school—and I did try. However, within a few weeks of starting school, the old routine began again with sleepless nights listening to Mom until all hours of the morning, and then trying to concentrate and keep up in class. Again I often found myself oversleeping and not attending.

At Corpus Christi there was a girl named Gracie who was the grade prefect. She wasn't like the other girls. When I was at school, she was always kind to me and showed empathy. She had charisma, charm, and a gentleness about her that I hadn't seen in a lot of people. I looked up to her. Gracie was sincere and always there for me. When other people made fun of me, she made them stop. Gracie would try and mitigate the impact of embarrassing situations that I got caught up in, such as the day I got my first period.

When I was wagging school, she showed up at my door and tried to encourage me back to school. One particular day, she advised me that if I didn't return to school the next day they intended to call the truant officers, which meant I would be taken away and put into a home. I really appreciated Gracie and her compassion and wisdom. She knew what was happening to me, but never made fun of me like the others. I made a decision there and then to go back to school, to turn over a new leaf, promising myself that no matter what happened at home, I was now the most important person. I realized that if I was to have any kind of life when I grew up, it was up to me to make that future happen. Gracie helped me come to those conclusions through her kindness and wisdom.

So every day I attended school and didn't leave the school grounds, thanks to Gracie, who had taken the time to come to my home and talk to me about everything. She understood and had promised me that if I came back to school she would be there for me. She was always there for me, in more ways than one ... Even in my future. Thank you Gracie; you were heaven-sent.

One day I woke up and Mom was still in bed. I shook her awake and told her she was late for work, but she said that she wasn't going because she felt sick. After I was ready to go to school, I told Mom that I would come home and make sure that she had something for lunch. She looked terribly ill. Mom told me not to bother coming home, but she knew that I was obstinate and would return to feed her. I asked Sister Albertus to let me go home and feed my mother as she was sick. I promised that I would return as soon as possible. I was given permission to leave the school grounds. After attending to Mom who was still in bed, I decided to go back to school. I had some spare time so thought I would take the long way around, and so I walked back to school via the hump. Everyone was there having lots of fun.

They all said, "Stay with us. Don't go back to school." But I had made myself a promise and I was determined to keep it. As soon as I started to walk away, a police car pulled up. Damn.

Funnily enough, as has happened several times in my life, it seems that when I make myself promises to be better or to stop doing something I shouldn't be doing, it is then and only then that I seem to get into trouble somehow. I started to run away, on instinct, but the police caught me and took me to the Preston Police Station. I was held there for several hours until they decided to take me to the Northcote Police Station because I was known there. Not because I had ever been caught doing anything untoward, but because of the attempted abduction case that I was involved in. They put me into the back of a police car and drove me down High Street to the Northcote Police Station … straight past St. Mary's! And, of course, I was spotted in the back seat of the police car, in my uniform, by one of the nuns.

Mom had to get up and come and get me from the police station. Needless to say, she wasn't happy. I implored her to listen to me and told her I was on my way back to school when they caught me. But she was sick and angry and basically over my out-of-control ways. Not that I even realized that I was out of control.

I set my mind to return to school the next morning, more determined than ever to prove Mom wrong and to show Gracie that I was serious about attending school. I was going to start a new chapter! And a new chapter it truly was going to be …

13
Expelled

∽

"Cry Me a River"

KEEPING MY PROMISE to myself, I dressed and prepared for school the next morning. I tied my hair back neatly and headed out the door with my school bag slung over my shoulder. Shoes cleaned, fingernails immaculate, and my uniform clean and pressed. These were the areas of my person most likely to be examined by the nuns that morning before class started. Yes, I had taught myself to iron and I could also sew, self-taught using my mother's old Singer sewing machine.

The bell rang and I took my seat in the classroom. Sister Albertus was late, which was unusual, so Gracie stood and directed the class. She smiled at me, happy that I had taken her words seriously. I was just about to start opening my books when Sister Albertus burst into the room. I could tell she was angry; her face always changed color. It started from the bottom of her neck and rose all the way to the top of her head, blood red. It was actually quite amusing. But this time it was not amusing as she was heading straight for me.

She grabbed me by the scruff of the neck, pulling my hair in the process, and shoved me towards the door. She walked slower than me, so when she caught up with me, she shoved me in the back again and continued like that until we were outside the classroom.

"You revolting little girl!" she boomed. "How dare you bring disgrace upon this school, driving past in a police car in full view of the parents *in your school uniform!*" I thought she was going to pop a vein. "Give me your blazer, now," she yelled.

"No, my mom paid for my blazer. It's mine, and I am not giving it to you."

She shoved me in the shoulder. "Give me that blazer … NOW!" she roared.

I heard scuffling coming from inside the classroom as the girls clambered to see what was going on. This only fuelled Sister Albertus even further and embarrassed me more. Then I heard Gracie yelling, telling the girls to return to their seats. I thanked her under my breath.

"Well, if you won't give it to me, I'll take it." She reached forward and in one foul swoop pulled the pocket with the school emblem right off my blazer, tearing a hole in it.

Tears smarted my eyes as anger boiled up. I knew how hard it had been for Mom to purchase these uniforms and now this nun had wrecked my blazer. I would never be able to use it again.

Without even thinking, my arm snapped out and I ripped Sister Albertus's wimple (head piece) off, revealing her ugly, shaved head and ripping some of the buttons off her white coif in doing so. She demanded I give her back her head piece, to which I replied, "No, give me back my pocket and pay my mother for my blazer."

Then I threw her wimple on the ground and stomped all over it. I was going to hell anyway, so I might as well go there with a bang! She pushed me roughly back onto a wooden bench and my head snapped back, hitting the wall behind. Ouch! Then she seemed to gather herself together (and her wimple) and told me to go to the social education classroom until my mother came to fetch me.

Oh no, not Mom, not again. Oh well, at least now I might be allowed to go to Thornbury High School with Kerry and Debra, and I will go to school, no matter where I am put.

I walked into the empty classroom to wait for Mom. Gracie emptied out my desk and brought my bag to me. She told me how sorry she was that it had come to this. I kept thinking that Mom would be so angry when she saw the tear in my blazer. I couldn't wait for her to tell Sister Albertus off for what she had done. I was sure she would realize that this was not my fault.

Well, I was wrong. Mom didn't understand at all. She was just as angry with me as Sister Albertus had been. I tried to explain to her, again, that yesterday I had only come home to feed her and that I was on my way back to school and should never have been taken by the police; but she refused to listen. We walked out of the school in silence and boarded a tram headed towards Northcote. I knew we were going in the wrong direction.

"Mom, where are we going?"

She didn't answer and I just followed along behind her. I thought we were perhaps going to her work. Less than twenty minutes later, however, we were sitting in the reception area of the Northcote Police Station, waiting for one of the detectives who was working on my abduction case to come and see us.

"Why are we here, Mom?" No answer.

I had not seen my mother like this, ever. She was being totally unreasonable. I couldn't understand why she wouldn't listen to me. Next minute a detective appeared from upstairs and Mom explained to him what had happened. He knew most of it from the day before.

Then she leaned forward and asked him in hushed undertones, thinking I couldn't hear, if he wouldn't mind giving me a good spanking because I didn't have a father figure to do it and I had just been expelled from school. He was happy to comply with her request.

He held onto my hand and led me up the stairs and into his office, where he shut the door. As he started to undo his belt, I began shaking like a leaf … *Is he going to have sex with me, rape me, right here in a police station, with so many people around?* … I was very frightened. I didn't know what he was going to do and who was I to know? After my life thus far, anything was possible.

Once he got his belt off, he grabbed me by the arm, threw me over his knee and gave me twenty of his best across my backside—I wet myself with fear. I still feared he was going to rape me after the belting. My backside was so sore.

But it was over.

I still didn't understand why I was the one who was supposed to have done something wrong. I didn't understand why I had been treated that way. I finally asked myself *Why me?* Why me was to become a constant in my life for a long time. I was maturing.

My mother wasn't talking to me, and after what she had put me through, I wasn't talking to her. The trip home was too quiet. The night was silent until she started to drink, and then it started.

"Bev, come here." The conversation though had changed this time. "You're such a bad child. You've always been a problem, a bloody thorn in my side. I've had enough, do you hear me?"

The way she said that got me nervous.

"You're out of control, Bev. I'm going to have to put you into a home where naughty girls go. What choice do I have? If I don't stop you now you're going to be off prostituting yourself on the streets next."

Finally, she was showing some concern for my life! I didn't deserve any of that. I had never been a disobedient child, not that she knew of anyway. [Well, I thought she didn't know.] I was told so many other things about myself that night.

I was …

… evil

… unwanted

… unruly

… disturbed

… dumb (that hurt)

The list went on until finally … "and no one loves you or wants you!'

I can't remember the next day, but I know that Mom took the day off work. I guess it was taken up by phone calls between her and my aunty regarding my future, as the next day I was summoned to Nanna's.

I can remember sitting on the couch and listening to it all again. I was berated, told how bad I was, told I was uncontrollable and that I needed to be locked away with other bad girls. Then I was told the news. I was going to be put into a Catholic convent for being so bad, and, get this, to *keep me safe*! Now they care!

I sat there, dumbfounded, a look of contempt on my face. I was quietly huffing and puffing and rolling my eyes. *For my own safety?* God, I had already got myself through the worst of it, or so I thought.

Where were they when I was "hurt" by Mary's grandfather? Was I kept safe then? No, my mother couldn't even *sense* that there was a valid reason why I wanted to leave that week-end. Like now, I wasn't being believed.

Did she keep me safe from Uncle Graham? And Uncle Ernie? And what about me roaming the streets and finally being brutally raped by that sixteen-year-old in the trench coat… not to mention numerous attempts at abduction. Then there was Ricky's father who had forced Ricky to have sex with me and raped me himself.

There was nothing else that could hurt me now, except this … this feeling of being so unwanted, so rejected by my family … to be disposed of … locked away, never to be seen again.

Remember the song, *Cry Me a River*, by Julie London? I think I did just that during that night as I lay on my grandmother's couch. I cried a river—a bloody big river. And you know what? I think a part of me never did stop crying.

I cried for the little girl hidden deep inside me who needed to be protected—even from her own family.

I cried for the innocence that I had lost along the way, for the cruel adults that had seen their way clear to take from me without permission.

I cried because all I wanted was a home, to belong, a mother and a father, and to be cared for.

I cried because I would never know any of these things; it was too late. That chapter of my life was closing. They had all but destroyed it. I fell asleep with the song by Gary Puckett playing over in my head—*This Girl is a Woman Now…*

I wasn't a woman, but the words were apt. The little girl in me was long gone.

I had no say in all of this. I was only twelve years old. All I knew was that the only life I had ever known until now was about to come to an end.

14
R.I.P. Saturday, 27 September 1969

"Don't speak. Don't ask. Just do what you're told"

THE TWENTY-SEVENTH of September, 1969—eight days before my thirteenth birthday, when other girls would be looking forward to teenage birthday parties and presents, frilly dresses and guests, was the official date Beverley Forster died, inside. It wasn't the child abuse that killed me, nor the sexual assaults, the mental abuse, the hunger or the rejection. It was the total abandonment of love, in every form.

On this date, I was admitted to the Convent of the Good Shepherd in Oakleigh, where I was to await transfer to the senior women's section of the Bendigo Good Shepherds Convent (also known as St. Aidan's Orphanage), called Maryfields. That's right, you read that correctly—the *senior women's* section, where the minimum age was supposed to be females of fifteen years of age ... I was twelve. Somebody couldn't count. I was to find quite a number of the girls there around my age, far too young.

What waited for me at the convent, I could not have imagined. I was not equipped to be put into this type of environment. Yes, I was street smart, but I was not emotionally ready to survive in this strange, unloving, unforgiving, systemized, sterile environment in which I was being placed. Not to begin with anyway ...

I was up early, washed, and dressed. I sat in the lounge room waiting for instructions on when I was allowed to eat. The night before I had been ordered not to move off the couch and I was doing what I was told.

Nanna called me out to the kitchen where she cooked toast for me. No smiles, no hugs. I can't remember ever receiving a hug from her, so nothing had changed. Mom came out to the table and sat, stone-faced also. It was a quiet breakfast.

Nobody talked at all, except for formalities such as "Pass the sugar, please" and "Can you pass the vegemite?" and so on. Mom and Nanna had their normal impasse.

After breakfast I returned to the lounge room where I sat with a little brown case in front of me. Inside were clean underwear, socks, a change of clothing, soap, and hygiene items, as they had been told not to send too much with me because everything was provided. No pictures or anything of a personal nature were allowed.

At around 9 a.m., my Uncle Bert came into the lounge room. He picked up my little brown case and reached his hand out to me... "Coming?" And he motioned with his head for me to follow him. Uncle Bert was an elderly man of few words—a loving and caring person. He would be the main reason why I got to see my mother most months. He would drive her the distance from Melbourne to Bendigo to see me on Parlor Days at the convent.

Uncle Bert cupped my back with his hand as he led me to the car. He opened the back door for me and I jumped in his little Hillman with my case. There were no farewells or hugs and kisses.

My aunty said, "I hope you behave yourself where you're going," and with that we were off.

I sat in the back seat with the window down and the wind in my hair, watching the trees and life go whizzing by. It felt like forever before we pulled up in front of an old, grey, brick building with large wooden doors at the front. It reminded me of something out of a scary movie, cold and dungeon-like, with its eerie gargoyles and engravings—a prison. My imagination was not far off.

Uncle Bert used the knocker on the large timber door, and a few minutes later a nun came to answer it. She greeted my uncle and my mother with a smile, but raised her eyebrows and gave me the once over with her eyes. We were led with enthusiasm down a long, highly polished corridor and were directed to sit on the chairs, which were neatly placed outside another door. Before long another nun appeared at the door. She gave me the once over also, looking me up and down with a look of contempt. I felt as though I was on a lunch menu. Mom and Uncle Bert were summoned into her office and I was told to stay put. I certainly did!

Shortly after, Mom and Uncle Bert emerged and they started to walk off towards the door. I stood up to go with them, but the nun pulled me back by the arm. Mom turned around and said, "Now, you be a good girl and do everything you're told."

With that, she turned and walked away.

It was Uncle Bert who turned three times to look at me as they walked the length of that long, polished hallway towards the front door. He waved goodbye just before they exited. Mom didn't turn around once. It felt like she was glad to see the end of me. I didn't know if, or when, I might ever see them again. I suddenly felt like a fish out of water. I had no idea where I was or what awaited me.

The nun pushed me back towards the chair again and told me to sit and wait. Before she left, she told me, "Don't get too comfortable. You are not staying. You will be picked up tomorrow and taken to another convent in Bendigo."

I was thinking, *Where in the world is that? Will they know how to find me?*

About twenty minutes later, a woman in a bluish grey uniform appeared. I'd eventually learn these ladies were called "auxiliaries", and most of them had been in a convent their entire lives without taking vows. She told me to come with her and led me down many more corridors, and up and down stairs, until we finally reached an area that was full of antique iron beds, all made up with blue and white bedspreads.

I later found out it was called "the infirmary". I was taken to one of the beds and told to shower and change into the clothes that were laid out for me on the bed and then to put my own clothes into the little brown case. The clothes they had placed out for me was a hospital nightie that was twice the size of me, but I did what I was told. With that, the woman was gone, giving no further instructions of any kind. So I examined my surroundings a little more. I walked to the door and tried the handle. Locked. I could hear children playing and making noise, so I went to the window and climbed as high as I could. There was a small, concrete courtyard below where heaps of children were talking together in small groups. I particularly remember that there were no games of any kind, no skipping ropes, no hopscotch, nothing—just groups of girls sitting around talking.

Not long after that I heard keys rattling in the door. A teenage girl holding a tray with food walked in, with a nun behind her. She placed the tray onto the trolley next to my bed.

"Hello," I said, but she didn't respond. Her eyes went straight to the ground and the nun rounded her up and shuffled her towards the door. She managed to catch a sideways glimpse of me as she left and I saw a slight smile on her face. I was so hungry the food went down without even touching the sides, and then I sat there bored again, swinging my legs backwards and forwards, staring at the wall. I didn't know how long I was going to stay there.

I'd be lying if I said that I wasn't frightened; waves of fear came and went throughout the day. I was living in a state of nothingness and didn't know what was to become of me. One minute melded into the next. Those minutes became hours and still nothing. I spent a fair bit of my time trying to see out the window to the courtyard below, but the noise that had been coming from the courtyard earlier had gone. There were no children to be seen anywhere, just the odd shadow moving from one place to the other every now and again.

Darkness started to fall and no one had come in to me. By now I found myself pacing backwards and forwards from the door to my bed. The room grew darker and darker, and then I heard keys rattling in the door again. I quickly ran to the side of the bed that I had been allocated. A nun stepped into the room and turned on the lights. They were so bright my eyes were blinded for a moment. Once they could focus again, I saw a young girl standing behind the nun with a tray of food. The nun instructed her to quickly put the food down and leave the room, which she did. Again, no eye contact. I didn't understand why they wouldn't talk to me. They were gone as fast as they had arrived. I hoped it was not going to be like this until I was allowed to return home again. When was that going to be?

I had heard of Mont Park, a mental institution at that time on the outskirts of Melbourne. My friends and I had often teased each other that that's where we were heading. Is that where I was? This all appeared to be just what I had imagined a mental institution to be like. I looked at the food on the tray and my stomach turned. What was it? I wasn't sure that I would be able to eat it, but I didn't know when my next meal might be, so I put my fork into the offering and touched the end of my tongue with it. It certainly didn't taste the best, but it wasn't bad enough to push away either. I didn't know it then, but I would have to get used to more offerings of food like this over many years to come.

I twirled my fork in the food and pushed the vegetables around the plate until finally it was a piled mess. I ate as much as I could fit in and then the keys rattled in the lock again. This time a woman in blue stepped in the door. She came over and looked at what I had done to the food.

"Don't let the nuns see what you've done with your food. If you're smart, you will eat it now before they come to take the tray away," she said in a very stern tone.

I eyed her up and down, trying to figure out how serious she was. I decided to push the rest of the meal down my throat, gagging with each mouthful. Thank God there was an end to it.

She fussed around, finding another gown and told me that I should have a shower and attend to my "hygiene needs". *Hygiene needs? Mmm?* She also told me that I needed to wash my underwear out and hang them at the base of the bed. Wash my underwear? *Huh?* ...

"Mom washes my underwear for me," I blurted out.

She immediately responded, "Well, you're lucky you have one. But she won't be doing your washing anymore."

I thought about that for a moment and decided I should do what I was told. I went and attended to my "hygiene needs" and returned to the bed. Hygiene needs in orphanage lingo referred to washing your face and hands or having a shower if it was your day. They never really cared if you brushed your teeth; the only thing you had to show them when leaving the bathroom was the crutch of your panties. It seemed crusty crutches were the ultimate sin!

I put my dripping wet underpants on the end of the bed where I had been shown. The water was dripping all over the place and there was a trail of water from the bathroom to the bed. She quickly grabbed them off the bed, took me back to the bathroom, and showed me how to wring them out. That was something new for me. I had just pushed them around under the water and put them on the bed as she said.

She checked the crutch area of my underwear and then showed me how to use my soap to clean it. Once cleaned, she rinsed them out and wrung the water out, ready to hang to dry. That way they were nice and clean for the next day. I took all of this in, but told her I had some more underwear in my suitcase that I could wear the next day. She just grunted at me.

It was only later that I would learn that some girls were only issued with one set of underwear on their admission to the convent, and five years later they were still wearing what was left of the same set. There was a girl who washed her underwear every night and wore them wet the next day as she didn't have any others, and none were ever offered because she was not a favorite of the nuns. If I had known that, I would have happily shared my underwear with her as I was lucky in having more than one pair.

Once I was in the new hospital nightie, she placed a dressing gown at the end of the bed and told me that I should jump into bed and she would see me the next morning. I asked her if I would see my mom the next day and she told me that she didn't know. With that, she picked up the tray, returned to the door, turned off the light, and said, "Goodnight." She was gone, just like that.

She had tricked me. I had eaten that horrible meal and I didn't have to. No nuns came to see me at all. Oh well, it was food and better to have some than none. I knew that all too well.

I lay there and watched the shadows from the dim lighting outside playing on the walls in the dark. It was scary. There was no one with me, no one to talk to or share anything with, no television to watch, no noise. Just deathly quiet and a pitch black room. Except for the odd movement of light here and there, there was nothing.

R.I.P. SATURDAY, 27 SEPTEMBER 1969

Then, as if by a miracle, just when I hit the height of my fear some little lights came on around the boundary of the room—night lights. I was relieved, but as the night wore on and sleep escaped me, they only served to scare me even more. There was the occasional bump and grind as the old building settled into the night, relieved to be saved from the heat of the day's sun. The lights danced on the highly polished vinyl tile floor. My senses were heightened and I heard skittering, but I didn't take too much notice as my heart was already pounding and felt stuck in my throat. I just wanted to go and turn the lights on, but if someone came I might get into a lot of trouble. I had never been scared of the dark, but this place scared me.

I crept from my bed to the door and tried the door handle again. Locked! So I returned to my bed, pulled the sheets up over my head, and tried to forget where I was. I thought of happier times when I was with Kerrie and Debra. I missed them. I hadn't seen them for over a week and I needed them. I needed Mrs. White to make everything okay. She would hug me and comfort me; she was the only one who ever did. My mom had refused to let me to see them on the Friday before I had left to go to Nanna's house. She blamed them in part for me wagging school. So they didn't know I was gone.

Suddenly something dropped on top of the bed. I felt the little thud as it hit my hip. I buried myself deeper under my blankets, letting out a little cry of terror. Then I bravely stuck my head up out from under the sheets and saw something skittering away across the floor. I watched as whatever it was scuttled around.

I got out of bed and put my dressing gown on, but I couldn't see where it had gone. So I got down on all fours and laid my head flat on the ground to see if I could locate it. All of a sudden I felt something run straight up the sleeve of my dressing gown. I let out a blood-curdling scream, threw myself backwards onto my bum and ran for the safety of my bed, only to realize that what went up hadn't come back down. I threw off my dressing gown and it landed on the floor. I patted my nightie all over and then quickly jumped back into the bed, where I laid staring at the dressing gown for hours until finally I fell asleep. It had been a mouse. My only company in the whole wide world was a mouse, probably kept a prisoner there also.

Rattle, rattle, rattle went the keys in the lock. Bang went the door.

"Time to get up," the nun said as I rubbed the sleep from my eyes. I was trying hard to focus on the black object in front of me when I realized that it hadn't all been a dream. I was in the same room, the same bed, and staring at the same nun I'd seen the night before. "Get up out of bed now and pick up that dressing gown, you ungrateful little girl. We give you nice things to wear and this is how you treat them," she said.

I scampered out of bed and hesitantly picked up the dressing gown from where I had thrown it the night before. Phew, nothing there. Whatever had been there had the sense to disappear overnight ... I wished it had taken me with it.

"Get yourself ready for church. I will be back in twenty minutes to get you," she ordered. Church? Me? My mind raced at one hundred miles an hour. Lucky I adapt fast; that was the first of many church days for me. I asked the nun if I would get breakfast as I was hungry. She told me that I should be grateful for what they had already given me out of their good charity. I learned quickly that sometimes I just needed to shut up and not ask questions. That was to be the pattern of survival for a long time. Don't speak. Don't ask. Just do what you're told.

Twenty minutes later, the nun promptly arrived back at the door. I sat waiting, with hair brushed, fully dressed, and shoes on and tied.

"Hmph, well, come on," she said. We walked down the many hallways and up and down the stairs until we reached the church. I was given a scarf to cover my head and was placed in the back row by myself. Every now and again some of the other girls would turn around and snigger at me. I smiled at them, hoping to make a friend. That was useless. Straight after church it was back to prison for me. I wondered if I would see an end to that room. I bravely asked the nun, "When will I be allowed out of here?"

She replied, "Oh no, we can't have you contaminating the other girls." And with that she was gone again.

Well, that had really hurt my dignity and the floodgates opened. It was just all too much. I started to cry, yelling at the top of my voice, "'I want to go home! I want to go home!"

Then I heard the keys in the door again. I slunk back to the side of my

R.I.P. SATURDAY, 27 SEPTEMBER 1969

bed. In came the same kind auxiliary who had spoken with me the night before. In her hands she held a tray of food for me, which she placed beside the bed. She saw I had been crying and told me, "It's no use crying. You need to get used to this now as your way of life and devote your life to the service of God."

I yelled at her, "But I don't want to be a nun!"

She laughed at me. "You could never be a nun. Nuns are pure of action and thought, and since you're so bad, you could never wear a habit."

She left. Feeling deflated by what she had said, I sat quietly and ate my cold breakfast—porridge that was rock hard, had cold milk with no sugar and was served with a cup of lukewarm tea. We all know how I felt about porridge not being cooked like Mom's.

The keys rattled in the lock again as the door closed behind her. I stared down at the tray of food and wished I could be anywhere else but here. What had my mother done to me?

15

The Not So Good Shepherd Orphanage

❧

> "Mom had come back to get me! She missed me and
> didn't want to leave me there. She had been
> only trying to teach me a lesson ...
> (Oh, just a dream.) Back to reality ..."

WHEN I WAS YOUNGER, my main security on those long, lonely nights by myself had been a radio, or as we called them then, a wireless. Then one day Mom was able to get her hands on a second-hand television. It became one of my main sources of pleasure.

Most afternoons I would run home from school or wherever else I might have been, just to see all my friends on television.

There was Kimba, Casper, and a myriad of cartoon characters, then the actors from *Lost in Space*, *Dr. Who*, and *Star Trek*. (Yes, I was obviously a nerd in the making). Later in the evening, *The Avengers* with Emma Peel, *Bewitched*, *The Monkees*, *My Three Sons*, and *I Dream of Jeannie* were my world. Wow, who didn't want to be Jeannie? All she had to do was blink her eyes, hold her arms up, and dream into reality whatever she wanted. I know I longed to be her; I still do.

Into the room she floated, as if she was standing on her own personal cloud. With one smooth movement of her arm, she beckoned to me to pick up my case and said, "Follow me." Perhaps I was going to meet all the other girls that I had seen at church that morning. Upstairs and downstairs, along hallways and through doors we ran; well, I did. She floated. I found it difficult to keep up with her pace; she floated so fast. Then we entered the main entrance where I had last seen my mom. My mind filled with imaginings and my heart with emotion. Mom had come back to get me. She missed me and didn't want to leave me here. She had been only trying to teach me a lesson ...

Back to reality ... Into the hallway stepped this tiny little nun, about 5 foot 2 inches. She was no Jeannie. She was skinny and had a lined, not-so-kind face with a cracked, forced, and crooked smile. She walked with a limp, which I later learned was caused by her club foot on which she wore a built-up shoe. With her she had two young girls who were introduced to me as Chloe and Maureen. The nun introduced herself as Mother Rita and told me that they had driven from Bendigo that morning to come and pick me up, and that we now would be returning to Bendigo. So we had to hurry up as it would soon be dark.

We all quickly marched towards the front door of the convent, with me carrying my little brown case, and exited through the doors into the outside world. I can remember I jumped up on a small fence and blinked like Jeannie, trying to change the situation, trying to bring my mom back, and my life. I was ordered to get into the car, a station wagon of some sort. I can't remember the model or the color, only the fact that it took me further away from where I wanted to be.

Chloe sat up front with Mother Rita and Maureen in the back with me. I eventually figured out that Chloe was most certainly Mother Rita's favorite little girl. She couldn't do anything wrong. I remember examining Maureen's face. It was warm and friendly but she was shy. She was a slip of a girl, thin to the bones like she had never been fed, not terribly talkative. But her eyes told me a whole different story. So I talked her ears off all the way back to Bendigo and she just sat and listened with a small shy smile on her face.

One thing I excelled at was talking. I can remember my mother bought a record when Dad was still with us; it was titled *You Talk Too Much*, by Joe Jones. She told me it was my song. Now I know why, and I agree. My granddaughter has inherited the same trait, and this is now her song too, she will tell you that quite proudly.

We stopped somewhere along the road and had sandwiches for lunch. Mother Rita asked a little bit about me, where I had come from, what school I had attended, and other bits of information. All the time she eyeballed me so that I couldn't lose her line of sight. Chloe whispered things to Maureen while we sat there eating. Then it was back to the car and onto the next step of the journey. It was coming on evening when we arrived at the convent.

Maureen leant over and said, "That's it," as we drove towards the top of the hill on St. Aidan's Road in Bendigo. St. Aidan's was huge.

It stood in its stateliness, reaching for the sky on top of that hill, majestic, pristine, eerily beautiful. We drove through the heavy iron gates at the front and up the long, winding pebble driveway, finally turning towards the left-hand side of the convent. Maureen explained that the orphans were on the other side and that she had been there herself, but now she was in this section with me. I gazed out the window at the sharply manicured and green gardens; everything was perfect. On my right-hand side there stood a grotto with a statue of the Virgin Mary. I can remember thinking it was pretty. Even though I had been such a naughty girl, I was at the same time reverent of all things religious.

We were let out at the front steps while Mother Rita parked the car. On her return, we all walked together up the stairs towards the front door. As she opened the door with her large bunch of keys, there was that disturbing rattling sound that told me that when I walked through that door, I was not coming out again. I had a sinking feeling in my stomach.

We stepped into the front room. Maureen explained to me that this was where the girls with families had visitors and that it was a special treat to be able to see them. We continued to walk through to the small hallway. The rattle of the keys as they locked the front door sucked the life out of me; I was overwhelmed with feelings of despair.

"Is the front door locked all the time?" I asked Mother Rita.

"Yes, it's to protect the good people of Bendigo from the likes of you," she said rather coldly.

The same thing happened again with the next door. Mother Rita walked past us and unlocked a door that led to a large verandah near some lockers. We walked through it and she quickly locked it behind us.

"Chloe, take Beverley and introduce her to Mother John," she ordered. And with this she turned to me and said, "We do not talk about our past here. You have nothing to be proud of. You are here to be repentant for your sins as all sinners should be." With that she was gone.

I was dumbfounded. *My past? Sinner? Repentant? Wow! Why? All I did was feed my mother when she was sick. Maybe it was because I had jumped on Sister Albertus's wimple?*

Chloe and Maureen turned around and stepped up into another entry area. Inside to the left was a staircase that led up to our dormitory, and then there was a door to the right, which was to be my group room. We lived in groups of around fifteen girls to one nun and an auxiliary. Chloe opened this door; it wasn't locked. We stepped in and immediately the whole room turned silent, I felt my face flush red and go hot as they all stared at me. Eventually, the dull level of noise started up again.

"Mother John, this is Beverley," Chloe stated before she went over to a group of girls who sat huddled, whispering and sniggering. I did not warm to Chloe as I had to Maureen; something about her nature put me on alert. I'm sure the feeling was mutual.

Mother John smiled and said, "Welcome to our group, Beverley." She directed my gaze over to the auxiliary and said, "This is Anne. If you need anything, just ask either of us." Mother John was a younger nun. She wore thick-rimmed, black glasses, had a gentle face, and seemed friendly enough; Anne was a lot older, in her late forties, early fifties. She wore a bluish grey uniform, had curly, greying hair, and a gentle but stern face.

I felt welcomed, but then Mother John turned, and with a more serious look on her face, stated, "We have rules here, Beverley, and they must be abided by. Has Chloe explained them to you yet?"

I shook my head to register a no ... No sound, nothing, escaped from my lips. All of a sudden I was extremely nervous. She explained when bedtimes were and that we got up at 6 a.m. sharp. As soon as morning prayers were completed, we would wash, dress, and head for our housekeeping duties, after which we attended mass and then had breakfast. We were all expected to pull our weight.

Was that it? What about the rest of the day? School? Did we get to go to school? Oh well, who cares anyway? To me school was not that significant.

Maureen was placed in charge of me and was expected to show me around, be my friend, and make sure I knew where to go and when. She introduced me to all the girls in the room, one by one. But I couldn't take my attention off one particular girl; her name was Irene. She had the devil in her, and I knew it as soon as I laid eyes on her—takes one to know one. We were kin, Irene and I. We were born from the same peapod, only to different mothers. There was an immediate attraction for both of us, and from that time we were inseparable. Irene was taller than me and was slim with stumpy, almost shapeless legs. She was still young and not developed. She had mousy, brown hair and an extremely good-looking, friendly face. Yep, we were going to be friends.

As soon as the introductions were completed, Irene made a beeline for me and me for her. We sat together and chatted. First the introductions and then the knowledge base. Where are you from? Why are you here? What did you do? And so on. We talked over each other in an effort to get it all out. There was such urgency in our conversation as if we were going to be taken away from each other. My heart was beating so fast to have found such an incredible friend in such a short time. Irene's mother had died and she was taken from her Dad as they, the Welfare, stated she was in moral danger. So she ended up at the convent, just like so many other children during that time who were taken from very loving families because one parent was absent or had passed away.

We all walked to the dining room as a group for dinner. I walked with Irene and Maureen. Maureen showed me how to line up and get a plate so that food could be sloshed onto it by the girls who were serving behind the counter. And then she took me to where I would sit. I was lucky because I ended up on the same table as Maureen, so I wasn't left with strangers. This place was so nice! Okay, so the doors were locked, but other than that it was wonderful. Much nicer than where I had been in Oakleigh. Everyone was so polite, the food was terrific, the group room was lovely, and I'd been informed that our group room had only just been remodeled, so we were the only group with a modern group room. We had a stereo that the auxiliary would play her records on. None of the other groups had one. I was so lucky given my love of music.

After dinner, we washed our plates in the sink, dried them and put them away, and then returned to the group room. Anne put on her favorite L.P. (a large vinyl disc album that was played on a record player to produce music the same way that CDs do these days; it stands for Long Play). It was Simon and Garfunkel. Later I would always be affected by two songs from the particular album she played, *Homeward Bound* and *The Boxer*. Each would always make tears pool in my eyes, but quickly I'd wipe them away so that I wouldn't be called a baby or sook by the older girls.

Irene and I sat in the corner … The conversation still hadn't stopped. We talked and talked until for some reason Irene poked me and said, "You're in."

We broke out into a game of tiggy and I chased Irene. I caught her, tagged her, and ran in the opposite direction yelling, "You're in."

She caught me and yelled again, "You're in!"

The whole time, Mother John was yelling at us. "Girls, stop it!" But it was too late.

Everything happened so fast. Irene was just starting to run through the chairs as Mother Rita arrived to see how I was settling in. Mother John stood to yell at us and my foot caught under the carpet square, catapulting me towards Irene with some momentum. Bang! She went down on top of one of the brand new velvet covered chairs. Crash! I landed right on top of her and the leg of the chair crumbled beneath us. As I tried to fix my position and push myself up, smash came this powerful thud from behind me. My head felt like it had been split in two. I wobbled and fell on top of Irene again. I stumbled to my feet, trying to make sense of what had happened. Then I saw the wooden hand broom in Mother Rita's hand and the same scarlet color that Sister Albertus used to get when she was in a bad mood.

I looked around me and everyone was silently staring at me, except for Chloe who was busily saying something to one of the other girls with her hand covering her mouth.

Mother Rita pulled me outside of the group room by the scruff of the neck and my hair. She yelled at me, telling me that my type wasn't actually wanted in her convent, but out of the goodness of her heart, and to the relief of my poor mother who had the responsibility of having to deal with such a terrible child, she had opened her doors to me. She told me that I would pay for the chair that I had broken and that I would not behave like that again, or I would be sent off to a jail called Winlaton, and that apparently was an exceptionally horrible place to be sent.

With that she called Maureen out and suggested that I be shown where the dormitory was so that I could settle in. Maureen was so kind to me. She told me I had to be careful not to do anything wrong in front of Mother Rita because she kept the hand broom underneath the front lapel of her gown, tied to her waist band, and she would not hesitate to use it on me again. It was one of her regular forms of punishment.

I was soon to find out that the beatings were routine, and the work we were expected to do, whether in good health or ill, was hard and laborious. But even worse was the lack of love, emotional support, or physical connection—all of which we craved and needed as young children.

The following extracts are reproduced from the Senate Community Affairs References Committee Report with permission from the Australian Senate.

FORGOTTEN AUSTRALIANS:

A REPORT ON AUSTRALIANS WHO EXPERIENCED INSTITUTIONAL OR OUT-OF-HOME CARE AS CHILDREN
August 2004 © Commonwealth of Australia
ISBN 0-642-71239-5   Extract of 3 paragraphs

CHAPTER 2 - INSTITUTIONAL CARE IN AUSTRALIA
All I understood was that I was away from my family, and as bad as they said that situation was, it was still my family, and it was the only way of life I had known.

INSTITUTIONS
2.1 Various factors have been used implicitly or explicitly to define institutions, including size, overcrowding, separateness from the community, regimentation, external control, residents who lack identity, choice and autonomy, and physically and emotionally barren environments. Institution is rarely to be taken to be a positive term. An oft-cited 1961 Goffman

definition of institutions includes: A basic social arrangement in modern society is that the individual tends to sleep, play and work in different places, with different co-participants, under different authorities, and without an overall rational plan. The central feature of total institutions can be described as a breakdown of the barriers ordinarily separating these three spheres of life.

2.2 Evidence to the inquiry described the atmosphere in many homes as emotionally and physically punitive, and where children were subjected to criminal assaults and had no emotional relationships with any adults or personal interaction with significant people in their lives. Apart from specific acts of emotional, mental, physical, psychological and sexual abuse, institutional life itself is inherently abusive.

2.3 Many Australian institutional settings for children and young people such as orphanages, group cottage homes, foster care, homes for children with disabilities and juvenile detention centers, have fitted the above negative descriptions. Of significance is that while children and young people need care, protection and safe environments, over time, many children were placed in institutions which not only did not meet these needs, but metered out cruel treatment and abuse.

16

The Daily Grind

❦

"Oh my God, for the love of Jesus; what's inside this sock?"

Maureen took me upstairs, advising me to be exceptionally quiet walking along the built-in balcony because the older ladies and mentally disabled people slept there and we were not allowed to disturb them.

"Do they always live here?" I asked. "It must be cold." As I looked at the slat glass windows, all I could think was that they were exposed to the elements, thinking back to my brother and the night he had been sent to Nanna's house.

"Yes," she said.

There were many that slept on this balcony and Bendigo had an unforgiving winter. With no heaters to warm them and only slat glass windows to protect them from the elements, they would wake up with their beds saturated from the rain that had worked its way between the slats.

As we entered the dormitory, I had to stop to take in how large it was. It was a long room, about forty meters in length, with row upon row of basic chrome beds. Each had similar threadbare chenille bedspreads, neatly tucked with hospital corners and one flat pillow. A free standing cupboard about a foot wide and six foot tall, stood next to each bed. Each row had approximately six beds. Along the wall with the windows that faced to the street was another row of about twenty beds. The dormitory was a regimented, sterile environment with only a few sparse personal items scattered here and there. No dolls or pyjama bags, nothing. Just a bed, wardrobe, bed, wardrobe, and so on. Every row was the same, with no variation in the color of the bedspreads. The lights made everything look washed out and old. The light of day saw no improvement.

Maureen ushered me towards the bed that I would occupy. She showed me that she slept nearby, which put me at ease. Since the others would be coming up to bed soon, she told me that I should hurry to get first dibs on the washroom because there was always a line up for the sinks. The convent had no heating and most girls just wanted to be warm in their beds.

I looked for my case but it wasn't there. Maureen gave me a nightie, a dressing gown, and a towel from the stockpile at the end of the dormitory. She then took me through what would become a nightly ritual for the next four years.

This routine was only broken by two showers a week, and if you were extremely lucky, one bath. Once the bath was full though, it was shared between every girl in the dormitory that wanted one, if there was time. Other than that, you washed with a face cloth in the sink, ensuring that you kept your private parts covered less they be exposed, which would bring down a swift punishment.

The bathroom was at the end of the dormitory and consisted of four large, steel wash troughs, which were encased in a tacky green granite marble counter. The troughs were side by side with cold water taps running down the back of them; the bare copper pipes reached to the ceiling. The overall look of the bathroom was retro—cream and black tiles, extremely high ceiling space, painted with a bland off-light green color. Something like you might see in a horror movie like *Psycho*. I stared around, oblivious to the fact that one day in the near future this room would become my torture chamber at the hands of Mother Rita and one of her lackeys.

Off to the back of the bathroom and pushed against the far left wall were two single shower cubicles. Showers were timed and there was little time for washing hair, along with other intimate places. You were made to feel selfish, dirty or just downright rude if you stayed in there longer than you were supposed to, getting up to "God knows what". If you were too far over your allotted time, an auxiliary or older girl would be sent in to make sure that you were not fornicating! As if that's all we had to do.

As you entered the bathroom door, straight ahead lay the room that housed the bath—the place that most longed to be but few ever were. It depended on timing and if you were a favorite. Favorites got first dibs at the bath tub with the warmest and cleanest water. I was never a favorite. Actually, I can't remember ever having a bath while I was there.

Maureen took the Velvet soap from the tray and showed me how you scrubbed the crutch of your underwear, just as I had done at Oakleigh convent the night before. This was the first time I had ever had to wash my own clothes.

I did as she said and squeezed them out to the best of my ability. They were supposed to be presented to the auxiliary, who in our case was Anne, before we could place them on the end of our bed to dry overnight. But as Anne had not arrived yet, Maureen told me not to worry about showing her that night and suggested that I put my underpants at the end of my bed so they might have more drying time. Maureen's underpants caught my attention as they were relatively small for her size, even though she was just a slip of a girl, and the material was quite worn with ladders and holes. Of course, I didn't ask why and I just focused on washing my own.

It was unusual for girls to be allowed in the dormitory without being supervised by a nun or an auxiliary, as it was presumed you might get up to something. However, as I had misbehaved so badly and we had been sent there by Mother Rita, it was a punishment that really turned out to be a blessing in disguise. I never could have absorbed all this new information without having time up my sleeve. If the others had come up with us, it would have been rushed and frantic.

After we finished with our personal hygiene and scrubbing our underpants, we both returned to our beds. You were not allowed to get into the bed until evening prayers had been said and the girls were now starting to appear in the dormitory from the group room. There was a flurry of activity as each girl set about her chores—going to the toilet, washing her face and underwear, and the presentation of the underwear to the auxiliary for inspection.

THE DAILY GRIND

Cleaning of teeth was never a priority and as a result most girls developed rotten teeth and then went on to have massive dental issues later on in life, even losing their teeth altogether, as I did.

After all those things were completed, we were directed to drop to our knees on the cold, hard, unforgiving floor boards and ask for forgiveness from our Heavenly Father for all of our sins. There were no mats on the floor, or carpet. I did as I was told and dropped to my knees. The auxiliary led us in prayer … *if I should die before I wake, I pray the Lord my soul to take. Amen*, at which time everyone scampered into their beds and the lights were turned out.

The only break to this routine was on a Friday night when we lined up in front of a nun and were given our weekly dose of castor oil. Each of us were given a tablespoon of this to keep us regular—with the same spoon. I don't know about regular, but the cramps I had in my gut all weekend were never so nice. We hated it!

I jumped into bed, happy to be there for the first time. I turned towards Maureen's bed and she gave me a little wave that I was just able to see through the moonlit dormitory. There were no curtains on the six foot high glass windows that faced out onto the upstairs verandah, so the moon caused the shadows of the tree branches from the garden to play on the walls around the room.

Apart from the moonlight, the dormitory was dark and still, but not silent. Every now and again, I would see a figure scurry silently across the floor boards and quickly jump into someone else's bed. I was soon to find out that some of the girls, who were best of friends, did this to continue conversations that they had been having. I was at first a bit naïve, but one night, a year later, when one of the girls came and got into my bed, I was to learn the *other reason* some girls were getting into bed with each other after lights out. This girl and I were not really friends and I had not been having a conversation with her that needed to be continued, so what did she want? It was only when she put her hand on my breast inside my nightie that I knew, with a shock, what she was there for.

My reaction was quick. "I'm going to scream unless you get out of my bed." She did! And fast. I had not had any sexual encounter with a female before, and I wasn't about to start. I knew then what they were up to, well some of them.

Night after night, as the girls settled back into their own beds, I would be lulled to sleep by the sounds of the sniffles and whimpering from the others around me. My first night was no different. My own sniffles and whimpering joined in with the symphony as I cried for my past life, the one where even though I was alone, unfed, and usually uncared for, at least it was familiar. I missed it. Here I was, scared; this experience was frightening, clinical, unloving, and unforgiving.

Next morning, I woke to a voice booming through the dormitory that quite frankly scared the shit out of me: "In the name of the Father, the Son, and the Holy Spirit" … Everybody threw themselves out of bed and onto their knees and joined in the chorus. "Hail Mary full of grace"… the voice continued to boom. I had no idea what was going on until my knees came into contact with the cold floor. I looked around quickly to make sure I was copying the others.

After prayers the girls grabbed their knickers from the end of the bed. Some folded them neatly and placed them into their cupboards; others shoved them into the pocket of their dressing gowns so that they could put them on again afterwards. I only had the one pair because I couldn't find my case, so I followed Maureen's lead and put them into my pocket. They hadn't dried overnight. Maureen came to me to let me know I had to make my bed and she showed me how to do it. Then I was to go straight to the bathroom to wash my face and get dressed ready for my jobs.

Jobs, me? What jobs?

No one had mentioned that before. Each girl had a pre-assigned job, which was to be completed before church. After church, we then went to the dining room to eat.

As it was my first morning, I was advised to follow Maureen until such time as I was told what I should be doing. I can't remember the first morning well, but eventually we ended up in the dining room. I was starving. We each grabbed a plate and lined up at the bain-marie where we were served equal portions of food.

I cannot remember what I ate that day, but it went down easily. Maureen took me to the drinks area where we were allowed to make a cup of tea. I had never had a cup of tea before, only the lukewarm one that I had been given at the Oakleigh convent, so I followed her lead. While carrying the cup and saucer back to my table, I tripped over someone's foot, which I am sure was put there on purpose. All eyes were on me—the new girl. I quickly collected myself, not having spilled a drop of my tea on the floor, and caught up with Maureen to tuck into my cup of tea at the table. I made mental notes for a later time when I may catch that same girl by herself.

I would find over time, though, that I was no match for these hardened, systemized, welfare children. They had been around the traps for a long time and many had learnt how to not only defend themselves, but how to cover their tracks well. A protection response from many years of having been victims themselves in most cases. I was however a fast learner.

After we ate our food and drank our cup of tea, I was shown how to scrape my plate into the pig's slop bin and then put my dishes in the pile for girls on dishes duty to wash for the next meal. Each girl was assigned a meal they were to clean up after before moving to their next assignment. Today our job was to head to the laundry. Not just any laundry; this was a commercial laundry that serviced a lot of the rural area, taking in Bendigo and the surrounding district. The convent received deliveries daily from as far away as Ballarat.

Maureen and I moved from the dining room into the yard, and for the first time I got to see my new surroundings properly. As we headed down the stairs in silence into the enclosed concrete courtyard, I noticed the gates that led to freedom. Made of heavy-duty corrugated iron and mesh fencing, they stood almost fifteen foot tall with razor sharp barbwire across the top of them. A chain fed through the two holes about three feet off the ground, locked up tight by a solid padlock.

I asked Maureen if the gates were ever opened. She said no, and so it was, day in, day out for a long time. Closed, padlocked, no access to the outside world, no freedom. Once someone from Bendigo, who had only seen the convent from a distance, mentioned how lucky we girls were in having such lovely gardens to play in. But we were kept under lock and key; we had no gardens to play in, just a small concrete courtyard.

After breakfast some of the girls moved to the laundry to sort through the newly delivered linen and clothing to be laundered or dry cleaned that day. I was to find out that this was not such a pleasant task, especially when dealing with the underwear delivered from a Ballarat boys' private school, or worse, the girls' boarding school. Ewww! Laundry arrived at all times of the day. Sometimes it was sorted before school, sometimes after school. The school clothing was delivered inside individually named laundry bags, which were also laundered. Each piece had to be handled, removed from the bag, the name tag found to ensure that the correct owner could be located once the item was laundered, and then returned to the school. Items were then counted and marked off a personal record sheet that accompanied them: four pairs of blood-stained underwear that belong to Sissy Jo; five pairs of white jockey shorts, name tag says "Jack Splatt" (toilet paper enclosed is free of charge); three pairs of black school socks … you get the idea. *Oh my God, for the love of Jesus; what's inside this sock? Do I really have to turn it in the right way?*

You needed a particularly strong stomach for this job as sometimes what was delivered could only be described as shocking and downright disgusting. The morning sorts were the worse. Having just eaten and then rushing to sort the laundry, your breakfast teetered on the edge of your stomach and threatened to join the dirty clothes in the laundry basket. The smell reeked through the air and it took all your strength to ensure that you kept your food down. Summers were worse, working in the heat under a hot tin roof with no fans. I am sure half of the clothes (and their contents) were cooked before we got to them; sometimes the smell was just too much to bear.

On my first day I joined a small group of girls sitting on the floor in amongst the piles of dirty clothing—sorting, marking, surviving. Job done! *Thank the heavens. To school!*

17

School Days

༄

*"It felt like the Christmas I'd always wanted! …
I had been given clothes!"*

School was a small room situated in the far right hand corner of the small courtyard, right across from the laundry and next to the boiler room. What a dangerous scenario! On 5 September, 1974, an explosion occurred in the boiler room of the Mount Saint Canice laundry of The Good Shepherd in Hobart. Seven people were killed and one died later in hospital. Seventeen people were injured, several seriously. We were, on any given day, just moments from possible death. But it was still only 1969 and I was only on Day One of the sentence imposed by my family.

Twenty-four hours was about the time it took for most girls to decide if you were a new friend or not important to them. And what you didn't get shown in that time, or find out yourself, you had to find out the hard way, which often included punishment for being wrong.

Maureen and I were chatting keenly as we walked up the ramp. We were hurried along by a small elderly-looking lady with very thick glasses. Mrs. Raeburn was to be my teacher for the following four years. There were no introductions to the class as had been the case every time I changed schools in the past. It was just, "Oh, you're new. I shall have to find you a desk. Here, come sit here," as she pointed to one of the desks stuck in the middle of the room. She fussed around me for a few minutes, saying that she would have to get me sorted out, and then her attention was dragged elsewhere as she got the rest of the class started on their daily lessons. She gave me a workbook that was a whole bunch of A4 pages stapled together with a pale blue cover. Inside the book were questions and lines on which to write your answers. I didn't know it then, but that book, or books like it, would really be my teacher for the next four years. (Really, we were teaching ourselves.) I stared at it curiously, wondering what I should do with it. It never was explained to me. A small woman appeared at the door and asked that I be released from the classroom as I was wanted by one of the nuns.

Mrs. Raeburn beckoned to me and told me I should go with the woman. I followed her to a room in the main courtyard where I was greeted by Mother Rita; very few words were exchanged. I was thrown skirts, blouses, jumpers, and cardigans to try on as well as enclosed black leather shoes, pre-loved.

After about twenty minutes, I was issued with my uniform, which comprised of a green Macgregor Black Tartan skirt, which Mother Rita advised I would grow into (well, I was used to that anyway), two pale yellow, thin flannelette long-sleeve shirts, well worn, a green tie, a wattle green jumper with a matching cardigan, three pairs of knee-length brown socks, and black leather shoes. I was told to take everything to my dormitory, put my uniform on, put the extras away, and return to the classroom, and not to dilly dally.

It felt like the Christmas I'd always wanted! ... I'd been given clothes! None of the items were new; they had all been pre-loved and were just part of the school uniform, but none of that mattered. They were mine! Most of the girls hated the uniform, but I didn't mind it. It was warm and that was all that mattered. I hadn't been too warm up until that moment.

I ran to the dormitory, put my uniform on, and was shoving the rest in my drawers as quickly as possible when I was disturbed by another nun who I would later find out to be Mother Mercy. She asked me what I was doing and wanted to know if I'd taken anything that didn't belong to me. I shook my head to indicate that I hadn't. She hurried me out of the dormitory and back in the direction of the school room. My laces were still untied and I fell clumsily onto my left knee when trying to run along the length of the balcony as she hustled me along.

She taunted, "Can't you tie your shoelaces yet? Are you a baby?"

I tried to explain that I could but hadn't had time, but we reached the end of the balcony. She pointed to the stairs and advised me that she had better not catch me in the dormitory again during the day or I would be in terrible trouble.

I hurried down the stairs and took a moment at the bottom to quickly tie my shoelaces. I put my leg up onto the post to do so and was quickly picked up by another nun, Mother Rose, advising me that young ladies do not raise their legs in public and I should learn to bend down to do such things.

She added, "... in a ladylike manner". And with a simple glide, she was gone as quick as she had arrived.

These nuns were bloody everywhere! Mother Rose often glided around the convent grounds, arms crossed underneath her front lapel. It was like she was on a hover board (or was she really a dalek like in *Dr. Who?*). She gave no indication by her movement that she had actually taken a step. Quite comical actually, although very talented when you think about it; she was obviously from good family stock. I thought it must have taken lots of deportment classes to make her walk that way.

I finally made it back to the school room in time for morning tea. Everybody mulled around outside the classroom on the very small concrete area, or they sat on the small brick wall in the morning sun taking in the warmth of the day. I couldn't see Maureen, but I did see Irene and we made a beeline for each other. She grabbed me and we jumped around in a circle. She told me how sexy I looked in my school uniform and we laughed as I twisted my shoulders and hips away from each other as a model would do.

We were inseparable from that day forward. Totally inseparable! While Irene was with me at St. Aidan's, it was bearable. When she left, my heart broke into a thousand pieces. I never bonded with any other girl in the same way. It was easier to remain distant because if they were to leave, and chances were they would, you would just become heartbroken again. This is where I learnt to walk away from relationships before I could be hurt.

What I did find out later was that Mrs. Raeburn was lovely, although she was not very switched on when it came to us girls and our shenanigans, or was she? When we returned to the classroom, Irene just simply swapped desks with another girl and sat next to me. Just that simple! She didn't get into trouble or get asked to move back to her original spot. She just stayed there and we chatted as much as we could, until eventually Mrs. Raeburn told us to "shh" because "girls are trying to learn".

I didn't touch my book that day because I didn't know what to do with it. Irene became my mentor more and more as the days drew on and my relationship with Maureen became more and more distant.

Irene explained to me that we did our schoolwork in the workbooks and if we needed help with any answers, we asked Mrs. Raeburn. Other than that, Mrs. Raeburn was really just there to babysit us through the days. Our schooling was done by correspondence and at the end of each week our workbooks would be gathered up and mailed for correction by a teacher who worked for the Victorian Education Department in Melbourne. In reality Irene was my teacher, Mrs. Raeburn my babysitter, and the invisible person on the end of the red pen, well, who knows what they were. They just wrote things at the end of each assignment and gave you a mark. There was nothing personal there at all.

Distance learning has changed throughout the years with the introduction of computers and videos. We could only have dreamed of such technology. We just stumbled along the best we could with what we had—a workbook. Each section began with reference notes. We were occasionally directed to read a book. That was a case of waiting in line for another girl to finish reading and return the book to the school library.

I was really good at fudging those assignments. I just guessed the answers. I've never been a person who enjoyed reading until recently. It didn't seem to really matter if I got it wrong. I just lost marks. Nobody yelled at me or sent me to the Principal's office. In fact, nobody really cared.

All I would get is a sentence in the back of the workbook: "Did you even bother to read the material requested?" from a person I had never met or spoken to, who was possibly hundreds of miles away and loved to wield a red marker. The nuns never checked, nor did they care. They never made comments, except for one made to me at a later date, but by then it was going to be a little bit too late.

One assignment that I had to complete in my next year, age thirteen, was to read a book by The Rev. David Wilkerson, The Cross and the Switchblade.

He wrote a series which consisted of *The Cross and the Switchblade*, *Hey Preach–You're Comin' Through*, and *Bury Me in My Boots*. This wonderful man worked amongst the poor and the forgotten drug addicts that existed in the back laneways and doorways, abandoned buildings, and other areas in most major cities. Reading these books had such a major impact on my opinion of drugs that I have never taken an illegal substance nor been tempted to for fear of what I might become.

※

Okay, that's it; school was finished for the day. We scurried like little mice to the dormitory and changed out of our uniforms. We then hurried to the dining room to get a cup of tea and a biscuit. We had fifteen minutes.

For afternoon chores, each girl was assigned a job; there were plenty to go around. My first job was to scrub clean the six toilets in Cozy Corner and wash the floor, then report to the laundry. When I say scrub, I mean scrub. Cozy Corner was the block of toilets used by us during the day from the classroom, and also by the female laundry workers moving to and from the laundry. St. Aidan's, Maryfields, not only housed young girls from age eleven up, it also housed a large variety of infirmed, elderly, and physically and mentally disabled people, most of whom worked in the laundry during the day.

On any given day I would find the toilets covered in excrement, urine all over the floor, s-bends blocked from sanitary napkins or bowel movements so large I do not know how they managed to pass them, and other various things. What could not be broken up and pushed down the pipe had to be removed into the waste bin—by hand.

I was issued with a scrubbing brush, Ajax powder, a bucket and cloth, and no rubber gloves. I learnt very quickly to do this job properly; the punishment was not worth it. One lesson of cleaning Cozy Corner with a toothbrush is enough. Let me tell you, Cozy Corner was anything but cozy. In each cubicle, you would press the button on the toilet first. You never knew what you would find in there. After this you would shake some Ajax powder into the bowl and then proceed to scrub it. You were not allowed to just scrub around the bowl; you had to keep slamming the scrubbing brush down into the bowl until the water had disappeared over the s-bend, so that you could shake in some more powder and scrub the s-bend clean as well. If there was a present left that could not be flushed, you would try to break it up or remove it, and then you continued with cleaning. Thank God there were not many presents, but on the days there were, I would scrub my hands with the Ajax powder until they bled when I had finished.

Once the toilets were clean on the inside, you would wipe all over the outside of each one. When all six toilets were clean, you would get hot water, disinfectant, and the scrubbing brush, and scrub the tiled floor on your hands and knees. If you were lucky, nobody would want to use the toilet while you were cleaning. If they did you had to clean it again. Looking back at it now, it was just plain wrong.

On my first day, Irene rushed into Cozy Corner and asked if I'd finished. She helped me finish off what I hadn't done and we headed to the laundry. We ended up in what was called the "Mangle Room" with Maureen. I felt I was lucky that day. I got to work with the two nicest people I knew, but the work was laborious and hard, and not for the faint-hearted. I didn't know it then, but I was to work in that laundry for nearly four years.

When I was thirteen, I was allocated a new job which was done in the morning. I was to scrub and polish the Apium Way. I did this in the morning before church and breakfast. There was no help, just me and this bloody long hallway. The Apium Way was approximately one hundred and twenty feet long and ten foot wide and ran from Maryfields to the nuns' quarters and the church which was the middle building of the three that stood on the grounds.

Every morning I would sweep the floor to remove the dust, fill my bucket with hot soapy water, grab a scrubbing brush, and scrub from one end of the hallway to the other on my hands and knees—ensuring I used a cloth to wipe up the residual water as I went. If a nun chose to walk to the convent over the wet floor while I was cleaning, I had to start again from the start to remove her footprints. They often walked this hallway, so repeating the work was common.

Once a week I would use two cups of ammonia in boiling hot water to remove the wax polish to prevent build-up. Again I would scrub this into the tiles on my hands and knees, no rubber gloves, just bare hands and bare knees, all the time wearing an apron to keep my uniform clean. I would hold my heavy pleated skirt between the top of my legs so it wouldn't get wet. I would then reapply the wax with a soft cloth and use a large industrial polisher to bring the hallway to a high shine.

I continued this job until the day I left the convent. By then I was extremely proficient at cleaning and was able to handle the industrial polisher well. In fact, towards the end, I would stand on the polisher and spin in circles to have some fun when I was sure I wouldn't get caught, and I would dodge the polish removal at least every second week. They never knew. How could they tell? By then I was becoming wiser.

I can remember one day, while cleaning the floor in February 1971, Mother Rita came by to check that I was doing my job properly; this was not unusual as we were often checked on. I had not long returned from Christmas break and had been wondering how my paternal grandmother was, as Mom had told me while I was home that she was quite ill and promised she would let me know if anything had changed. I had not heard anything, so I assumed her situation was the same.

Mother Rita casually said in passing, "Oh, your grandmother is dead; I got a letter from your mother a few weeks ago and forgot to give it to you." My grandmother had died on the twentieth of January, 1971, and the letter had been sent a few days later. It was now nearing the end of February.

I was gutted. Even though I had only met my father's mother once when I was about three years old, she was still my grandmother.

It wasn't unusual for Mother Rita to open our mail. All letters to any resident within the convent were opened and read by her, and in some cases censored. All outgoing mail was also censored before it left, so we didn't let out any secrets.

18
Penitents

"Bad girls do the best sheets."

To the nuns we "wayward girls" were penitents; it didn't matter that many of us were only twelve years old. A penitent is someone who feels or shows sorrow and regret for having done wrong; they repent of their sins and wrongdoings and seek forgiveness from God. Penance (symbolic payment of your sins) in the Catholic Church normally took the form of having to say a certain number of Hail Marys or The Lord's Prayer. At St. Aidan's, it was laundry work and prayer: I must have been extra bad!

As I was placed into the Maryfields side of St. Aidan's, which was officially a complex for fifteen-year-old women and over, I was thereby deemed old enough to work in a commercial laundry for the profit of the Catholic Church; no sorry, not for the profit of the Church—for the sake of the remission of my sins as a penitent. It was suggested that doing laundry was a symbolic cleansing, a search for purity! We worked so hard, I can tell you, there was no time for any sinful thoughts!

At St. Aidan's laundry we didn't just wash grubby clothing from private schools. We girls were responsible for hundreds of sheets, pillowslips, and linen tablecloths from hotels in and around Bendigo each day; this amounted to many thousands per week.

According to an article in The Sydney Morning Herald in 2003, titled *Bad Girls Do the Best Sheets*, our Irish counterparts were regarded as "fallen women come laundry slaves". In Australia we were considered to be a milder version—"women in moral danger" laboring in laundries. What did they know? It wasn't them slaving, pulling steaming hot items off the large, spinning metal mangle under a tin roof in 40 plus Celsius heat every day. No, there was no difference between ourselves and our Irish sisters, except our age as most Irish girls were much older. (Sydney Morning Herald, April 14, 2003 Alan Gill) Believe me, it was bloody slave labor! [You may be interested in having a read. <www.smh.com.au/articles/2003/04/23/1050777303111.html> or Google "Bad girls do the best sheets".]

So let me tell you some more about that laundry!

The Mangle Room was extremely large in area, almost vacant except for two huge machines that stood left and right to the back of the open space. Along the right-hand side was a brick wall, behind which was the area with all the industrial washing machines. To the left was a huge wall of large glass windows that looked to the outside world, and beneath them were long, narrow folding tables, often packed with piles of folded sheets, towels, and pillowslips. Below us, other than a fruit crate to stand on, was a polished wooden floor and above us a tin roof and steel girders. As you entered the room, to the left was a small lunch room used by the older workers—the elderly, disabled, and mentally handicapped women who slaved in the laundry all day, sometimes without breaks.

My introduction to the Mangle Room was to stand on a fruit box and try to remove the scolding hot, wet linen off the large, heavy cloth roller on the machine in front of me, known as a "mangle". The mangle was used to dry and press linen—mainly sheets, tablecloths, and pillowslips. These things were delivered wet from the laundry after being washed and starched. They were wheeled into the Mangle Room in a large cane basket on wheels.

First, they had to be untangled, separated, and shaken out to straighten them as much as possible for their journey through the mangle. We would do each sheet individually, folding it in a zigzag pattern of four folds, ensuring it could be easily fed through by little hands. Each item would then be fed into the mangle and peeled off on the other side by us. Then we would pick up the heavy pile of wet, hot sheets and take them around to the girls who were feeding the mangle, so they could put them through again. We would then run back around to the other side and jump back onto our fruit crates to begin removing the items from the mangle once more.

This was repeated three times until they were dry enough to be folded. Why not just leave them on the mangle and allow them to go around until dried? The end of the sheet would overlap the start of the sheet, making it very near impossible to remove it, short of stopping the machinery.

The mangle was about twelve foot across the front and approximately three to four foot deep, and stood about six foot high. Imagine the metal plate on the bottom of your iron at home covered in a light material, and amplify that into a roller, approximately four feet in circumference, which is solid metal. Then place another metal plate about four inches thick on which the roller is cradled and turning slowly. That is the mangle that we fed sheets and other items into. Two girls stood at the back to feed sheets in, and two girls, sometimes three, at the front to take the sheets off.

The feeder area consisted of constantly turning cotton conveyor belts, which assisted the girls feeding the sheets and linen into the machine, so it was easier for the mangle to pick up the product and pull it into the drying and pressing area as described above ... It could also take in your arms and fingers if you were not careful.

On the removal side there was a wooden bench, approximately one foot deep. Each article had to be removed as it came around on the mangle. If you missed an item and it went around twice, it caused all sorts of problems, and on occasion that did happen, even when we tried our hardest to remove it. The starch on the sheets would stick to the woolen surface of the mangle, making it difficult to get enough of the sheet corner for us to grip onto to pull it off. Every article stuck to the mangle, hard, and you were constantly using your fingers to pick at the corner to try to get it off before it would go over the top of the roller and couldn't be retrieved.

My friend Maureen has had to have some joints replaced in her hands due to this work at such a young age. She is very limited in what she can do now. My own hands are also affected by arthritis. I struggle to open lids and find it hard to grip things that I need to. I will often drop items as the muscles in my hands give way.

Reaching for my first sheet frightened the hell out of me. I was standing on my box but distracted by the disabled young girl beside me who was standing silently on her box but constantly swinging her head from side to side. When I reached up to grab the sheet from the big hot roller, I burnt my hand on the steam that was pouring off it. As I quickly pulled my hand away, I pulled the corner of the sheet with me and it rolled over the top of the roller, so I was unable to regain my grip to take it off. Round and round it went until someone finally managed to pull it off the mangle. I was in trouble and I knew it—confirmed by the sudden thud to the back of my head. Wham! Mother Rita! Somehow whenever you did anything wrong, that woman would always be behind you. With one swift motion, up had come the hand with the hand broom extension! Straight across the back of my head.

"You stupid girl. What are you? An idiot. Even retarded people don't make such stupid mistakes. Now get back up there and don't let it happen again."

I climbed back onto the old fruit box with tears in my eyes and allowed my hands to burn while trying to pull the corner of each wet sheet off the mangle roller so that the sheet did not go around a second time. The steam poured off the wet sheets in front of me, burning my eyes and face. Maureen showed me the tips of her fingers and guaranteed me that soon I would have callouses to protect me from the heat, like hers.

After the third feed through, you got a break while you moved to the folding table to fold the sheets, one by one, until the next load of fresh wet sheets appeared from the laundry. It was constant; you were either sorting, stacking, pulling linen off the mangle, or folding. You were never left idle.

Folding the sheets and table cloths was much better than taking them off the mangle. Of course, there was a system that you had to abide by. Corners on the ends had to meet exactly. Once the corners were in place then you folded the sheet in half again, making sure that the corners still lined up perfectly. At this point you grabbed the folded edge on one end and the person on the other end did the same. The sheet was flicked like a whip to ensure that it fell into place nicely for the final fold. One girl would swing her arm out, grab the middle of the sheet and swing around to grab the opposite end. She would then move with the sheet to the folding bench, ensuring that each sheet got an additional three folds and that the corners lined up perfectly. Twirling and swirling like a well-choreographed dance—each pile uniformed, perfect, corner to corner. That's right, if the corners didn't match, you guessed it, the wooden hand broom. Wham! I cannot tell you how many times I was hit with that bloody thing. I'm amazed I'm not brain damaged. (But wait, maybe I am?) Then you started the process all over again.

When I worked with Maureen on the folding table, sometimes we were lucky enough to recognize her sisters walking past the windows on their way to the pool. Maureen had sisters who were kept on the orphanage side of the convent as they were deemed too young to be in Maryfields. We were told it was a sin for us to look upon these innocent angels; they did not want the likes of us introducing sin into their souls. If we were spotted even gazing at them sideways as they walked past, the punishment was the hand broom on God knows what part of your body—just whichever part it connected with. So Maureen played a dangerous game each time, just trying to catch a glimpse of her sisters while I kept look-out. Maureen couldn't risk being hit by a hand broom; it would have broken her frail body. Recently I found out that the children on the other side called us, "the overs". They knew us to be the bad girls.

We were not supposed to talk to each other in the Mangle Room, just work and silently ask God's forgiveness for our sins. Relationships overall were frowned upon, as the nuns did not want us forming bonds with the other girls. I think the nuns were scared of us forming relationships. Maybe they understood that the times were changing and that somehow in the future we would start to talk about our experiences and this would lead to the cover being blown off the Catholic Church and its so-called care of minors during our time. Unfortunately, some of our Irish counterparts are still in some cases too scared to talk about their incarcerations and treatment at the hands of these "tender loving creatures". [Excuse the sarcasm, but can you blame me?]

Or perhaps relationships were frowned upon because within an institutionalized environment with a patriarchal, or in this case "matriarchal", hierarchy of control, individualism and a sense of self must be stamped out to maintain control.

Caring relationships bring power to people and that could pose a threat. Bugger it. It's probably just because they figured that as "fallen women" we didn't deserve any love, care, or friendships.

Anyway, that did not prevent us from doing just that. Human beings, no matter where they are, will seek communion with others. Maureen and I, as well as Irene and myself, formed pretty strong bonds, even though away from the laundry Maureen and I did not have a lot to do with each other. In the laundry we were close, and, in fact, sometimes we even managed to have some fun while doing our job.

The best thing I remember was when we taught Margaret, the young woman with the disability who swung her head from side to side, to sing *Barbara Ann* by the Beach Boys. We sung it over and over again to teach her, ensuring we shut up when we saw the black habit coming around the corner. But all day she would stand there singing the words to the chorus, over and over again. It must have driven them mad—mission accomplished. However, we were very proud of her, and she loved us being in there in the afternoon working with her. We were always greeted with the biggest grin. I think back now and remember her tenderly.

For years I slaved in the Mangle Room, sometimes in over 40 Celsius heat (104 degrees Fahrenheit on the old scale) with no fans or air-conditioning. There was no knocking off if it got too hot. It was unforgiving, and many nights I nursed blistered and burnt hands. Eventually though, my hands did get calloused as Maureen had promised, making the job easier.

When I got older, I was chosen to move into the ironing and pressing room; this was the hub of the laundry. It was where all the shirts and personal items of clothing were ironed and pressed. The drying room was also attached to this area, and that was a really nice, warm place to be in winter. When you walked into this area, for as far as the eye could see, there was bench after bench of irons and young girls. There were a few shirt sleeve presses in the center, and off to the right were dry-cleaning presses for doing pants and so on. I didn't last very long in this area and eventually was sent back to the Mangle Room.

I don't think I was well liked by the nun who looked after that area. I was ready to return to the Mangle Room anyway. I knew the work, the expectations, and we were left alone most of the time to just get on with the job, unlike the ironing room where you were scrutinized and watched almost every minute!

Today I still get frustrated when ironing, trying to ensure that an item looks like it has just come from a mangle or an ironing press rather than a household iron and ironing board. If something should become creased while ironing, I lose it, ripping the item from the board and throwing it back in the washing pile to be washed all over again. To take away this frustration and anger, my husband—God bless him—has taken over ironing his shirts in most cases.

19

Double Trouble

"Irene was my little bit of home."

My mate Irene, my soul sister, my sister from another mother, my rock, my confidante, my friend—I miss you. I always have.

What can I say? Irene and I were two peas from the same pod. Where there was trouble, Irene and I followed, or in our case were the cause of it. St. Trinian's, eat your heart out. Funny how songs remind you of a person. For me Irene's song has always been *Little Town Flirt* by Del Shannon. You see, Irene was like me in more ways than one. We both craved the affection and attention of men and boys, the love we missed at home I suppose. We had similar upbringings, only Irene had been taken from her father, who was trying to do his best to raise her after her mother died, and was placed into St. Aidan's by welfare. Eventually, she would return to him, being released years before me to go home, or did she? But in the meantime, we got to have lots of fun, and these times are so imprinted on my heart that I can't help but dedicate a whole chapter to our antics together. Here are some of my more memorable moments with Irene.

Dear Dori. One of Irene's favorite things to do was to upset Dori. Dori was an older lady who lived in one of the cubicles on the cold balcony opposite our dormitory. She was a grumpy old soul, but who could blame her; I actually remember her with fondness. Dori was hardly ever seen by anybody, but when she was you knew who she was. She was very top heavy, with tiny little legs, and walked like the hunchback of Notre Dame, hunched over and swaying. She smelled; you could always smell her as she walked past. She had one turned up eye which disfigured her face. When you walked past her cubicle, you just knew she was in there because her favorite pastime was to constantly mumble sentences with lots of "bloody this" and "bloody that".

Instead of just walking gently past Dori's cubicle, Irene would stomp past and kick the wall, causing Dori to start yelling in a jumble, "gunnakickyabloodygutsin" and "kickyagutsout yabloodystopit"—which Irene would happily imitate, making Dori even madder. We would then run off giggling as cruel school children do.

This happened four times each day: on the way to morning chores; on our way to change out of our school uniforms; on the way back when we were heading to the dining room for afternoon tea; then once more on the way to bed. We always had to make sure we were ahead of the pack so that we didn't get caught.

I saw the funniest thing one night. Irene had just started to stomp past Dori's cubicle when out came a leg from under the curtain that was her doorway. Kick! "That'll bloody teach ya," the voice mumbled from inside the cubicle. Irene tripped mid-stomp, which made her stomp harder.

Mother Mercy yelled, "Stop making all that racket up there; you'll disturb the residents."

In 1971 Dori was sadly found passed away in her cubicle. An ambulance was brought into the concrete yard and the ambulance officers carried the stretcher with Dori's body on it down the stairs, across the grounds and to the back of the ambulance. Irene had left by this time, but all the girls gathered at the windows of the dining room to see what was going on. Dori's body, which seemed more petite than usual, was covered by a white sheet and loaded into the back of the ambulance. With that she was gone. She was now free of this hell hole.

Mother Mercy yelled at us from the microphone, "Move away from the window and leave the poor woman in peace."

Nobody moved; we were glued to the scene. I can remember a tear came to my eye as I wondered if that was how I would have to leave there also.

I was to learn later that Dori really felt the bitter Bendigo cold, so she had worn close to thirty or more jumpers and tops to try and keep warm. She hadn't been fat at all. Seeing her on that stretcher made me happy in a way as she had been able to spend her last year in peace, without having to put up with Irene's antics, and, of course, any chance of me continuing them.

During my first weekend at the convent, Irene tried to convince me that Mother Peter's violin lessons were great fun, and, without my permission, Irene skipped forward, asking Mother Peter if I could also attend violin classes. Mother Peter was ecstatic, always ready to encourage another penitent to learn a skill that may come in handy one day. Besides, she had a few unused violins. There were only six of us in her group. Mother Peter was a tiny woman who stood about four foot nine inches, was very elderly and always looked over the top of her glasses. She had a warm and beautifully angelic face and an even nicer smile. She was tender and caring and had a wonderful aura surrounding her.

I happily headed off to the class with Mother Peter, only to realize that Irene had not accompanied us. That's right! The violin lessons were so much fun because Irene got to play hide and seek with Mother Peter every Sunday morning. Mother Peter was extremely patient when it came to looking for Irene, and it took great skill to avoid her clutches, as I would soon find out. I tried unsuccessfully to hide from her for four weeks in a row; apparently a breathing curtain is not normal. She didn't growl at me when she found me. She would just call me a scallywag and tell me we'd be late.

I enjoyed the two hours of violin lessons I received every week for the next two years (thank you, Irene), at the end of which all I could play by rote was *Twinkle, Twinkle, Little Star*. That was it— just those four bars! Guess I was not equipped to be a violinist. If the girl band, Bond, had been around then, now, that would have been an incentive to put more effort in. Such amazing talent I had—not! Mother Peter would just stand there, waving her finger around like some awesome orchestra conductor; her eyes closed so she could soak up every sound we made. Oh, it was awful—the whining and off-pitch notes we hit with those violins. I think she was somewhere far, far away.

❧

Irene desperately wanted to have her ears pierced and saw her chance when a new girl arrived from another home. We huddled together scheming and talking during sewing class. The new girl assured Irene that she could pierce her ears and she wouldn't feel a thing. With that we skulked off to another area so that we could have some privacy. I'm not sure what they used to clean the ear before the needle pierced it; however, I do remember seeing Irene's already pasty white skin turning whiter. She looked quite ill. The needle went in, out spurted the blood, and down went Irene. It was hilarious. Irene had passed out and girls scattered in every direction. They left her lying there, bleeding like a wounded pig. From memory I believe Maureen was involved in this little escapade. Eventually, somebody went and got a nun because Irene was not coming around and we all thought she was dead.

Well, we all got to stand for meals for a little while after that, having our chairs removed from the dining room table. A small price to pay to have my friend back alive and well!

One of my saddest memories of my friend was watching Irene every Parlor Day. We would wake up, as we did every other morning, go to church, do our chores and eat, then together we would sit in the concrete yard and just wait to see if our names were called for visitors. Parlor Day was visitor's day and happened once a month. Some girls had to stay on the grounds with their parents or family. Others like me were allowed off the grounds to go into Bendigo, to the lake and surrounds. And then there were those like Irene who got dressed and prepared every Sunday to wait for a family that usually never arrived. Her sister came to get her on occasion, but mostly we sat together and waited. Sometimes I was able to briefly let her share my mom when she came.

Visitors in general, though, were not encouraged. If they did come every weekend, they were told that they would disrupt the girl and make her homesick. So they were told once a month was more than enough to see their child. If we had known that, we wouldn't have had such high expectations and such major disappointments every weekend. If midday came and went and nobody turned up for us, we would change out of our good Parlor Day clothes and attend whatever activity was going on that day.

Sometimes, if it was raining, Mother Mercy would allow us to play records in the hall and dance. How we prayed for rain! Other days we would just play board games in the group room, or sit and listen to Anne's Simon and Garfunkel album.

There wasn't really much else to do except go for a short walk around the sixty meter by forty meter concreted playground and talk about the family that never came.

But talk we did; we talked and talked. I'm not sure what we didn't talk about; we knew everything about each other. There are so many more things to say about Irene, but I must move on to my final moment with her...

❧

From memory it was the 1970 Christmas holidays. We all gathered with our small bags, waiting for family to come and pick us up so that we could go home. Those who did not have a home to go to sometimes went to the homes of "good Samaritans" in Bendigo, and some stayed behind in the convent throughout the Christmas period. I always went home as I was classed as a boarder. Not only did they collect money from the government to have me there, but my aunty paid annually also, and I earned my own keep by working in the laundry. Talk about a triple bite at the cherry.

Irene and I were excited and jumping up and down because she was going home for the holidays also. She was called to the Parlor Room first; her family lived locally, so it didn't take them as long to get there. We made promises to remember everything so we could exchange stories upon our return.

The nuns never gave you pre-warning when you were leaving forever. You were there one minute and gone the next, even in the middle of the night, or you went to the Parlor Room and never returned. In Irene's case, she went to the Parlor Room and never returned.

When Christmas break was over and we all returned to the convent, I sat on the seat outside the Parlor Room door waiting with anticipation to share my Christmas holidays with Irene. As darkness closed over the verandah from the setting sun, I realized she wasn't coming back. I don't know how long I cried for, but it was very difficult to fill the gap in my heart that was Irene. In fact, I'm not sure that it has ever been filled.

To this day I have never seen her again. Many times I have thought about her and tried to find her. I remember our special antics. They had helped to take away the pain and suffering of being so far from home. Irene was my little bit of home. *Seasons in the Sun* by Terry Jacks always reminds me of her.

In a way, Irene's departure was the beginning of a new chapter in my life as a penitent at the convent. After that my broken heart spiraled out of control. A new me was born, one who was a little more cunning, slightly more grown up, and definitely more aware of what I needed to do to survive.

20

The Great Escape

"It was now or never."

If IRENE WAS NOT THERE then I was not going to be there either. I had heard girls talking of a gate at the back of the laundry, which was easy to climb. A lot of girls had gone over it to escape, and that's exactly what I planned to do. Escaping was not uncommon. Many ran away and very few returned. In my innocence I thought that they had been ejected from the convent and sent home. I did not realize that a lot of them had been caught by the police and had not been accepted back to St. Aidan's. So they had been sent on to other homes and government-run institutions.

I plotted my escape carefully over the next few days. I had been at the convent now for over a year and a half and had become trusted by the nun and auxiliary circle. It wasn't unusual for Sister John to say yes to a request to retrieve something from the dormitory at seven o'clock in the evening, especially once a girl had earned her trust. I knew that would help me in my plot to escape.

The big day arrived. It was now or never. I anxiously composed myself and asked permission from Mother John to go to the dormitory. She replied with a yes but added for me to hurry up. I walked out of the group room door, ensuring to shut it after me so that nobody would see me head in the direction of the yard, instead of the dormitory. I stayed in the shadows of the dimly-lit balcony, hoping that I wouldn't round the corner and come face to face with Mother Rita, which was always a possibility as that nun was everywhere. What would I say to her? My heart was pounding and my stomach churning so much that I wanted to puke. I was scared but very resolved in the fact that I was not going to stay another minute without Irene. Why hadn't I just told my mother about life at the convent and begged her forgiveness so I could stay at home? She wouldn't have believed me for one moment. Nobody would believe how we were treated. I would have been called a liar and told that I should be ashamed of myself for telling lies about nuns, and that I would probably burn in hell for that too.

Whatever ... I figured I was going there already anyway. I was going to burn forever at this rate.

With that I ran the length of the small yard, staying out of the moonlight and sticking as close as I could to the walls. I thought that I heard someone coming, so I hid behind the wall that covered the entrance to Cozy Corner and held my breath. Then when I was sure that the coast was clear, I bolted across the yard as fast as I could and ran for the protection of the balcony at the other end of the laundry. Now I had to be careful. Nuns often walked the balcony from the Apium Way to the convent at night. I stopped to catch my breath and slowly lifted my head above the railing to see if anybody was in pursuit. There was nobody coming, so with that I slipped between the small gates and turned the corner only to be confronted by twelve foot high, steel meshed wire gates with barbed wire on top looming ahead of me.

My heart was beating so fast I thought I would die. My fight or flight reactions had cut in. The idea of scaling the large gate seemed a daunting task indeed, but my resolve took over and the tomboy in me came out to play. I scurried up that wire fence barely touching it. Once I reached the top and unhooked my leg from the barbed wire, going down the other side was smooth sailing, and I mean sailing. I cannot remember being able to get a grip on the wire at all and almost fell all the way down. I used to find it very easy to climb the large walnut tree, which had stood in our backyard. I loved climbing and was always rewarded with lots of fresh walnuts to eat at the top. So this fence shouldn't have posed any problems.

Once over the fence, I ran along the back of the laundry, making sure again to stick to the walls so as not to be seen. Not that I expected anyone to be lurking around in the darkness; however, I couldn't take any chances. If I was caught at this stage, I would be in so much trouble. That was enough to spur me on to freedom, to ensure that I didn't get caught and punished.

The sideway to the convent was an issue, as was the front of the convent. Three group rooms of windows with the prying young eyes of those incarcerated within threatened to trip up my journey to freedom at any given moment. I tiptoed silently along the gravel, up against the wall and down the driveway, heading for the front gate—freedom so close. Luck was on my side. As I reached the final window in the driveway, the lights from the group rooms went out and I knew that this meant the girls were heading to bed. That meant there would be a lot of noise on the stairs, so they were unlikely to hear my footsteps on the pebbles underfoot. I ran! I covered the short distance from the corner of the building to the large iron gates that held my freedom. I walked through, or should I say ran.

As I reached and crossed the street, relief spread over my entire being. I was free! I also felt a certain sense of pride. What I hadn't expected was the next feeling that overwhelmed me—a sense of utter despair. As I looked around me, I realized that I had no plan, no idea where I was or how to get home. I walked on anyway, being sure to duck for cover if I saw car headlights coming. The nuns certainly would have called the police by now as they did every time a girl ran away. Especially as the dormitory lights were all on, they would have surely done the head count by now and noticed me missing.

I made it the seven or so kilometers into Golden Square, Bendigo. I was very pleased with myself. I stopped to get my bearings, attempting to figure out how to head towards Melbourne. The next moment a man fell out of the hotel, nearly landing directly on top of me. I was frightened, but not as frightened as when he started saying, "Come here, sweetheart," beckoning me to go to him. When I didn't, he began to follow me.

I had nobody to help me and nowhere to go. I didn't know which way to turn. I was confused, frightened, and just wanted to go back to the convent. Crying and shaking, I made my way to the police station that I could see in the distance. It had all become just too much for me. I walked up to the constable and advised him that I had run away from St. Aidan's and asked if he could please take me back. He advised me that they had not had a report of a runaway. He took my details and headed to the phone to call the convent and enquire from the nuns if I had actually run away. The response was a resounding no!

"They're wrong!" I yelled at him. "I've run away. If I'm standing here in front of you, how could I also be there?"

"Listen, kid, you don't want to be in a place like that; only bad girls are kept there. You should run along home to your parents."

Now I was angry. I yelled at him again. "I did run away and you should take me back immediately, or Mother Rita will be really angry with you."

That got me into a police car straight away, and he drove me out to St. Aidan's.

We were greeted at the front door by Mother Rita, who initially looked a little shocked then quickly planted a pleasant smile on her face for the benefit of the police officer who had escorted me back.

"Oh, thank you, officer. Beverley does belong here. Thank you very much for returning her," Mother Rita said sweetly. "Where did you find her?"

"She just walked into the police station asking for protection from a drunk," the police officer explained. And with that he was gone and the front door was locked.

Mother Rita swung around and glared at me with her beady little eyes. Her entire attitude had changed in a split second, like a schizophrenic. She grabbed me by the back of the hair and charged me into the wall, smashing my forehead hard against the concrete. Wham! Immediately an egg-shaped lump appeared. Needless to say it hurt.

She sneered at me. "You are such an idiot." Then she teased me like a young school girl. "You are so stupid you can't even run off properly! You're thick, do you hear me? So thick; it's no surprise that your mother doesn't want you."

She pinched my arm in several places, quite hard, hard enough to hurt. She banged me against the walls several more times as she pulled me along by my hair, forcing me up on my tiptoes as we went to the dormitory. Mother Rita stomped along, her breath was coming hard and fast by the time we arrived at the dormitory door.

Before she pushed me in, she told me that I was not to leave the dormitory the next morning *under any circumstances* until she came to see me. And then she hissed, "If you open your mouth to anybody tonight about what has happened, your punishment will be a *lot worse* than what's it's going to be."

I knew she meant it. Perhaps coming back wasn't such a good idea after all. The drunk was starting to look a little more appealing.

The lights were out and most girls pretended that they were asleep. Several people were brave enough to whisper welcome back, except one, who told me I should have received more punishment than I got for what I had done. I didn't care what she thought anyway—nobody did, actually. This particular girl was always crawling up to the nuns to get what she wanted. I quickly put on my little cotton nightie and jumped under the covers, where I cried myself to sleep. I didn't know what to expect tomorrow, but I knew it was going to be bad—that's what I did care about.

The next morning Mother Mercy came into the dormitory, lights on and bellowing, "In the name of the Father, the Son and the Holy Ghost ..."

We all fell to our knees on the familiar cold floor, wiping the sleep from our eyes.

Mother Mercy walked towards me as all the girls busied themselves getting ready for chores. "You are to stay in your nightie and not move from the dormitory until Mother Rita arrives." She looked at me sadly, and with that she hurried the other girls up to wash, dress, and leave the dormitory.

I made my bed and sat, silently waiting for Mother Rita to arrive. She didn't come immediately. She liked to oversee the chores that the girls did and supervise breakfast. I presumed that was to ensure that no girl took more food than they should.

My stomach was tied in knots. I had already felt Mother Rita's wrath on more than one occasion, but nothing compared to the night before. My head still ached. I knew she could be a vindictive person. I wasn't sure why I was to stay in the dormitory or in my nightie for that matter. I guess if I was in my nightie it would be harder to run away again.

Another girl had tried to run away from the dormitory. She had tied sheets together and attempted to climb down the brick wall, but she fell from the top and was taken to hospital, not to be seen again. I wasn't about to follow in her footsteps.

It was about 9.30 a.m. when Mother Rita burst into the dormitory shouting, "Why are you sitting on your bed?" With that she walked up to me and slapped me many times across the back and head, yelling the whole time, "Why, why, why?" until she could finally compose herself.

I was also asking myself by that stage *Why, why, why?*

Mother Rita ordered me to clean the showers—no big deal, right? ... With a toothbrush ... My toothbrush! I was thirteen years old at this time. I scrubbed that shower forever with my toothbrush and Ajax, ensuring that there was no mold or dirt anywhere. I scrubbed without stopping, as I was told not to stop until she returned. After scrubbing for *three hours* she came in to inspect my work. She had another child or auxiliary with her—I can't remember which. This was not uncommon.

Mother Rita said accusingly, "Look, you hopeless child; there is still dirt there," pointing her crony, withered finger at some miniscule black mark on the bottom left corner of the shower recess. *Of course, there is still a spot of dirt in the seventy year old shower!* I thought. But any smart alec thoughts didn't linger ...

Suddenly I felt myself heading for the floor as Mother Rita shoved me hard in the center of my back, pushing me towards the floor and almost splatting my nose into the wall.

"Clean it! Clean it! Clean it!" she screamed over and over. I started scrubbing for my life at that tiny speck. Then suddenly cold water was pelting me from the shower. She had turned on the tap.

Whack! She began to beat me uncontrollably across the back and the back of my head with her trusty old wooden hand broom. I could hear her grunting with each hit while I cried and whimpered beneath the blows. She must have hit me around fifteen to twenty times, until either she was exhausted or she thought she had gotten her point across. I do believe that she simply could not control her anger.

She walked out, leaving me beaten and drenched. I sat huddled in the base of that shower for about an hour afterwards, shaking from the cold and the trauma of what had just happened. I was totally cried out. I wasn't brave enough to venture out and get something to dry myself off with, so I left my wet nightie on in case she came back to hit me again for getting dressed.

I never did clean that spot off the shower recess, and she didn't even notice when she came back to inspect my work again before I was allowed to be served lunch—a bowl of clear broth and one slice of bread. My nightie eventually dried from my own body heat.

This incident in the shower is one that I will never forget as long as I live. I can neither forget it nor forgive her for it. This would be the deed that set me up to be a target for bullies of all kinds for the rest of my life. Just show aggression of any kind towards me and I fold; you can walk all over me. Although, I slowly am gaining the strength I need to say enough is enough; it has taken me over forty years to do that though. I have never had a voice. This incident took away my voice for a long time, but not my ability to speak up against injustice towards others—just never myself. But now, I'm talking, through this book.

I spent two long days in the dormitory. I was supposed to be doing penance, cleaning the dorm from top to bottom, praying to God for forgiveness, and begging him to save my soul from the burning fires of hell, which I was assured by Mother Rita I would feel lapping at my feet in the very near future. What I did do was daydream of being home. I wished that I had never been put into this home and that I could take all my bad behavior back. I knew what I would say to Mom if I saw her …

"I can prove to you I am a better child now, really. Please give me a second chance and I p-r-o-m-i-s-e you, you won't be sorry if you keep me at home now."

After two days I was allowed back out to mingle with the other girls, none of whom were allowed to speak to me. The bathroom was sparkling.

I wasn't the only girl to experience being locked in the dormitory. Many girls had been over my time at the convent—some for running away, others for transgressions that only Mother Rita was privy to. When they were released from the dormitory, it was hard not to notice that they were always anxious and depressed, and you could tell they had cried a lot. Now I understood why. I wonder if they had to clean the showers too. I'm sure some suffered a worse fate than I.

Whenever this happened nobody talked about it. In each case we were told not to interact with the girl until they knew how to behave correctly. And that's what happened to me. It was the old concept of a public shunning. The instructions were usually given at breakfast over the microphone, to ensure everyone heard and that the public shaming for the transgressor was maximized—just one more way to put you down regardless of how much penance you had performed in the dormitory. The older women would stand by the food servery, shaking their heads in disgust that we could treat the nuns so poorly after all of their kindness for taking us in.

I still daydreamed of my mom coming to my rescue and letting me go home. In fact, I was going to tell her the next Parlor Day about what had happened. That is, I wanted to, but Mother Rita warned me off with her poisonous tongue. She told me that I should be grateful to them as they had taken me in and given me food and protection when nobody else wanted me.

"Your mother certainly doesn't want someone like you around. That's why she got rid of you in the first place. Even if you tell your mother what has happened, she will certainly not believe a little liar like you. Your mother has told me how much of a liar you are." Apparently, that's why the nuns could not trust me.

Well, after thinking about it, I accepted that Mother Rita was more than likely right and I was wrong. I probably hadn't given my mother respect, so why would she believe anything I said? Thus began a pattern of giving up my own thoughts to those who "must be right". After all, I was bad and stupid.

Even if I had told my mother, in hindsight, she most probably wouldn't have believed me, as she hadn't believed me when I told her that I had been returning to school the day the police picked me up at the hump. She would have just been embarrassed by my running away from the convent.

Still, I was looking forward to seeing her. The prospect of seeing her was cheering me up after what had been one of the most difficult periods to date at the convent. Parlor Day seemed to come around quickly …

21

Goodness, Gracious Me

*"SNIP! 'Now nobody will want you;
you're as ugly as sin.'"*

WHEN I LOOK BACK at my life in the convent, I see some parts that were comical, to the detriment. In particular, if one of the nuns did not like you, you could pretty much guarantee that another nun who didn't like that nun, would like you. I call that petty and think that they did that to piss each other off. What it did do was leave a door open for manipulation, and some children used it to get what they wanted—a survival tactic that naturally develops in any institutionalized environment.

As such, because Mother Rita didn't like me and Mother Mercy didn't particularly like or agree with Mother Rita in some areas, it appeared that I was a slight favorite of Mother Mercy. I think she saw a little of herself in me, a little of the rebellious child she may have been before she took her vows. When I did stupid things, as I was always the clown, I would see her mouth form a soft smile that she would try hard to suppress. I guess it was a smile that she wanted to publicly show. She was always quite caring towards me but not to others. Conversely, Mother Rita was also caring of some girls and gave them extra preferential treatment over and above all other girls who were there; I was not one of them.

Each nun was the same; all had their favorites. Every girl knew who they could play. With me it was definitely Mother Mercy. She showed me certain kindnesses that were not given to other children. She was going to play a small comforter role in my life for the next few months. However, as I was called to the Parlor Room one day to be greeted by Mom who had arrived with Uncle Bert to take me out, I could never have guessed the role that Mother Mercy would play in the days following their visit.

※

Usually on Parlor Day I bolted to the door to get out of that place. But this Parlor Day in particular I felt a little more subdued. I wasn't sure what I would be greeted with when I went inside that door. I knew Mother Rita was in there, as she always greeted the parents with her nauseous fake smile and fake laugh, and a part of me was a little scared that maybe in the end she had told my mom what I had done, albeit an edited version.

There was an awkward silence as I entered the parlor—none of the prolific chit chat that usually ensued—just silence and worrying looks. *Uh oh. Mother Rita has told Mom I ran away. I'm in deep shit* I thought. The heavy atmosphere indicated that something was definitely wrong. Mom's face was not angry but rather looked deeply concerned about something. The same with Mother Rita, who was anxiously rubbing her hands together. Mom put her arm around behind me and pushed me towards the door, assuring Mother Rita on her way out the door that she would take care of it.

Take care of it? What? If she knows, why isn't she angry?

Now I was really scared. What was she going to do with me? Hadn't I been punished enough?

Uncle Bert waited by the car door in the driveway and ushered me into the back seat behind him. I did what he said, without question. Normally, Mom would be talkative on our way into town, but not a word passed her lips this time. As I leaned forward and placed my chin onto the front seat (we didn't bother with seat belts back then), I could see she was still anxiously rubbing her hands round and around in her lap. Uncle Bert kept his eyes straight ahead on the road as always and tried to strike up the occasional conversation with me about the past month since their last visit.

We reached the Bendigo Lake where we went every Parlor Day. We jumped out of the car and I turned to Mom and bravely asked what was wrong. She told Uncle Bert that we would go for a short walk as she wanted to talk to me alone and we'd be back soon. That made him happy. He pulled out his flask from the boot and started to prepare the small picnic area that we had stopped at, so that we could eat lunch together on our return. I think Uncle Bert really enjoyed Parlor Days.

Mom and I walked for a few minutes in silence, and when she was sure that we were out of Uncle Bert's view, she stopped and offered me a cigarette. I was surprised and wondered if she was testing me. I had smoked sometimes with friends, but Mom didn't know that.

She pushed the pack forward, urging me to take one. "I know you smoke, so don't pretend you don't."

Now she had a slight irritation to her voice, so I took one. I felt slightly uncomfortable. I felt like I had been caught red-handed with my hand in the cookie jar, but that was nothing compared to my mother's next statement.

"That Tony boy visited me."

My breath caught under my ribcage. I wasn't sure where she was going with this conversation. I hadn't seen Tony since he raped me. She told me that he had come to the backdoor at home and she had refused to talk to him, telling him that I had been sent off to a convent and that I no longer lived there.

With that he had pushed his way inside the house and stormed past her into the kitchen. He scared her just like he had me. He was very tall and heavily built for his age, and as it stood, he was then around eighteen years old. Mom was only slight in build and stood at around five foot three inches, so he would have towered over her as he had me. I could understand how she would have been frightened, but I feared what she would say next. I wondered if Tony had done to Mom what he had done to me. I prayed not.

"Then do you know what he did, Beverley?" Mom asked. "He threw a packet of rubbers at me." Her facial expression changed to one of defeat and her shoulders slumped. "And then he asked me if I knew how to use them!"

I was too scared to say anything and twirled the cigarette around in my fingers, burning myself slightly on the index finger as I looked anywhere but at her face. What were rubbers? She went on to explain that he had been quite aggressive.

Mom continued. "Then he told me 'You should learn to use them and then teach your fucking daughter to use them too because the fuck'n little bitch gave me syphilis.' And with that he left."

Mom said that she fell back into her chair with shock. Well, I felt like I was about to do that too, onto the grass, especially when she asked the next question.

"Bev, is he the only boy you've had sex with?" …

The question seemed to hang in the air for a moment. I was so embarrassed that I wanted the earth to open up then and there and swallow me up. I hung my head in shame. I was silent. A part of me wanted so much to tell Mom what had really happened. Actually, I wanted to tell her *everything*. But at the thought I instantly felt panic overtaking me. I was so scared of the trouble I would get into. I was already in a home for wayward girls based on supposedly not walking back to school directly one day. I didn't know what kind of punishment she would or could dish out next—or Mother Rita for that matter—for something like sexual sin.

Mom took my silence as my answer that there had been more, but she didn't question me further. I couldn't tell her that Tony had raped me; I figured she never would have believed me … I was a liar. That was what she had told Mother Rita. I wonder if she had hugged me if we both would have felt better.

Uncle Bert was not aware of our conversation, or of what had transpired before the visit. I doubt Mom had told anyone. Her embarrassment at having a daughter with syphilis was enough to keep her quiet. She told me that Mother Rita had agreed to have me checked by a doctor and that she would not make it public knowledge; so I was not to tell anybody. I was shocked at Mom's attitude towards what had happened. She was really calm. Maybe she knew about the other abuses I had gone through but wasn't telling me … Maybe it was her guilt as well that made her so understanding … I experienced a side of my mother that day that I had never seen before. She just seemed so despondent and not angry as I thought she would be. Although it was never said, and I could not assume at the time, I now believe that my mother knew there was much more to my encounter with Tony than he had mentioned to her that night. Whatever the reason for Mom's attitude, I think that day was the saddest Parlor Day that I ever had at the convent.

I was returned to the convent early that day and kept separated from the other girls. Mother Rita ordered that I go straight to the dormitory and to bed. Alone with my thoughts, I couldn't understand how Tony had the audacity to do that to my mother after what he had done to me. *Did I really give him whatever it was he said I had given him? Or did he give it to me? He is much older than I am, so it must have been him. I'm gonna slap him in the face next time I see him on the street ...*

None of the others—Uncle Ernie, Uncle Graham or his father, Ricky or his father—had said anything to me or my mom, so they didn't have it, whatever it was. *What is it anyway? Is it going to kill me?* I had so many questions and nobody to ask. I was scared and felt very alone.

Dinner was brought to me in the dormitory on a tray. The auxiliary said nothing, handed me the tray and walked away, coming back to collect it about twenty minutes later. *Does she know I have this "thing"?* I was so embarrassed and didn't know who knew. When the girls came to bed, I was not allowed to talk to them. They were accustomed to me getting into trouble and being confined to the dormitory, so it wasn't really a surprise to see me there. A couple were concerned and stopped to ask what was wrong. But they were shuffled off fairly quickly by Mother Mercy, who actually stopped briefly by my bed to check I was okay and that I had everything I needed. Such compassion; I hadn't had that at all since I had been put in there.

Usually if you were confined for punishment, you were not allowed to get into your bed. But those who were sick were sent to the dormitory and confined to their beds for the whole day. You had to be *really* sick for that to happen. So I knew I was really sick, but I had no idea why? I felt normal.

The next morning Mother Mercy instructed me to get up out of bed only after the other children had left the dormitory. I was to dress but to not use the shower or bathroom to clean myself. Instead I was given a bucket and told to fill it with warm water from the tap and to cleanse myself in that, tipping it into the toilet to empty it after use. A new block of Velvet soap was left with me to use and a fresh towel. I was instructed not to leave the Velvet soap lying around in the bathroom for the other girls to use. It was to be kept by my bedside for later use, and the towel was to be immediately placed into the dirty towel basket. We washed, dried, and folded towels in the laundry every day, but we girls only got one clean towel a week to use. So throwing out a clean towel straight away was not normal.

She then instructed me to wait for Mother Rita to fetch me after I was dressed. After I was ready, an auxiliary brought my breakfast to the dormitory and came back to collect the tray just before Mother Rita arrived. I had no idea what Mother Rita was going to do to me. I knew what she had done to me for running away, but for having sex with a boy the penalty would have to be worse than death.

She walked in the door and signaled for me to follow her, mumbling as we marched along, "You'd think I have nothing better to do than to run around all day after a tramp like you. You had better not have given this to any other girl or you're out. You should be whipped for such lowly behavior. Only prostitutes have sex with men without being married. Are you a prostitute?"

Mother Mercy was ordered to guard me in the Parlor while Mother Rita brought the car around. At first I had no idea where we were going, but then I remembered Mom telling me that Mother Rita would take me to the doctors.

I sat in the back seat as we drove down the long road towards town, the same road I had used to attempt my escape only nights before. It looked different in the daylight. We drove towards a large red brick building near the center of town. Mother Rita parked the car and ordered me to follow her. She did not walk—she marched! Short, quick steps, a dozen to a yard. It was quite comical actually. If you've ever watched an episode of *The Roadrunner*, you can imagine Wylie E. Coyote's legs spinning around as he was winding up to speed after the Roadrunner. Well, Mother Rita's legs moved in the same manner when she was on a mission, and it was clear that she was on a mission with me in tow.

We entered the building through a small glass door that opened up into a foyer. Mother Rita approached the woman behind the high wooden counter and asked if she could please consult with a doctor for one of her charges.

Then she spoke in very hushed tones. I couldn't make out what she was saying, but they both looked over at me. I could see disgust on their faces. I was still sitting on the seat, in the spot that Mother Rita had pointed to when we entered. Shortly afterwards my name was called by a short, round man with glasses and thinning hair—the doctor. He looked over his glasses at me and raised his eyebrows. He directed me into a small cubicle and pulled the curtains shut. Mother Rita spoke with him in hushed tones outside in the hallway.

Upon their return, Mother Rita took a seat at the end of the bed. The doctor instructed a nurse to bring stirrups to the cubicle and attach them to the bed. He then instructed me to remove my underpants and jump up on the bed.

I was so scared because I still did not know what was wrong. My face blushed. It must have been beetroot red because the doctor looked over his glasses at me and said, "Now, now, surely you can't be embarrassed to remove your underpants. You've been removing them for boys for how long?"

My eyes looked to Mother Rita and I saw her start to wag her finger. I knew she was becoming agitated with my hesitation, so I did as I was told. While looking down to the floor, I removed my underwear and climbed up on the table. With that the nurse grabbed my left foot first and placed it up in the air in the stirrup and the doctor did the same with my right foot. They tied my feet so I couldn't remove them.

The nurse opened a large, green cloth that she had placed on a small table beside the doctor and handed him some sort of medical instrument, which he forcefully pushed inside me. It was metallic and cold. I writhed with pain as I felt it tearing through my insides. It felt like a million small blades cutting me all the way in. All I could do was scream as tears rolled down the sides of my face.

I looked first at the nurse who was expressionless, then to the doctor who was busy concentrating on what he was doing "down there". And Mother Rita? She had a mocking smirk as she sat at the end of the bed with a full view of the proceedings as she would not allow the doctor to draw the curtains for fear that he would interfere with me. I knew what was going through her head; I could feel it to my very core. Or maybe she was just enjoying the view. Either way, she was right there, right in the mix getting into the action with a prime viewing seat. I felt so embarrassed.

"Goodness gracious me," the doctor exclaimed. "Goodness gracious me. This is one of the worse cases I have ever seen, but we cannot be certain before we get some results back. In the meantime, we are going to start her on some penicillin." He told Mother Rita that she could bring me into the hospital for every injection or he could show her how to do them and they could be done at the convent, but I would require months of treatment. Mother Rita opted for the convent. At least that way she would not have to bring me to the hospital every day (and I figured she could enjoy torturing me better by giving me injections).

He said that every sexual partner would need to be notified, but I refused to say anything, knowing that if I did I would be in more trouble than I was already. One boy, one time! That was it. As far as the doctor was concerned, he estimated that I had contracted syphilis several years earlier. It had been in my system for a long time. As far as Mother Rita knew, it was only two years before, just before I entered the convent.

On the way back to the convent, Mother Rita warned me that if any other girl in the convent had contracted this disease from me, I would be made a ward of the state and sent to Winlaton.

"You are the worse kind of sinner for giving your body to men outside of marriage. You will never be forgiven. If you thought you were going to heaven, well I can tell you right now, girlie, forget that notion—because it will never happen!"

Yes, it was hell for me, no chance of redemption. God had spoken. She told me I was never to speak of this to anybody. If I did, I would be put into solitary confinement. I wasn't sure what that was, but she seemed to be referring to something different to being locked in the dormitory. She told me to go to confession and to confess my sins and to hope that the good Lord could forgive me. Any privileges that I had up to that point in time were now gone. I couldn't think of any, so that really didn't matter much.

All because I was raped ... and somehow it was my fault. Yep, this all sucked, big time. It was no surprise to me that I would be blamed though.

I felt so low; I was gutted actually. What I needed was someone to put their arms around me and let me know that it was all going to be okay. Even just explaining to me what it was that I had would have been a great start. My mom was not there to hug me, not that she would have done that anyway. She had had her chance on Parlor Day. Nobody was there, nobody understood, and I was groomed enough at that stage to believe that somehow I deserved this because I had been such a bad child.

To add insult to illness, when we returned to the convent, Mother Rita pulled me into her office by my hair. She pulled me around to the back of her desk and opened her drawer. Using one hand and holding my pigtail with her other, she took a pair of scissors and SNIP—gone.

My hair was all gone!

I was only just registering what was happening when I heard her say, "Now nobody will want you; you're as ugly as sin." With that she pushed me out the door, shutting it in my face while telling me to go to the schoolroom. I was already full of self-loathing and self-depreciation, and now every time I looked in the mirror I was to see an ugly, horrible, freckle-faced idiot, with rat shit hair who was not worth anything to anybody. I was being tutored well in my own worthlessness.

That night I found myself standing at my dining room table with no chair to eat my meal; this signaled to all the girls that I had done something wrong, but I could not tell them what. My chair was removed for a week, probably to be disinfected and fumigated, and I was to be given extra chores so as to truly be ashamed of my sins.

I lay in bed that night with a high fever. I was sweating profusely then nausea took over my whole body and I could not stop vomiting. Now I know that it was a reaction to penicillin, and many similar nights were to follow. My bed was wet from sweating so much that it looked like I had wet it. I didn't want them to think that's what I had done and receive a punishment for bed wetting as well. Children who wet their beds were made to stand with their wet sheets over their heads. They were made fun of, mocked, and made examples out of.

Mother Mercy came in the next morning with her burgeoning voice … "In the name of the Father, the Son …" All the girls were already on their knees reciting the prayers that had been drummed into them, even non-

Catholics. Mother Mercy stopped short when she saw me struggling to get out of bed and quickly moved to me. She felt my forehead and grabbed me by the shoulders, pushing me back into the bed and covering me up. A few girls smirked at me as they walked past the bed.

"Faker," one sneered!

"Bitch," I retaliated.

"There's nothing wrong with you, bitch," another mumbled under her breath.

Some of the girls could be so nasty. None of them knew what was wrong with me; none of them were allowed to know. Two hours later, Mother Mercy came and got me. She helped me into my dressing gown to keep my dignity as she led me to the infirmary for my injection. All the girls were hard at work by now, so there were none around to see where I was being taken. When I walked into the infirmary, I was told to face the wall, pull my underpants down and bend over the bench facing away from Mother Rita. She had one of those old stainless steel hypodermic needles in her hand, which looked about a foot long. She made the sign of the cross on my butt cheek and then, just like throwing a dart, she took aim and threw the needle into my rump. Shit! After emptying its contents into me, she ordered me to get dressed, do my chores, and make my way to school.

Well, that was the only time I heard the nuns clash with each other. Mother Mercy actually went at Mother Rita, telling her I was too sick to take part in my daily activities and I should be put back to bed. Mother Mercy's pleas for leniency fell on deaf ears. All Mother Rita would say is "She brought this on herself. Now she deserves everything she gets. It's God's way of letting her know that she has done wrong. Mother Mercy was angry but had no choice than to be compliant. After all, Mother Rita was the Mother Superior of the Convent.

The initial injections lasted for a week, one every day for the first seven days. Then three times a week for three more months. Every time, Mother Rita blessed my butt before putting the injection in. She must have thought that by doing so it would save at least one part of me. No, seriously, I found out later in life there is a quadrant on the buttock that must be identified before giving an injection, so she was drawing the quadrant physically to ensure that she didn't inject the wrong place. But my theory sounded good, didn't it?

I returned to the dormitory, got dressed, and completed my daily chores, despite feeling sick. In fact, I was going to feel sick for quite a long time, but I just had to do what I was told. After that I went to the classroom to complete the weekly schoolwork that I was already behind on. Several girls asked me what was going on, but I refused to talk to them about it. I knew that the punishment was not worth it. I know that there would have been a lot of chatter around the place about what was wrong with me. It was all too cloak and dagger not to be noticed. The girls thrived on gossip; after all, we had nothing else. In later years, I have heard the girls talk about "that girl" that had syphilis, but none can remember who it was. I have still not broken Mother Rita's golden rule about sharing what was wrong with me. I suppose this blows it right out of the water though.

Later on that day, Mother Mercy quietly took me out of the Mangle Room, to a spot underneath the stage in the large hall. There she sat me down on a chair and tried as hard as she could to style my hair. Again, I was sworn to secrecy. She didn't have much to work with, but it looked a lot better than it had before she started. Then she sent me back to the group room because work for the day was finished. Bless her for one of the only kindnesses I was ever shown in that convent by the nuns.

22

WEDDINGS, FROGS & TOADS

" … my hands were firmly clasped around her neck! …
Welcome to the family!"

EVEN THOUGH I WOULD return home to the boring normality of daily life at Mom's place every Christmas, I still looked forward to every holiday. Holidays were a break away from the daily mundane and systematic routine of the convent and gave me some freedom and time to find myself again and remember who I was. There was still the drinking to be considered and the nights of being pulled out of bed up to twenty times to hear about how bad, mean, and horrible everyone was. It was still mostly stories about my father and what he had done to her before he left. It was monotonous, and the older I grew the more I understood what was going on and the less I appreciated its continuance. I did not have a bed or a bedroom of my own as the place was just too small, but it was enough for Mom to survive in without me.

Typically, I did everything I could to stay away from the house when I was home. I don't think Mom missed me too much either, as she was used to me not being there anyway. So life just went as normal for her.

I made holidays fun, as best as I could. In fact, it was during these times of freedom from the convent that I was to start spreading my wings and touchdown into dangerous territory again. The rebel was slowly emerging. I would head back to my old haunts with the kids that I knew before I was placed in the convent—Kerrie and Debra. Or I would head to Stoke Street in Preston to visit my old friend Carolyn, my pea-in-the-same-pod friend, who not only looked like me but got me into some awfully bad trouble at times. I also had a new friend to visit—Cheryl—who had come into my life at the convent. She was a different type of girl, the new breed who was afraid of no one—a "take-no-prisoner" type who lived less than five kilometers from me. When the nuns told her what to do, she didn't ask "how high" like me, she just ignored them. From the start I felt Cheryl really "got me", and she still does.

One night when I was supposedly visiting Kerrie's house and she mine—well, you know how it is—we were picked up by a group of four young guys driving around in a ute. Hmmm I could say they were picked up by us! Kerrie and I were feeling pretty confident and a bit adventurous. After we talked for a while, they asked if we wanted to go for a ride to the beach. For some reason they seemed really trustworthy, so it didn't take us too long to accept their request and jump in with them.

It was really cool sitting in the back of their hotted-up Holden ute, cruising down the main strip of St. Kilda on our way to the beach. They had some alcohol with them in plain brown paper bags, but we refused their offers to drink. They were true to their word and took us to the beach. There was no funny business, just fun times with a great bunch of guys. We ran around, chasing each other, jumping over things, and screaming at the top of our lungs until eventually we were exhausted and built a camp fire. We sat around the fire, just talking, until the early hours of the morning. They had never met a convent girl before and were quite curious about my life and stories of survival behind the convent walls.

There were five of them: Robert, Brownie, Steve, Bruce, and a young guy who was particularly cute. He sat in the back with us, along with Bruce and Brownie. I took a shine to him straight away. He stood about five foot six inches tall, had strawberry blond, shoulder-length wavy hair and blue eyes. His smile was gorgeous and his nature gentle. He even put his jacket around me as the night wore on to keep me warm because the night air had really set in and I was feeling chilly in my crop top and shorts.

His name was Ernie. Funnily enough the song *Ernie (The Fastest Milkman in the West)* by Benny Hill had just been released at that time and was in the

Top 40. I can remember telling my friends earlier that same night that I'd never go out with a boy named "Errrrrrrneee". The real reason was, of course, because of Uncle Ernie, but I didn't tell them that. But before our night at the beach was over, I was hopelessly in puppy love with this young boy and my nickname became "Trigger" from that night forward. Why Trigger? Well, it was to do with that song. Trigger was Ernie's horse!

We found out that these guys were from Keon Park and they asked if we wanted to go up there the next day and hang out. We eagerly agreed, but when morning came Kerrie wasn't interested in going. I was though; I wanted to see Ernie again. So I went by myself. He was just as nice the next day as he had been the night before.

We all went to Ernie's house as his parents were at work and we had the run of the house. In a teenage way he was eager to have his way with me—boys will be boys and they all try at some stage. Ernie and I separated off into his bedroom.

He fumbled around for a while, but luckily nothing happened. After what I had been through, I was not taking any chances and made it rather difficult for him to succeed in getting to home base. Nevertheless, he seemed satisfied just to have had a girl in his bedroom.

I didn't see him again that holiday. I was keen to go to Keon Park again, but hanging out with Kerrie seemed the right thing to do. The holidays flew past. I had a fantastic summer of fun, though I pined for Ernie. Before I knew it, I was on the old red rattler train heading back to Bendigo.

As the train pulled away from the platform, I waved eagerly at Mom who was standing on the platform waving back at me. Then I settled down into my seat for the long journey back. We hadn't gone very far when the train came to an emergency stop. I stood up and looked out the window and could see the platform in the near distance. I wondered why the train had stopped, but figured it would start again soon and continue on its way to the convent, back to the life I had now become accustomed to. It was welcomed in some ways. I knew the routine and I knew I would be fed. The work was hard and Mother Rita was cruel, but there were really no surprises. It's interesting how I could switch so easily from the freedom of my holidays with Mom straight back into convent life and all that it entailed. I had become systemized, almost robotic in some instances. My expectations of any other type of life had gone; it was really all I knew now.

I was surprised and a little nervous, to see a police officer approaching me, showing me his badge.

"Are you Beverley?" he asked.

"Yes." *What have I done now?*

Another question came. "Is that suitcase yours?" He was pointing to the suitcase above me on the overhead rack. I nodded in confirmation and he pulled it down. "Come with me."

I quickly rifled through the flashes of memories from my holiday to figure out when I had broken the law. I knew that if I had broken the law, I could be made a ward of the state and handed over to the wardens of Winlaton, which I knew by rote to be far worse than being at St. Aidan's. In later years I was to find out that it actually wasn't worse and it was easier to be there, or so some say. But for now my fears were very real and founded on warnings by Mother Rita.

The policeman alighted from the train and lifted me down onto the track ballast, assisting me to walk the length of the train back to the platform where Mom was thankfully still waiting. She rushed to meet us once we reached the platform and insisted on knowing why I'd been removed from the train.

Once we were safely up on the platform, the whistle from the conductor sounded and the train jolted as it moved forward, continuing its trip to Bendigo without me. *How did the police even know I was on the train?* I figured they must have rung the convent and asked Mother Rita when I would be coming back. Who knows … They had found me and now I didn't know what I had done. All I could think of was the punishment I might receive once I was back at the convent. Mother Rita did not like me returning in police cars. It was all rather nerve racking.

It turned out that I'd done nothing wrong at all. I was required in court as a witness for that attack on Kerrie and I and her nearly successful abduction, when I was eleven. The hearing date had arrived and we had both been subpoenaed to appear at the County Court in Melbourne as witnesses or complainants.

The court case lasted several days, and each day Kerrie and I appeared. First, we sat outside the courtroom. Then once we had given evidence, we sat inside.

Even though Kerrie and I were still very young, we were made to feel like we had committed the crime instead of the three men now facing the court. We were asked questions of a personal nature, about sex and other private things, and were reminded that we were under oath. We felt like we were on trial. Thankfully, the judge at the time reminded their lawyers that we were both young girls and should be respected as such, eventually calling an end to the line of questioning that the lawyers were taking.

All were found guilty. One was sentenced to serve out a period of time in Pentridge as it was a second offence and the other two were convicted but given suspended sentences. One of them had already been dealt with in the children's court as he was under sixteen years of age.

In hindsight, I thought they were treated rather leniently. Their intentions at the time of the attack were not very nice—and that's an understatement. In fact, I believe that if the car had not broken down outside Kerrie's house and her mother hadn't heard my screams and come out, Kerrie may not be here now.

As we left court that day, one of the guys caught my eye, even though the judge had instructed them not to look at us. He formed a pistol shape with his fingers and slowly lifted his hand to his lips and pointed it at me. He then pretended to shoot me. It scared the life out of me. After that I would dream at night that I was being chased and he would eventually catch me and shoot me. At times I would wake up in a pool of sweat. This dream continued into my early twenties.

A week later, I was back on the train to Bendigo. I was greeted by Mother Rita at the door with the same statement I received each time I had a major issue arise.

"This is nobody's business and as such you will not mention what has happened to any other person." Ya da ya da ya da.

I was also informed that I would not be returning to Mother John's group as we had "made her have a heart attack". So now I would be in Mother Theresa's group. I was sad but excited at the same time. Mother Theresa's group dormitory had been refurbished with individual cubicles and lovely new bedding and lime green bed quilts. Each cubicle contained a bed with a small wardrobe beside it, each with a set of drawers and a mirror. And each cubicle had a curtain that could be pulled across for privacy.

We had always felt like the poor cousins when we walked past their doorway of an evening. The bathrooms were all brand new and the girls had access to several showers, which would make bathing easier and faster. You could even pull the curtain across the front of your cubicle to get changed, instead of doing it out in the open!

There were some nice girls in her group. Mother John's group had been dispersed across all the groups, so there were some girls from Mother John's group still with me. Mother Theresa's group room was spacious and full of natural light, with carpet on the floor and a huge table where we could all sit and do our homework. There was even a small kitchenette.

I think I'm going to like it here was my immediate thought as I headed up to my new bed for the first time that night. I felt lucky to be given the corner bed right next to the window. *Hmmm or is it because they think it will be too cold here and I'm being punished? ...*

My belongings had been removed from my previous cupboard by one of the senior girls and put into my new wardrobe. It wasn't much, but it was mine.

The only downside of my move was that Mother Theresa didn't like me very much, and I was pre-warned my first night back not to put a foot out of place because she would be watching and waiting. That's why I wondered about the cubicle I was given. I had heard stories about how strict she was and I had seen some of that in the ironing room where she was one of the nuns in charge. I don't know why I rubbed people up the wrong way. Hell, I still do it today. But back then I didn't even have to open my mouth. She reminded me very much of Sister Albertus, the nun who expelled me from St. Mary's and started me on the journey to this hell hole. I suppose Mother Rita thought that Mother Theresa would be able to control me.

At every given opportunity I yabbered on about Ernie. I said I was going to marry him and live happily ever after. Cheryl continued our friendship, promising to go to Keon Park together and hang out with the guys on our next holidays. Rhonda was also Cheryl's friend, but she lived too far away to be able to come. Nevertheless, the three of us became a tight little group. We didn't work in the laundry together, but we were together every moment we could be in our own time.

One Sunday morning, I wondered, as usual, if I was going to receive visitors. My name was called out and I ran to the Parlor Room, expecting to see my mother waiting there. Instead, there stood my brother Daniel in his Army uniform! Tall and all grown up and fresh from war-torn Vietnam. I ran into his arms. Such a great feeling. I was so happy to see him and so glad that he had made it home and came to see me. Me!

I was so proud of my brother in his uniform and wanted to show him off to everybody. So I asked if I could take him in to meet Mother Dorothy. I must have introduced him to over twenty girls on my way to the group room. For weeks afterwards the convent buzzed about him. There were a lot of very young, hormone-driven teenagers at the convent and the added bonus of a uniform had tongues wagging.

Afterwards, he took me into town and bought me a hamburger, chips, and a milkshake. What a brother! We sat and talked and I told him how every morning I would listen to the death and casualty list from Vietnam on the radio in the dining room while I was eating my breakfast, hoping to God I would not hear his name. He had some good news for me. He had met a girl named Maree and had asked her to marry him. I was thrilled. Then he told me that he was going to bring Maree to meet me. Me!

A couple of months later, Daniel was true to his word and did just that. Maree was so nice; I loved her straight away. She had a warm face and welcoming smile, and you could tell how much she loved my brother by the way she looked at him. Yep, I liked her right there, right then, and nothing would ever change my mind. Maree asked me if I would be her bridesmaid at the wedding, and with that her fate was sealed—I was going to be her sister for life. She told me that they would get married in Cobar, which is a small country town in outback New South Wales. Maree and Daniel were asked by Mother Rita to have a talk to me because I had not been very good, but I don't remember the talk at all. I was too excited by the fact that I had a new sister *and* I was going to be a bridesmaid. She measured me up for the bridesmaid dress, and with that they were gone. But I knew it wouldn't be for long.

⁂

One day one of the older nuns asked me to help her shift some boxes in what was the old uniform shop under the balcony and dining room. It was a very dark, dingy, catacomb of rooms, with concrete walls that were paint-chipped and moldy. A musty smell lingered heavily in the air. I had never been down in this area before and was slightly scared. I had heard girls talking about the fact that it was haunted, and that was enough to keep most of us from straying down those stairs at any time.

However, while I was down there, I noticed that the external door to the uniform shop and the outside world was *not* locked. I took that in as a point of interest, stored for another time in the future when that type of information may be needed.

I quite enjoyed one activity at the convent—being part of the choir. We had a fantastic choir. Our girls had a wide range of voices, and together we were anything but ordinary. I'd have to say we were amazing. We had a lot of practice and were taught by Mrs. Lyons, who was with the Bendigo Operatic Society.

I had a particularly strong and extremely high soprano ranged voice and would often be pitted against the choir for blending purposes. This was one situation where I seemed to be of value. The nuns made good use of us to do their civic duty, and at Christmas time we would be shuffled around the old people's homes in Bendigo to sing Christmas Carols for them. I loved singing, so this was a real pleasure for me.

On one such occasion the hospice had arranged for a local boy band to attend and play also. We sang one or two songs and were seated while the boy band took the stage. I was pretty excited that we were getting to see a boy band and drifted off into my own little world, until I heard them start to play *As Tears Go By* by the Rolling Stones. I instantly became alert and emotions that I had buried long ago starting bubbling to the surface. I had never heard that song before, but it reached down to my very core and touched me in a way that music had never touched me. I openly cried as I listened to them sing the words.

The music took me to the place that was the convent where in my normal daily life there was little time for play. I recalled the beatings from Mother Rita, the hard work in the laundry, the burning of my fingers from the steam of the mangle, the sore knees from scrubbing floors, the lack of love and affection, and in particular—no freedom. Being locked behind heavy steel gates, away from a world that was passing us by.

I cried for myself and I cried for every other girl at the convent. Every time I hear that song, it will stir very deep emotions in me, even more so now than back then. Perhaps that's what happens as we get older.

※

Christmas holidays and the wedding arrived. I was quite excited. I was picked up by Uncle Bert and put on a plane to Sydney where my brother picked me up from the airport and took me to his home in Manly. Maree and I had to share a bed that night while my brother slept in the kitchenette. I went to bed quite tired, ready for a good sleep. I remember feeling happy.

But halfway through the night I was woken by the feel of my brother's strong hands pulling at my shoulders. Through the haze I realized that I was sitting straddled across Maree's chest! Not only that, but my hands were firmly clasped around her neck! She was trying to scream but was struggling to breathe. Somehow, in my sleep I had tried to strangle my new sister to death. *Welcome to the family!* I couldn't believe it. I felt really embarrassed.

The next day Maree said I had freaked her out and I felt terrible. I was worried she would turn against me, but to her credit she didn't. We agreed to put the strange goings-on of the night before behind us and we travelled to Cobar where I met Maree's mother and father, and her sisters and brother. We visited the farm and went swimming with yabbies. I knew they were in the water because I felt them nip at my bum while I was clambering through the mud trying to escape them. I was not impressed.

The young guys in Cobar were fantastic, and as I was the new girl in town I was much sought after. I loved the attention. I visited the pool nearly every day, showing off my new pair of bathers. Yes, Mom had bought me new bathers just for the trip, and I loved them. They were awesome, as close as I would ever come to wearing a bikini. They were the latest baby doll fashion with separate pants and a bra that clipped at the front, just under the bust, and a long skirt that opened down the front. On my return to the convent, they would be cut off me and thrown in the bin by Mother Rita as they were considered "disgraceful". Well, she couldn't throw my great memories away!

One of the local boys offered to take me horse riding. He was quite trusted by Maree's family, so when we rode off bareback on the horse, up the road and into the bush, they didn't worry at all. It was so exhilarating riding on a horse ... and being with a good looking guy. What a good story I was going to be able to tell the girls back at the convent. I felt like Lady Godiva but with clothes. We rode for a very long time. Eventually, he came to a stop, jumped down, and helped me off the horse. Then he turned to me and said rather matter-of-factly, "Ride for ride or you walk back."

What the ... Up until now I had thought this guy had a fantastic personality. I could see why most of the girls in town crooned after him. But suddenly he was showing an ugly side, a nasty side.

I tilted my head to the side and said, "No, no, you take me back now or my brother will not be very happy with you at all. He's in the Army, you know, and he will kill you."

Again he said, "Ride for ride or you walk back. I'm not scared of him; I have a gun."

So I turned and started to walk, trying to follow the trail that we had used to get there. It was hard to see with the long grass and bushes. I found myself very frightened at what could be in the grass. So when he came up behind me on the horse and said for the third time, "Ride for ride or you walk back," I did the only thing I could think of.

I told him with resignation, "Okay." *What's one more guy?* And besides, I didn't want him to shoot my brother. Daniel was the only person who truly cared about me.

But I still had a bit of fight in me. I ended up making it so difficult for the boy to have his way with me that he gave up in frustration and eventually took me home without getting what he wanted. I was becoming an expert in evasion. After this he continued to hang around me, probably hoping that I would change my mind and go horse riding with him again so he could finish what he started. But that never happened because I knew what he expected of me. I wasn't stupid. I knew nothing comes free, so I never gave him that second chance.

Over the course of my holiday, I often snuck out to the dunny and sat to have a quiet cigarette where I would not be disturbed. By now I was smoking a fair bit. Having been offered that cigarette by Mom, I knew she allowed it. Daniel and Maree had no idea that I smoked, so I thanked my lucky stars that they had an outhouse to smoke in.

One night when I was doing just that, I shut the door, pulled down my knickers and sat. There it was—something lumpy and slimy! I had plonked my bum right on top of it. I jumped up, screaming at the top of my lungs and hitting my head on the side wall in the process. I stumbled around in the dark, with the cigarette in one hand and with my other hand fumbling to pull my knickers up to get out the door—all the time wondering what the hell I had sat on.

Meanwhile, my brother had heard my blood-curdling screams and was heading my way fast, believing that I was being attacked. Once I had managed to get the door open, I bolted out of the toilet, smoke in hand, knickers twisted in a knot at the top of my legs and tears pouring down my face. The last time I had sat on something on a dunny seat it had been a tarantula, and it had bitten me. Not that I blame it, mind you.

This had felt like a snake and I couldn't keep it together long enough to explain that to my brother. All I could do was point.

Daniel lit up the toilet with his cigarette lighter and there, right on the seat, sat a huge, gruesome looking ... tree frog. Didn't they know they're not supposed to hang out in toilets? New South Wales had been in drought for a couple of years, so water was scarce and the days were a putrid 45 Celsius plus in the shade. The tree frog had found his water source and he was not giving it up for me, or for anyone else. Daniel had to fight him for the toilet.

That is how I got caught smoking. I told Daniel that Mom had let me, so he was fine and allowed me to continue smoking in front of him and Maree, but not in front of the family. Good enough for me.

The night before the wedding, I slept in Maree's bedroom—very brave of her after the last experience. We had to share the fan because of the heat. The excitement of the following day, combined with the heat, had me tossing and turning for hours. It took forever to finally fall asleep. Once again I awoke feeling my brother's strong hands on my shoulders as he pulled me off Maree's chest. Her mother was prying my fingers away from Maree's throat and people were all around us, yelling and panicking. My brother growled at me, but I had no idea what I was doing. To this day I still do not know why it happened. Deep down I must have feared losing the only person I thought truly cared about me ... I don't know ... I should have been happy that I was gaining one more who would care about me, just the same. Luckily, Maree had a heart big enough not to hold it against me—again—which meant I adored her even more.

The next morning was a flurry of hair appointments, make-up sessions, and getting dressed to be ready to accompany the beautiful bride to the altar. We arrived at the church and the first person I saw in the crowd was my father! What a surprise. I forgot all about why I was there—I suddenly had a mission. I was locked on target and not about to let him out of my sight. I ran straight to my daddy, stopped right in front of him, and said the only thing I could think of. "Hello, Daddy."

He asked, "Is that you, Bev?"

"Yes," I replied as I leant forward to give him a cuddle.

"My you've grown," he said.

"I know." Then I commenced to fire a myriad of questions at him; some he answered and some he didn't. But at no time did he cuddle me back or tell me he loved me. In fact, other than the quick cuddle I stole, the closest I got to my father that day was to stand beside him, about a foot apart.

Dad had apparently been invited, but they didn't expect him to turn up. Dad and Mom both ended up drinking quite a bit at the wedding. I remember walking out into the foyer of the hotel where the reception took place to see them having a loud discussion.

Daniel stepped in and asked them to remember where they were and told them that it was his day, his turn, and his time. I found out later that Mom had discovered that Dad had not arrived in Cobar alone. Dixie was in a hotel in town with their young son. Until then my mother didn't even know that my father had another son. I can only imagine that she would have been devastated and her only refuge was beer, lots of it. And she always turned nasty when she drank a lot, lashing out at whoever was her focus for that night. I certainly knew that from experience.

I didn't bother to stick around after that. Dad had made it clear that he didn't care about me, and Mom had too much booze in her. The formalities were over and nobody was going to miss me. Bridesmaid dress and all, I went and found some fun out on the main street with the other teenagers in Cobar who were hanging around. It was a great night until we got home after the wedding. Mom and I had a dreadful fight; I don't even know what it was about now. I ended up walking out of the house, shouting, "I'm going to go to my father!" I knew he was in town somewhere and I wanted him to take me to where he was living, to care for me, and stop me going back to the convent, and Mom. Maree's father quickly came after me.

He had a very adult talk with me. I think he saw in me what everybody else didn't—that fact that I was messed up and unloved. We sat outside on the front fence for a long time talking.

"Bev, sometimes adults are not responsible for their actions, especially when they have been drinking. So you need to not take your mom and Dad's behavior to heart," he explained.

Of course, I have since learnt that adults *are* responsible for their actions, always, regardless of whether they have been drinking or not. But that was enough to settle me down that night. Then he put his arm around my shoulder and said, "Come on, let's put you into bed." He was a real salt of the earth fellow, Maree's dad. I had only ever felt safe with one man, my Uncle Bert, until I met him.

Shortly after that I returned to Melbourne. I did have some awesome memories of my holiday that overshadowed the disappointment in not having a better experience with Dad. I actually wasn't to see or hear from him for another couple of years.

23

Changes in the Convent

"… From today onwards you will be taught to be young ladies."

WHEN I RETURNED TO the convent after Christmas holidays, Mother Rita wasn't at the door, ready with her spittle of warnings for me. In fact, Mother Rita was gone! Apparently, Mother Superior had visited from Ireland, and even though we did not see her or get to talk to her, the other nuns had lodged complaints against Mother Rita for her appalling treatment of them. It seems she was just as bad toward the other nuns as she was to us children. Mother Rita was removed as head and was moved to a convent where she would never be in charge of nuns again. Forget us kids; we were just collateral damage.

The day Mother Rita left St. Aidan's was one of the most exciting days in my life. No more beatings. No more sour face and nasty words … *Yep, without Mother Rita this place is going to be a breeze. But wait … Who or what is going to take her place?*

Mother Rose was put in charge of us. In reality, I only recollect tiny flashes of this period. Obviously not much changed at all in our discipline or working conditions. We still slaved in the laundry and did chores before and after school as well as on Saturdays. After church and morning chores on Sundays, we either had a rest day or a Parlor Day. In our systemized, institutionalized life, one minute normally melded into the next, one hour into the next, one day into the next day, and so on.

But one very unusual event stands out—something that was totally out of the norm and was to herald change at the convent—real change. This is the type of defining moment that is memorable.

On this day, we were told before we left the classroom to gather as quickly as possible in the small concreted area outside of the hall, in front of the verandah. What a nuisance. We all knew with the delay that we may not have time to get our afternoon tea before having to report to the laundry. However, assemblies were very rare. In fact, I'd only been told to assemble once before, and that was when one of the older nuns had died and we were being informed. The normal scuffle of girls running to get a cup of tea and biscuit before starting work at the laundry was replaced with steps of trepidation at what we were being called together for.

As we walked the short distance to the assembly area, we all noticed that the big iron gates at the back of the convent were open, wide open. Whispers flew wildly around us as we pointed towards the bottom end of the yard. We could all run out and what could they do to stop us? But we didn't, of course. We did as we were told and hung around, waiting.

A group of nuns, including Mother Rose, appeared from the dining room door. I noted a new face, a younger, kinder looking face. She was very tall. To a teenage girl she appeared to be about six to seven foot tall. My first thoughts were, *Shit, if she hit me she'd knock me flying*. She wasn't a large nun by any means, just very tall. It was the fact she towered over the other nuns that made her stand out. I was only about four foot six inches tall at that stage, which may have emphasized her height. She had a softness about her face, which was unusual amongst the nuns, most of them hardened, supposedly from years of looking after troublemakers like us.

Mother Rose had her normal flushed face as she stepped forward to make an announcement.

"Girls, this is Mother Catherine," she said, gesturing to the tall nun. "She is now the head nun at the convent and is in charge."

With that Mother Catherine stepped forward. She didn't smile, but still her face retained its warmth.

I can still remember her opening statement. She looked over the general assembly and said, "Good afternoon, girls. My name is Mother Catherine.

It is not my intention to keep any of you girls here who do not want to stay here. You may have noticed that the back gate is now open. Feel free to leave any time if you wish to. You will also find the front door open if that is more to your liking; however, it will be locked at night."

With that she began to tell us some of the changes that would take place. "My first instruction is that you will no longer be required to work in the laundry. From this day on, you do not have permission to enter the laundry for any reason."

A cry of sincere appreciation went up from all the girls gathered in front of her, especially from those of us who had already spent the better half of our younger years slaving in the heat and filth of the laundry. Mother Mercy hushed us from behind her, putting her finger to her mouth. We started to fidget, jiggling from foot to foot, restless with with both excitement and apprehension. We waited quietly to hear what she would say next, each of us with some kind of stupid grin on our face.

"Secondly," she continued, "from today onwards you will be taught to be young ladies. We will provide teachers, models, make-up artists, hairdressers, and elocution teachers to show you how to look after yourselves. And if you are going to insist on wearing those miniskirts, we will teach you how to bend over and sit down in them."

Oohs and aahs hung in the air. Excitement was building amongst us all.

She pointed to one of the older girls and asked her to move forward. "Twirl around for me, please," Mother Catherine said, as her long finger spun in the air, indicating for the girl to spin.

The girl complied and twirled around. Mother Catherine turned to the other nuns and asked, "What era are these uniforms from? We can't have this." She looked us all over and said, "On Monday you will all be individually fitted for an updated, modern uniform, one you will be proud to wear. One that will be recognized as St. Aidan's, no matter where you go."

Just what we need, I thought. New clothes sounded good, but the "being recognizable" didn't leave a good taste in my mouth. A part of me wanted to be excited about all this, but I felt a little wary. Even though Mother Catherine appeared to be nice—she sounded nice and seemed to be very giving—she was an unknown quantity and as such had to be treated with caution until such time as she was deemed worthy of my trust. But, true to her word, the gate stayed open, the front door was unlocked, and on the following Monday we reported one by one to the cookery room to be measured from head to toe for our new school uniform.

Yes, some did take advantage of the gate being open and left. I don't know who made the uniforms, nor do I care. But I remember the excitement amongst us girls when they were finally delivered a couple of weeks later and we were able to put them on. No more pleated skirts in heavy tartan swinging halfway between our knees and our ankles. No more matching wattle green twin sets, which had included a jumper and cardigan to weigh us down. Instead, we had these beautiful synthetic sky blue uniforms, with rounded white collars and short sleeves. They were measured to exactly three inches above our knees, and nobody but us had ever worn them. We were issued with two pairs of brown tights and a pair of new shoes that were not heavy and bulky, to complement the uniform. The only downfall was that we retained our wattle green cardigans and wore them on cold days. Even though I loved the new look, how I appreciated the warmth that the older uniform had given me during the colder winter months. The new uniform looked good but didn't offer a great deal of protection from the cold.

More important than all of that was the fact that there were no more laundry duties. It was heaven! We still had to do our normal range of jobs for the upkeep of the convent, the church, and the nuns' quarters. But other than that, we had much more time on our hands. Mother Catherine made us more responsible for our groups, encouraging us to work together with the nun in charge of our group. We cooked meals together in our group rooms and sat together, as a family would, to eat around a table, with enough seats to seat us all.

Our groups were given different names. Mine was "Shalom", meaning peace. By now all of the new dormitories were built and everybody had a separate cubicle to sleep in, except the old ladies and the mentally disabled who still slept out on the balconies in the cold.

One of the things that Mother Catherine was particularly concerned about was the fact that many of us had alcoholic parents. So she arranged for the local Alcoholics Anonymous group to come to the convent and each week we were herded into the Parlor Room for the meeting. I went willingly as I wanted to try to understand how to live with my mother. The only benefit I got from those meetings was the free ice-cream at the end of the night. The meetings went right over our heads. They weren't designed for children at all. But the ice-cream was good and it was nice to know that people did care.

Mother Catherine introduced movie nights. If we behaved, we got to watch movies on a large screen in the hall; when I say large I'm talking about a pull up screen about four foot wide that rested on a metal bar. We watched movies such as *The Sound of Music, A Man for All Seasons, The Girls from St. Trinian's* ... Whoa, back up, hang on a minute ... Now you're talking. I can remember the look on Mother Catherine's face when the St. Trinian's girls really got started. I truly believe that she thought it would be a convent just like ours. How wrong was she? We snickered up our sleeves and poked each other when the funny or raunchy bits came on. Yes, I think it was a bit saucy for us but nothing really new to us either. Needless to say, we didn't get to finish watching that one, even though Mother Mercy complained because she really wanted to see it.

A lot of girls were now passing through the convent. It was more transient than it had ever been. Many girls remain in my memory, and I often wonder what happened to them: Leah, Rhonda, and Rosemary (sisters), my beautiful friend Irene, and young Mary. The front door became like a turnstile, in and out, faster and faster.

Don't get me wrong; I was glad the girls were getting out of there. But how I wished that somebody loved me enough to fight for my freedom also. People do not realize how it feels to be locked away from society in your early adolescent years, and the scars and repercussions that it causes in your later years. Some parents were amazing; they went to great lengths to get their children out of there, most not wanting their children there in the first place. One mother didn't listen when told visits were only once a month. She was there every second week, travelling by train all the way from Melbourne to see her daughter, with her younger children in tow. Yep, some people were just really lucky and some parents were very devoted.

Girls were coming and going around me and I felt like a brick in the wall, doomed to stay there forever and ever. There were several of us like this, but most were not there very long at all. Some were lucky enough to go home; others were shuffled sideways into other convents or sent back to state government homes like Wimberra and Winlaton, for whatever reason. Sadly some died or were killed shortly after they were released. I remember feeling desperately lonely as time went by. When was I going to get out of here too, for good?

Mum and Dad in Melbourne just after they met in 1943. This photo was taken just before they were married on 12 February 1944.

Dad (on the far right) at his anti-aircraft gun on HMAS *Australia* during World War II. This very same gun is now housed outside of the Australian War Memorial in Canberra ACT, Australia. My father's initials, A.F., can be seen etched into the steel underneath the gun.

Dad, Mum and my Grandma Forster, with me in front. This is the only time I met my grandmother, who lived well into her seventies. Such lost opportunities for me to have a real family.

Me playing in the backyard with my best pal, Tiny, and Lambchop our sheep. Dad stole Lambchop from a paddock on his way home from a fishing trip. Tiny and I were the best of mates. He was my confidante, my life, until someone cruelly took him away from me.

Here I am sitting on top of Mum's camphorwood box, which Dad brought home from China. The photo was taken the night of my sister's sixteenth birthday. She spent all day curling my hair so I would look pretty and feel special too.

St Aidan's Orphanage Bendigo, Victoria, Australia. St Aidan's comprised three sections. Maryfields was for girls aged fifteen and over, but I worked in the Magdalene laundry at the age of twelve, along with many other underage girls. There was also an orphanage, and the nuns' quarters in the middle to keep the two areas totally separate.

My father and me outside the church at my brother's wedding in January 1972. It was the first time I'd seen my father since he had walked out on us when I was a young child.

Afternoon chore time at the convent. Yep, that goofy-looking one hiding behind the nun, that would be me. Note our sexy aprons.

Me at Bendigo Park on visiting day at the convent, more commonly known as "parlor day." Mother Rita had cut off my ponytail in anger because I was ill with a disease I did not deserve.

Happy-go-lucky Sandi, at the height of the disco era in 1979 just before I met Shaun. Taken at Menzies Hotel in Melbourne, Victoria.

In 2011 I revisited the site of my accident, Sylvia's Cutting, Tarcutta, New South Wales. The National Truck Driver Memorial was placed at Tarcutta in memory of the many truck drivers that have lost their lives on this very spot.

One of my most favorite moments with the best person I know in this entire world: Shaun and me on our wedding day in May 1981, in one of the few photos I have of Shaun in our wedding album where he's not kissing me.

Shaun and me renewing our wedding vows on our twenty-fifty wedding anniversary, 6 May 2006, at the Palazzo Versace, Gold Coast. Queensland. Shaun reaffirmed his love for me, and I for him.

24

The Three Stooges

> "We were instructed, 'You three are never to speak to each other again, nor gather in a group of any sort.' Yeah, right, that is never going to happen. Not in our lifetime anyway."

LUCKILY THERE WERE term breaks. While on holidays in the next break, I went to Cheryl's house to pick her up so we could go to Keon Park together, but she wasn't home. Her brother, Michael, invited me in and told me I could wait for her if I wanted. While I sat on the couch, waiting, I was immediately attracted by Michael's dark chocolate eyes; they pierced right through me. I sat there trying hard not to stare at him. I loved the way his chestnut colored hair curled and framed his face. He was gorgeous and seemed to be quite gentle.

Michael had his mates over, but I noticed his eyes catch mine every now and again, and that would send my heart fluttering. I also noticed he was showing off in front of me, which was a good sign.

The room felt electric. Michael was very attentive, making it clear by the end of the hour that he was interested in going out with me, and I gave him the subtle signals that I was interested as well. So from that moment on, we had our sights set on each other and knew that we would become an item. I felt that this was the beginning of my very first real relationship with a guy.

Basically, anybody that showed the slightest interest in me back then became "the love of my life", so I was out of love with Ernie and now in love with Michael, although this felt different.

Cheryl came home and reluctantly I headed off to Keon Park with her.

But I made more effort to go to her place and be with her over the following days, trying to see more of Michael. Ernie had long since lost interest in me, so I was a free agent.

Cheryl and I had great fun those holidays. We hung around with the gang during the day and sat by a camp fire with them in the vacant fields of a night. We then started the whole thing again the next day. It was tremendous fun, day in, day out. Nobody to stop us, no one to tell us what we shouldn't be doing. We were free! We were a very tightly knit circle of friends. Mom still showed no interest in what I did every day, so I did what I wanted.

When the holidays were drawing to a close, the guys from Keon Park asked us to go up there to say goodbye to them on the Sunday afternoon. Mom agreed as long as I was back in time to get the train to Bendigo. We spent the entire afternoon in the park drinking Ouzo and Coke, smoking until our lungs hurt, and running riot. We rode around on the back of Harley Davidsons—God, I love those bikes—and by the time we had to leave to go home, both of us were totally smashed. The boys escorted us to the train station and we boarded the train to go back to Cheryl's house.

Cheryl had taken the rest of the bottle of Ouzo and tucked it under her jacket. When we got back to her Mom's place, she quickly hid it in her suitcase. Her Mom, Mrs. Kirchener, realized we were both drunk and although she was not happy, she was far more liberal than what my mom would have been. I guess the saving grace was that it was late and since Cheryl's Mom was driving her to the train station (as she wanted to say goodbye), she said she would take me as well. Because of the tight timeframe to get to the train, it meant that I couldn't linger at Mom's house.

We just dropped by quickly and I picked up my suitcase and said a quick goodbye to Mom. I tried as hard as I could to act straight and not let on that I was drunk—it worked. When she asked me what the funny smell was, I replied that it was liquorice and off I went. She gave me a quick peck on the cheek and waved goodbye from the back door.

At the station the train was almost ready to leave, so it was a quick goodbye to Mrs. Kirchener and onto the train. We walked the length of the train, trying to find Rhonda who we knew would be onboard as well. The old red rattler that went between Bendigo and Melbourne had separate compartments, each with two long seats on either side and some tin foot warmers. The door could be closed to each section, providing privacy. As soon as we found the compartment that Rhonda was in, out came the cigarettes and the rest of the bottle of Ouzo. We also put aspirin into our Coke cans and drank that, although now I know that was useless. So the effects we were experiencing were undoubtedly from the high level of alcohol in our bloodstream.

Within the hour we were hammered again, including Rhonda, and we ran riot on the train. We didn't hurt anybody, but we had a lot of fun stirring passengers up and basically just making idiots of ourselves. Apparently, we did some things on the train that night that we should be really ashamed of. We were reported to the conductors by other passengers, and they radioed ahead. We were met by the police at Bendigo station, who were more than happy to give us a lift back to the convent. Here we go again!

Well, what can I say? Mother Catherine greeted us at the front door where we stood rather disheveled but happy with ourselves. We were smirking sideways at each other, trying very hard not to laugh. We really didn't give a shit about what the repercussions were going to be. Oh, the bravado that alcohol afforded us. Mother Catherine merely told us that she was very disappointed in us. But she was still an unknown quantity. I had never been in trouble with her before, so I did not know what to expect.

Needless to say, we were all duly punished. Privileges were withdrawn and the three of us were told that we would stand to eat all meals in the dining room for the next three weeks, and our chairs were to be removed. You'd think they didn't have enough chairs for the nuns up at the convent dining table the way our chairs continued to vanish.

Funnily enough, I had feared that the punishment would be more severe, remembering my time in the dormitory. Was it more forgiving because they were pandering to the new breed of child coming into the convent, or was Mother Catherine genuinely caring? Though not as extreme as previous disciplines, we had to be made examples of.

Our lives were made a living hell with additional jobs, standing for meals, and no privileges; to naughty teenagers it seemed so unfair at the time. So, we reacted, as teenagers do. Within two weeks, Cheryl, Rhonda, and I were out that opened door of the Uniform Shop that I'd discovered under the verandah and we were hitting the highway to home in the early hours of the morning. Hmmm. I don't know why we just didn't leave through the gates that Mother Catherine had said anyone could do at any time.

We walked for what seemed an eternity, hitchhiking where we could. The time went fast. We talked and mucked around most of the way. Then after about two to three kilometers, we were lucky to be picked up by a businessman who drove us all the way to Kilmore. We chatted eagerly with him, making up some kind of story about who we were and where we were going, and then he pulled the car over to the side of the road and informed us that he had to head in the opposite direction. We thanked him, jumped out, and kept heading into town. We did not realize that he actually had gone in that direction also.

After some discussion, we decided just to walk straight through the town instead of hitchhiking, so that we wouldn't arouse the suspicions of anybody that could be a police officer. Also Cheryl insisted that it was better to walk straight past the police station, as they wouldn't be suspicious then. So we did. I won't listen to her again!

As we were walking through Kilmore we were surrounded by three police cars. Sprung! The nice businessman, who had given us the lift, was a detective from the Kilmore Police Station. They picked us up, took us back to the police station, and locked us up in the cell out the back.

Time marched on and it was getting close to lunch and we were really hungry. We hadn't eaten breakfast before we left. So we demanded that they feed us, reminding them that prisoners had rights too. In fact, we were quite boisterous and made ourselves well heard. So well heard in fact that the policemen came out the back, stuck a hose through the cell door, and hosed us down. They were laughing their heads off at us and thought it was a great joke. But Rhonda, who was quite animated, pulled the hose into the cell, spun it around, and turned it on them. I wouldn't have had the guts. Well, game over! They got pissed off with us and lunch never arrived. They were saturated though, and we pissed ourselves laughing, congratulating Rhonda on her quick thinking and wit. Perhaps the hunger was worth it.

By 4 p.m. Cheryl and Rhonda had been taken in a divvy van back to Bendigo. The already small cell, which was really a cell just big enough for one prisoner, seemed to become even smaller without the other two girls. Any boldness I may have had had vanished with them also. The thick concrete walls kept the cell cold and the heavy wooden door reminded me of the front door at the convent, except for the small barred window in the middle of it. It had one bunk bed, which hung down from the wall and had been our seat for the entire day. The fact that I hadn't been taken back with the other two girls worried me a little. I couldn't understand why we had been separated. I waited and asked anybody who came near the cell what was going to happen to me. The sun was starting to go down and there was a winter chill in the air. My clothes were still quite damp from the hosing down I had received earlier in the day and there was nothing in the cell to keep me warm.

I began to think that I just might not be welcome back at the convent, and surprisingly a fear engulfed me unlike anything I had ever felt before. What would I do? Who would care for me, especially who would feed me now? I now know about Stockholm's Syndrome and I imagine the feelings that I experienced that day were similar to what sufferers of Stockholm's go through. I wasn't aligned with the police, but rather with the nuns. I was scared that after all these years of being their captive they would not take me back.

About an hour later, there was movement in the camp! I was placed into the back of a divvy van and driven to Seymour, where I was transferred into the back of a second divvy van to continue the journey. The police officer with me felt sorry for me and bought me a pie from the shop on the side of the highway. I wolfed that pie down; I was starving. I think it was the most delicious pie I'd ever eaten! Then I was driven back to the convent.

Rhonda and Cheryl were already there when I arrived, which was right on dinner time. I was guided roughly into the dining room with Mother Catherine's hand firmly in my back. All three of us had to stand while trying to eat our dinner. We could feel eyes burning into our backs. Mother Catherine boomed over the microphone that the other girls were to have nothing to do with us and should go as far as to turn their backs on us as we walked past—because we were a disgrace. We were instructed, "You three are never to speak to each other again, nor gather in a group of any sort."

Yeah, right, that is never going to happen. Not in our lifetime anyway. And what happened to Mother Catherine's statement when she had first arrived? "You can leave if you don't want to be here." Well, we didn't like it and we had left. Obviously she hadn't meant what she said.

Actually, in some ways I think Mother Catherine was a softie as she didn't always follow through. Even though we three girls were instructed to never speak to each other again, Mother Catherine still gave permission for me to go out with Cheryl and Mrs. Kirchener on one Parlor Day when Mom did not appear. Uncle Bert was elderly and starting to get sick. There were a few times when he just couldn't make the trip to bring Mom to Bendigo. Mother Catherine knew that I had been to Mrs. Kirchener's house on holidays and that Mom had allowed her to take me to the train station. So when Cheryl's Mom was happy for me to go out with them, Mother Catherine agreed. She seemed to encourage days out away from the convent, although not every girl had an opportunity to leave like me.

Mrs. Kirchener drove us to the lake in her blue and red station wagon. We sat in the back and listened to the music blaring from her car radio. Mrs. Kirchener seemed much younger than my mom, so therefore was much more hip in my eyes. She understood us. I looked forward to her visits as much as I did my own mother's. We ended up alternating visiting days. Sometimes she would bring Michael, other times not. I loved it when Michael was there, and of course he tried harder to be with her after we met. We always kept it pretty low key when his mother was around as we hadn't actually cemented the relationship in any way during the holidays. So the glances and the sideway smiles between us were kept up, and occasionally our hands would brush past each other while sitting at the picnic table. There was definitely electricity between us.

In Mother Catherine I felt I had finally found an advocate. She had forgiven my shenanigans, without the extreme punishments of Mother Rita, and she had allowed me to experience some care from Mrs. Kirchener. As a result I followed her around like a puppy, always eager and at the ready to try to please her no matter what she wanted me to do. This strange new nun, with the exotic background, deserved my loyalty. I'm not sure "exotic" is the way to describe her, but she had worked for many years in overseas missions, and to me that sounded romantic and exciting, I guess anything other than the monotony of everyday life at the convent was exciting. I was so inspired by her that at one stage during the year I even informed her that I was thinking about becoming a nun, after a young novice had been introduced to the convent. She laughed, shuffling me out of her office and said, "You do not have the makings of a nun, Beverley. You need to consider another line of work." I was devastated … but not for too long. There was too much mischief to get up to yet.

Life was definitely much brighter since Mother Catherine's arrival, although I craved to go home now more than ever. I could see a light at the end of the tunnel and a part of me wanted to zoom towards it. I was now in my fifteenth year and I knew that the trauma of being locked away would soon be over. Yes, I know that the gates were open during the day; they may have been unlocked but we were still not free. I knew that leaving was not an option for me. And daily life was still regimented. Mom had always said that I could leave the convent when I turned sixteen, and that was only five months away. I had so much to look forward to, and a really cool new boyfriend to boot.

25

Jealous Guy and Sweet Sixteen

*"You always get three chances at finding true love.
Michael was my chance number one!"*

My final year, Grade 10, Form IV, was turning out to be pretty cool. Being senior to most of the girls at the convent meant I *could* boss others around the way I had been, but I didn't really take advantage of being top of the pecking order of inmates. I wasn't really the pushy type. Mother Mercy was also tending to turn a blind eye to my shenanigans a little more than usual. All seemed good with the world. We had time to learn some new skills. I learnt to knit and crochet and how to do floral artistry and pottery.

These things replaced working in the laundry for hours every day. My school work was average. I struggled with some subjects and didn't really get much help with them. I excelled in history and had chosen to do various types of history for my final year. Everything else I couldn't really be bothered with. I had my sights firmly set on leaving that place and being with Michael. That was the only thing I could concentrate on.

One day a group of us congregated under the stage, which was in the large hall. Costumes were kept there that were used as part of our drama lessons to create plays such as *Brigadoon* and *Salad Days*. In the latter years, parents would be invited to watch us, as would honored guests from Bendigo who financially supported the convent. Everything you required to put on a show was housed under that stage: props, make-up, furs, pants, dresses, and the list goes on. It was also away from the nuns, a place where we could smoke and not get caught. That day there had to be at least ten of us under the stage, all having lit up at the same time. We were messing with the costumes while we lolled around, smoking and laughing at our own antics. Then out of the blue a burly fireman came rushing down the stairs, yelling, "Are you alright down here?"

We all looked at each other and burst out laughing. We knew we had hit the jackpot. If anything was going to make Mother Catherine upset, this was going to be it. Red faced, and aware of how much trouble we were in, we climbed the stairs, each one of us greeted by the not-so-happy face of Mother Mercy at the top. If Mother Mercy herself had not shown me this spot when she had fixed my hair a few years ago, I would never have known it was there to show the others. Mother Catherine didn't really have a lot to say about our antics; she just advised us that we would be punished. We were given extra chores to do around the place for the following week, but there were no bashings or hair cutting involved. We respected her for that.

As it turned out, Mother Mercy had been walking past the entrance door and had heard the carry-on from below the stage. But when she stepped into the hall to investigate, she saw smoke coming through the floor cracks in the stage from underneath. She believed we were screaming because we had been engulfed in flames. So before attempting to extract us, she had run to the main office to call the fire brigade, who speedily arrived before she made it back to the hall. Talk about priorities. We were not very popular after this. Mother Mercy virtually ignored me for several weeks, but she returned to her old self eventually.

We made a concerted effort not to gather and smoke in such numbers from that day on. We got cigarettes from visitors or by going to the shop when we were out with our parents. I was to find out in later years that Cheryl and Rhonda just blatantly walked out the door and went to the shop whenever they felt like it. Even though I was close to these two girls, I had absolutely no idea they were doing that.

Our favorite place for smoking was now under the trampoline. Mother Catherine had purchased a trampoline, which had been set up outside the back gates of the convent, near the laundry windows. You could be seen clearly from the laundry during the week; however, when the trampoline was not being used, it had to be covered up with a tarpaulin. The tarpaulin provided the perfect cover for us to sit under and smoke.

September school holidays arrived and Mrs. Kirchener picked us up from the convent to take us home to Melbourne. She dropped me off at Mom's house. I'm not sure why she bothered because I was in and out the door in two minutes, already walking to her house to see Michael. He wasn't there and I was disappointed, but Cheryl and I went to Keon Park and met up with our group there.

Over the holidays we had fun and we still hung out after dark in the fields near the station. We had our small fire while we chatted and smoked and the guys drank. But we didn't frequent there as much as we had in the past. I didn't really want to go now; I was more interested in whatever it was that Michael and I could share.

One day as I walked through the lounge area at Cheryl's house, Mr. Kirchener turned to Michael and said, "Great child-bearing hips."

I smiled. I knew that was some kind of compliment, even acceptance, by him.

Then I heard Mr. Kirchener ask, "Well, have you asked her yet?" to which Michael replied, "No, but I'm going to tonight." My heart did a quiet flip flop.

I went into the kitchen and sat down while Mrs. Kirchener was preparing dinner. Little Randy, Michael and Cheryl's younger brother, walked in, fresh from playing in the street with the other kids.

He innocently asked his Mom, "What are we having for dinner tonight, Mom?"

Mrs. Kirchener, quick as a whip, turned and said, "Little boys' sausages," while holding out the knife and tongs as an indication that he should put his little sausage out to be cooked too.

Randy ran screaming from the kitchen, covering his groin, and I just had to giggle. When dinner was dished up, he wouldn't touch the sausages. I'm sure he had a phobia about sausages into his adult years. (RIP Randy 2012.) But that was life at the Kirchener's—fun and love whenever Mrs. Kirchener was about.

After dinner we watched some television, sitting together on the lounge room floor in front of the fireplace to keep warm. We were playing a game together with the other children. All during dinner my stomach had been fluttering, remembering Michael's words that he was going to ask me something tonight. I knew what I hoped it would be.

Finally, just before we were going to bed Michael asked me. "Bev, will you go out with me?"

I gestured yes to him by eagerly nodding my head. "Yes, I'll go out with you, Michael." *Yay! We're going steady!*

"Good. I'll take you to the pictures on Saturday night then. Do you think your mom will let you go?"

My stomach sank. "Yes Michael, she won't care," I responded. I tried hard not to show him how deflated I was. I had thought that asking me to "go out with him" meant he was asking me to go steady, to be his girlfriend. It was just a first date ... Of course, silly me, didn't realize that at that point Michael already considered me to be his girlfriend. I'm slow to catch on sometimes.

Saturday came and I arrived at Michael's for our date. In I walked with my daggy jeans on. And him? He stood there decked out in what could only be called his Sunday best. He even had a cravat around his neck. Slightly old world, but it was nice that he cared enough to dress up for me. He was *handsome*!

Actually, I know I've said this before, but Michael was so handsome, with his dark brown, curly, shoulder-length hair, olive skin, and the darkest, deepest chocolate-brown eyes that you could imagine. He stood about five foot four inches at that point and was of a solid build. He was certainly mature looking for his age, although he still only had bum fluff on his chin. He normally kicked around in jeans and a t-shirt, which suited him better— he was looking a bit too formal— but I went along with it and we walked to the station to catch a train into town.

We saw a movie called *Bangladesh*, a tribute concert given by George Harrison to help support the starving multitudes in Bangladesh. It was fantastic—and I don't just mean the movie. I would soon realize that Michael was really into two things: the Beatles, just like I was (and everyone else!) and me. We petted and flirted with each other throughout the entire movie.

Afterwards, on the train heading home, Michael reached over and grabbed my hand. I felt bolts of electricity shoot through me. Woah! I kept my hand in his and he put his other arm around my shoulder. It felt nice. We talked about the movie, the Beatles, and God knows what else on the trip. It was clear we were well-matched and were meant to be together. We snuck into the house as it was late. Mrs. Kirchener had left the lamp in the lounge room on for us, to light the way. Michael quietly closed the lounge room door, as he didn't want to wake everyone, and we sat and whispered for what seemed like ages in front of the fire. We watched it flicker away until there were only hot ashes left.

They say you get three chances to find true love. Michael was my chance number one! He stood up and reached down to me. I took his hand and he helped me up. Without a word he kissed me warmly and passionately; the kiss did not have the urgency or hunger of a teenage boy. Then he led me through the kitchen, out the back door, and into his bungalow. I nervously recalled a really bad time in my life when I had willingly followed a boy into his bedroom, and so I sat on his bed hesitantly. I momentarily feared history was repeating itself as he put on his latest album, *Imagine* by John Lennon. Of course, he was unaware of my fear, and why; that was my secret.

Michael moved towards me and I stiffened initially to his touch. But he lay down on the bed beside me and pulled me down gently into his arms. There was no struggle, no hesitancy on my behalf, and no force on his. I gave myself completely over to him. Michael gently guided me through the mine field that was playing out in my head, knowing how wrong it all was but at the same time not wanting it to stop either.

John Lennon's *Jealous Guy* was playing on his record player. Michael pointed out to me that *Jealous Guy* was his favorite track on the album and tried to sing it to me. He looked down at me and could see tears were falling from my eyes. He stopped and told me that he didn't want to hurt me, and if I wanted to, we could stop. I told him that I didn't want to stop. I was crying because I really loved him. So we continued. I had been in that situation many times in my life, never under good circumstances. But this felt like the first time in my life. I felt like the giggling, shy, school girl that I was, experiencing young love for the first time. And all the natural feelings that came with it: excitement, hesitation, fear, and lust. I think Michael felt the same as he led me very gently through every step.

We had found ourselves in this situation so naturally; however, I was still very inexperienced at being a willing participant. Michael had no idea of my past and I could never tell him, from sheer embarrassment alone. How would I tell him that I was generally submissive in sex, as my tormentors took what they wanted from me? He was neither hurried, nor rough, and he cared enough to make sure I was happy. No words had passed our lips to suggest that we would end up like this; it had just happened. There was no question of "Will you …?" He had just taken me by the hand and led me. Michael was a great lover, quite mature for his age. For the first time I felt fulfilled in a very innocent and immature way. I spent the rest of the night wrapped up in his arms with my head on his chest, listening to his heartbeat, until I fell into a heavy sleep.

When we woke up, it was about seven in the morning. Michael jumped out of bed. "Shit, quick. Get dressed before they find us."

But it was already too late for that. Mrs. Kirchener knew that I wasn't in the room with Cheryl because she had already checked. I threw on my clothes and ran for the back door to see Mrs. Kirchener already active in the kitchen. I put my head down and tried quickly to head to Cheryl's room, without Mrs. Kirchener noticing how untidy I was.

Without looking at me, she said, "Stop."

I froze in fear. Memories came flooding back of what had happened after Gary's dad had caught Gary and I kissing.

"Where did you spend the night?" she asked. She knew where I had spent the night, but she wanted to hear me say it.

I stammered, "In Michael's bungalow." I just choked. My heart was pounding in my throat and my stomach turning so much I thought I would throw up. *I'm gonna get in terrible trouble.*

She must have caught the expression on my face because without even looking at me, she just said, "Go and get fixed up and don't let Mr. Kirchener know."

I could tell by the tone of her voice that she was not very happy about it. Not that I had expected her to be. But she didn't punish me. The big rod didn't come down on my back. Just feeling that I had let her down and that now she would not think the same of me left me feeling devastated enough. She was like a mother to me and I didn't want to lose her.

Once I was in Cheryl's room, I could hear Michael and his Mom discussing the situation out in the kitchen. Her main concern was not so much that we had spent the night together, but more so the repercussions of what could happen, like me getting pregnant. That hadn't even entered our heads! I had been told two years before by the doctor who had diagnosed my syphilis that it was highly unlikely I would ever conceive, let alone carry a baby to term. I didn't understand what that meant at the time. I would only find out later in life.

Cheryl's reaction to hearing what had happened? "Oh, fuck. Yuck, you didn't? Not with my brother?" She gutted herself laughing and threw herself around so much she fell out of bed.

Holidays over.

※

I tried so hard to settle back in at the convent. I admit I was boy crazy, always craving the attention of boys wherever I went, but Michael was someone special. I couldn't get him or our night together out of my mind. I would lie in bed at night and sleep would elude me. I wondered what our next time together would be like.

One night while I was lying awake, I heard this commotion coming from outside the dormitory window. There were a couple of guys standing next to a car, yelling up at the windows. We all snuck out of bed and rushed to see what was happening. It was quite common place for the boys in Bendigo to swing by the convent on a Friday night, to yell obscenities at the "whores" who lived inside the walls. The obscenities that those guys yelled would curl the hair of the most seasoned sailor.

This was a little different though. They were too far away to make out what they were saying and it was too dark to see them properly; but they were not yelling obscenities. We were herded back to bed as soon as our auxiliary realized that we were at the windows. A week or so later, I found out that it had been Michael with his mate. They had stolen a car in Melbourne and driven to Bendigo to try and break Cheryl and me out of the convent. My hero!

But my hero had ended up driving the same car into the Bendigo Lake that night. The police caught him and charged him. He was eventually sentenced to several months in a juvenile remand center, not far from Bendigo. So, on some Parlor Days I was able to see him during visiting hours if Mrs. Kirchener came to take us out. It wasn't long before he was released and found himself in trouble again and was back behind bars for the second time, just before I was released from the convent. It seems my Michael had a bit of a bad boy streak in him.

I didn't dwell on that, though. I had something more important happening. My sixteenth birthday! *Happy Birthday Sweet Sixteen.* It's strange what crosses your mind when you know you have finally reached the light at the end of the tunnel. I now knew that legally they could not keep me there; I was sixteen, not in the care of the state, and effectively a private boarder, supposedly with rights. My upkeep was paid for, so at any moment I could have walked out the door and there would not have been a damn thing that they could do about it. Well, I knew that in my head, but it was my sense of morality and fear that stopped me.

My birthday came with a mixed bag of emotions. All day I was shunned by my own group. These were the girls I spent most of my time with, but not one would talk to me. When I went into the group room, I was yelled at by Mother Dorothy and told to go back outside and stay there until I was called for. I sat in the courtyard outside and cried. I felt so lonely, so lost, and so not in control of my situation, or my life. Sixteen was such an important number. I could now leave the convent, but would I?

As I thought about leaving, I started to shake with fear, imagining the worst of scenarios happening. So many questions came to mind. *What will I do? Where will I go? Who will look after me?* I didn't know how to look after myself. Then I hit on an idea. *I know. I will get a job. But how do I get a job?* I knew how to dress for an interview, how much make-up to wear, and even how to sit in a miniskirt. But I didn't know how to get a job. I could cook, but where would I get food? I knew that if I returned to live with Mom, nothing would change. There would be those long, endless nights of her calling me out of bed. I would have no clothes and no food. What to do …?

There were lots of questions I couldn't answer. It was at that moment I realized I couldn't leave there. I didn't know how to. So I decided I would stay. I was not leaving. I would do my higher school certificate and wait until I was at least eighteen. *By then I might know how to look after myself.* This decision momentarily calmed me down until I realized there was more probability that I would leave … and then the fear came back again.

Yes, I had a lot of time to think that day. It was turning into quite an emotional roller coaster. It was starting to get dark and the air was turning cold. I covered myself up with my cardigan, pulling my sleeves down to protect my hands.

The circus of thoughts was interrupted by one of the girls from the group room, who came to tell me Mother Dorothy wanted me. I walked into the group room with my head down, thinking what a bunch of bitches they were. *Why are they so nasty to me on my birthday?* I was not happy and I was determined they would feel my wrath later.

But what happened next was far beyond even my wildest imagination. As I opened the door to the group room and stepped inside, everyone yelled, "Happy Birthday!" I looked up to see balloons and smiling faces and a table filled with small cakes and other treats. I could not believe what I was seeing. I had been in that convent for a very long time and never had I celebrated a birthday, not for any girl let alone for me. Then Terry the auxiliary put a record on, the one I would eventually drive all my own children mad with— Neil Sedaka's *Happy Birthday Sweet Sixteen.* De ja vu! Tears welled in my eyes as I remembered my sister's birthday so many years before. She had had a normal birthday party with friends at home, with Mom and Dad. She had dressed me up so prettily. I had always longed for the same but knew that it would never happen. Not now, not ever. I looked around the room at the happy and glowing faces of the girls in front of me, and I knew this had to be the next best thing.

My own children often wonder why I find it hard to celebrate birthdays or special occasions, like Christmas and Easter. It is because we didn't normally celebrate them in the convent. They are just days to me, although I do work hard to try and make it different for my children and grandchildren. I don't always succeed.

But this was a birthday to remember. This was the only birthday party ever held for me in my entire childhood. The girls sung along to the song, replacing some of the words with "from now on you're gonna be Michael's."

The picture of this, with all the smiling faces and a celebration just for me, will always remain in my mind as one moment frozen in time. My very first birthday party—and my last for many decades to come. It was a defining moment. One of those "stand-out memories". The party strengthened my resolve to stay there. I was sure I never wanted to leave. I had no reason to want to leave. Michael was now in Pentridge and there was really nowhere for me to go that I wanted to be.

I'll just stay here.

26

Going Home to No Home

"I had seen this coming like a steam train full blast before I had even left the gates of the convent, but I had been in denial."

THE YEAR 1972 WAS drawing to a close. Exams were upon us and that meant that school holidays were just around the corner. My thoughts turned to home. I was excited that I would be able to go and see Michael, even if he was in Pentridge, and also the guys from Keon Park. More lazy days without a care in the world. Cheryl and I would have some great times together, though tinged with sadness because Cheryl would not be returning to the convent. Me? I was staying, at least until I was eighteen. *Or was I?*

All these thoughts clogged my brain while I should have been concentrating on studying for exams or doing whatever else I should have been doing. I loved daydreaming; that was my escape. I could daydream my whole life away, minute by minute, forever changing the circumstances that surrounded me into something nicer. Don't get me wrong. Mother Catherine had done a wonderful job of changing the overall atmosphere of the convent, even to the point that it was now tolerable to be there. Hey, I was even thinking of staying, voluntarily! However, my daydreaming took me to exactly where I wanted to be, somewhere nice where I felt protected from all harm, and loved, in Michael's arms. Some habits are hard to break, and so it was that on the first exam day I sat in the classroom, pen in hand, paper in front of me, doing nothing until I heard Mother Rose say, "Five minutes."

Oh shit.

Scribble, scribble, scribble.

I handed the paper in and left the room so as not to disturb others doing their exams.

Ha! Who needs it, anyway? This isn't going to do me any good.

On the last day of exams, I walked in, sat at my desk and waited for the timer to start. We had been sitting in that room for two days in a row, mulling over answers, not talking, divided, and unable to bounce ideas off each other. I quickly gazed through the exam in front of me, ticked some boxes, wrote some sentences, shut the book, and handed it in to Mother Rose who sat at the front of the class. I had completed the exam in less than five minutes.

As Mother Rose looked at me, she said, "You never put effort into anything you do, Beverley." As I was leaving the classroom she screamed after me, "You'll amount to nothing, you lazy, lazy girl. NOTHING!"

I turned and looked at her, shrugged her words off, and exited the doorway with a smile plastered on my face. *What is she going to do? Keep me locked up for another year? I don't think so. I am sixteen and I am free …* But did I want to be free? …

I slowly wandered up to the play equipment. We were having our exams on the orphanage side of the convent and we were not allowed to leave the area by ourselves. So I had to sit and wait for everyone else to finish. As I sat on the equipment pangs for home started to creep over me. The words Mother Rose had said were starting to cut, despite my bravado. *Maybe I should just go; I'm not wanted here either*, I thought.

A day or two later, Mother Catherine gathered us all together in the concreted playground. That always meant some sort of announcement. She turned to us and informed us that the convent would not be receiving any girls the next year. *Receiving any girls?* I was puzzled. What did she mean? We all looked from one to the other, slightly confused.

"Some of you will be redistributed to government-owned facilities and the rest of you will be sent home."

Home? No! I don't want to go home. There's nothing there for me. I was suddenly filled with fear. *No. No. I want to stay now. Can't I stay?*

We were also advised that the convent would be saying goodbye to every girl *that weekend*. There were some hoorahs, but there were also a lot of sad faces. I could not comprehend even today how the children who were wards of the state felt, hearing that they would have to move again to another home. Things had only just started to get really good at the convent, even to the extreme of being enjoyable. Some were used to the way of life that the convent offered now; it was unfair. Me? I was confused what I wanted. After all the years of hardship and no freedom, particularly in Mother Rita's days, I should have been shouting with joy at the chance to leave. Yet, there was fear. I still didn't know if I could look after myself in the world, and I knew I couldn't rely on Mom to look after me. The thought of leaving what I had known for four years was scary.

After her speech, I went to her and told her that I didn't want to go home and that I wanted to come back the following year and continue my schooling. She said that was impossible. The convent would be closed to all boarders except the elderly, infirmed, and mentally disabled.

We all spent two very sad days, walking around, chatting to each other, hugging and reminiscing, taking each other's addresses, and hoping that we could meet up again on the outside. We were told to pack our belongings, and on the last day we were to strip our beds, clean our cubicles in the dormitory, and wait to be called as parents and authorities arrived to pick us up.

Recently, I learned that around that time the Federal Government ceased paying a weekly/monthly allowance to religious organizations for each child that they housed or had in care. So that would be why so many of us were let go.

At around 10 a.m. on the Sunday, I was called to the Parlor Room with Cheryl. Mrs. Kirchener had told Mom that she would take me for my final trip home and she was there to pick us up. So into the back of the blue and red station wagon we piled and homeward bound we went. I remember lying in the back of the station wagon and staring down the road at the three tall buildings in the distance as they got smaller and smaller. What once had loomed large and foreboding was now small and insignificant.

Mrs. Kirchener turned the radio on and we dialed up the volume! The radio was blaring and banging out hits like *Children of the Revolution* by T Rex and *Hey Jude* by The Beatles. I can remember sitting in the back of the station wagon with Cheryl, driving down Spring Street in Regent, yelling at the top of our lungs, nah, nah, nah, nah nah nah nah … Ha ha! Leaving the convent was suddenly not as scary as I had thought it would be. There were going to be good times ahead! I was sixteen and was all "grow'd" up. I'd done my time in hell and now I was *free*, free at last to create my own life and future without constraints. A happy future, one of my own making.

It's funny the things you remember. As we were driving down Spring Street, Regent, not far from home, I noticed a light blue and white S Series Valiant driving in front of us. I said to Cheryl, "Look at that car. There's no-one driving it!"

"Nah," Cheryl responded. "It's a guy from Regent who lives around the corner from us. All the girls are after him for his car. He's so small I've never seen him." I laughed. So small his head couldn't even reach above the steering wheel it seemed!

On we drove until we reached the front gate of my house. I gave Mrs. Kirchener a quick hug and thanked her for bringing me home. When I walked in, I found the back door was locked. We still lived in the half a house that Mom had rented many years before and our entrance was at the back of the house. I sat on the small brick fence with my suitcase and waited. Nothing! So I slid the louvres out of the small kitchen window and shimmied in, like I had done many years before when I was twelve. I hadn't grown much, so I still fitted.

As I sat in the kitchen, I thought about all the things I had to do the following day. Get up early and somehow go and find a job. I thought about all the places that I would go to and ask. Then I heard the familiar footsteps coming up the sideway. Mom had a very heavy step and I could always recognize it. I too have the same heavy step.

Mom walked in and I scared her half out of her wits. She wasn't expecting me to be sitting in the kitchen. She demanded to know how I had got in, so I told her that I had climbed in through the louvered window. She wasn't happy but said, "I suppose that's okay. I didn't realize you were coming home today." I felt like an intruder in what I considered to be my home.

I settled in, as it was late afternoon and there was no rush to be anywhere now. I had the rest of my life to do as I pleased. Things had changed in the time I had been at the convent. By then, instead of Mom drinking till all hours at the pub, she would bring her booze home and drink there. At around 10 p.m. after having sat in the kitchen listening to Mom go through all the usual stuff, I let her know it was time for me to go to bed because I had to get up early to find a job.

"Ooh, la-di-da!" came the reply.

"No, Mom. It's just later than I am used to going to bed and I have a really big day tomorrow." I tried to reason with her. I was so tired. With that I got changed and climbed into the bed that I had shared with Mom as a youngster. It didn't take very long at all for things to return to normal.

"Beverley!" came the yell from the kitchen. It woke me from the very beginning of my slumber.

"Yes, Mom."

"Come here. I want to talk to you."

I knew there and then that Mom was caught in some kind of weird time loop and nothing had changed. I was still to be the little girl who did as I was told every night, and I would probably not get to sleep until three in the morning. If tonight was going to be like normal, then I would be the lazy arse kid who wouldn't help herself and go get a job.

We played this game until about one in the morning, when I finally turned to her with tears of exasperation in my eyes and said, "Mom, that's it. I can't do this anymore. I can't stay here with you if you are not going to respect me and let me sleep."

She went crazy, accusing me of all sorts of things. "You're bloody hopeless. I didn't ask for you to come home anyway. Nobody wants you. That's why I had you locked up! If I had my way, you'd still be there!" She spat out every word like a knife, but there was more…

"You're a troublemaker," she hissed, her face getting red. "You're not worth shit. I had to work bloody hard to keep you at that convent and you don't even appreciate it."

The many faces of my mother. There was nice Mom who didn't drink and then there was ugly Mom when she was sozzled. This was ugly Mom, the one who could not be reasoned with, who did not understand reasoning. No, it was no use even trying.

I couldn't take it anymore. I walked into the bedroom, grabbed the bag that I had brought home with me, packed a few of my belongings into it, and walked back out into the kitchen.

I gave her one last chance and begged, "Mom, I don't want to leave you. I have nowhere else to go and nobody to go to, but I can't go through this every night. I want to be able to get a job and help you, but I need sleep to do that. You constantly calling me out of bed every time I put my head on the pillow is not helping me. I'm begging you to stop, please stop."

I knew if I walked out that door there was no coming back. But she made my decision for me that night.

She yelled at me over and over to get out of the house. She screamed after me. "You have no respect for me or anyone else. You're a spoilt little bitch, Bev, just bloody spoilt. How dare you talk back at me and put me down when I've given you everything. Think you're bloody better than everyone else. I'll show you better…"

As I walked down the dark sideway into the night, the screams continued … "You're gonna end up pregnant just like your sister, and when you do, don't ever bother coming back! In fact, don't bother ever coming back here again, ever, you're not wanted!" And the back door slammed so hard the house rattled. Mother Rita's words likewise rattled around in my head. It was like she was standing beside me and repeating into my ear, "Your mother doesn't want you."

By then I had made it to the front gate. I turned and looked at the old house, the place I had called home for so many years, when in fact it wasn't home. I didn't have one. I never really had one. I was unwanted and unloved, and now I was by myself.

I felt the emptiness that I had always had inside me bubbling up into my throat. I couldn't breathe. I wanted to go and bash on her door and seriously tell her what I really thought of her. Adrenalin surged through me and my heart pumped furiously with anger. Damn having been brought up with so much respect for those older than you. Damn society's restrictions. I felt so empty in the end. I no longer fitted here. I couldn't return to the convent—I didn't belong there either—and I had nowhere else to go. Tears and snot smeared across my face as I walked away that night. All my dreams of a bright future dashed, gone with the empty bottles of beer that tomorrow would be thrown into the trash.

The lyrics to *World*, a Bee Gees song, sprung to mind as reality set in. I walked away and just kept going. I didn't turn around. I didn't dare look back. Forward was the only way for me now.

∽

I had known nothing would change. Actually, I had seen this coming like a steam train full blast before I had even left the gates of the convent, but I had been in denial.

Even though I knew Michael wasn't there anymore, I went to the only place I knew where people would help me. I walked the four kilometers alone, no stranger to the dark, with my suitcase, arriving at Cheryl's bedroom window at about 2.30 a.m. I tapped on her window and woke her from her sleep. She pushed the window up as far as it would go and helped to pull me in. I whispered to her what had happened.

"Don't worry. Mom will help," she reassured me. "We'll talk to her in the morning."

I jumped into the bed opposite and laid there for the rest of the night, wondering what was to become of me, again. I was so scared that I would get into trouble for being there, but I couldn't stop myself from sobbing. Mrs. Kirchener heard the ruckus and came into the bedroom. She wrapped her arms around me in a big hug.

"Honey, you're welcome to stay. How can I throw out the girl my son loves?"

But she had rules that we would discuss in the morning, and they were to be followed. First was to get a job. At that I broke down, again, and told her that I didn't know how to get one.

Next morning Mrs. Kirchener sat with both Cheryl and I at the kitchen table and showed us how to go through the job section in the paper. Then she told us both to get dressed and she took us to our local employment office. At the employment agency we were able to inspect all the jobs that were available for us on the board. It wasn't long before I was interviewed by an employment officer. He looked at my skills and the fact that I had just left school. I could type and my typing speed was excellent. I typed over one hundred words per minute with one hundred percent accuracy. However, I did not have the results of any exams to prove it, so secretarial work was out of the question. They did have an opportunity for a clerical telephonist at a small goods factory, a few suburbs over. They rang ahead and arranged an interview time for me. It was for the next day.

Cheryl had a similar interview with a different company. Mrs. Kirchener took us shopping and bought us both some clothes for the job interviews. After that she said, "Now you are on your own. I think you'll both do well." I wished that she was my real mother. I really needed someone like her in my life, but hopefully one day she would be my mother-in-law and then it would be the same anyway.

The new day dawned and I was up early, dressed, and ready to go to the interview. It was exciting. Cheryl's was later than mine, so Mrs. Kirchener drove me to my interview and waited for me in the car.

I walked into the office. It was a very small rectangular office that had three desks pushed up against the small far side wall. One was a small desk at the end of the room, and then there were two larger desks. The desk at the top of the room next to the separate office, which housed the office manager, had a small six-holed plug and cord PABX next to it. The small goods factory of Allenby's was not large. It was quite small with a butcher's shop attached to the front of it for sales to the public.

The stench overwhelmed me when I walked in, but it wasn't so gross in the office with the door shut. I stood in the doorway and was beckoned to the small office at the end by a woman who sat looking over the top of her glasses at me. She had papers around her desk everywhere. In fact, there was a lot of paperwork everywhere.

I sat in front of her, making sure I did not cross my legs and kept my feet tucked gently to the side and back under the chair, indicating to her that I was a lady. She asked me some questions about my schooling and my typing, and then she told me that I had the job. She said that I could start on

Monday, although she wanted my exam results as soon as I received them.

I thanked her for the opportunity and told her I would not let her down. I was introduced briefly to the two other girls in the office and was shown the very small desk at the end, which was where I would sit. With that I was ushered out of the door. I stood there for a moment taking it all in. It was unbelievable! Then I ran to the car to let Mrs. Kirchener and Cheryl know I got the job. I was so excited. I was on my way. I would prove to my mother and all my other critics that I was something, someone, that I did exist and I could make it, even if I was alone. Then it was Cheryl's turn to go for her interview. I believe she got the job, but I can't clearly recall.

The weekend came and went very quickly. Both Cheryl and I had headed for Keon Park and mucked around up there the same as we always had. Monday was upon us before we even knew it. I dressed for work and took the train from Regent to Northcote, ensuring I was at least fifteen minutes early for work to impress the boss.

One of the girls spent the day with me, showing me what needed to be done. I caught on very fast and after that was left by myself. The following Friday I received my payment for the week—nineteen dollars and ten cents. I couldn't even begin to determine what to spend it on, but I knew that I had to pay Mrs. Kirchener some board for looking after me and for the clothes she had bought me for the interview. I was left with enough to make it through till the following week. I had never had so much money in my life. It was a great feeling.

Again, the weekend was fun, hanging around, just being a kid, doing the things we loved to do. Then we headed off to Keon Park to run amok. However, this night there was a notable difference. As we sat by the campfire in the fields near the railway station listening to the radio, Robert, who was one of the regular group, began to act a little weird. He'd had a bit too much to drink and became angry as I think that he and his girlfriend had fought with each other and may have broken up. Anger was not normal for him. He was generally cool, even tempered, and easy to get along with. Everybody liked him. He was just incredible. But tonight he was different; he was upset, indifferent, and angry.

I'd had a little crush on Robert since the first time I had seen him many years ago. He had the most charming smile, beautiful brown eyes, and a curly mop of dark brown hair on his head. He walked with animation and had a bounce to his step that was so cute. He had a tremendous personality—all of us girls liked him. Sometimes at the convent I had daydreamed about us being together, but then I put it out of my mind because I knew he would never be interested in me. Besides, I was Michael's girl now and I would wait patiently for him to get out of jail.

Robert got up and stormed off into the fields away from the others. One of the guys started to go after him, but he was grabbed round the wrist and told to just leave him alone and he'd get over it. I stood up to go and make sure he was okay. I have never been one to sit back when someone else is hurting and leave them to it. I walked in Robert's direction. He had walked a fair way as the light from the fire was dim in the distance. I could just see the glow from it and a few people moving around.

I stood and looked down at Robert, who was sitting on the ground, and asked, "What's wrong?"

He looked up and then without a word, grabbed me and pulled me down to the ground like he was possessed by something. I tried to scream and he put his hand over my mouth, saying to me, "You know you want me to do this. You always have. I've seen the way you look at me." He fumbled with the fly on his jeans and ripped at my underwear. I struggled to stop him and bit him on the hand, but eventually he had me pinned down and my underwear far enough down my legs that he could enter me. I immediately went into my submissive zone and just stopped and lay there, staring at the stars and wishing I could be someplace else. In the distance I could hear the Bee Gees song, *I Started a Joke*, playing on the small radio as it travelled unimpeded through the night air. I thought how appropriate that song was for me at that very moment in time. Tears were streaming down the side of my face.

Once again someone had made me feel less than human. Once again someone who I had trusted had taken a part of me that I could never get back. I hadn't noticed that three more of the guys had followed me into the field and were now waiting in line to take their turn with me. For the first time while being around these guys, I was frightened. I had known them for nearly four years. Nothing like this had happened before. Nor had I seen them do anything like this. But time had passed and really we were strangers. They were no longer boys. They were young men; testosterone was pumping and pack mentality was taking over. In hindsight I can see these guys were not bad; this was just a situation that was starting to get out of hand.

Then when I thought that my situation was hopeless, a strong hand reached down and pulled Robert off me. Brownie, who was another long-term member of the Keon Park gang of boys, had followed the others into the field. He stood above me with his fist still firmly gripping the clothing around Robert's shoulder and said to Robert, "You don't want to do this, mate."

Robert shoved him away and pulled himself together, mumbling under his breath as he walked off, making his way back to the other group. Brownie then turned to the others and said, "Fuck off, it's not going to happen." He then reached down, grabbed my hand, and helped me up. He also helped me sort myself out and we walked back to the fire where I told Cheryl that I wanted to go home. Brownie understood and nodded to me as we stood up together to leave. She couldn't believe me when I told her what had happened. I would never return to Keon Park again.

Another week came and went. I was good at my job and enjoyed it. I also loved to stir the guys in the factory as I went out to grab the bookkeeping files. I made sure to work it as I walked towards the ladder, stirring them up all the way. I had to climb a short ladder to get to the files, and it was the era of the miniskirt. I always got massive wolf whistles until my boss would make an appearance and look at them with contempt. She had made it her personal crusade to protect the innocent angel who had been raised in a convent from the likes of those horrid men who worked on the factory floor. Little did she know I encouraged the conduct, just not when she was about. I felt that a little flirting couldn't be too dangerous in the workplace. Nothing would happen, not with my personal protector around.

Another weekend rolled around and Cheryl and I sat there looking at each other. What to do? I was not going to go to Keon Park after what had happened; I would rather die. We decided to walk to the phone box and call around to see if people were home that we knew. We *intended* to go visiting. Of course, more often than not, things don't always go as planned.

27

JACK

✥

"If that's the way she wants it then she's lost her daughter."

As Cheryl and I walked to the phone box along Spring Street, I noticed the S Series Valiant that I had seen weeks earlier parked by the side of the road.

I poked Cheryl and said, "Look, there it is. He must live there."

She shrugged and dragged me forward. We walked across the road to the phone box and I stood there with the door open while Cheryl made the phone calls. Next minute I saw this guy standing at the gate of the house where the car was. He was beckoning for me to go to him. I shook my head from side to side. He beckoned again and I shook my head again.

This went on for about five minutes. Then he yelled out, "Come here!"

"No!"

He shouted back, "What are you, a scaredy cat?"

"No, I'm just busy!" I yelled back.

Again he yelled for me to go to him, but this time I yelled back, "I'll meet you halfway." So when I saw him start to walk towards me, I started to do the same.

Cheryl cocked her head out of the phone booth. "Oi, where do you think you're going?"

"I'll be back in a minute, hang on."

As I got closer to the guy, I found myself mesmerized by his blue eyes and cheeky smile. He had brown hair halfway down his back and stood about five foot two, not much more than me. I had reached my halfway point, so I stood and waited for him to reach me.

"Hey, I'm Jack."

"I'm Bev."

"What are you girls up to?" he asked as he rubbed his hands together.

"Oh, we're bored," I replied. "We're ringing around friends."

"Well, why don't you come for a drive with me?"

Yeah, why not? I told him I'd have to ask. I walked over to the phone box and asked Cheryl if she wanted to go for a drive. She said no and kept talking on the phone.

"Well, I want to go," I said

"Bev," she said, putting her hand over the mouthpiece, "it's not a good idea." Why didn't I listen to her?

I begged her to cover for me with her parents and she reluctantly said she would. She knew she wouldn't change my mind. With that, Jack and I jumped into his car and just cruised around for ages. He told me all about himself. He was single and his girlfriend had recently dumped him and he was still upset. He said her name was Diane and that she was a nurse who worked in the country. He was unemployed as he had contracted industrial dermatitis from his plumbing apprenticeship, which he had been doing with his uncle. He finished his explanation with saying that he lived with his Mom and her boyfriend, and he too was bored.

"Do you drink?" he asked.

"No," I said because I didn't really drink. I had some drinks at Keon Park and wiped myself out—that was enough for me.

"Do you have any money on you, so I can buy some beer?" he asked. I handed him a dollar from my pay and we drove to the bottle shop. He grabbed a couple of bottles of beer and said, "Let's head somewhere quiet."

We drove out onto the Hume Highway and turned off down a dirt road, where we sat talking in the car while he had a few drinks. He reached across to put his arm around me and I lamely told him that I had a boyfriend who was in Pentridge but would be home in a few months' time.

That didn't deter him. He reached across and pulled me over to him.

Thoughts of "ride for a ride or you walk back" came into my head. When he kissed me, it was intense, but the whole time my stomach turned because his breath reeked of beer. It was a smell I just could not tolerate from years with Mom. He kissed me again and I did my best to kiss him back. At that moment I felt I had gone too far to turn back. I had broken what I had considered a sacred trust between Michael and me.

I was feeling upset with myself but kept going anyway. Perhaps it was some excitement I was looking for. Just having the comfort of another person's attention, particularly a male's, even for just a moment in time, seemed worth the trouble. And let's not forget Jack's Valiant. I think the main thing I found appealing about Jack was his car, and his car only. (You have to remember I was only sixteen!)

Well, one thing led to another and before long Jack put the front seat down, which flattened out to make the perfect bed. I knew what was expected of me next, and of course I was perfectly obliging. I knew the score in these situations. *One more doesn't matter*, I thought with resignation. That's what my early childhood experiences had led me to believe. I didn't know if this was going to be a once off or if I would see him again, and honestly, after I had crossed that invisible line in the sand where I could no longer give myself honestly and faithfully to Michael, I just didn't care anymore. I was so angry with myself and that anger boiled over into resentment for the person who had helped to put me into this position—Jack! Quite frankly I didn't care if I never saw him again. After he finished doing the deed, he put the seat back up and drove me to the end of the street where I was living.

I quietly made my way in, showered, and put myself to bed. I knew I was late and had broken curfew. Cheryl was still awake and whispered to me, "What happened?" I told her we had just driven around and then he dropped me off.

I had arranged for Jack to pick me up from work the next night, and he did. He drove me back to Regent, but not so close to home that I could be caught with him. I gave him some money for petrol because he told me he didn't have much. He asked if he could have some more money for drinks later too. So I gave him a little extra.

Later that night after dinner, he picked me up near the telephone box again. Cheryl didn't want to come, so she stayed home. Mrs. Kirchener asked me where I was going and I made up some lame story. I felt terrible lying to her. If she knew that I had been late the night before, she hadn't mentioned it.

Why in the hell am I back in this bloody car? What is the attraction? Nothing!

Again we picked up some beer and drove out to the same place on the Hume Highway. We did the deed again and returned somewhat later than the night before. I say 'did the deed' because, really, it felt like a chore. This became a nightly event until finally Mrs. Kirchener questioned where I was going every night and why I was returning so late. I couldn't lie to her.

"I've been driving around with this guy, Jack," I said, rather sheepishly.

The look on her face showed me she was not very happy with me. "You're grounded. You are not to see this Jack again. You're Michael's girlfriend and you should respect him and your relationship."

Deep inside I agreed, but how could I tell her it was already too late?

"If I have to keep you locked up in your room until Michael gets out of jail, I'll do it, my girl." I didn't doubt her.

The following weekend Cheryl met up with some friends on the Saturday night and slept over, which left me with nothing to do. So, again, I snuck out of the window to meet Jack.

I don't know what it was that kept me going back to meet him. He didn't make me feel happy, excited, or even loved. I think somewhere deep down inside me I had a need to be used and abused. I had no self-esteem and certainly didn't believe I was worthy of any better, so why not just give it out to whoever wanted it. At least that ensured that I got the attention I needed. I mistook sex for love, and even though I wasn't quite sure what love was, this was as close to it as I thought I was going to get. I didn't deserve any better and I shouldn't ask for any more than this.

When I woke up Sunday morning, I got up to go to the bathroom and I found the bedroom door locked. I was shocked. I knocked loudly on the door until eventually it was opened.

"Why is the door locked?" I asked Mrs. Kirchener.

"To make sure that you're not sneaking out at night." Suddenly I felt like

I was a prisoner again. I panicked as I couldn't cope with the feeling of being locked up again. So I did the only thing I knew: I ran. I got dressed, packed what little I had in my bag, and escaped through the bedroom window. No goodbyes, no "thank you for having me". I felt guilty, but all I knew was I had to run.

I ran down the street, crying, towards Jack's place. I knew I could never go back now. I would not be forgiven after all she had done for me. Anyway, it was now too late for Michael and me. How could he ever trust me to be faithful if I couldn't trust myself?

I was dressed in a pair of hipster jeans, with a tiny crocheted crop top. My hair was long, halfway down my back, and fell loosely into ringlets. I had no shoes and my face was stained by tears. I was a slip of a thing and looked like nobody loved me, which was not far from the truth. I carefully opened the gate at Jack's house and stepped inside, closing the gate behind me. I walked up to the door and rang the doorbell. A small woman opened the door. She had a grumpy face and her hair had tight curls in it like it had been in curlers. She stood there, looking me up and down.

I squeaked out, "Is Jack here, please?"

She answered, "No, nobody by that name lives here," and closed the door in my face.

As I turned to step off the small porch, I noticed Jack's car parked in the backyard. I turned and rang the doorbell again. This time when she answered, I told her that I could see Jack's car in the backyard.

She looked at me with beady little eyes and said, "That is my son John's car. No Jack lives here," and she closed the door in my face again.

I got the distinct impression I was not welcomed, so I left her yard and went down and stood at the phone box, hoping that Jack would come out. He didn't, of course, until very late in the afternoon.

I was to later find out that after he dropped me off, he would go home and drink the beer that his mother provided for him on tap. He would argue with her until the early hours of the morning, often abusing her. When he went to sleep, he would sleep until early afternoon—something he would continue to do until the day he died.

I ran to Jack and told him what had happened. He put my bag in his car and we got in and drove off. I told him that I didn't think his mother liked me, and he agreed. He said that his mother had yelled at him when I had left and told him to get rid of the little slut. He also told me that if she had her way, he would just stay at home for the rest of his life and be her little boy, and he didn't like it. (So he said; in fact, I was to discover that Jack was quite happy to be treated like a boy and be taken care of.)

Never did I stop to think why it had taken him so long to come out of his house to see where I was. He asked where I was going to live and if I could go home to my mother's house. I told him I couldn't and that I had nowhere to go. We discussed my situation until late in the night when he decided that I would just live in his car. He said that after his Mom left each morning to go to work, he would sneak me in so I could get dressed and get ready for work. Then he would take me.

So that is what we did for a week or so. We slept in his car at night in a vacant lot near the Hume Highway, and each morning we would drive to his place where I would shower and get ready for the day. Then he would take me to work and he'd go back home to sleep.

One morning I was just waking from my sleep when I heard rustling around the car. A police officer put his head through the front window.

"Good morning," he said in a deep, gruff voice. "Beautiful day. So what are you two doing all the way out here?"

Jack sat upright and explained to the police officer that he had been drinking the night before and rather than attempting to drive home drunk, we had pulled over and he had slept it off. The police officer thought that was quite reasonable. The officer then went on to explain how factory workers had reported seeing a car parked there every night. Jack said it wasn't us, stating we had only been there the one night.

"Well, you'd best be on your way then. But if I see you here again, I'll do something about it."

I don't think he believed our story, but at least he was giving us a warning. I was only sixteen and Jack was twenty-one, and without parental consent Jack was actually committing a crime by having sex with me—carnal knowledge—which to my understanding is still a crime today. Since our parking spot was no longer available, we had to find a new area for me to sleep. Jack found a deserted piece of land just near the river that ran by the new Northland Shopping Center.

After a week or two, money started to get scarce because my pay didn't seem to go as far as it used to. Probably because I was paying for Jack's beer and petrol. He was now spending more time with me in the car every night and less time with his mother at home. Then he started to show a nastier side. He asked for more and more beer money, and in return he would talk to me like I was a bit of dirt, push me around, and yell at me if I wore something he didn't like. If I threatened to walk away from him, he would become really nice again, promising me the world. It was all very confusing, but in some way familiar. In my sixteen years I hadn't really seen what a healthy relationship looked like.

My bond to Jack tightened as he became the epitome of everything that was familiar; again I felt comfort where I should have felt fear. In the midst of a huge fight in the car one night, I needed to go to the toilet. Jack told me to get out and go behind the car, but I sensed danger. The hair on my arms and the back of my neck stood on end and I refused to get out, demanding that he take me to the nearest railway station so I could use the facilities.

Again he refused and the fight worsened. He reached across the front seat of the car and punched me in the face as he yelled at me to just get out and do it there. Tears rolled down my cheeks from the shock and pain. I just sat there and stared at him. I was sorry for being so demanding. I figured I deserved it as I shouldn't be causing him so much trouble.

I opened the door and got out of the car. Jack asked, "Where are you going?"

"To the toilet!" I replied as I stumbled in the dark to the back of the car. I wiped the trickle of blood from my lip, pulled down my underpants, and started to pee. As I started to feel relief from emptying my bursting bladder, I suddenly felt a hand groping at my crutch, ripping at me. It all happened so fast. I turned around really fast in the direction of whoever was groping me, losing my balance on the loose gravel. The dark figure that I could only just make out was now trying to force his way onto me.

"Jack!" I screamed. "This isn't funny. Get off!"

Now I had pee and dirt all over me. If this was a joke, it had gone way beyond funny as he was now hurting me. I went to pull his hair to get him off me and there was no hair! All I could feel was a bald head. I screamed a blood-curdling scream as I realized that it was not Jack. My senses had been right all along. Somebody had been watching us in the dark. I think that had been my very first experience with ESP, as I like to call it, which now seems to happen to me a lot.

At first on hearing my screams, Jack had thought that I was mucking around, given that I had told him I thought there was someone outside the car before I got out. But when I let out the blood-curdling scream, he put his foot on the brake pedal, which lit up the rear of the car so he could see in his rear view mirror. He saw two figures at the back of the car, not one, as I had fought my way back to my feet and was leaning on the boot lid. With that he jumped out of the car and ran like hell after the guy, who was too fast for him and got away. Jack ran back to find me still standing at the back of the car. My crotch area was bleeding, my hair had been pulled out in clumps, and I had urine and mud all over my backside and legs, which were now all housed safely back inside my jeans.

I knew something was terribly wrong. "I need to go to the hospital."

He put me in the car and drove to Preston and Northcote Community Hospital (PANCH) as fast as he could. We reached the emergency center and told the triage nurse that I had been attacked. I was taken into a cubicle straight away. I was cleaned up and stitched, blood tests were taken, and the police were called. After several hours of waiting for the police to appear to make my statement, the doctor came back into the cubicle. He closed the blinds behind him and walked to the side of the bed. "You are a very lucky girl. You could have lost the baby."

Baby? Baby? Baby? I repeated blinking my eyes in disbelief. That last word rang out in my head, over and over ... *Baby*. I could just hear my mother.

"But I'm not pregnant!" I cried back at the doctor.

"Yes you are, and by my estimates about six or so weeks. But I can't be sure. Is the young man outside the father?"

I said, "Yeah, I suppose so."

The doctor asked if I wanted him to give Jack the news. I told him that I would, so the doctor left the cubicle, drawing the blinds on the way out. Jack came in and looked at me, quite scared after what we had been through. I didn't know how to tell him, so I just blurted out, "I'm pregnant."

He did not respond well. "Aren't you on the pill?" he asked tensely.

I thought about it for a second then turned and asked, "What's the pill?" I really had no idea. They didn't talk to us about that at the convent.

"Oh fuck, no," came his reply. "You fuck'n bitch. You trapped me. You set this up from the start, didn't you?" It was more a statement than a question. "Mom was right. She told me that was all you were after."

"No!" I cried. "I don't know what the pill is; I don't."

He walked out, leaving me there in the hospital all by myself. The police came and took a statement, but I couldn't really give them much information. It had been dark and I hadn't really seen the man's face. So all I could tell them was that he didn't have any hair and he was about my height.

In the early hours of the morning, I was released from the hospital. There was a chill in the air and Jack had all of my clean clothes. I was barely dressed and had nowhere to sleep. I walked from the hospital to Jack's house where I could see his car in the backyard. There were no lights on in the house, so I knew his mother was asleep. She slept in the room next to him, so there was no way I could even knock on his window without her hearing.

My clothes were in Jack's car, but I couldn't go to his car without getting caught either. So I walked back to the cluster of shops just near his house and curled up in the doorway of one, trying to keep warm. It was the middle of March 1973 and the nights were starting to get cold. The next morning I saw his mother, Mona, and her boyfriend, Charlie, head for work. They were officially "not living together", as she was a "good Christian woman" beyond reproach.

I waited until they were out of sight and then ran to his front door. I kept ringing the doorbell, trying to wake him up, just so that I could get my clothes because I had to go to work. He wouldn't come to the door.

I went through the back gate into the backyard and tried the car doors one by one; the passenger side was unlocked. I quickly jumped in and grabbed my stuff, then climbed over the back fence to make my escape. It was obvious that he didn't want to see me anymore, so the farther away from him the better. At the same time I was petrified he would catch me. Jack had already started to show me a brutal side of himself and I didn't feel up to fighting him off that morning.

I bundled all my worldly goods, which was a handful of clothing that I had managed to acquire in my short time since leaving the convent, and I didn't look back.

I walked down the street towards the railway. I was exhausted. I had no money for food and I felt physically sick in the stomach. I didn't know where I was going to go. I had nowhere to go and now I couldn't even go to work. I hadn't been able to wash from the night before and there was blood and dirt on my clothes and they stunk like urine. I walked up onto the platform of the train station, making sure to stay near the end of the platform. Morning commuters were busily coming and going, so by boarding the train at the end carriage in Regent, when the train pulled into Thornbury station, I knew I could just jump out and remain undetected.

I wandered around Thornbury aimlessly, not knowing what to do. I ended up back at Mom's and sat on the small brick fence that edged the path leading to the back of the house. Even if I could speak to my mother, what would I say? "Hello, I'm pregnant." Regardless, I sat and waited. I waited all day and into the evening. I didn't dare go into the house. I wasn't wanted; I didn't belong there anymore. I leant my head against the fence, hoping with all my heart that my mother would take me back, that she would help me. I didn't know what to do. I was sixteen, pregnant, and homeless, with not a soul in the world to help me.

Then I heard those familiar footsteps coming up the sideway. I knew it was just a matter of moments until I would have to confront her. My heart started pumping, the adrenalin rushing around my body preparing me for imminent conflict. As I stood up, my mother's nose went straight into the air.

"Mom," I said.

"What do you want?" was her response.

"I need to talk to you for a minute," I replied.

"What? Are you pregnant or something?" she retaliated, accusingly. My head was spinning. *What? How did she know?*

"Yes," I cried.

"Well, serves you bloody well right. You know best, don't you Miss Know-It-All?" came her reply. Before I could even answer she continued, "Get out of here and don't ever darken my fucking doorway again. I want nothing to do with you, not even when the baby is born. Don't bother telling me or trying to see me to get me to give in—'cause I won't. Now *get lost!*"

By the time my mother finished, I was gulping so hard I could hardly breathe. My world, what was left of it, was crumbling around me. All the dreams and hopes for the bright, happy future I had envisioned were slipping away faster and faster, out of my reach. It was tearing me up inside that my mother could just pass me over like a piece of garbage on the street, and for what? Why? Because she had a drinking problem and couldn't admit it? Because she had forced us into this situation by having no control over her actions and by blaming me for them? I was totally gutted. I could not believe that my own mother would speak to me like this, and she really meant it.

In my entire life, I had never heard her swear. Is this how she had treated my sister? … What was I to do now? Her words had cut me to the bone, more than anything else that Mom had ever done. More than when she hadn't believed me about walking to school when she was sick. More than when she sent me away to the convent, disowning me. My heart was shattered. As I walked away, this time I also felt something I hadn't felt towards Mom before. I felt anger, very, very strong anger, tinged with hatred.

If that's the way she wants it then she's lost her daughter. I will never, ever forgive her for this. Ever!

28

Homeless

"… a young woman in moral danger."

WHERE TO GO? I remembered that on the way to Mom's I had passed some double story flats being built a few doors up from Mom's house. The brick walls were up and the basic concreting had been done. The plaster was on the walls, but they had not yet closed the entrance doors.

I headed back there now and walked up the stairs to the top level, glancing in each doorway to find something to lie on. It was dark and cold. I still hadn't eaten, but truthfully my stomach felt so queasy I don't think I could've stomached anything. Water out of people's front taps was enough to sustain me for the moment. Then I spotted a tarpaulin on the ground with some paint tins and other items. I pulled it over to the wall and sat down, pulling the tarpaulin over me to keep off the cold. It didn't take long for me to doze off. Sleeping was uncomfortable with my head against the brickwork. So I rolled up the end of the tarpaulin to use as a pillow and lay down. It wasn't long before I was fast asleep.

The next morning I awoke with a big stretch. I opened my eyes and found myself looking straight into the faces of two strange men. They looked down at me with quizzical expressions on their faces. I sat bolt upright and stood up so fast that my head started spinning and I had to lean against the wall. I wanted to run but couldn't find my feet. Fear had my feet glued to the floor.

They were painters and were both talking at me at the same time. I couldn't understand a word; I think they were speaking Italian. It was hard to tell. I was feeling really woozy. Suddenly one of them grabbed my arm and I panicked, thinking they were trying to apprehend me to call the police, and I jerked my arm away.

Fearful thoughts were flashing through my head. I was in a very precarious position. I was classed as *a young woman in moral danger*, and that was enough to have me put away into another institution, probably Winlaton, as a state ward until I was eighteen. I'm surprised my mother hadn't reported me, knowing I was pregnant and homeless. If I were to be put away, they would also take my baby when it was born. I didn't want to go to Winlaton and I certainly didn't want them to take my baby away. When the other man pulled out his lunch sandwich and offered it to me, it was only then that I realized they were merely trying to help me, not harm me; the other man had been just trying to steady me.

They helped me back to the ground and thankfully made me eat. I scoffed down that sandwich. Afterwards, they offered me a hot coffee from their thermos flask. The coffee was strong and nasty, not really to my liking, but I thanked both of them for their kindness and drank it. I then quickly made my way out of the building and to the station so that I could clean up and go to the toilet.

I sat on the toilet for what seemed like an eternity as I pondered my next move. I think maybe I was praying for a drip dry situation as well, as station toilets were not very accommodating back then. Now they have lovely soft toilet paper. Back then they used to rip up old phone books. With the stitches intact from the attack, wiping myself was quite painful. I had no personal care items with me as I had left them behind in Jack's car. My hair was a mess, so I brushed it back with my fingers and tied it into a knot to neaten it up.

I walked out of the station and drifted towards High Street, the main street of Thornbury where shops and shoppers lined the street every day. I felt grubby, like a street person. Well, I was a street person, as I had nowhere to live.

I found myself treading familiar ground as I walked through St. Mary's school and church grounds, my old school. Parents were dropping their children off to school. I must have looked quite a sight as most parents pulled their children away from me. I rounded the corner into Kerrie's street and walked up to her house and knocked on the front door, even though the door was never closed I always respected their home by knocking first.

Mrs. White yelled from the lounge room, "I'm in here!"

I walked down towards the voice and rounded the corner to see Mrs. White nursing several sick kids with spots.

"Oh, poor little things," I said. "They look so sick."

Mrs. White responded, "Yeah, they have German Measles."

"Oh," I said. "I had my vaccination for that, so I shouldn't catch it. Do you need some help?" My German measles vaccination was the only vaccination out of the many that we were given at the convent that I was told the name of.

Mrs. White raised her eyebrows and looked me over quickly, saying, "You've been doing it rough." I nodded and then broke down in tears and told her the whole story. When I got to the part about being pregnant, she said, "You can't be here. The kids have German measles; the baby might catch it." I assured her it was all okay; my vaccination would protect me. She reached over, grabbed me, held me tight, and just let me cry it out.

I was home!

Mrs. White was gorgeous. She had eleven children and more room in her heart for every blow-in that came along. With that she said, "Go and have a bath or a shower, put your stuff out in the back room, and share the top bunk with Debra. Kerrie had moved out to live with new husband Ian already, so there was a spare bed. She also had another of the girls' friends living there as well, who was also pregnant but was staying with friends until the house was cleared of German measles.

I made myself at home. I finally felt like I had a home. It was just accepted that I would stay there until whatever arrangements I could make for myself came to be. I was happy again.

I had not seen Kerrie for so long, so when she dropped in later in the day it was like a huge reunion. I told her what had gone on and she said that Ian would take me up to Jack's house to talk to him about it all. She said Jack had to step up and accept responsibility for what had happened; it takes two to tango. I agreed and Ian drove me to Jack's house to see him.

He went in and got Jack, telling him that he needed to sort out what was happening. After Ian spoke with Jack for nearly half an hour while I sat in Ian's car, Jack climbed into his own car and drove off.

Ian came back to me and said, "Sorry, I tried. He doesn't believe it's his."

We drove back to Kerrie's house in silence. Kerrie gave me a cuddle and reassured me that everything would work out. Debra and Kerrie closed ranks around me to protect me. They were great friends. I realized I had missed them a lot.

A few nights later we tried again. Ian drove me to Jack's place and I sat in Ian's car while he went in to talk. Then out of character Jack turned and started to walk towards Ian's car. He asked if I would come to his car, so I did. Ian waited in his for me to finish.

Jack and I spoke and yelled at each other for the longest time, and then Jack agreed that he would support me through the birth but that was it. He would prefer I had an abortion.

I was elated. He asked for Kerrie's address, so I gave it to him and he said that he would come and see me the next night. I jumped back into Ian's car and we drove back to Kerrie's house.

I was greeted with a very cold reception from Kerrie. "Where the hell have you two been? What have you been up to? Why did you take so long? Are you playing up together?"

I was shocked. "Kerry," I answered, trying to reassure her, "we've done nothing like that at all. I just spent a lot of time with Jack trying to sort out our differences. Ian waited for me in the car to bring me back home. I'm sorry it took so long."

I wondered why Kerry, my friend, could even think like that. This was as far from the truth as you could get. I respected Kerrie—she was my best friend—and hitting on her partner was something I would never have considered. In our absence the woman from across the road had come over and put the idea into Kerrie's head that Ian and I were having an affair because we were taking so long. I was livid.

Only the night before I had confronted this same woman—let's call her the *bitch* (you can tell I didn't have much respect for her)—about her affair with Mr. White, Kerry's father. I told her she should back off because he was married to Mrs. White, not her. I had only found out because I caught him with her. I felt protective of Mrs. White who was in my eyes my savior and the epitome of a perfect Mom and wife.

Well, the night got worse. The bitch across the road, who was obviously stewing over my accusations to her the night before, came over for a showdown. She demanded that I come out the front and confront her.

Debra warned, "Don't go; she will really hurt you." But I knew I could hold my own in a fight. I'd been there already in the convent and I wasn't about to back down now, especially not after she had convinced one of my best friends that I was having an affair with her husband. I was fuming.

A time was allotted with Kerrie as mediator and I fronted outside. True to her word, the bitch arrived with her oldest child in tow, all puffed up in the chest, spewing verbal crap everywhere.

"You need to shut your mouth and stop telling lies about me," I said.

"Or what?" she asked, nose up in the air.

"Or nothing. You just need to stop telling lies and face up to what you're doing yourself." At no time did she deny her relationship with Mr. White. Besides, everyone seemed to know what was going on.

The next minute I felt this really hard blow to my stomach. I doubled over in pain but not before grabbing a fistful of skin from her neck and hanging onto it for almost the entire fight. It was on for young and old. She punched. I punched. She bit me and I bit back, after telling her that only dogs bite. She tried to scratch my face and I left her with four scratch marks the length of her cheek. She backed off before I did and spewed a barrage of abuse towards me as she tripped over her own feet trying to get across the road to crawl back into her hole.

As soon as she was gone, a massive spike of adrenalin hit me and I started shaking. I shook so hard I'm sure my teeth almost fell out. Debra came running out to help me as I stumbled back inside.

"She had no right to hit you in the stomach. She knows you're pregnant," she said.

Shit! For that short time I had forgotten I was pregnant. Anger had overtaken me and I forgot about the precious life that I had within me. I would never forget again.

The next night, true to his word, Jack arrived to pick me up. I ran out to the car, happy to see him as I thought that now I wouldn't have to do this all alone. I went to wrap my arms around him, but he pushed me off.

"You're not wearing that fuck'n outfit out with me," he said. "It makes you look like a whore. Go and get changed."

I had a dress on that was a mini but was loose and felt comfortable. It was a maternity dress I had borrowed from Kerrie. I dutifully turned and did as I was told immediately, coming back out in a pair of jeans and a jumper. Once in the car, he growled at me.

"Don't you ever dress like that again or I'm gonna belt you one." Lovely.

Then he told me something nicer that got me excited. He told me we were going to the drive-in. I'd never been to the drive-in before. My excitement built even more as we got closer to the drive-in.

Then he turned into the street at the back of the drive-in, and, to my surprise, pulled over and parked. He turned to me and said, "Roll your window down or we won't be able to hear it."

"But I thought we were going in," I said, perhaps a little whiney.

"You're not working anymore. How do you expect I can afford the drive-in?"

"Well, when are you going to get a job, Jack?"

"Are you stupid? I told you I have dermatitis. I can't work." And that was that.

I reminded him that there were other jobs.

"No there isn't," he said. "I'm going to be a plumber." He continued, saying that he couldn't do anything else, so he would just have to wait until he got better.

I could tell he had already been drinking and he had another bottle open now. I had to persist with the line of questioning, didn't I? … "How much have you already drunk?"

"You should mind your own business."

He reached over and I stupidly thought he was going to pull me closer and kiss me. I'm a Libran and a true romantic. Instead, he opened my door, turned sideways, shoved his foot in my hip, and kicked me out of the car. He then drove off, leaving me on the nature strip.

There were other cars there, but nobody took any notice or came to help. That's the way it was back then. I stood up and brushed myself off. I waited for a while, hoping he would come back, but he didn't. So I turned and started to walk the five kilometers home to Kerrie's. My hip was hurting where he had kicked me, which made walking a little difficult.

I arrived home at about eleven o'clock and Mrs. White was in the lounge watching late night television when I walked in. She commented that she hadn't heard the car.

"I walked home."

Mr. White was across the road with the bitch and the kids were all in bed. Mrs. White beckoned for me to come and sit by her and chat.

"Do you really feel it is wise to stick with Jack? He doesn't treat you very well."

I looked sadly at her, knowing very well where her husband was. She was obviously speaking from years of her own experience.

"I've got no other choice," I replied

"But honey, you can get unemployment benefits and make your own life."

Unemployment benefits? I hadn't known I could get that. I told her I would go tomorrow and sort it out. The convent didn't prepare us for life at all. I hadn't known about the pill and I hadn't known about the dole. All I knew was how to pray (and I didn't do that) and how to sit properly with a miniskirt on and put on make-up. I was soon to find out there was even more I didn't know.

I went to the local job center the following week to apply for unemployment benefits. After talking with the unemployment officer behind the desk for a little while, she advised that because I was expecting a baby, I could not receive unemployment benefits and quite simply they had no other means of helping me.

In fact, I now know that legally I had been entitled to unemployment benefits until nine weeks before the birth of my baby, but I had been facing the bias of the day embodied in that unemployment officer. I was pregnant and *unmarried*. I might as well have been a leper. It was a case of the employee taking government policy into her own hands to suit her own agenda. She advised me that the local courthouse may be able to give me ten dollars a fortnight for hardship.

She deliberately did not tell me my rights. She advised me that there was no help available at all. There was no unmarried mothers benefit until a few years later. I took that clerk's word as gospel, of course; she was the authority, the one behind the desk.

The very next morning I woke up feeling pretty sick. I had a temperature and felt like I had a cold. Mrs. White came out to check on me and when she pulled up my nightie to check my stomach, she gasped and put her hand to her mouth. "I thought you said you had had the German measles vaccination." I told her that I had definitely had it

"You have German measles. You need to go to the doctor."

I got up and got dressed, and then Debra took me to the local doctors who confirmed Mrs. White's prognosis. He told me that as I was expecting, the baby may have problems due to the illness and I should prepare for the worst. I didn't know what to do.

Jack showed up about a week later, chucking orders around, telling me that I was leaving the Whites and going with him, and added that because I had stayed in the bloody hovel, I had jeopardized his child's life.

I couldn't believe it. I just looked at him and yelled, "You don't bloody care, anyway. These people do, and you continuously do bad things to me and think it's alright. These people don't. Don't you dare put them down; you're not willing to help or support me, so fuck off." Oh, how I was always so willing to stick up for others but not myself.

I turned on my heel to march back inside the house but was suddenly painfully stopped in my tracks as my head was yanked back by the hair and Jack pulled me hard towards the car. He growled at me in a very low, menacing tone through his two top teeth as they bit into his lower lip, "Don't you ever walk away from me again." He had the look of a madman in his eyes. Then he spun me around by the hair, opened the front door of the car, and shoved me in. "Don't fucking move."

He went around the other side of the car and got in. He then drove really fast to the end of the street and braked recklessly. He spun out the wheels as he turned the corner into High Street. I thought he was going to kill us. When we arrived shortly afterwards at his mother's house, he got me out of the car and dragged me inside. When we reached the kitchen where his mother Mona and Charlie were having a cup of tea, he announced, "She's pregnant and it's mine."

His mother wasn't shocked at all. She just calmly got up from the chair, looked me up and down, and said, "I knew it. I knew that little harlot would trap you."

I didn't dare say a word. This was a power play between Jack and his mother.

Then Mona said, "Oh well, we'll have to find you somewhere to live, won't we? Can't bring up a baby in a car, can you?" directing the question at me. The statement was accusatory, and why it was only directed at me I don't know. This was her son's baby and I reckoned he should share some of the responsibility—but I daren't say anything. She had known all along that I was living in Jack's car.

As she pushed past me to leave the kitchen, she stopped and looked at me and said in a low, quiet voice, "You know, he throws ashtrays at me and bashes me, don't you? Now it's your turn, and I can't think of anyone else who deserves it more."

I was shocked. I stood there with my eyes wide open. Charlie didn't say a word. Jack didn't retaliate or protect me either. I felt like I had arrived in a mad house, and, boy, I was not far from wrong. I spent the night in Jack's car in the backyard, alone, as his mother had told me she couldn't possibly have us sleeping in the same bed under her roof—we were not married—unlike herself and Charlie who were exempt. At least at Mrs. Whites I had had a warm bed.

The next few days moved quickly. Before I knew it, Jack's mother had paid the bond and rent on a flat and fully furnished it. She chose all the furnishings and the finishes, sparing nothing for her precious boy. And then the baby stuff started to appear.

Shortly after we moved in, I received word from my sister Robyn that my father was going to be visiting her and wanted to see me. So Jack took me to Lalor to visit.

When we arrived, Robyn directed us to sit in the lounge room, while everybody else was sitting in the kitchen. I could see my dad and Dixie with a little boy, who I would later find out was my younger, half-brother Mark. My sister and her husband were in there also. It was all so very formal, not like a normal family gathering. Something was up.

Dad came into the lounge room first, but not straight away. He closed the double doors over before he turned to us. Jack stood up and shook Dad's hand. I thought that was a good start. I wanted so badly for someone to accept our situation. Dad sat in the chair and talked about what was going to happen to us. He spoke about how unprepared young people are to be parents and how a child impacts on your life in ways which you couldn't possibly imagine. Lack of sleep, irregular feeding hours, no more freedom and, of course, the amount of attention that the child will need while growing up. He didn't think that we were up to the job.

But I thought *Who are you to judge? Aren't you the one who walked out the door when I was a youngster and left me to starve?* I didn't feel he had a right to preach to me. He then said that he had come down to help me. He wanted me to go back to Forster and live with him. They would arrange an abortion and I could go back to school. *Too little too late for my liking.*

Abortion? "I don't want an abortion. I want to have the baby."

I would have gladly got in the car with him that night and gone anywhere if he had told me that I could keep my baby. I believed having an abortion was a mortal sin, and there was no way I was going to hell, not for him, not for anybody. Besides, the life growing inside me was a baby, my baby, someone who I believed would love me forever, no matter what. Finally, someone to love me and accept me.

Of course, I was wrong. It was wrong and selfish of me to want to bring a baby into this world for the sole purpose of having someone who would love me, warts and all. At such a tender age, and with a lack of life experience and nothing but hardship as a teacher, this seemed like logical thinking. Really, at sixteen, was I mature or equipped emotionally enough to have a baby? No, I wasn't, but like any teenager when I had an idea in my head, I stuck with it.

Every person then came in individually and spoke to us. It was like an intervention. Where were they all the other times I needed help? Finally, I stood up and advised them all that Jack and I needed to go out to the car and talk privately about what we wanted to do. Dad said to take our time. We left the house and when we got to the car, I said to Jack, "Go. Take me home." As we drove past the shops, I got Jack to stop the car at a phone box. I rang Robyn and told her that we would not be coming back and we had decided to keep the baby. I could hear the disappointment in her voice. I found out some years later that if I had gone back, my father would have kidnapped me.

Even though, during the sixties, attitudes to marriage and sexual relationships were broadly changing, with the pill available and many young unmarried couples deciding to live together, this was yet to be reflected in the provision of social support for unmarried mothers.

An Abstract from the Website of the Council of Single Mothers and Their Children:

> 'There was little income support for single mothers, either through the Commonwealth Social Security System or through services provided by the states. Under the Commonwealth Social Services Consolidation Act (1947-1970), the mother of an illegitimate child [was defined] as a person who does not qualify for any other pension, benefit or allowance, who is unable to provide for himself and his dependents without assistance. These women would sometimes be entitled to special benefits at the discretion of the Director General; however, the rate was not to exceed that of sickness benefits and was usually varied according to age. In effect, women could receive special benefits for a period of 12 weeks before the birth of a child and six weeks after (this may be exceeded if a woman was prevented from working due to breast feeding).

The only Commonwealth benefits for which single mothers were automatically eligible were the Maternity Allowance, on the birth of a child, and child endowment, a non-means tested payment to all mothers with dependent children, irrespective of their marital status.
www.csmc.org.au Reproduced with permission.

29

My Rollercoaster Pregnancy

"Please attend the hospital immediately for urgent admission."

ONE DAY LORRAINE, the other pregnant girl who had been living with Mrs. White, visited me and asked if I had seen a doctor for the pregnancy yet. When I replied that I hadn't, she asked if I would like to go with her to a pregnancy clinic the following week at the local hospital. I happily agreed. Quite simply, I hadn't known I should go to one, so I was glad that she had told me. It seems like there was always something new for me to discover out there in the world. Seriously though, one of my convent friends told me that when she was told she was pregnant, she wouldn't believe them because she wasn't married. The nuns told us that you had to be married before you could have children.

Lorraine arrived quite early and before long we headed off to the hospital. Jack had gone out so he wouldn't know I'd gone. At the hospital, Lorraine stuck with me through the process, waiting for me while I collected a small sample of urine and helping me fill in forms. It felt like Lorraine was my mentor; she took me under her wing and protected me for this part of my life's journey. After a short wait I saw a doctor. He felt my stomach, did an internal, arranged a blood test and told me that he wished to see me again the following week. As Lorraine and I headed home she promised she would come with me again. She went her way home and I made the rest of the way to the flat by myself. My stomach started churning the closer I got to the flat.

I didn't really know what was waiting for me. When I walked in the door, Jack was home.

"Where have you been?" he asked gruffly.

"At the hospital. I saw a doctor about the pregnancy," I explained, somewhat warily. He didn't say anything about it. *Phew.* He just returned to his bottle. Jack had recently started drinking three to four bottles of beer a day. His mother paid for everything including weekly deliveries of beer, so all he had to do was drink. On this day he had started early, so by late afternoon he was pretty drunk. I sat on the lounge quietly. I had learned that it did not take very much at all to tip him over the edge when he was in this state.

We just sat there. Ten o'clock came and I stood up and told Jack that I was going to bed because I was tired. I'd had a big day, walking to the hospital, a good seven kilometers each way.

"Sit back down," he ordered.

"But I'm tired, Jack. I walked to the hospital and back," I pleaded. His demeanor was different. Going to bed before him was something he hadn't minded until that night. It was a power play. He had to prove he was in control of everything I did, including my sleep.

"Pfft, go and put yourself to bed then," he said grumpily. It felt like Mom's all over again. I got into bed and was just falling asleep when I felt my head being ripped off the pillow by my hair. Jack had come into the bedroom and was pulling me out of the bed. Then up came his other arm and wham! His fist thumped into my face.

"I didn't tell you that you could go to fuck'n bed, slut! Nobody goes to bed before me!" he yelled. He dragged me back out to the lounge room and threw me towards the lounge. I sat down and did not move a muscle—I was petrified. My mind was telling me to go, to run away as fast as I could, but run to where? I could go back to Mrs. Whites. She would take me, but he would come after me there and he might hurt the kids. Who would protect me? So on the lounge I sat, until about 4 a.m. when he decided that he'd had enough to drink and he got up to stagger to the bedroom. He hadn't told me that I could go to bed, so I stayed on the lounge, staring at the bedroom door in case he rushed back out at me. I was in fight or flight mode. It was only when dawn broke that I allowed myself to finally drift off to sleep, sure that he would not come after me now as he was in a heavy sleep.

The next day after he left, sometime in the early afternoon, I checked my face in the mirror. I was sporting a bruise on my cheekbone just below my right eye where his fist had connected. He had warned me when he left to have his dinner ready when he got home. I prepared chops, mashed potato, and peas, which I would figure out was just about all the guy would eat—steak, sausages, chops, mashed potatoes, and peas for breakfast lunch and dinner, except for the occasional egg in the morning. Today was chops. His mother would bring more food tomorrow; until then it was all we had left. Jack never gave me any money for groceries. The only food we received were weekly groceries delivered to the door by his mother and her boyfriend.

At 6 p.m. sharp his food was ready, as ordered. I sat there waiting for him to come home. Six o'clock came and went and there was no sign of him. So I did what I had seen his mother do. I put the plate on top of a pot of boiling water and covered it with a lid to keep it fresh and hot.

At 10 p.m., which was the closing time for hotels back then, he rolled in the front door with his best mate, Keith. I didn't know where they had met up; I didn't ask. The less questions the safer. He staggered to the table and demanded that his and Keith's dinner be put on the table immediately.

"I don't have enough. I've made yours, but I don't have any for Keith. I didn't know he was coming home with you," I said.

Throughout my explanations, Keith was trying to apologize for keeping Jack out so late, but his words were just background noise. Jack jumped up from the table and backhanded me across the face, throwing me backwards across the room. I lost my footing and tripped over the small coffee table and landed flat on my back. He was yelling at me to get his fuck'n dinner *now* and that I better have enough for his mate too.

Keith turned to Jack and said, "Come on mate, that's not right. You shouldn't be doing that. She's pregnant." He tried to stop Jack coming at me. I got up and scrambled to the kitchen. Jack sat back down at the table and waited, staring at me with a look that said he could easily have killed me there and then and he wouldn't have cared. He felt embarrassed that his mate had stuck up for me but saw it more as an affront by me for simply breathing. I got another plate out of the cupboard and divided Jack's dinner in two, putting one chop onto Keith's plate and dividing the mashed potatoes and peas. I had nothing else to cook. Keith was telling me it wasn't necessary because he wasn't hungry. In the meantime, Jack was telling him that it was and he should sit down and eat. He was being quite forceful, so Keith did as he was told to.

I returned with the two plates in my hand and put them on the table in front of them.

"What's this shit?" Jack asked.

"It's your dinner."

"Where's the fuck'n rest of it?" he yelled, while standing and pushing his chair backwards so hard it fell over onto the floor.

"You told me to give Keith dinner too, and that is all we…" My words trailed off because I realized he was running at me with his fists up. I took off, running really fast towards the front door, tripping over the chair as I went. He tripped over the chair also, which gave me a small lead so that I could get out of the flat. We lived in a top story unit, so I ran around the balcony and turned the corner to start down the stairwell. By the time I reached the top of the stairs, Jack was right behind me. Up came his fist again, bang right in the side of my face. I lost my footing and fell the full length of the stairwell. Keith came out just in time to see Jack hit me.

He'd been Jack's friend for a very long time, but he turned to Jack and said, "You disgust me, Jack. You'll never see me again," and with that he stepped over me at the bottom of the stairs, helping me up. He said to me, "If I were you, I'd be leaving too." Then he left.

The rest of the night was pretty much more of the same thing because now I was responsible for the loss of his friend. Jack hit me at random in various places around my chest, back, and stomach. Eventually, he fell asleep in a drunken stupor. I just sat on the couch and looked at him until I thought it was safe enough to doze off. I never mentioned the beatings the following day because I didn't want him to start up again.

A couple of days later, I decided to make roast rabbit for dinner. I had watched Mom do this several times, so I felt confident that I could too. I made the stuffing, got the rabbit, cleaned him out then filled him with stuffing and sewed up his innards. I put the roast on early because I wanted it to be cooked just right. I knew that the vegetables had to be cooked for about half an hour; however, I really had no idea about the rabbit. So I put him on at about one o'clock, thinking that would be enough time to have him on the table at six o'clock. *Yeah, five hours should do it.* It smelt so good. At half past five I put the vegetables in and by six o'clock everything was cooked. For the first time Jack complimented me on my cooking, saying that it smelt so good he couldn't wait for dinner. He rubbed his hands together in eager anticipation. I pulled the vegetables out of the tray and made the gravy. Then, feeling really pleased with myself, I unwrapped the rabbit from the tin foil to carve him up. Everything was on the plate waiting to go. I put the knife into the rabbit to start carving and … he just fell to bits, crumbling into a pile of ashes. The only thing that was solid about him was the stuffing.

My heart started pounding and my head was spinning. I was once again in fight or flight mode. I knew what was going to happen, but strangely enough the sight of the rabbit crumpled there in front of me made me laugh. For the first time ever Jack laughed with me, or I should say at me. For the rest of the night I heard what an idiot I was, how I couldn't cook, and so on.

And then came the evening beating.

It didn't matter how much I tried to avoid it, he always found some reason for it to happen. Now I knew what his mother had been talking about. It was my turn.

This was my life, every night the same. Jack would sit at home drinking, and after he had a belly full of beer, the beatings and abuse would start. I just couldn't imagine a different life. As a child I was used to being mistreated, so nothing new here, just bigger and more painful. I was getting used to it and I couldn't comprehend that there could be a better life out there for me. Nobody had ever really shown me that there could be.

⁂

The next week came around quickly and Lorraine arrived to take me to the prenatal clinic for my follow-up appointment. I sat in front of the doctor as he explained to me that they had received the results of my blood test and I was *not* pregnant. I shook my head in disbelief. I had this rounded belly and it certainly wasn't from over-eating. I was lucky to get food.

"I have to be pregnant," I stated.

"Well, I'm sorry but you aren't. Sometimes phantom pregnancies happen when a woman wants a baby bad enough," he continued. Believe me, the last thing I had wanted at that stage of my life was a baby!

Lorraine stood up and said, "You're a quack. She is bloody pregnant and I'll be taking her somewhere where she will get proper care."

With that she dragged me out the door, stating as loudly as possible for everyone to hear, "Phantom pregnancy. Fuck'n quack."

We left the hospital and boarded a tram for East Melbourne. Lorraine paid. Shortly after, we arrived at the Mercy Maternity Hospital. She walked me through to their emergency department and told the doctor what had happened. They agreed that they would look into it and started the procedures—first the urine test and blood tests and then the internal. I hated the internal as they always hurt me a little and were uncomfortable. Lorraine said that this was where she was having her baby and that they were wonderful. She assured me they would get to the bottom of it.

And they did. The doctor returned and told me that from physical examination I was definitely expecting, around three months. But they would have to wait for blood tests to confirm this, as the urine test was negative. He told me to go home and made an appointment for me to attend the prenatal clinic the following week.

The next day I received a telegram that read: *Please attend the hospital immediately for urgent admission.* Jack snatched it from my hands and read it too. Surprisingly, he agreed that I should go and said he would take me. I put together two nighties and some toiletries. I didn't have a dressing gown or slippers, so I went with what I had. Jack dropped me at the front of the hospital and drove off. I walked inside to the reception desk and waited until I could get the attention of the clerk. When she turned around, I went to show her the telegram but before I could she said, "Beverley? Beverley Forster?"

MY ROLLERCOASTER PREGNANCY

"Yes," I replied. And then I recognized her! "Gracie!"

I was gobsmacked. It was my friend from St. Mary's before I had gone to the convent. We had so much to catch up on, but when she spotted the telegram, she deemed that to be more urgent and said she would come to see me in the ward later on. I was directed through to emergency and prepped for admission. The doctor I had seen the day before came to see me. He explained that my blood test had come back positive, but only just. I had low estriol levels.* There are a range of issues that can arise from a mother having low estriol levels, from mental retardation of the fetus to threatened miscarriage. After I was admitted, I had a drip threaded through my body from my arm. I was told I would need to stay on this drip for the duration of the pregnancy. It went into my arm and was fed up through my shoulder then down through my abdomen and into the fetus. I was not the one that needed to be treated—the baby did. A couple of days later, Jack turned up to visit. He had a few drinks in him and got a little noisy when I told him that I couldn't go home with him. He tried to take the drip out of my arm and was asked to leave by nursing staff. Amazingly, he did what he was told—with the assistance of a security guard.

Things were going well with the pregnancy and the treatment was working. The only concern was the amount of weight that I was stacking on. The doctors decided that I could have a two-day break each week now that levels were coming back to normal. So Saturdays and Sundays I was allowed to go home for the weekend. Charlie would come and pick me up and I would come back by tram on the Sunday afternoon, when they would re-insert the drip again.

The weekends were scary, but who did I have to tell? I hoped that the doctors would cancel them, but at the same time I was scared that if they did, Jack would go off the deep end. My blood pressure was on the rise and by the time I got back on Sunday afternoons, it was through the roof. After talks with the matron, who was concerned for my safety, the doctor told me that I was not allowed out on weekends anymore. She had seen the bruises

---

* Estriol is one of the three major naturally occurring estrogens, the others being estradiol and estrone. Estriol is produced almost exclusively during pregnancy.

and the state in which I returned to the hospital after each visit, and noted that it was getting worse. She also had sat on my bed and held my hand while I cried after each weekend visit home. I had told her that I was really scared that Jack would do something stupid. She said not to worry, that I was okay, and he couldn't hurt me there.

One Saturday night after lights out, around 10 p.m., I felt a strong tug on my hair. Then a fist came down into my face. The tearing at my hair got stronger, pulling me out of the bed.

"You fuck'n bitch. Think you can hide here, do you? You're coming home now. I need my dinner. Why aren't you there cooking me my fucking dinner?"

Jack had come into the hospital and was assaulting me at my bedside. I let out a scream and the night nurses came running. Security restrained him and escorted him from the hospital. He was told that he was not welcome back anymore. The nurses resettled me and the next day a lock was placed on my ward door. Jack was officially informed by the hospital that should he do that again, they would take out an injunction to prevent him coming into the hospital. He only came into the hospital once more after that—a couple of days after the baby was born.

A few weeks after Jack's assault, when I was eight months pregnant, I asked the doctors if I could please go home for the weekend. I was feeling cooped up—cabin fever. It started to feel like when I was locked away in the convent, and I wanted a break. Looking back I can see that being in the flat would have been just as confining. But at the time it was familiar territory and it was mine. Anyway, they agreed as I kept pestering.

While I was back at home, Jack kept disappearing throughout the day, and on the Friday night he didn't come home at all. The next morning I saw him leaving another flat across from us. A young girl named Brenda lived there. I realized he had been having a relationship with her while I was in the hospital. I found out from the lady downstairs that it had been going on for quite some time.

When he went out on the Saturday, I confronted her. "Do you know that he has a girlfriend—me—and I'm pregnant, with his baby?"

She said, "Yeah, so what? He doesn't want the baby and he doesn't love you. So why should I stop seeing him?"

I told her that she needed to back off or else. In hindsight, I should have let her keep him. But I could see whatever security I had for my baby's and my own future disappearing.

Late on the Saturday night, he came home. He had been to Brenda's house and she was not happy that I had gone there. She had given him the "me or her" choice. He was angry and riled up and went straight for me as he walked in. He grabbed me around the neck, banging my head up against the wall. "How dare you go and see my girlfriend. Who the fuck do you think you are?"

I told him that I thought I was his girlfriend, since I was living with him and having his baby. He opened up the door and pushed me out, telling me to fuck off.

I said, "Okay, if you want me to go, I will." I started to walk quickly towards the stairwell to leave. He ran up behind me and shoved me so hard in the back that I lost my footing, sending me face first down the stairwell. Here we go again. Bang, bang, bang. Down I fell, feeling each step hit my eight-month pregnant belly on the way down.

"You're not leaving with my baby," he said. He ran down the stairs and grabbed me by the scruff of my neck hair, using it to drag me back up into the flat. Then he closed the door. He ranted and raved at me for such a long time until he fell asleep. Then I realized that I was in trouble. Pain was shooting across my stomach and I thought I was in labor. I walked out the door and up to the telephone box in High Street, where I called an ambulance. I waited there for them to come and they took me back to the Mercy Maternity Hospital. Thankfully, he had done no harm and I wasn't in labor. I was just experiencing pain from the fall and possibly false contractions—these days known as Braxton Hicks. I was not allowed to leave again … until Gracie's wedding.

I was nine months pregnant and Gracie was getting married. She invited me to her wedding and I really wanted to go. I promised the doctors that no harm would come to me and that I would be back first thing on the Monday morning, so they let me go. Jack dropped me off at the wedding; he didn't want to go. Besides, he wasn't invited. It was a fantastic night. We danced and ate lots of continental food. It was laid on as you would expect from an Italian wedding. Every morsel was a melt in your mouth moment. Everybody wanted to touch my belly and feel the baby kick. I felt really special. Then during the night I must have been enjoying myself so much I wet myself. Unbelievable. I was so embarrassed. This pregnancy stuff … I rushed into the toilet and stayed there until the tide had subsided. There was a little bit of blood in my knickers, but I dismissed it. I walked home and put myself to bed. Jack wasn't there. I guessed he was over with Brenda. I actually didn't mind now; it gave me a break.

On Sunday morning I woke up and still no Jack. So I got out of bed and pottered around. I was feeling off but no contractions. It still seemed so far away for me. Later in the day, Jack came home. He had been with Brenda—I could tell as he was happy. But his mood quickly changed. He started throwing sexual innuendos at me, asking me how many men I'd fucked at the wedding. I begged him to leave me alone. I could see a beating coming. I told him that he could harm the baby if he hurt me. That didn't seem to matter to him.

I was walking through the bedroom to go to the bathroom when he grabbed me from behind. He pushed me face first into the bed so I could hardly breathe. He then pulled down my knickers from behind, held me down firmly at the base of my neck, and raped me. He had so much strength; I couldn't fight my way out of his grip. So I just stayed still, hoping that the attack would be over soon and that he wouldn't feel the need to hit me along with it. There was one difference this time. When he had finished with me, I couldn't move. I was in so much pain. I knew he had hurt me in some way. I knew I wasn't in labor because the pain was in my back. I didn't give a shit about his rule this time. I just climbed into bed, pulled the sheet over my head, and cried myself to sleep. He left the flat and returned in the early hours of the morning.

Around eight o'clock the following morning, I woke to Jack's foot in my back pushing me out of the bed. He yelled, "Get out of bed and cook me breakfast, you lazy, fat, fuck."

I pushed his foot away. "I can't. I'm in too much pain. I can't move. You'll have to make breakfast yourself." A part of me couldn't believe I said it, but I really felt I couldn't move. Well, that didn't go down well. I felt a full-on kick to my back and I landed flat on my backside on the floor.

"You're fucking useless!" he yelled. He stormed out of the flat and shortly after I heard a door slam on the other side of the complex. It looked like somebody else would have to cook his breakfast. I sat there for a very long time until finally I pulled myself up and got dressed. I grabbed my things and made my way to High Street to catch the tram. The conductor realized that something was very wrong with me and asked me where I was going. I told him I was trying to get back to the Mercy Maternity Hospital. He assumed I was in labor, so when we got to the stop where I should get off, he jumped down and flagged a taxi driver to stop. He and a couple of passengers helped me off the tram and into the back seat of the taxi.

The taxi driver wasn't very happy with the fare and sped to the front of the hospital. He jumped out and ran around to open the door and pulled me out of the back seat. He helped me to the curb where he left me sitting in the gutter at the front of the hospital. Unable to find anything to help me to get up, I just sat there crying. At the exact same time, Gracie was on her way to morning tea and had seen the whole thing happen. She ran to me and said "Stay here. I'll get help."

I couldn't move anyway. Next moment a doctor and several nurses with a trolley were outside with me, and before I knew it I was in the emergency center where, after examining me, they told me that my waters had broken. They asked when it had happened. I couldn't tell them. I had no idea. I couldn't bring myself to tell them I had wet myself on the Saturday night—too embarrassing. No-one had forewarned me about this waters breaking business. So much to learn!

When I got back to the ward, I confided in the matron that I had wet myself at the wedding. She explained to me that my waters had broken and that I was very close to moving into stage two of the birth. When that happened, I would be taken to the labor ward. They gave me something to help me sleep.

In the early hours of the morning, I woke up to blaring lights in my eyes, and nurses and a doctor around me. I heard the doctor say, "Take her down now. She's ready to deliver."

With that I was pulled off the bed and over onto a trolley, which was then wheeled to the labor ward. Everything was blurry because of the drugs they had given me. I would wake up and look at the clock in the closed-in room and it would say two o'clock. I would wake up again and it would still say two o'clock. I looked around. There were no windows. I didn't know if it was day or night. I didn't know how long I had been there or what day it was; it was quite disconcerting. All I could see were instruments, gas masks, and nurses coming in and out. In the background I could hear women screaming as they delivered their babies. The only mainstay was a young man who sat beside me, and every time I woke he would try to comfort me, telling me that he would be with me the whole time. He held my hand until I fell back asleep. (Poor bugger. I found out later he was an intern and he needed my birth as his last one to qualify. It was an interesting experience, having a male hold my hand gently to reassure me. There's always a first time!) I would wake up and my legs would be in stirrups, the doctors all looking into my crutch, shaking their heads and one saying, "We'll have to do a manual turn." Sounded like a driving lesson. I was in lots of pain.

Another doctor arrived and told me that he wanted to put a spinal block in my back to stop the pain. He said it was a new procedure and it could pose some risks, but it would stop all the pain. Stop the pain? Yes, please. I readily agreed. The doctor told me that I had to touch my head to my knees, but as hard as I tried I couldn't do it. I was huge. But after a couple of attempts he was able to position the needle and the good stuff started to take away all feeling I had from my chest down.

They still kept me heavily sedated, though I remember waking at one point to hear the doctor ask, "Have you managed to get in touch with anybody yet?"

"No," said a nurse.

"Keep trying," said the doctor, "we don't have much longer."

"Much longer for what?" I groaned groggily at him. Dr. McAfee, who was my obstetrician, sat beside my bed and explained to me that the baby would soon be in fetal distress and that I was showing signs of maternal distress. He went on to say that my mother would not answer the hospital's calls and they could not get in touch with my boyfriend. Because I was a minor they needed an adult to sign a consent form for me to be given a caesarean section. He told me there was no way the baby was coming out, alive, by himself. I had been in labor for five days, not counting the Saturday night and the Sunday when my waters had broken. It was now Friday afternoon of the following week.

About an hour later my blood pressure spiked to very dangerous levels. The doctor believed that the placenta may have ripped from the wall of my uterus—placental abruption—and it was collapsing under the stress of the labor. My baby's heartbeat was too slow; in fact, it was dangerously low. Dr. McAfee, who hadn't left the area, said to me, "You have two options as I see it: You can stay here for another hour or so and you will give birth to a stillborn baby, or we can take you to theatre now for a caesarean and he will live."

To me the right option was obvious. "I haven't laid here for five days for nothing," I said. "I want my baby." I believe when it becomes a life and death situation, the hospital has the power to operate on a minor without permission from a parent or guardian.

"Prep her. Theatre. Now!" he yelled as he pulled the stethoscope away from my stomach. "Your baby's heart is giving out. We need to deliver him now." He tried to comfort me with a gentle touch on my hand, and then people ran around everywhere.

Nurses came running in and a trolley was pushed in and placed next to my bed. They then grabbed my sheet and thumped me unceremoniously onto the trolley. After that I can only remember the ceiling lights flashing by as I lay on my back on the trolley as they navigated the corridors on our way to the theatre suite, ten floors up. As I looked up at the roof, the trolley was travelling so fast that the nurses had to run to keep up. All I remember is crashing through the theatre door.

Dr. McAfee was already waiting. Before I knew what was happening, I heard him announce, "You have a wee, bonny, bouncing, baby boy." I didn't hear my baby boy cry—Jason.

It wasn't until days later that I was awake to a point where I could remember what happened. I was kept in a single room for intensive care as my blood pressure remained worryingly high. Finally, Jack arrived. I think it was the only time I had ever and would ever see Jack sober.

"Well, your baby is born, so you can fuck off now," I said, while I tried to hide my face away from him.

He said, "I know. I've seen him." That cut through my heart like a dagger. I felt tears welling in my eyes. *He's seen him.* I hadn't even seen my baby and Jack didn't even want him. Next minute a nurse arrived.

"Is everything alright in here?" she queried.

"Yes, why?" I asked.

"We just had an alarm. Your blood pressure is going up," she said. She asked Jack to only stay a little while as they were concerned for my health. I knew they were concerned about a little more than that, given Jack's history with the hospital.

Two days later I was put into a regular ward. I sat in the bed expressing my milk, which was then sent to the special nursery. Jason needed to be in intensive care as he had been born with an enlarged heart, fluid on the brain, meconium aspiration, and dislocated hips. The little man was fighting death and winning every day. He was a survivor. He was always touch-and-go, so I was advised daily. The milk that went to the nursery to feed and nourish him was the only contribution I could make. And it wasn't a lot because my milk never really came in.

Gracie came up to see me after about a week. She was so happy that he was born and that I was okay. She congratulated me and then I broke down crying. I told her how I hadn't seen him yet. I was distraught. She couldn't believe it and turned on her heel, went and saw the nurse, and within a few minutes returned with a wheelchair. She helped me out of bed and into the chair, and then she wheeled me down to the special nursery.

I stood up at the window and the nurse wheeled him over for me to see. He was in a humidicrib. I put my hand on the window and big tears rolled down my cheeks. He was beautiful—8lb 7oz according to a sign. He was a big boy—his only saving grace apparently. We stayed there for as long as I needed to. I just wished I could hold him, but there was more bad news to come. Shortly after I went back to the ward, I was advised that Jason had caught gastroenteritis in the special nurseries. Now normally that would not be too bad, but for a special needs baby it was life threatening, and so it turned out to be. For another week or so, Jason fought the gastro virus, almost succumbing to it three times. When he recovered sufficiently, I demanded that I be allowed to hold him.

It was that very day that I received a visit from Mother Catherine. Mother Catherine was very informative. She sat with me and explained what had happened with the emergency delivery and Jason's deteriorating health. She asked me if I really thought that taking him home to an uncertain future was in his best interest when there were families that he could be placed with who would love him and give him everything that I couldn't. They would be prepared and mature enough to accept his ongoing health issues head-on. She was very convincing to the point that I even started to consider it. But, as if I had been struck by lightning, I spun in my seat to address her straight on.

"Mother Catherine, I will never, ever, give my baby up for adoption," I said resolutely. I stared into my lap for a little longer, watching my thumbs chase each other around and round. "Nobody is going to take my baby away from me—*nobody*. There is a little golden string that binds us together, and he loves me."

I guess she thought that I had turned hostile as she did not stay for long after that. There was no way I was giving my baby away—never, not under any circumstances. Little did I know what the future would hold. If I had, I might have thought differently. But for now I just wanted to hold my baby. So later that night I was finally taken to the special nurseries, after three weeks, I held my baby for the first time.

I was very fortunate that my baby was not forcibly taken away. Many babies of single mothers were forcibly put up for adoption in the '50s, '60s, and '70s. The Hon. Prime Minister of Australia, Ms. Julia Gillard, formally apologized to those affected by this on March 21, 2013. Because I was in a defacto relationship at the time of Jason's birth, I was saved from this.

And perhaps it was because of my stoic rejection of Mother Catherine's suggestion to adopt him out ... Though I was to wonder many times in life whether Jason might have been better off adopted out ... for his own sake. Let's just say life has not been kind to him.

I approached the nursery door with some nervousness and trepidation and pressed the button as the sign instructed. A courteous and encouraging staff member, all dressed in hospital blues, greeted me and directed me to a sink where she told me to wash my hands up to my elbows with special soap. I then had to put a gown on over my night clothes and a mask on my face.

"We don't want him getting any nasty bugs again, do we?" she said.

You should have thought of that before.

Once I was ready, she helped me into the room and told me to sit in the cream leather chair that had been set up for me. I barely had time to sit before she placed my little man into my arms. The blanket was swaddled tightly around him. I looked at him with wonder as his big brown eyes curiously searched my face and mine his. My stomach tumbled over and over and my heart was trying to burst out of my chest. I had the smile of a Cheshire cat spread from ear to ear as I gently unwrapped the top of his blanket and touched his tiny fingers. They immediately gripped around mine. I had never felt such joy in my life. He was very dry and flaky; a sign that he was "well-cooked". But to me he was just beautiful. My beautiful baby boy; that memory will stay burnt in my mind for as long as I live.

The nurse interrupted my introduction to my son by telling me that Jason's head was enlarged, but the swelling was subsiding and they felt a drainage tube was not going to be necessary. She further explained that his enlarged heart was now settling into the correct side of his ribcage and his legs were still heavily bandaged to hold his hips in place. I was very careful with him. I was scared that I may do something that would do more harm to him.

At the time I did not completely understand the severity of his condition, in particular the fact that an enlarged heart, also known as *cardiomyopathy*, happens when a heart fails to pump blood effectively, which can lead to a syndrome known as *congestive heart failure*. Nobody explained that to me, and back then they did nothing about it either. It is only with maturity and the ability now to research on the internet that I now know how grave his situation truly was and that every day he has lived is a blessing. If I had realized at the time that Jason could have died in my arms at any moment, I would have died too! I would have been inconsolable. He had to be monitored regularly for seven years after his birth because of his condition.

The nurse helped me to introduce my nipple to him and he gripped on well for the first time. But it was never going to be a successful venture. Women who have caesarean sections often do not produce a reasonable supply of milk and find themselves supplementing their child's food intake with formula, as was the case with me. I fed Jason religiously after our first meeting. Every feed time they would come and wake me we would go through the same procedure—washing, scrubbing, donning hospital gowns, and putting a mask on. Each time we would just sit and stare at each other for the longest time, his big brown eyes full of wonderful innocence, hope, and love. And I loved that his love was for me. I longed to have him with me in the ward but was firmly told, "No."

And so it was until about a week and a half later, four weeks after his birth, when we were both cleared by the doctor to leave the hospital and go home.

Charlie, Jack's pseudo step-father, came to pick Jason and me up from the hospital. He did not take us home but took us instead straight to Mona's house. He told me that Jack would swing by later to pick us up. I quizzed him to find out where Jack was. It was a Saturday morning, so I couldn't understand why Jack couldn't come and get us. It was not like he had anything to do. He didn't work. What was he doing? Was he with that Brenda? They were molly coddling him, so he didn't have to be responsible for anything still, even though he was. He was now responsible for both his son Jason and me.

So to Mona's house we went. Jack finally turned up to pick us up a few hours later. In that time I had to contend with Charlie staring at my boobs when I was trying to breastfeed Jason. I would get up and go to another room and he would come and stand in the doorway of that room and watch me. It was very disturbing. I hated it and I couldn't produce any milk for Jason while he watched. My stress levels were through the roof by the time Jack finally arrived. I just wanted to go. I wanted to go and start being a family. My family was going to be better than anything I had ever known.

30

MOTHERHOOD & MEMORIES

"Tammy ... Tammy ... Tammy ..."

MOTHERHOOD WAS GREAT. I can say now that I was a natural. I enjoyed the fact that I had someone who unconditionally loved me and I loved him in return. Nothing was too much for my little boy. The nurturer within me came to life at such a young age. From the moment I held Jason in my arms, I knew that I would never be able to let him go or harm him. I instinctively knew that I had to protect him with my life, as a lioness protects her cubs.

It took no time at all for me to get some sort of routine going and do whatever was best for Jason. He was a great baby. He hardly cried and slept well, unless disturbed by Jack fighting with me. At the height of these fights, the yelling would startle Jason and he would need to be pacified by a cuddle or a bottle. He was not a demanding child, unlike his father who was much harder to deal with than our young son.

I had to contend with Jack's continual ups and downs and drunken mood swings both day and night. He would abuse me after his heavy drinking sessions every night, which was mostly just before he went into a stupor and spent the rest of the night dribbling on his t-shirt. I would just sit and watch as I was too scared to go to bed until I had his permission. A pattern had been set in motion. He would also take it out on me in the morning when he woke up like a bear with a sore head. But I had a baby to fear for also. I had no idea what Jack could be capable of if I was to make him angry. He had proven he could do a lot of damage to me when I was pregnant, which told me that he was more than capable of doing something drastic to his son also. There was just no reasoning with him when he was drunk. I had to stay alert and ready. Many times he threatened to harm Jason. He saw Jason as a contender for my attention, rather than an extension of himself that needed a father to love him. He also knew that if he hurt Jason, it was the ultimate way to hurt me as he knew how much I loved and needed Jason. I had somehow believed that Jason would be the magic Band-Aid to make Jack love me. That was obviously not happening.

I remember this time in my life to be very tiring. I was constantly exhausted, but I dared not lie down during the day to get some much-needed rest, lest Jack return home and find me asleep. I would have to suffer his anger for being lazy. So I survived on minimal sleep. Lying down during the day was not even a consideration, even after staying up until three or four o'clock in the morning while Jack slept in a drunken stupor on the couch in front of me and I sat there frozen.

I found myself becoming overwhelmed. Jason had special needs due to his birth complications. Then there were Jack's constant demands that saw me jumping immediately when spoken to and doing what I was told. When Jack wanted something done, it was not a request, it was an order, and one that had to be met immediately or consequences would follow. Day or night, twenty-four-seven! He didn't work and as such was underfoot most of the time, unless he disappeared to Brenda's for a few hours, more often than not. That was my only reprieve, and I knew better than to complain about his "friendly" relationship with her. All I could do was wish that he would stay there, so I could get some much-needed peace.

There was no reasoning with him when he was around. His demands came thick and fast, and our son's requirements were not a priority to him. He could do absolutely nothing for himself. I became an extension of his mother, not his wife. Other than the normal housekeeping rules, like keeping the house spotlessly clean, which I had learned to do so well in the convent, I also had to fetch bottles of beer for Jack who just sat on the lounge and shouted orders. He demanded that his jocks were starched after being washed and that they be ironed and folded in a particular way—the way that his mother did them. In fact, all his clothing had to be treated exactly as his mother had done it. Each piece of linen had to be folded in the same way so that it sat neatly in its pile and everything lined up. Sheets and pillow slips were starched and pressed; even towels and face cloths had to be ironed. Here again my training in the convent's laundry, including the "work hard or get hit in the back of the head with a wooden hand broom" came in really handy. So getting the linen right was a given. Even so, what I did was still not approved of and often would be redone by his mother.

In the morning, Jack's breakfast had to be on the table, hot—when he turned off the shower, not when he was ready to sit at the table and eat it. No, when the shower went off. This meant that he had a reason to start a fight with me first thing in the morning, every morning, because his meal would get cold in the time it took him to dry off, brush his teeth for nearly five minutes, and brush his hair—and that in itself was a task because it was almost to his hips. Then he had to get dressed and make his way to the table, which he always took his time doing.

He took longer in the shower than I did. His clothes had to be laid out on the bed, fresh each morning. A pair of jocks, jeans, t-shirt, singlet, and socks, all ironed and starched. Nothing was ever re-worn. And his shoes had to be down beside the bed, so he could just slip into them. If any one thing was out of place, that was also a reason for him to lay into me.

Breakfast each morning consisted of chops, sausages, or steak and eggs with toast and a cup of coffee. You could tell he didn't pay the grocery bill. He would always make me cook him a fresh breakfast after the morning fight because he would inevitably pick up the plate from the table and throw it at me. Sometimes I managed to escape and it would miss me. It would then smash all over the wall and floor. But normally it would hit me and I would end up with his breakfast in my hair and all over my clothes. It was a routine, one he excelled in. If it did miss me and land on the floor, he would sometimes pick up the egg and hold me against the wall while he rubbed the egg into my hair and face. Then he would call me a dirty, fat slut for not washing myself before breakfast.

Sometimes Jason would be in my arms, but I had learnt it was best not to have him there in the morning. So I found myself propping Jason's bottle up on a pillow near his mouth so that he could feed himself while this type of thing took place. I felt it was safer that way, but it robbed both Jason and me of much needed bonding time. Every time I propped his bottle up and couldn't pick him up in my arms, a part of me died inside. Even so, it kept him safe from being hit by something. Both of their mealtimes coincided, and of course Jack always came first—his number one rule.

It didn't matter what Jack did, his conduct was always enabled by both his mother and Charlie, who would rush to replace what he had destroyed and continue to provide food and beer on tap. Jack was on the dole, but I never saw a cent of it. He would occasionally leave some change around and I would squirrel it away in case I needed to get Jason to a medical appointment at the hospital, as he had many in his first few years. He was a very sick little boy.

Jack would be so drunk he wouldn't remember the change that he would put on the bench or left in his pockets. The only money I never dared to squirrel away was the two dollar note that Jack kept in his shoes. This was kept there because if he was ever picked up for drunk-and-disorderly, he could not be charged with vagrancy also. Two dollars was the magic sum that by law kept him out of the lock up for the night. Not that he went out and drank anymore. No, he would just sit at home and guzzle it down, night after miserable night. Jack wouldn't go out and drink at the pub because he would always end up in a fight. He was a very nasty drunk.

On the rare occasions that I could get out of the house with Jason, I was so proud of him. I would dress him up and put him in his pram, which was a very old-fashioned 1940's buggy that Charlie had found at one of his clean-up sites. Charlie worked for the Victorian Housing Authority and went in after tenants had left to clean up their mess. He was supposed to dump the garbage that was left behind, but most of that rubbish ended up at our place. Most of our furniture had come from these clean-up sites. It was better than nothing though, and who was I to complain? I had nothing to offer.

Charlie had dragged this buggy home, and he and Mona hand-painted it white with a lilac matt trim. They told me it would do. I knew it was going to be more than helpful, but at the same time I could only cringe, thinking about my trips to the hospital and how I would lift it on and off the trams, let alone up and down the stairs to our flat on the second level.

On one such trip out with Jason, I was happily walking up the street with my beautiful baby boy lying in his pram. He was swaddled in his blue bunny rug with his lemon pram set covering him over to keep the winter chill from hitting his little face. As I neared the tram stop I positioned the pram next to the bench, where two older ladies were sitting to wait for the tram. They slid the length of the bench to get away from me, as if I had a disease, saying things like, "Disgusting, obviously out of marriage", and "Tramp, you should be very ashamed of yourself". They tutted and continued their tirade at me until finally I broke and yelled at them to mind their own business, while I walked away to wait at a different tram stop. Shame on them for their narrow-minded, bigoted view of the world!

I continued my journey to the hospital where Jason was given the all-clear once again. He was thriving and doing well. His head size was reducing and his heart was now fully lodged on the correct side of his ribcage, although there were still serious issues that had to be monitored, and his hips were fine. What better news could I ask for? They insisted, though, that they would still monitor Jason until he was seven years old.

It was clear to me that Jack's mother idolized her grandson, although when she visited she did not stay very long. When Jason was six months old, Charlie arrived one Saturday morning and told me that he was going to take Jason for the day. I asked if he wanted me to put some clothes, nappies, and bottles together for Jason, but he said no. He told me that Mona had everything that she needed, and with that he scooped Jason up and was gone. Mona provided everything for Jason's daily needs—food, clothes, nappies, and toys. There was nothing I had to buy or needed to get for him. It left me feeling empty. Part of the joy of having a baby is preparing for their arrival and picking up little bits and pieces along the way. But there was never any money.

I can hear some of you thinking *Woo-hoo lucky girl. But what a bitch for thinking so poorly of such a wonderful mother-in-law. I wish I had one like that.* My response would be that you can have her with my blessings. She was the reason that Jack was totally incapable of any kind of responsibility. He was her only child and very precious to her. Nothing was too much for him. She doted on him and enabled his sick, child-like dependency, in effect disabling him. She continued to do that even though it was obvious that he didn't want to do anything for himself any longer. She doted on him until the day he died just recently—December 2012. Jack knew he could use his mother and milked her for every cent he could. Why not? He had money on tap and didn't have to do a damn thing to earn it.

By disabling Jack with her love and taking control of our family, she denied me the right to have the husband and family that I truly needed and deserved. In the process she also removed my choices and abilities as Jason's mother.

Finally, I found out that I could apply for child endowment. (Mothers in hospitals are lucky now as they're handed all the Centrelink forms before discharge.) I think it was two dollars a month. They would not pay it into Jack's account as he demanded, only into mine. Every month he would harp on me to give it to him so he could buy more beer, but I wouldn't. On this point I bravely held my ground. That two dollars a month gave me a sense of normality. Besides, it was for my child and it gave me such a great feeling to know there was something I had control over. The very first time I received it, I bought Jason a beautiful pair of blue booties. I was so proud of myself.

It wasn't long before we received our marching orders from the flat. It appeared that the neighbors did not really appreciate the constant yelling and other noises that came from our abode. Not that any of them would come and help me at one and two o'clock in the morning. Another flat was found for us to live in, and the first time I saw it I was relieved to see that it did not have a staircase. We were on the ground level, so no more struggling with Jason in the pram. I longed to have a pusher, a small pusher like other women had. It would be so much easier for outings, not that I went out a lot. But I did need to go and buy milk and take trips to the hospital. One of those would have been perfect. I'm sure that Jack's mother worked in cahoots with her son to make my life as difficult as possible so that I had to stay at home.

The new flat had a small kitchenette, barely large enough for our small two-seater table, but it would do. There were two bedrooms. One was off the lounge room, which would be Jason's room. It was close and I would be able to hear him if he needed me. The flat did not have a laundry. There was a common laundry next door, so it wouldn't be too hard to run in there and do the washing when I was there by myself with Jason.

I enjoyed moments by myself when Jack was not there. It gave me time to think and time to play with Jason, to count his fingers and toes over and over. To see him smile. I loved his smile. He was such a happy baby and I loved being his mother. It would have been so much easier without Jack, so very easy. The thought crossed my mind on a few occasions to leave him. But where would I go? Who would help me? It wasn't any use anyway because he would come after me.

Every couple of weekends Charlie would come and collect Jason and sometimes I would not get him back until the Sunday afternoon when we went to pick him up. It was obvious that Jack's mother did not want to give Jason back. She treated him as if he was her own, and the visits were becoming more frequent. The little things that I would get for him with my two dollars would be gone and replaced with clothing purchased by her. I never got them back.

On the days he went to their place, I learned not to have him dressed in anything I had purchased. Jack's mother had lost one or two children before or after Jack was born. I think Jason was like a replacement baby for the ones that she had lost.

Jason's first birthday quickly approached. He was growing so big. One look from his big, brown eyes and I would melt. I wanted to give him the world, but with no funds I couldn't even give him a birthday present. Jason struggled with each first step. He was behind in most of the normal developmental stages. His first words, his motor skills—everything—was a struggle to the poor little man, but his beautiful, happy, and cheeky smile was always there, from very early on in his life. Jason's first birthday was spent at Jack's mother's house. A few of Jack's family members came over and brought some presents for Jason. We had a cake, sung happy birthday to him, and it was all over. Back to normal. Jack drove us home and life continued. Back to Jack's dungeon of pain, torture, and misery!

Jason was very unsettled one night. It was lucky I didn't sleep anyway, but Jack yelled at the top of his voice over his shoulder from the lounge room, "Shut that little bastard up!" He was having problems trying to listen to his record player, which he was playing as loud as he could. *Stairway to Heaven* by Led Zeppelin blared out from the speakers while Jack cried into his beer glass, trying to follow along with the lyrics to the song but sounding more like a wounded dog baying at the moon. It was his favorite song. He said it reminded him of his one true love, Diana. Diana had sense enough to run away very fast. I wished he would just go and drink at the pub like other guys did.

Jason was distressed. I walked the floor in his bedroom, rocking him to and fro, until eventually he fell asleep with his little head on my shoulder. It would have been a whole lot easier had I been allowed to shut the door to keep the noise out, but no!

He was so hot and I was extremely worried about him, but it was a long way to walk to the hospital and I wasn't sure whether Jack would let me take Jason there. I knew he certainly wasn't going to drive me, not at one o'clock in the morning and not in the state he was in. And because I valued my own safety and sanity, I wasn't going to ask him to take me either.

The next morning Jason was no better; he was hot and had broken out in spots overnight. I dressed us both and walked the long distance to PANCH Hospital. The doctor assured me that Jason would be okay. He told me that Jason had German measles and advised me to keep his temperature down, to put him into a dark room, and not to take him out into the sun. I did my best to cover the front end of the buggy, to keep the sun out of his eyes while I walked him the long distance back to home. After I settled him into his bedroom, I pulled the blinds and walked out to the lounge room. I felt an overwhelming need to rest; I felt dizzy and spent!

The midday movie was just about to start, so I curled up on the end of the couch. Jack was nowhere in sight; he was probably at Brenda's house.

So I took full advantage of the few minutes with nobody demanding my time. The movie started, and as the movie title flashed up on the screen, the movie's theme song started when I heard the words sung by Sandra Dee to Tammy's in love …

Tammy … Tammy … Tammy … I felt a flutter.

I put my hand to my stomach and felt the flutter again. A smile mixed with trepidation flashed across my face and tears welled in my eyes. *A girl, wow, a girl. I'm pregnant and her name is Tammy.* And right on cue, I bolted to the toilet and promptly threw up.

Here we were full circle. Jason was in the bedroom with German measles and I was pregnant again. When Jack came home, I told him what had happened.

"Jack, I'm going to have another baby!" I said with excitement.

But he didn't share my joy.

"Get rid of it or I'm gonna kick you in the guts."

I took several steps back, shocked. It was the way he had looked at me when he said it. It scared the shit out of me. His scowl sent chills up my spine. How could he be so heartless, so cold?

"I'm not going through this shit again," he screamed at me in a high pitch voice. "Get rid of it, because if you fuck'n don't, I will. I mean it!" His words spewed out, disjointed and mean, and then he came at me swinging.

This life growing inside me was part of him also. How could someone not want their baby? I ran from the flat, down the street, and headed for the main road. I wasn't sure where I was going to go. He didn't follow, and then I remembered Jason. Jason was still at home and he was sick. He needed me.

So I turned around immediately and headed back home. I opened the door and entered the flat. Jack was sitting in the lounge room, watching television and drinking a bottle of beer. He didn't say a thing to me. I was blinded by the tears in my eyes as I started to prepare his evening meal. I could not believe his attitude, and I didn't know how to get rid of the feeling that he would do something to harm the new baby. Abortion went against the grain of everything I stood for, everything I had been taught in the convent. I didn't want to have an abortion anyway. This life that was growing inside me was precious, more precious to me than life itself.

I had been warned not to have another baby for at least four years, due to complications that could happen because of my caesarean section scar and the fact that it could rupture my uterus. What could I do? Tammy was here now, and in my uterus she would stay.

Later that night, once the booze had taken hold, I was bombarded with hours of put-downs about myself, my family, and the way I looked, acted, and spoke. Then came the beating, which was worse than ever. At one point he raised his leg to kick me in the stomach but fell backwards because he was so drunk, which saved my baby's life I believe.

The next morning as I prepared Jack's breakfast and placed it on the table, immediately after the shower was turned off as directed, I knew that he would take this opportunity, once again, to create a fight and maybe try to finish off what he had tried to do the night before. I waited anxiously in the kitchen for his arrival, and as expected, he grabbed the plate and shoved it down the table at me yelling, "It's fucking cold! Make me another lot."

From nowhere a feeling of boldness came over me. I picked up his plate from the kitchen table and walked towards the open windows in the lounge room. I threw the plate through the window and out onto the driveway, where it smashed to smithereens. I turned to him and yelled, "Well, if you don't want it, the fuck'n dogs can eat it," as I stomped off towards our bedroom and slammed the door. I had no idea that the girls who lived opposite us were on their way to work, and when the dish had come flying out the window, I heard them giggle. One of them said, "Well, it looks like Jack was having bacon, eggs, and chops this morning."

"Was having, I think," the other said. I giggled to myself, proud of the fact I had stood up to him. But that joy came to a sudden halt as I felt my hair being ripped out of my scalp as I was pulled from behind. And then as he spun me around by the hair, a fist caught me right under my left eye.

Jack spent the next ten minutes or so struggling with me to try and push my head down. He had his hand firmly placed across the back of my neck, trying to knee me in the face. I was holding my stomach, scared he would connect. I stepped backwards, round and round in circles. I struggled to get away from him, and when I did, I ran to the kitchen.

I grabbed the large kitchen knife off the bench and ran towards him yelling, "Don't ever fuck'n touch me again!" He lunged forward to run at me, so I ran into the bathroom.

He raised his fist once more to hit me in the face, and as he did I raised the knife. I had no feelings. I was mentally numb, exhausted. Adrenalin was the only thing pumping through my veins. I wanted this nightmare to end, and at that moment I didn't really care how. I plunged the knife forward towards his chest. He grabbed the handle to the bathroom door and pulled it shut *really* fast, leaving the full force of the knife to pass through the door to the hilt. Had he not shut the door, I have no doubt that I would have killed him that day.

"You're a bloody mad woman!" he screamed. Then he disappeared for a few days. I must have scared him.

Shortly after that I was admitted to hospital with extremely high blood pressure and a high amount of protein in my urine. I lived the next six months with the risk of losing my baby from pre-eclampsia. I was bedridden and not allowed home for any weekend breaks. My blood pressure never subsided, no matter what they tried. It was not known then that I had a genetic and terminal kidney disease and that chronic renal failure would shadow my life from age twenty-eight. It was probably the cause of my issues in both pregnancies.

It was a very long hospital stay. I appreciated any assistance given to me by nursing staff and other people's visitors. Day after day I sat in that bed looking out the window, thinking about my little boy, wondering how he was, what he looked like now. I hadn't been allowed to bring Jason into hospital with me. Nobody came. No Jack, no Jason, no Mom, nobody. I felt quite deserted. One of the sisters had taken a liking to me and laundered my nighties and underwear, as there was nobody to help even do that.

Finally, the day arrived. Tammy was going to be born. I sat and waited in hope that Jack might turn up, but to no avail. I had rung his mother's house and told her that Tammy was expected to be delivered, but I was given a very cold reception. The hospital had chosen to deliver her, as I teetered on the very edge of danger with my blood pressure. The nurses arrived with the trolley to take me to theatre. Everyone wished me luck—all the long-term stayers who had supported me through my sojourn in the hospital. As I was pushed out into the corridor, the nurses were asking me for names for the baby.

"Tammy," I said.

"But what if it is a boy?"

I smiled and said, "She's not. She is a girl and her name is Tammy."

"But you can't be certain," they stated.

"I am. She is a girl and her name is Tammy."

Rather than fight with me and raise my blood pressure further, they accepted that if I delivered a girl her name would be Tammy, and if I delivered a boy, I would name him later.

Several hours later, I awoke in the maternity ward at the other end of the hospital. The nurses came in with a bowl to wash me and I grumbled through sleepy eyes, "Where is my daughter? I want to see her." After the traumatic time I had with Jason, I would not accept or believe that she was alright until they had put her into my arms several hours later.

She was beautiful. She had tufts of dark brown hair on the top of her head and around her ears, with a particularly long piece in the middle of her crown. Her skin was warm, soft, and pink. She was a chubby little thing—8lb 6oz.

Her eyes were open and fully focused on trying to make out my face. She scrunched up her own little face in concentration. I unwrapped her from her swaddle and checked her from head to toe, and only when I was happy that she was all there and everything was okay, I relaxed. I wanted to keep her with me, but they insisted that because she had been born by C-section, she must remain in special nurseries for twenty-four hours. I wrapped her back up in her bunny rug and watched as she struggled to get her hand to freedom. That is something she would always do, no matter how tight she was wrapped. As I watched Tammy being wheeled from the room, the song, *My Eyes Adored You* by Frankie Valli, was being played on my little transistor. It would always be her song.

The next day I was informed that Tammy was failing to thrive and that she would need to stay in special nurseries just a little longer. She was losing weight dramatically. Gracie came up and wheeled me down to see her. I wasn't allowed to hold her and could only look at her through the glass.

The song … *My Eyes Adored You* … continued in my head as my mind drifted off, reminiscing about holding her, smelling her beautiful baby scent, putting my nose into her hair and breathing her in. Tears rolled down my cheeks as I remembered the ordeal with Jason, teetering so close to death for so long. I didn't want that for my daughter also.

"When will I be allowed to have my baby with me?" I pleaded with the nurses.

"When she starts to drink properly," came the answer.

Tammy was only taking 10 ml or thereabouts each time she was woken for a bottle. Every four hours the report came back to me—10 ml, 5 ml, 10 ml. One of the other mothers in the room leaned over to me and said, "Demand that they put her onto demand feeding. I bet she drinks then."

"I didn't know that I could do that," I said, raising my eyebrows in surprise.

I rang the buzzer and told the nurse that I wanted Tammy to be placed onto demand feeding. She fussed over it as if it were a discussion.

I said, "No, she is my baby and I want her on demand feeding." I felt strong as I said this, in control for once in my life. I was eighteen, which is probably why the nurse had such disdain for my request. Most mothers at that age were still having their babies forcibly removed.

"Okay," came the reply.

It was approximately 6 p.m. when I made this request. I rang the buzzer at 11 p.m. as I had not heard anything from the nurses.

A nurse came and said, "I'll call down to special nurseries and see what is happening."

I was told Tammy had not woken up for her feed yet. The next morning at 6 a.m., I rang the buzzer again—the nurse came and gave the same response. Tammy had not yet woken up for her bottle and they were concerned that she may dehydrate. They wanted to wake her. The woman beside me shook her head subtly from side to side so the nurse wouldn't notice.

"No, I don't want her woken. When she wakes herself, she can be fed."

At 2 p.m. that day, nearly twenty-four hours after the decision had been made to demand feed Tammy, she woke and guzzled down a full bottle, the whole 60 ml. I watched at the window as they fed her. I just wanted to go in and hold her and let her know I was there. I was happy that she was feeding, but a part of my heart was breaking as I couldn't hold her yet.

The room slowly started to fill with mothers and babies as each of the old gang from the previous ward delivered their babies. Once Tammy was feeding every four hours, she finally joined me. *At last.*

Jack had still not been in to see her—nobody had. It had now been four days since she was born. Apparently *my* decision to fall pregnant and have another baby when I couldn't look after the first one was truly looked down upon, and my second pregnancy was rejected by all concerned. Mona had had as much contempt as her son for the child I had been carrying and had even asked Jack if he was sure that the baby was his. According to her, this child could have been anyone's.

One day I was sitting in my hospital bed holding Tammy and I commented how she looked like Jason. One of the women turned to me and asked, "Who's Jason?"

I responded, "My son."

They didn't know I had a son.

"How long has it been since you've seen your little boy?" one of the other mothers asked.

"Just on six months," I sighed.

"Six months? Why haven't you seen him?"

I told them that I hadn't had any visitors, that nobody would come and bring him in to see me. Just as I said that, I looked up and saw a little boy toddling along the hallway. He had beautiful, medium-blond, curly hair and was dressed in a little sailor suit. I smiled, thinking that Jason would be about that age. I got teary.

Everyone was looking at him, stating how cute he was. Hearts were melting everywhere. Then I spotted Jack's mother. Oh my God! It was Jason. I didn't even recognize my own son!

"Jason!" I screamed. His head snapped towards my voice and he starting running to me, falling over his own little feet. But he picked himself up and still headed towards me. I tried to pick him up onto the bed, but with the cut from the caesarean and my inability to bend sideways, I struggled. But he was not to be stopped. He pulled the chair over and climbed into my lap.

He cried, "Mommy, home." Jason had not seen me for months, yet he still knew who I was. His little hand reached up and cupped my face as he looked into my teary eyes.

"Yes Jason," I said, as tears streamed down my cheeks. He rested his head against my chest and would not have a bar of Mona when she tried to take him from me, smacking her hand away and saying, "No, my mommy."

I think that Mona had enjoyed not having to share Jason with me. It had been a dream come true for her. Not one visit in the whole time I was in hospital; but, this day was different. It was Mother's Day. She must have felt compelled by some sense of decency, or maybe she was curious to see if the new child had any resemblance to her son. My feelings of contempt for her were obvious. The scowling faces of the other women in the ward showed their criticism also. After they left, I was surrounded with kind words and support.

"How could they do that to you? You are his mother? How dare she?"

Not long after this, I was well enough to go home. Jason did not make a return visit, and on the day I was due to leave, Charlie picked me up—no Jack in sight. Again, it was straight to Mona's house. She had to have her fill of the new baby before I was allowed to go home. She was obviously convinced it was her grandchild.

Jack arrived at about six o'clock that evening in a drink truck to pick us up. I put Tammy in a carry basket on the front seat and Jason on my lap. Jack had been drinking and it was one of the scariest trips home I think I had ever had.

While I had been in hospital, he had gone and gotten a job. I wasn't sure why, but the beer didn't flow into the house as freely from his mother anymore; however, food still did. He had no responsibilities, none! They even paid our rent. The income he earned was allowed to go straight to the pub, and it did.

We had also moved house, compliments of course of his mother, who thought we needed a house now because Jack drove a drink truck and it couldn't be safely housed at the block of flats. Forget the fact that we now had two children who needed bedrooms.

Things changed a little, but not for the better. Jack became more verbally abusive, more destructive with things around the house, more possessive and controlling, and he learned to hit harder. I was not allowed to leave the house, not even to go to the shop around the corner to get milk for the babies. On the odd occasion that he did allow me to go, he followed me, hiding behind bushes and fences. He was paranoid about me meeting other men, or any people for that matter. And when I got back home five minutes later, I was bashed because apparently I'd had sex with someone at the shop.

I couldn't talk to anyone about this; nobody would believe me. I was just so alone. My mom still wanted nothing to do with me. If I tried to talk to Jack's Mom about it, she would call me a liar and tell me I was making up stories. Her beloved son could do no wrong, ever. Once when I turned up at her house with a black eye for her birthday party, she asked, "What happened?"

I said, "Your son punched me in the face for wearing some makeup."

She retorted, "He did not. You walked into a door, liar."

I was obviously not going to get any help from her. Amazingly enough, just a few years ago she had told me how he used to throw ashtrays at her and a whole range of other things. How quickly one forgets. I was to learn later that Jack had paranoid schizophrenia, and I suspect Mona does too.

Jack's beatings always made me feel so low, but truly, I think the put downs had a worse effect than the beatings. Physically, I could heal; mentally it would be years before I would ever be able to look at myself and see a human being as deserving as any other. Because of my life to date, and his put downs, I was a true victim, with a victim mentality, able to be manipulated, groomed, and discarded at anyone's pleasure.

I hated him for bringing my family into it every time he could. My mom was a "fuck'n drunk" and "no-hoper", my sister a "selfish loser" and "stuck-up bitch", and my brother an "idiot". If anyone was paid out on, Danny copped it the worst because he was in the Defense Force, and Jack hated Defense Force people. He would always say they were homosexuals. His taunts would be "your brother's a poofter; he takes it up the arse".

Yes, he was truly such a wonderful person. I was sickened by it and every day saw me sink lower and lower until there was so little of me left to hurt.

Yet he would find new things to put me down with all the time. His family … well, they were all so perfect and wonderful and beyond reproach. And don't dare open your mouth and say one word to the contrary for fear of being murdered.

31

To Die or Not to Die

❦

*"I suddenly felt a sense of calmness come over me.
This was something I had never felt before."*

NOT LONG AFTER Tammy's birth, I'd had enough. I waited for Jack to go to work and quickly scurried around the house, putting some of the children's clothing into a bag with a few things for me. My heart was pounding so hard I thought it would leap out of my chest. I was scared as I wheeled the pram with the children out of the house and down the street. I cannot describe in words the anxiety and stress of the next hour as I ended up running with the pram along the street, trying to get away because I was scared that he would come after me and do something terrible to the three of us.

I found myself heading towards the only person I thought would help me—Michael. I knew Michael was married to another girl and had a daughter of his own, but I had nowhere else to go and nobody else to turn to. I am not sure what drove me towards Michael's house. It just seemed like the right thing to do at the time.

After a very long walk, I arrived at Michael's house and was not disappointed. He took me in.

Cathy was more than happy to have me there also. With their help and advice, I found myself gaining better health and courage every day. I was finding it hard to support the kids as the courts only offered ten dollars a fortnight to help separated or single, unmarried parents, and when I left I had not been able to take much. So each time I needed something it had to be bought.

I was told that if I had been married and separated, I would have been entitled to a small benefit from the government each fortnight, after a waiting period of six months. But as I was an unmarried mother, I had no entitlement except for a small ten dollars a fortnight contribution from the local courthouse, which did not go very far at all.

Michael suggested that I get a job and that Cathy would look after the kids for me during the day—so I did. Once again, as soon as I applied for a job I got it. I must present well! I got a job at the local grocery store as a check-out chick, for menial pay, most of which I gave to Michael and Cathy for food, board, and child care. I was making it without Jack, with Cathy and Michael's help of course.

One Saturday I washed and dressed the children. I was living around the corner from Jack's mother's house and as yet had not been seen. I have always been a fair person and I did not think it was right of me to keep my children from their grandmother. I knew that she loved them. So as I headed off with the pram that morning, I had great imaginings of her doting on the two children.

After she opened the door, I was met with a scowl. "What do you want?"

"I've brought your grandchildren to visit you," I explained.

She looked past me at the children and said with blood as cold as a snake's, "What grandchildren? I don't have any." And with that she turned away and shut the door in our faces.

At first I was taken aback by her attitude. I was young and couldn't understand why a grandmother, who I had perceived to love my children so much, would do anything else but welcome them when given the opportunity. But what did she do? She wouldn't even admit that they were hers. She knew how I was being treated. She knew what Jack was like; she had warned me herself. So why the hatred towards us? This experience actually cut really deep. It hurt that she could refuse her grandchildren like that and that they had to experience that kind of rejection so young in their lives.

As it turned out, it was a blessing in disguise, for if I had left them there that day, and I would have trusted her enough to do that, I would never have got them back. I didn't know it then, but Charlie tailed me that day to see where I lived. He was one very creepy man. I first walked the distance to my mother's house. She had never seen the children. I had such a strong need to be accepted by my mother, but I didn't hope for much. After my visit with Jack's mother, I thought I might as well get the rejection from my own mother out of the way as well.

I walked down the sideway to Mom's door, and as I entered the yard I heard her behind me. She had just returned from doing the shopping.

"What do you want?" she said with a frown on her face.

"I thought you might like to meet your grandchildren, Mom," I said softly.

Mom immediately looked down at the pram and I watched her heart melt. And then mine melted towards her when I heard her ask warmly and with a smile, "So, who do we have here?"

Both Jason and Tammy beamed up at their grandmother's smile. Jason gave her killer smiles, enough to melt the hardest heart.

"This is Jason and this is Tammy," I said.

Mom invited us in and we had a lovely visit. I told her that I had left Jack and I was living with Michael and his wife for the moment, I had a job in a supermarket, and my intention was to never go back. She was so happy to hear me say that. She had been worried about me, it was obvious. But being as stubborn as she was, there was no way that she would have given in first. I was so happy that I had made this move to try and reunite with her. I had missed her.

Mom gave me her new phone number, as she had finally got the phone connected, and told me if I ever needed her, to call. Wow, the day couldn't have got any better. I said I would stay in touch and then I left, content in my heart that my mom had finally accepted my children's and my situation. She had finally accepted me. I wore a silly grin all the way home to Michael's.

About an hour after dinner there was a kerfuffle at the front door.

"I want to see my fuck'n wife," Jack roared at the door, stumbling on his legs, sozzled.

Charlie had told him where I was. Michael suggested, rather demanded, that he come back when he was not drunk and pushed him off the property. Jack got in his truck and left.

The next night he came around, again half-tanked and ready for an abuse session. Michael put him in his place and strongly suggested to Jack that if he were going to turn up there again, that he be sober. Then he sent him packing. Jack would never hit a guy; he was too chicken.

The following night Jack turned up again. This time he just sat in the truck outside Michael's house and kept beeping the horn until it became so annoying that Michael asked me to go and talk to him. I did as Michael asked and went out to see Jack. He wanted me to get in the truck, but I wouldn't. I wanted to be in the open to make a quick escape if I needed to.

He begged me to get in and I continued to say no. He told me how much he missed me and that he wanted me back home. He promised all manner of things, including that he would stop drinking.

He reached out to me and I ducked, thinking he was going to hit me. But his arms went around me instead and he begged me to come with him. I spoke to him for about an hour and told him that I would come back home with him, on one condition, and that was that he didn't drink anymore, or hit me. He promised that he wouldn't.

I went back inside and thanked Cathy and Michael for having me. I told them that I was going to go back to Jack's place. Michael looked worried and said I was making a huge mistake. Still, he helped me out to the truck with my stuff and the children, and then we drove off. Jack didn't say anything all the way home. He was intensely quiet. He helped me in with the children and shut the door. Then he backhanded me so hard across the face my nose started to bleed. He said in a low, terrorizing, detached kind of voice, "Don't you ever leave me again, do you understand, bitch?"

Then he reached up and grabbed the back of my hair with his left hand as he brought his right fist up to hit me again. I shied away from the hit and begged him not to hurt me in front of the kids. He stopped. He demanded to know how many times I had fucked Michael while I had been there. No amount of reasoning was good enough that night.

I put the kids to bed and moped around. He had fooled me. I was ordered to get his dinner, get his beer, and do his washing. It went on and on and on until about 3 a.m. when he finally fell asleep on the lounge chair. I sat on the couch waiting to be told I could go to bed.

When he left for work the next day, I packed the kids up and made my way to Cathy's so that I could drop them off and go to work. I was only at work for about an hour when there was a loud altercation at the top of the store near the registers. I had been busy packing shelves at the rear of the store.

"Where the fuck is she?" Jack yelled at the top of his voice. He was angry.

My blood ran cold and I started to shake. *Why? What have I done?* I tried to think; my mind raced.

The manager came to the back of the store and told me that he thought it would be better if I was to hand in my uniform, resign, and take my husband home. I was devastated. For the first time in a very long time I had had my own little taste of personal freedom. Having my job meant everything in the world to me, but to Jack it meant less control. If I had any money, God knows what I could do.

With great disappointment I did as requested and climbed into Jack's truck, which was parked outside. I remained just out of arm's length so he couldn't hit me. We picked the children up and went home, and that is where he stayed for the rest of the day, watching me, making sure I didn't leave the house.

Nothing had changed.

A short while after this, Jack went to his uncle's for the day. It was a Saturday. I expected him to be home for his dinner and it was prepared and on the table, ready for the evening fights that would eventuate because it wasn't cooked like his Mom made it, or it was too cold, not enough, too much ... It didn't matter what I did, it would be wrong.

Eight o'clock came and went, with no Jack. Ten o'clock, still no Jack. Midnight, no Jack. I put myself to bed, thinking that I'd be in just as much trouble when he got home, so I might as well get some sleep.

The next day I woke up and Jack still wasn't home. I immediately thought he might have been hurt in a car accident because he would have driven drunk as always. I packed the kids up in the pram and walked around the corner to the phone box. I called his mother's house—no answer. I called the police and asked if there were any accidents and gave his description. None!

I went back home, bewildered, and sat playing with the kids until it became dark again. I fed, bathed, and put the children to bed. I didn't bother making dinner as I wasn't hungry. I wasn't sure if he was coming home anyway, so why waste the food. Another night with no Jack! He had never been gone this long before without any contact. Something must have happened to him. My mind was filled with all types of imaginings. I know it's nasty to wish ill on people, but I was glad that he wasn't home. I didn't care if he didn't come back. I was just starting to feel comfortable with those thoughts when it occurred to me that he may have left me for someone else. *Oh well.* The thought crossed my mind and then it was gone. *Let them have him. Hope it's Brenda; she deserves him.*

I was shaken out of my thoughts by a knock at the door. It was his Uncle Eric.

"Where's Jack?" I broke down.

Uncle Eric had a very serious look on his face and told me that there had been an accident. All I could imagine was that Jack was dead. He said that Jack had been taken to the hospital and that he was expected to be released that day, but he just wanted to prepare me for it. He looked surprised that I didn't know. I told him that nobody had told me. Jack's uncle was one of the nicest men that I had ever met. He had a kind heart and he was nothing like Jack's mother. He was understanding and compassionate, always. He said that he had been following Jack because he'd had a fair bit to drink when Jack's car veered off the road and hit a power pole. Jack wasn't physically hurt in the accident, but when the police and ambulance officers arrived, Jack became abusive and violent and had to be restrained. He was taken to the Austin Hospital for observation and had been there for two days.

After Eric left, I immediately went to the phone box and rang the Austin Hospital. I wanted to know what was wrong with him. They put me through to the Psychiatric Ward. *The Psychiatric Ward?* I explained to the nurse who I was and she advised me he would be released that day, and that his violent outbursts had settled down. They said they had explained all of this to his parents. So they did know where he was and they hadn't bothered to tell me. I was so angry with them, and Eric, for avoiding telling me that he was locked up in the Psych Ward, not just in observation.

Jack had been arrested by the police at the scene because of his violence towards them and had been admitted into the Austin Hospital for psychiatric evaluation, where he had been kept because of his severe outbursts of anger. The doctor said that he would require follow up with a psychiatrist, and it was important that he kept the appointments. I thanked her and hung up. I went back to the house and waited for Jack to come home. I have no idea whether Jack was ever diagnosed, but it became extremely clear to me later in life that Jack was paranoid schizophrenic. The signs and symptoms were there from such an early age. He also had a whole pile of other issues due to alcohol abuse.

Charlie and Mona arrived with Jack. When I asked them why they had not told me, they denied that any of it had taken place. I told them that Eric had visited that day and told me. They said he was lying. I said, "So the nurse at the Austin was lying too, was she? Or maybe the doctor that I spoke to was also lying?" They would not enter into conversation about it.

All Mona would say was, "There is nothing wrong with my son; he was just upset."

Such an enabler, always the enabler, always his advocate for bad behavior! They didn't even offer an explanation for his forty-eight-hour absence. But I knew the truth anyway, so it didn't matter. In fact, knowing he had been locked up in a psych ward made no difference to me either. Life continued as usual and it was never mentioned again. No, he didn't make those follow-up appointments as he had been ordered to do.

The next morning was an eye opener. He accused me of sleeping with every Tom, Dick, and Harry from Preston while he had been in hospital. He told me that I obviously didn't have enough to do if I had time to sleep around, and with that he tore the house to bits.

He up-ended clothing from drawers, throwing it all over the floor in every room. He pushed everything off every shelf in the house. He pulled every bed to bits and pulled the mattresses up the back end of the yard, placing them against the fence, and so much more. Chillingly, he said to me before he left the house, "If you do not clean up this fuck'n mess by the time I get home, I will kill you." He had never threatened to kill me before. I suppose there is always a first time. I was scared.

After Jack left I sat on the pile of clothing in the hallway sobbing, with Jason crying in my arms. The front door was wide open and just at that moment my mom popped her head in the door.

She looked at me then around at the mess. "My God, what happened?"

I told her everything in between my sobs.

Up until that time, Mom really had no idea what my daily life and struggles were with Jack. Now she begged me to leave him, telling me that if I didn't, she was scared he would end up killing me or the kids. She helped me to put the house back together and was gone before 3 p.m., as I expected Jack home by 4 p.m. and I was petrified that if he found her there, he would do something rash. He hated my mother. As she left, she begged me again to leave.

I looked at her and said, "But Mom, where would I go? I can't do this by myself." I paused, waiting for her to offer a solution.

Nothing. She had no other option. I was hoping she would offer me the bungalow, but she just shook her head sadly and headed out the door. Shortly after Jack arrived home, he picked on something really small and made it into a mole hill. I guess anything would do as an excuse to fight with me, to hate me, to put me down. But at least I wasn't beaten. I guess Mom and I had cleaned everything up enough.

The next morning the same thing happened, although not quite to the same extent. I quickly worked to put things back together as my mother's words rang out in my head: "He will kill you!"

Again, I grabbed the kids, put them in the pram, scribbled a quick note to Jack, threw a few things together, and headed out the door to Cathy's and Michael's. I couldn't think of anywhere else to go, but I knew I couldn't stay there. Mom's words were clear and I had no doubt that my demise was not far away.

Again Cathy and Michael took me in.

This time I couldn't find a job, so I depended on their generosity and what I could get from the local court house. There was, however, a difference this time. Michael and Cathy were on tenterhooks. Something was happening with their relationship as well, and I was sure that I was not helping the situation.

One day I said, "I'd better leave."

But Michael said, "No."

Then the very next day Cathy left. She left behind her baby as she had been admitted to hospital. Even though it had never been my reason for seeking Michael and Cathy's help, it didn't take very long before Michael and I fell back into each other's arms. I needed so much to be loved and wanted, like he must have also.

But this was not the past. My thoughts were that we could just pick up where we had left off, with three additions. I made no consideration for the fact that what we had together had been short-lived. We had only ever had sex once and my love then had not been strong or mature enough to survive our separation in the first instance. It was only teenage love. There was no consummation of our second union.

When you are young and stupid, like I was, you do not think like an adult. You do not put things into perspective and you can make stupid decisions based on falsities, or worse, based on need.

The very next morning I woke with an intense pain in my left side, which I could not explain. It seared through me from front to back. I couldn't move. Later that day Cheryl took me to see a doctor who said I had a kidney infection and that I should go back home to bed rest. So, that's what I did. Michael had to take care of the three kids while I rested, that's if you can call not being able to move an inch without massive pain sweeping through your body resting.

A couple of nights later, Jack was on Michael's doorstep demanding to see me. Michael was frustrated because he was trying to care for the three kids and, unfortunately, he was seeing my lying in bed as just laziness even though I was deathly ill.

Well, it wasn't long before the whole scenario fell into a hole, and it took one last visit from Jack to coax me back home. He promised again to change, to give up drinking. Because I was in such a bad situation, I fell for it, hook, line, and sinker. I knew in the future I could not run to Michael. Too much water had gone under the bridge and Cathy was returning to him also. Childhood loves should always remain just that.

Again, as before, the drinking did not stop, the nightly bashings continued, and the abusive and sometimes physical breakfasts happened every day. It wasn't long before I felt at my lowest point. There was no escaping him. I had nowhere to go, nobody cared. From within that darkness, one day I suddenly felt a sense of calmness come over me. This was something I had never felt before. Everything seemed so very clear. I had a plan of action that was obtainable—one that would bring peace. And it was so easy.

I slowly walked to the kitchen and reached for the tablets in the pantry.

I slowly walked to the sink, filled a glass with water, and took the tablets, one by one, until they were all gone.

I slowly walked into the lounge and sat, just staring at what I was married to. Dribble ran down his face and froth was at the side of his mouth as he snarled words at me with a wild look in his eyes, barely able to stand—but he still would have been able to deliver a good right hook.

Oh, did I forget to tell you that I actually did marry him? Well, I did. It was as exciting as that. The reason? To make me an "honest woman" and give the kids a name. It was so important to his mother that it had to be done. No roses and violins, or proposals on bended knee in a romantic setting. It was more like, "Mom has booked us in to get married at the Registry Office on…" You know, I don't even remember the date.

I closed my eyes, and before I knew it he was on me.

"Who said you could go to fuck'n sleep?" I found myself fighting the urge to sleep, scared of being bashed one last time before I left this earth. Then I collapsed.

I don't remember getting to the hospital. I don't remember much at all except for waking up and the nurse telling me I was a very lucky girl. I turned my head to face the wall and a single tear rolled down my cheek towards the pillow.

I mumbled, "Lucky in whose book?"

I was no stranger to this hospital. My file was over two inches thick with all the attendances for "falls" that I had taken, walls I had walked into, and all the other excuses I had come up with over time. The nurse looked at me with pity and I just cried. After a psych consult, I was allowed to go home. The psych said it was all just circumstantial.

I was discharged and left the hospital, but when I returned home, the door was locked. I couldn't get in. I called for Jack to come and let me in, but it was little Jason who pulled his chair to the front door and opened the lock. I walked in and Jack attacked me as soon as I walked in, yelling at me, wanting to know who I had been with, who I had fucked. He was relentless, never wearying from his goal. He was insane.

I am still not sure what made me go to the extent that I did—to attempt suicide. I just saw it as the only alternative to my situation. Our neighbor had committed suicide only the week before and it had worked for him. My mom had tried and failed, but obviously I still felt it was an option. Actually, it was quite easy to do in that calm space I had found myself in.

My next visit to the hospital wasn't too long after. Another overdose. Another failed suicide attempt. This time a stern warning from the psych came that if it were to happen again, they would have to lock me up for my own good.

Then a miracle—actually the first of a few! The first miracle was winning two tickets to see the Bay City Rollers, which Jack refused bluntly to let me attend. So I thought if I put up a notice in the local milk bar, someone might get some enjoyment out of the tickets, as I certainly was not going to. When Jack left for work, I headed to the milk bar around the corner less than fifty meters away, with the kids wrapped up in the pram, to see if I could put a note in the shop window. I also had to grab some milk.

Bingo. When I walked into the shop, three young girls were standing there. I would learn their names later: Leah, Sharon, and Josephine. I asked if they wanted the tickets because I wasn't allowed to go.

Sharon laughed at me and said, "Get a life."

At first I thought that was quite rude, but they all laughed and saw the hilarity in it. The Bay City Rollers were not everybody's cup of tea. They asked who I was and where I lived. I was only a year or two older than them. I introduced myself and invited them to come around some time, pointing out that if Jack's truck was there, they shouldn't come in.

Another miracle, and one which would ultimately change the direction of my life, happened the very next day—the girls came to visit. It was so nice to have people around I could talk to; although adrenalin pumped through my veins the entire time they were there, in case Jack came home or Charlie was parked down the road spying on me, as he did.

They could tell I was on edge and Sharon's response to that was "Fuck him." I told her it wasn't as simple as that.

They came and went a few times over the next few weeks, keeping me company during the day, until one day Charlie came while they were there. He didn't say anything, but he ran like a weasel and snitched to Jack as to what he had seen. The very next day, Jack came home early to catch me out. My heart was in my throat as I heard the truck pull up. I knew he was not going to be happy at all. He didn't like anyone being there during the day when he wasn't home. In fact, he didn't like me to have any friends or family around. Nobody! I had been cut off from every person I knew.

I was shocked when he came in as he was as nice as pie to the girls. They could sense my anxiety though and immediately took their leave. Within minutes of the girls leaving, I became Jack's punching bag.

"What. Have. I. Told. You. About. Playing. Up. On. Me. Bitch!" as each punch connected.

I had a beautiful black eye the next day when the girls arrived. They cared for me, looked after the kids, did the housework, and told me I should leave him. I told them I had tried but failed a few times already as I had nowhere to go and nobody to help me.

So a pattern was set. Each day after Jack left, the girls snuck in. They knew what time to leave before Jack got home.

Eventually, Sharon got brave and wouldn't go home. I pleaded with her to leave but she said, "No. He can't make me; this is your house too. He's not going to hit you tonight," and with that she didn't budge.

This then became a daily plan. The girls would stay, refusing to be frightened away by Jack. He was learning to share me, but he hated the lack of control that he wielded over me when they were around. You could see it in his eyes. So each night when they left, he turned from Mr. Nice Guy into Dr. Jekyll and Mr. Hyde. The routine remained in place. The girls went home, the beatings came thick and fast, the verbal attacks spewed forth.

The lack of sleep from fear of being bashed again kept me on the edge of my seat.

I knew what to expect, so one night while the girls were there, rather than go through the consequences when they left, I again took an overdose of tablets. This time though, without realizing it, I took something that would not harm me. The girls called an ambulance and the ambulance attendant said that they couldn't take me to the hospital if I was refusing to go. They checked me and assured everyone I would be okay. I was screaming out for a solution to my problem, a solution nobody could give me except myself. But first I just had to accept the inevitable, and I wasn't able to do that.

Several months on when my resolve was totally depleted, again I tried to end it. This time I took a huge number of tablets and was rushed to the hospital unconscious. Jack was good enough to call my mother. When she picked up the phone, he apparently said, "Your fucked-up daughter's done it again—tried to commit suicide, but she's so stupid she can't even do that right." And he hung up.

Mom called Uncle Geoff and he called the police. The police found out that I was at PANCH Hospital, so Uncle Geoff drove Mom there. They paced the floor outside in the waiting room while the doctors worked to save my life. They pumped my stomach and then forced me full of medication to make me vomit. After hours of working with me, Mom and Uncle Geoff were allowed to see me. Mom cried, "Why?"

"I can't take it anymore, Mom."

"Leave him."

"Mom, can I come and live with you?" I asked. "Will you take me and the kids in? Can I rent the bungalow from you?"

She said no because she needed the rental money.

I turned to her and said, "Well, it looks like I just have to stay with Jack because I have nowhere else to go."

The doctor was willing to release me into my mother's care, and Uncle Geoff drove me home. Before I got out of the car, Uncle Geoff turned to me and said, "Please don't ever make me go through that again. First your mother and now you. I couldn't stand to lose either of you."

He got out of the car and gave me a hug and then I walked inside. The front door was open, the lights were all on. Jack was dead drunk and asleep on the couch. I was over it. I could have easily taken another bunch of tablets, but Uncle Geoff's words rang in my ear. I remembered also how I'd felt when Mom had almost died when I was just a little girl. I didn't want those memories for my little boy and girl. Finally, I snapped out of it. I knew there would be another way out of this situation, one that wouldn't leave me dead and my children motherless. But what?

32

The Last Straw

"You have not been hurt bad enough if you are not willing to change your situation."

Answers were not immediately obvious to me. Life went on and the kids got older and were starting to see things now. Jason reacted every time Jack raised his voice and spent the night banging his little head against his bedhead to comfort himself. I was not allowed to go to him once he had been put to bed. When he was awake, he clung to me, as did Tammy.

Life was horrible. Jack's mother became more possessive, not only over Jack but now over the two children. If she was invited for dinner, which Jack did often, she brought dinner with her, stating that he preferred her cooking over mine. This was followed by a smug smile, even when I had made an entire meal for them. It was pushed out of the way and hers was dished up.

Mona and Charlie did the gardening, mowed the lawns, emptied the garbage, cleaned up the yard, and even took the washing if it was already done and would do it again.

The baby's nappies were often taken and put through the copper to keep them white. I appreciated her doing that because I had an old, beat-up washing machine that had been salvaged from a refuge, which Charlie had cleaned out. It was broken more often than it worked, and, besides, I loved the look and the smell of the clean, white nappies on a baby's bum.

So when it was broken, the nappies were soaked in a bucket until picked up by Jack's Mom and then taken to be laundered at her house. She preferred it that way anyway. Nappies were plentiful at our house; I would go through at least two dozen each day.

These two people ran our lives. Jack was not capable of running his own. I was, but he gave them permission to dictate to both of us when he allowed them to provide everything for us, and I mean everything.

One Saturday Jack had gone off to the football with his uncle and the girls asked if I'd like to go into the city with them and see a picture, their shout. They thought it was only fair. Jack was out so why shouldn't I have a bit of fun also? I do not know what gave me the idea that this was going to be a good thing.

I wanted to jump at the chance; I had never been out with the girls. Actually I had never been out, but I had no one to look after the children. Then I had an epiphany—my mother. Mom had offered to look after the kids for me at one stage. I thought it would be nice if she could have some grandmother-grandchildren time, and I could finally have some me time. It was the one and only time Mom had ever been asked to look after the children. She jumped at the chance, and within the hour she arrived at the house. I told her I would be back before Jack got home. The girls and I quickly headed out and jumped on a tram headed to the city.

When we got there, Sharon said we should drop into the hotel and have a drink together. The last time I had had a drink was when I was fourteen and spent the afternoon in Keon Park. I agreed, and we walked into the hotel and ordered drinks. There were a group of sailors there, and it didn't take long for them to take notice of us four girls together, alone. New blood. Before long they were shouting us drinks and we were having a fantastic time. We never did get to the pictures.

One sailor in particular had taken a shine to me, and I had to tell him that I was married and had children. It didn't stop his advances. It felt so good to be desired. The attention was very welcomed. In what seemed like a very short time, I looked at the clock and died of shock. It was nearly six o'clock in the evening. Time had flown, but we hadn't seen it because we were inside a dim bar.

I knew I was going to be in serious trouble, but I was also terrified for my mother, who now would be at home alone with Jack. Mom wouldn't just leave when Jack got home. No, I knew she would stay to make sure that I was okay. After all those years of neglect by Mom, after she saw what Jack was doing to me, her protective streak was finally starting to show through. I made a call to the house to let her know that I was on my way and to apologize for losing track of time. She was fine with the fact that I had lost track of time, but in a low voice she told me not to come home.

"Don't come back to the house, whatever you do. He will kill you."

Then she was gone. Jack had pulled the phone out of her hand and yelled, "Where are you, bitch? You'd better get your fuck'n, whoring arse home now."

I turned to the girls and said in a panic, "I have to go, NOW!" The urgency in my voice scared the girls. We quickly stood up, said goodbye, and headed straight for the tram. All the way home the girls were saying, "Oh fuck him," and "Why don't you just leave him?" They didn't understand it just wasn't that easy.

When the tram stopped at our street and we got off, the girls asked if I wanted them to come home with me. I answered no. With that I put my head down and hurried towards the house. It was about seven o'clock when I walked in the door, which was wide open. When my mother heard my footsteps on the verandah, she stood quickly from her sitting position in the lounge room and let out a blood-curdling scream. "RUUUUUN....!" I didn't need to be told twice.

I saw the look on her face and then the look on Jack's. He was like a wild man, eyes wide open, and pupils dilated. He looked possessed.

I ran out of the house, down the stairs, out the gate, and towards the main road. I don't know where I was running to, but I had hoped that being on the main road and being visible would deter him from hitting me.

I was halfway across the main road when he grabbed my hair from behind. It felt like he was ripping my scalp off. He swung me around, tripping me over and smashing me into the road. Then the kicks and the punches started. I could hear my mother screaming at the side of the road, begging him to stop. He continued to kick and punch.

Cars drove past and around us and nobody stopped. He had me on the tram tracks. I was completely aware of where I was. My head was hurting badly, my side was hurting, my back was hurting. I could hear my mother screaming at him, but I couldn't stop him. All I could do to protect myself was curl into a ball to stop him kicking my stomach.

Mom ran to the local phone and called 000. She begged the police to attend. Their reply? "Sorry, Madam. It's a domestic dispute between a husband and wife and we can't intervene."

"Then you had better send an ambulance because she's gonna be dead when he's finished with her," she shouted down the phone. They did!

The kicks and punches stopped. Jack walked off and left me lying in the middle of the road, unable to move. He was getting more brazen, daring to bash me in front of people. That was a scary progression to his abuse. What would he do next?

The world was spinning. I'd taken six or more good kicks to the head with his steel capped boots, although my arms had been able to block the brunt of them. Mom was there, holding my hand and crying the words, "I'm sorry, but I couldn't do anything to stop him." Red lights were flashing and some nice men were lifting me onto a stretcher to put me into the back of the ambulance.

Things were rushed at the hospital. An intravenous tube was placed in my arm immediately. A barrage of tests and x-rays were run and pain medication was administered. Before I knew it I was sleeping. The next morning when I woke, I was black and blue. My eyes were swollen and bruised; there was blood on my face; my flank areas were heavily bruised; and the pain was intense. I was kept in intensive care for twenty-four hours in case of bleeding as they said that my kidney had ruptured, although my spleen was fine. I was then sent to a ward.

Mom came to visit and said she had been back to Jack's to try and get the kids, but he wasn't there. Obviously he had taken the kids to his mother, far be it for him to take care of them. In fact, I don't think he would even remember what he had done the night before. It seems that because of the alcohol he had a memory problem.

I was at the hospital for four or five days. In that time I was poked, prodded, and photographed. The police attended but told me that it was domestic battery and as such they could not lay charges against Jack.

If I had not married him, it would have been a different story. Life is so different these days. Back then men who bashed their wives had free reign to continue. It was a "domestic issue". It was "He is entitled to do it" or "What did she do to deserve it?" never "He shouldn't be doing that." Yes, they were dark days. I'm not saying that all men bashed their wives, and I'm not saying that some wives didn't bash their husbands. I'm just saying it was acceptable, very wrong, but acceptable, nevertheless.

I was a victim of domestic violence, but I was a victim who was suddenly gaining resolve, something I had not really had until that moment. Before my only option seemed to be suicide. But now a sudden surge of adulthood flowed through my veins. An intelligence that had escaped me for years suddenly came flowing into my life, like a lava flow, thick, fast, and inescapable. While I sat there in that hospital bed, still in pain from the assault, I knew one thing for sure. No matter what, I had to leave Jack. I had to go very far away from him, so he could never find me again. I could not stay with Jack for another minute. He had beaten me severely in public and even the Police Force wouldn't protect me. The next time I could very likely be killed. And then what would happen? My poor babies would have no mother. There is a saying that "you have not been hurt bad enough if you are not willing to change your situation". Well, now I was ready, whatever it took. The final straw had been bent, the final gauntlet thrown down … or so I thought.

On the day I left the hospital. I put my bloodied clothes back on, as that was all I had. Jack had not been near me, or his family. I walked home and knocked on the door. I could hear the kids inside and Jack's truck was parked in the sideway, so I knew that he was in there. I begged him to let me in and he told me over and over to go away. When I told him I would not go without the kids, he told me that I was a deserting mother and had no rights.

I could hear Jason trying to unlatch the door to let me in, but Jack was stopping him. I told him I wasn't going anywhere and I sat on the doorstep and waited. I waited and dusk settled. I waited and night time came. I waited into the cold hours of the night. Eventually, morning came and I was still waiting. Jack opened the door and beckoned for me to come inside.

As I did he went to grab my arm and my head snapped towards him. For one brief moment, I tasted insanity; anything could have happened. My eyes followed his every move, never straying, never blinking, and my voice came out cold and forbidding. "Don't. Touch. Me," I warned as I pulled my arm away.

He backed off.

"The only reason I've let you in is because I have to go to work and I've got nobody to look after the kids," he said.

I looked him in the eyes. "Jack, I'm leaving you, once and for all. I don't know if I will be here tonight when you come back."

He quietly left the house and didn't say a word.

As soon as his truck pulled away from the curb, Sharon was inside. She took one look at me and said, "You have to leave this bastard; he can't keep doing this to you." I didn't need to be told. I was already busy packing a few of my personal possessions into a box, my hands shaking so badly I could not still them—a symptom of the shock that I was still suffering.

Sharon looked at my yellowing bruises and asked, "Where are you going to go?"

"I have no idea, but I can't stay here any longer."

We left the house and together we walked the length of Plenty Road, attempting to find a rental that I could take up. But I had no job, no deposit, and no rent. It was impossible. I was crying and Sharon was trying to reassure me.

"It's okay; we'll find something," she said with a confidence that I couldn't muster for myself. Then we happened across a small real estate who said it must have been our lucky day. He had a property that a bikie gang had just moved out of, and he told me that I could take it and live rent-free for three months if I cleaned it up. A third miracle. He explained how he couldn't put anybody else in it for fear of the bikies returning and doing bad things. But if I was willing to cope with that, then I could take it.

We went and had a look at it. There was oil on the floor and the place stunk. Graffiti covered the walls and the backyard had one meter high grass. It was bad. The stairs were rickety and dilapidated. I had nothing—no furniture, no belongings, no bed, no refrigerator. I wasn't sure how I was going to survive, but I would. I died inside when I realized that I would not be able to take the kids. It was no place to bring the children; however, it would be okay for me. There was also no way I could look after them. I actually believed I couldn't. All these thoughts ran through my head. *I'm not capable. I'm an idiot, a low-life, a big fat whore who doesn't deserve them. They deserve much better than me or what I can give them, which is bloody nothing. This sort of place fits me, but not my sweet babies. Where would they sleep? I have no beds for them? How can I feed them?* So many thoughts, none I could share. In the days that followed, as the girls spoke to me about leaving I just went along with the status quo for the ease of conversation. They were all too young; they didn't understand at all.

I had no money and no job, and even if I had a job, I had nobody to care for them while I worked. So many questions and thoughts spun around in my mind. No, they were better off where they were.

I rang my mom and told her that I had found somewhere to live and that I was leaving Jack, but I had to leave the kids because I had nowhere safe to take them.

Later that night my brother arrived at the door with Maree. Danny told Jack that he wanted to talk to me *alone*, and Jack didn't dare say anything. Danny shut the door to the kitchen and we sat and talked about what was going on. Mom had been in touch with Danny. I wasn't sure what he knew, but it seemed Mom might have told him everything. I was so embarrassed. My brother begged me to follow through on my plans and leave Jack. But when I told him that I wouldn't be able to take the kids with me, he was devastated and begged me to reconsider leaving the kids, and to take them with me.

I explained why I had to do it this way. Besides, there was also the fact that Jack would never let me take them. "I can't, Danny, even though I want to. I have nowhere safe to take them. The house I'm going to live in is a wreck and dangerous. And I've got nothing to take with me and no-one to look after them if I find a job. Jack's Mom will make sure that they have a good home and will never want for anything. Jack will take them to her as soon as I leave. He always does … *And* if I stay here, he might kill me."

I'd figured it all out. All I had was a dangerous, dilapidated house to live in, no furniture, no money, no job. And I didn't tell Danny this bit, but if the bikies came back they might cause trouble. It would be okay if I was in the firing line, but not my kids. I might even end up on the street. I knew how well I had coped before, or not coped on the street, didn't I? And now it was even worse. Now I was also hopeless, stupid, and naïve—believing everything Jack said about me was true. But I didn't tell Danny those thoughts either.

I asked Danny if I could bring the children and live with them until I got on my feet. Danny and Maree couldn't offer me an alternative. Living with them was definitely not going to happen, so after an hour they left, exasperated.

The next night my sister arrived to talk to me and, again, the same thing—no alternatives were offered. It seemed it wasn't anybody's responsibility to take care of my problems. I got myself into this, so I alone had to make it better. It didn't matter how much I begged everybody to take my problem and help, they couldn't—or wouldn't. Everyone had their own lives, their own problems. None offered us refuge. I felt I shouldn't expect them to solve my problems, anyway. Besides, I had a plan now and I knew what I had to do.

If I lived, maybe one day I could be a parent to my children again.

If I died, well, I would never be there for them again.

The answer was obvious.

I had no idea, though, how hard it would be for me to get them back again when I was on my feet. I hadn't really thought that far ahead. Again, my lack of knowledge and maturity was to let me down. If the same thing happened today, I'd have been with my kids in a refuge with all sorts of services helping us.

Every day for the next few days, Jack came home early or at lunchtime and didn't lay a hand on me. But he was still trying to show control and manipulation by his words and actions. I think I had put the fear of God into Jack with my ice-cold words the day I came home from the hospital. And perhaps my family visiting had unnerved him. The girls were not dropping in as much as they usually did—they were too scared. They didn't like what they saw. They knew Jack was capable of much, much, more, and they didn't want to be his victims as well or even be involved, except for Sharon.

One night he crossed the line. After I cooked his dinner, which I had not done for him since my return, he threw it at me then came at me to follow through with his usual. Suddenly my arm shot out and I grabbed him around the neck. In a moment of mental desperation, I gathered strength from deep within and spun him around, smashing his head over and over into the light switch in the dining room until I saw blood running down the back of his neck. Then I pushed him off and again said, "Don't fuck'n touch me, again, ever."

"You're a fuck'n crazy person and should be locked up!" he cried.

"Oh, yeah?" I replied. "Go ahead, call the police. They won't come—it's a domestic matter."

I refused to make him another meal and told him instead that if he wanted to act like a dog he could eat off the floor. Then I walked out of the kitchen and left him to it.

Even though I put on a brave face, I was very, very scared. I felt like a rat caught in a trap. I could feel his eyes on me every time I moved. I was living with a time bomb that had a very short fuse and, at any moment, it could explode. I knew it was only a matter of time before he did, and he would kill me, if I didn't kill him first.

I decided that the next day was the day for me to make my move. I had put it off for so long because the stakes were high. I had to leave my babies and it was the last thing on this earth that I wanted to do. I sat on the couch and watched Jack as he drank himself into oblivion. He bad-mouthed me all night with various put-downs about my life, my family, and just me in general. I slept on the lounge chair with one eye open, ready to move at any second. But eventually he fell asleep where he sat and I knew he would stay that way until at least 6 a.m. when his usual shit would start again. I relaxed enough to get a few hours of sleep before we would start again.

As Jack was walking out the door to go to work, I told him that I was leaving that day. He stopped and said, "Over my dead body, and don't think you're taking the fuck'n kids because I'll hunt you down and kill you."

I said, "And? What would you do with them Jack? You can't even look after yourself." A part of me was hoping like hell that he would say "Take them then" and let me walk away with them. But I knew that he saw me as his possession to control and that he would never say that, and even if he did, I could never take the kids where I was going. I knew that I could not give them the quality of life they needed. I could only give them everything that I had—which was me. I knew that I wasn't enough. He turned one last time, looked at me with daggers, and said, "Don't you dare fuck'n leave me, I mean it. I'll come after you, I mean it!" he yelled as he stormed off towards his truck.

I yelled back at the top of my voice into the street after him. "Fuck you, arsehole. You can't tell me what to do." I was no wilting daisy. I had the mouth of a gutter snipe and had always been told by my elocution teacher at the convent that placement of words was my specialty.

Why did Jack want me to stay? It was not that he loved me in any way. I was merely a possession, a puppet that he could maneuver and control at his whim. Someone to take his anger and tirades out on, who normally wouldn't fight back for fear of retribution. If I left, it would not be me that he grieved for, it would be the control that he no longer had over somebody, anybody.

The girls came around and grabbed my little box of goods. They knew where I was going and that I had no hope of getting the box out of the house when the time came. So they took it for me. I didn't pack much, just enough to support myself. A few clothes. Well, all I had, which wasn't much. I had never been allowed to buy any. Some underwear, shoes, a towel, one plate, a cup, a knife, a fork, a spoon, one pot, and a tea towel. That was it! The total sum of my life, to that date, in a small box, the size of a small book packing box.

Jack came home early again. I had Jason and Tammy in bed for their afternoon sleeps. They looked so peaceful. I had sat on the floor of their bedroom for ages, just staring at them both. Jason's fine, blond locks were curling around his face and ears, his little chest rising and falling with his soft, whispery breaths. Tammy's face was serene and soft. Her pink hair bow, which had come undone, fell across the side of her face with her dark brown locks in tow. Their bedroom wasn't that big and their beds were side by side, close together. From where I sat on the floor I could hold each of their little hands. This was my final gesture of goodbye. I didn't know how long it would be before I ever saw them again. I knew one thing for sure; Jack wouldn't make it easy. All I could hope for was that one day in the future, they would come and find me, and when that time came, I would hope to make up for all the missed years. I knew it was going to be hard—I didn't realize how hard. I knew that Jack would use the kids as pawns to manipulate and control me. But first he had to find me.

I heard his truck pull up, so I immediately stood and kissed each of the children on their cheeks and whispered softly, "Goodbye, I love you." I gently brushed the hair from their faces and then I left the room. Right there, right then, my heart was torn in two—a wound so deep that it would never heal. I hated Jack then more than I had hated anyone or anything at any other time in my life—I still hate him. Through his actions he had taken from me the two most valuable things that had ever been given to me. Without his help I couldn't take care of them, but to stay would be putting my life in jeopardy because of his control issues.

When Jack came in, I told him that the kids were asleep and that I had to quickly run and get milk before he went back to the depot. I said that I would then come back and get his afternoon tea. I had written a letter to him earlier in the day, telling him that I had to leave him and why. I don't know what I said in the letter, but knowing me, I would have been trying to make him feel like he was the good guy and I was the monster. All I know is that I hate leaving people feeling bad, and even though I hated him, I didn't really want to hurt him.

I didn't listen to Jack's grunts and arguments, not wanting to look after the kids for all of five minutes while I ran to the shop. It was in that moment that I had to summon all my courage. He wanted me to take the kids with me. I just looked at him and shook my head. I grabbed my bag as I walked out and quickly glanced sideways, blowing a kiss to my angels as I walked past their room and out of their lives through the front door.

I didn't turn around.

I didn't dare stop.

I didn't wipe the tears that were now running down my cheeks.

I threw the letter into Jack's truck window, knowing he would find it when he got back in. I knew I had to be strong and keep moving forward. I got to the corner and I ran, and I didn't stop running until I was safely in the door of the house that would become my home, for a short while at least. It was some five or six kilometers from where Jack now was with my children. I cried like I had never cried before ...

33
Hello Sailor

*"She couldn't understand the driving need I had
inside, the demons that pushed me ever
onward to find ... him."*

For the very first time in my life, I was alone. Totally alone! Responsible for nobody and, in turn, nobody was responsible for me. I looked around me at the dirt, the filth, and the graffiti and slid down the wall to sit on my haunches. As dusk fell, I had a heightened awareness of every sound around me, both inside the house and outside in the small laneway that went up the side of the house. The front door to the house was accessed via this laneway. It was also used quite often by people on their way home from High Street to the street behind. Drunks fell into the laneway and used it as a urinal, often dropping their bottles of booze and sending them smashing all over the concrete. I hate to think what other unsavory types of characters used the lane. I just know it was a busy place of a night.

The house was attached to a shop and the front bedroom looked out onto High Street, a busy main road. There were three or four main bedrooms upstairs and a lounge room, kitchen, outdoor bathroom, and toilet downstairs. The front door was not very reliable, probably due to the number of times it had been kicked in by the police when the bikies had lived there. The staircase was rickety and the floorboards squeaked, but it was now home.

There was a knock at the door and the girls were yelling at me to let them in. I ran to the door. It was so great to see them; I had felt so alone. Tears stained my face again, and many still fell at the idea of not being with the kids. Leah informed me that Jack was in his truck looking for me everywhere. He had asked Josephine to mind the kids while he looked. Josephine was the only one who had no idea where I had gone; she didn't agree with me leaving. In fact, she may have even sided with Jack a little. They had gone to the house to see if I had left yet and Jack was angry, really angry—but only angry at being left with the kids.

Sharon said, "You did the right thing, but I'm still not sure about the kids." I knew that they had reservations, as did I.

I was thankful for all their help, but I knew that they too would soon walk away from me and leave me in the too hard basket. Then I feared I'd be back to square one and have to return to Jack. No. I had to cut the umbilical cord and stay away. Jack was no good for my future or my life. He had already proven that. I had to make sure that whatever I did now was sustainable, for myself, for my survival. I couldn't depend on anybody else to make sure that my future was secure. These were the sorts of thoughts running through my mind.

As it got later into the night the girls said they had to go. They had previously told me they were going to move in with me, but it seems they had forgotten those words already as nothing was mentioned. Let down number one. I sat on the floor in the lounge area. Sharon had remarked that I had no electricity. I told her I didn't know how to put it on, and if it cost money I wouldn't be able to. She said she would bring me some candles the next day from her home, and they left.

I sat cross-legged on the floor with my back against the wall. I had nothing to sleep on or to keep me warm. I rugged up as best as I could and huddled myself into a ball, rocking myself backwards and forwards. The tears came. Images of Jason and Tammy flashed through my mind for the better part of the night. Several times I thought, *Fuck it*, and stood up to go back to Jack. But I would get to the door and berate myself for being so foolish. I knew that going back to him would not improve the situation. It would only make it worse. It would confirm to him that I couldn't live without him and it would put me front and center as his punching bag for however long it took for him to end my life.

I had so many thoughts ... *Those children deserve a far better mother than me ... Now they will have one ... Mother Catherine was right; I should have adopted Jason out when he was born, then this wouldn't be happening* ... But even if I had, Jack still would have hunted me down and never left me alone. He was controlling and dominating, and even without the baby he would have found me and ruled over me. I had been ripe for the picking. My convent years had made me submissive, as had the many rapes in my childhood. By the time I had turned sixteen, I was ready for a master. I was ready for someone to come along and tell me what to do, where to go, when I would do what, and how I would live.

Right on cue along he came, horns, tail, and pitch fork. He controlled me like a slave, a battered slave. The abuse was daily—mental, physical, and sexual. "No" did not mean "no" in our household. He was small but very powerful, and I could never fight my way out of his grip. Yes, I was abused in every way possible. Every way! If Jack wanted it, he took it.

I knew Jack's mother would take care of the children after my departure and that she would never allow any harm to come to either of them. It wouldn't take long for Jack to hand them over to her. (I was to find out later that I wasn't wrong there.) I also knew one more thing for sure: she would never let me see them again. That thought sent me into another spin of despair and sadness. I was not thinking in any sort of logical capacity. I started feeling sorry for myself—*poor me*. And then I couldn't accept the fact that the kids would grow up without their mother. *Poor Tammy and Jason, poor kids. What have I done?*

It was heartbreaking enough that I had walked out and left them, but I didn't even have a picture of them. The only things I had were two small bluebird name badges that belonged to them, and I clutched them in my fist all night. As I sat and looked around in the cold of the night, at the dirt and grime, I shook my head in defeat. I knew I had done the right thing. I couldn't bring them here. Fuck, I couldn't even feed myself, let alone the kids. What would I have done with them?

In the dark of that night I longed for the touch and the smiles of the two little people who were left behind. I remembered how I used to sit with them and play during the day. I would rock them to sleep when I could slip away from Jack at night. Sometimes when Jack fell asleep on the couch, I would sneak into their room and pull their sleeping bodies up into my arms and hug them for a while, until I would hear him stir. These memories weren't comforting me at all.

After a very cold, dark night alone, the next morning I looked like a wreck. I grabbed my towel from the small box and some fresher clothes and headed to the bathroom. I turned on the shower and the water was stone cold. That's right—you need electricity for hot water. Oh well, I had to wash. I couldn't be dirty. I had to find a job, so I jumped into the cold shower. It took my breath away and for a moment I wished that it would take my breath away forever so I didn't have to accept what I'd done. But it didn't! In fact, a part of me has never accepted nor forgiven myself for walking away and leaving my children the way that I did, although I know situational issues had to be taken into account. My staying alive for just one more day was a major consideration. I never considered myself to be much of a mother. Let's face it, how good can a teenager actually be? I had tried to be the best mother I could be in the circumstances. I gave it my best until I could give no more. I hoped that one day I would be reunited with my angels.

As one does when confronted with extremely cold water, I washed as fast as I could and jumped out to dry myself off even faster to get some blood flowing. I dressed and headed out the door at 8 a.m. to attend the local unemployment office. I was really lucky that there was a job going as a coffee maker at a stall at Flinders Street Station in Melbourne City. They gave me enough money to attend the interview and I got the job. One thing is for sure, whenever I look for work, it's always there. This was a start, a little start, but a good one. At least I was moving forward. It meant that I had to get up very early some days for the next week to walk for a couple of hours from Northcote to the city. But after I got my first pay packet I was able to use the tram. Sometimes I got a few tips during the day, which meant I could catch the tram home, or even get the tram to work the next day.

Over the next few weeks I was able to have the electricity connected to the house and I cleaned it up a little, getting rid of the oil off the floor with my expert floor cleaning skills gained from the convent. The girls helped when they came around, and eventually it was all starting to come together.

My mother had come to see me and took me to St. Vincent's. She explained my situation to them and they gave me a double mattress, some blankets, a table, and a couple of other bits and pieces. My mother purchased a second-hand refrigerator off them, also, and gave it to me. After a couple of weeks, the girls came to see me and asked if I wanted to go into the city with them again. I jumped at the chance.

I borrowed clothes from them and off we went. That started the first of many trips into the city. We went in search of the sailors that we had met that day weeks ago. We found them, but not the one who had been particularly attracted to me—Scottie. Apparently, he had moved on, having left HMAS Cerberus, the Navy training base in Victoria, to go to his ship posting in Sydney to continue his career.

Over the next few months, I would grow well acquainted with the Navy, its customs, and in particular with the guys at Cerberus. I moved from guy to guy in search of someone who would take me for who I was deep down inside. Someone who would accept me and take me in his arms and tell me everything was going to be okay. I was still looking for someone to solve my problems. I wanted someone who would help me to fight for my children, who I hadn't seen since the day I left.

I look back now and I see a little girl, lost after many years of abuse and abandonment, who was searching for that one person who was going to make it all worth it. I searched and searched, going through sailors like they were water. I had lost all self-respect. Using and abusing them, all the while allowing them to think they were using and abusing me! My home became a refuge for them, and on weekends we could have up to a dozen or more sailors there, all looking for companionship and affordable accommodation. They were all great guys who would put themselves out for me. They would buy me food and give me a few dollars for letting them stay. It all helped to get me on my feet. I'm sure the local police thought that my home might have been a little more than a quiet suburban house given the comings and goings that went on. But they never bashed down the door or approached me in any way, so they must have been happy that all was normal and that I just had a lot of visitors.

Emotionally and mentally, though, I was still locked in a prison of insecurity—never good enough, ugly, fat, awkward, dumb … Yeah I knew it, but why these guys didn't, I'll never know. Why did they keep coming back? Couldn't they see who I was? It got around that I was an easy lay, and I suppose that was a fair call. I deserved it given how many of them I had slept with. My background and insecurities did me no favors. I didn't want to be an easy lay; I just looked at every person who showed me any attention as the one I should give my all to. And of course if you give your all, most people will take it, regardless of whether they deserve it or not. I was looking for the one who would take my love and respect it for what it was. Not a label.

And then I met one, a really nice guy named Tony. Before long I was expecting. After being checked out by the doctor I was advised that I should seek an immediate termination, sooner than later, given that I had already had two caesareans very close together. I was told that having another pregnancy on top of that would more than likely tear my uterus, which could cost me my life. It was unlikely that I would have a successful pregnancy and I would put both myself and the fetus in danger.

After much reluctance and with a very heavy heart, I booked into the hospital for a termination. Another child gone! I was doomed to never have the family I so desired. Tony accompanied me to the hospital along with his mate Bruce. We were very upset.

As they were wheeling the trolley along the hospital corridor to the theatre, I heard a booming voice yelling out, "Stop, you can't terminate that baby. You have to have permission from its father."

I looked sideways and saw Charlie running towards us—creepy man.

He pulled the nurse's arm and said, "Didn't you hear me? She can't have the baby terminated; it doesn't belong to her."

The nurse and orderly continued to push me along. Tony and Bruce broke away from the trolley and stopped Charlie from harassing me, stonewalling him in the corridor. My heroes!

"Fuck'n low life bitch," Charlie yelled as I was wheeled into theatre. I could hear him outside the theatre doors yelling out, "You'll pay for this. You'll get yours, you fuck'n whore. You're never going to see your kids again."

I was just about to break down, but before I could contemplate any of it

I was asleep. There was nothing he could do to stop the termination. It was classed as a medical emergency due to my circumstances and was requested at the insistence of a doctor. The baby was not Jack's baby anyway.

Shortly after that Tony and I parted ways. Tony wanted a family and it was obvious to him that I could never give him that. I think memories of that day ate away at his insides, making him more and more uncomfortable with our relationship.

More men came and went, and then another good one came along. Edward was a few years younger than me. Sharon was at her wits end by the time I met him. She had watched me go from guy to guy and was disgusted. She couldn't understand the driving need I had inside, the demons that pushed me ever onward to find ... him. But now I thought I had found him. Edward was everything I ever wanted. Attentive, social, funny, supportive, and a great listener. Sharon had to admit that I was finally onto a good one. He even talked her into trying to get the kids one weekend so that we could see them. Did I mention he was absolutely gorgeous as well? Six foot four, dark hair, blazing green eyes, a face and body to die for. Yep, pretty good, really.

Sharon arranged to mind the kids for the day and as soon as Jack was out the door, so was she. It was the best weekend of my life. We spent the day at the house, walked them to the local park, and played with them for a while. It was all over too quickly. Sharon had to have them back to Jack's by a certain time. The kids kicked and screamed as Sharon pulled them away from me to get them back to their father. It brought it all back again, all the emotions of the first time without them. I sulked for a week, not wanting to leave my bed.

One night after I had returned from work and bunkered myself down for the night, the guys from the Greek shop across the road came over and asked if I would assist a young Greek girl who had been abused by her parents—the abuse was horrific. She had to leave and find somewhere to go. It would only be for a few nights until they could rehouse her. I was thrilled that they had asked me and trusted me. I had been in the Greek shop several times to buy a souvlaki for dinner, but I didn't even know that they were aware I existed. Apparently, they had always silently looked out for me.

Sabah didn't take anything with her when she had to flee her parents' home. She was very young, sixteen or so, but seemed even younger mentally and emotionally. I made her comfortable on the couch downstairs, which was the only other area where a guest could sleep. I slept upstairs in the top room at the front of the house.

I had an exhausting day at work and when I came home, Sabah was already asleep downstairs. So I snuck up the stairs and quietly put myself to bed so as not to wake her. I drifted off to sleep fast as I was exhausted. I woke to a familiar rocking, and as my mind struggled to emerge from sleep into the here and now, I realized that I had a man on top of me—inside me—and he was rocking backwards and forwards as he engaged in sexual intercourse without my consent. I froze with fear as I looked at his face and couldn't recognize him. At first I thought I was dreaming and I tried to dismiss it from my mind; but no, I was being raped.

My thoughts were spinning at a phenomenal rate. I felt terrified, but my first thoughts were for Sabah. *What should I do? Where is Sabah? Is she alright? Should I scream? Will the guys in the Greek shop across the road come if they hear me?* I felt sick; I wanted to vomit. Flashes of my childhood played out in my mind also, adding insult to injury. What to do? I could smell his beery breath all over me. He ripped at my breasts and continued his barrage of shoves.

"You're lovin' this, ain't ya babe? I knew you'd be a good fuck." Then as if a miracle had happened, he just stopped. He pulled out of me and said, "I'm just gonna go get another beer, want one?" I looked at him, stunned. And then it hit me. *Just play along with him. That might get me out of this.* All the while my mind was screaming silently, *Where is Sabah? What the fuck is going on?*

Then I heard it. Bang, crash, crunch. He had fallen down the stairs. The bastard had come into my home, put his beer in my fridge, and taken me without my permission. And he thought all this was alright—he was acting as if he was an invited guest.

"I hope you broke your fuck'n neck!" I yelled, anger overtaking my fear. I jumped out of bed and quickly pulled my clothes on. I looked out the window and couldn't get anyone's attention. The only way to solve this was head on. I moved quickly down the stairs to the lounge room and saw Sabah sitting wide-eyed on the end of the couch. This bastard was laying naked the length of the couch, swigging on a bottle of beer with one hand and holding her arm with the other.

"Sabah, come to me," I said softly.

"Where the fuck do you think you're going?" he slurred.

"I just thought you might enjoy a hamburger before we get going again," I said as I winked at him.

"She stays with me," he stated firmly.

"No, I can't do that. You see Sabah is very young and I can't leave her with strangers. But I swear I'll just duck over and get a hamburger and come right back. Do you want one? How do you like it? Beetroot?"

He slurred, "Yeah," in agreement. With that I grabbed Sabah's hand and we slowly backed out of the lounge room heading towards the front door.

Once we hit the front door, I said quietly, "Run and don't stop." She did as I said and we ran towards the Greek shop, which was less than two minutes from where I lived, terrified he was chasing us.

"Rape!" I yelled as I entered the shop. A couple of the guys ran to Sabah, while the rest headed out the door to my house. He was gone, but how? In less than five minutes he had disappeared, no trace of him. Then the worst shock of all. He had raped Sabah also. Before he had come to me, he had been in the house for hours and this poor kid had sat there like a church mouse, too scared to move. Well, the Greek guys scoured the neighborhood for the rest of the night while I walked the distance with Sabah to PANCH Hospital to have her checked out. God knows what would have happened if they'd found him.

The nurses took swabs and did the usual rape kit test of the day on both of us. The police were called and so were Sabah's parents. She had been listed as a missing child. When Sabah's father arrived, I tried to tell him how sorry I was that I wasn't able to protect her, but he just spat on me and walked out. I never saw her again.

Sabah's parents did not want to press charges if the police caught the guy, and when I said that I wanted to, I was asked, "Really? Are you sure you want to do that? You know that they will make you out to be the bad one in this. They will bring up all sorts of things from your life and it will be all over the papers."

That was enough for me to drop that idea. All I could think of was seeing it all in the papers and Jack finding me. Then I wouldn't be rid of him from my life.

I was stunned that someone thought they had the right to do this to someone else and would get away with it. Anger boiled inside me as I walked home from the hospital by myself, each step harder than the first. My heart was so heavy. Then through teary eyes I looked up at the night sky and thought, *No, no. I am not going to be a victim.* I had been a victim for years and it had got me nowhere. So, no, not anymore. I put it to the back of my mind as just another experience, another hole in my heart that I would put a Band-Aid on and tuck away safely, until one day I would be strong enough to deal with it.

One day not long after, I went to pick up a friend from where she worked as a steam press operator in a drycleaners. And that's when I recognized him—the guy who had raped me and Sabah. He was standing at the back of the store. I felt sick to the stomach and wanted to start screaming "Rapist," but I held it together. I wanted him to recognize me so that I could see the guilt on his face, but he didn't look at me. There was no excuse for what he did, and I knew it was him. My gut was heaving and I wanted to throw up, but not before telling everyone. But I couldn't do that either. *What if it wasn't him?*

But it was! "Bastard!" I yelled as I left the store.

I later questioned Leah about the co-incidence of him working with her and she told me that she had spoken about my exploits at work. So he took it upon himself to partake of my body and got Sabah as a booby prize in the process. I went to the police immediately to inform them, hoping they would do something. Still nothing was done. It was my word against his and, again, I was convinced to walk away.

After Edward found out what had happened, he travelled the distance from Westernport, where HMAS Cerberus was located, to Melbourne every night to stay with me and keep me safe—except when he was on duty. It was much better having him around. I felt safer as I could not fall asleep in the house by myself after that. I still have problems to this day being alone at night, but over time I have gotten better. I have never felt safe since. Later in life when I would be left for weeks on end by myself at home, every night I would sleep on the couch in the lounge room and I would tie rope to every door handle so that they could not be opened from the outside.

Determined to put the rape behind me and not be a victim, I threw myself back into life. Weekends were great. We always went to town and danced the night away until the early hours of the morning, talking—or yelling—drinking, then falling back home off the tram. Or if we missed the last tram home, we walked if we didn't have the money for a taxi. Usually the times spent at nightclubs were drink sessions, and I learned to drink as good as any sailor. It took away the pain. It also gave me the bravado needed to interact socially on a peer-to-peer level—something I did not have the confidence to do under normal circumstances. Any self-confidence that I had when I left the convent, and I know it was very little, was stripped from me while I was married to Jack.

I loved the weekends as the world's woes disappeared and with it my woes. It didn't mean that I didn't care. It just gave me a little bit of freedom from my daily worries. I didn't realize at the time, until the girls pointed it out, that I was being watched from a distance. Charlie had found me and every night he sat in his car down the road, watching, and probably counting how many sailors came in and out of my house. I hope it was fun for him. It did freak me out a little and I considered reporting him to the police as a stalker, but I never did. It was only a matter of time before Jack would appear on the doorstep.

A few months before I had left Jack, an Aboriginal teenage girl I had known at the convent had caught up with me. She told me of the abuse in her marriage and the fact that she wanted to leave her husband but had nowhere to go. I knew how she felt. I told her that she could stay with us for a while. I knew Jack would mind, but I didn't care; it was only for a little while until she got on her feet.

I did not realize that Jack held such racial hatred towards Aboriginal people. I had grown up with her; I accepted her. I was more mature now and any misadventures I may have had with her while in the convent, for my part, were dead and buried. While we had had our differences, we certainly were past that period in our lives now. I welcomed her with open arms and she saved me for a little while as well.

Every night Jack sneered at me when she was out of earshot. "Get rid of that black bitch out of this fuck'n house," and "Fuck'n useless abo bludgin' off me." It broke my heart. I wanted to help her more than anything, but ultimately it became too much and I had to ask her to leave. It really was for her safety, as I could see Jack was reaching boiling point and was going to explode. Up till then he had done well to hold his anger in check, a rage that he would eventually take out on me. I don't think she ever did see that part of him; he was so different in front of other people—such a two-faced mongrel.

One Saturday morning, I woke up and left Edward sleeping while I snuck downstairs to get a coffee. I stepped over the numerous bodies on the floor and said good morning to those who were awake and able to talk. I went into the kitchen and yelled, "Who wants a cuppa?" Conversation buzzed in the lounge room, and then everything went deathly quiet. I heard a voice that I didn't recognize come from the lounge room.

"Where is the fuck'n bitch? Come out, ya bitch. You got business with us." As I walked towards the door with the kettle in my hand, I looked at a wall of sailors who had all jumped up from the floor to form a chain across the lounge room that nobody was going to cross. There they stood, staring down four Aboriginal men who now stood in the doorway of the lounge, having entered by kicking in the front door.

One of them piped up, "If you want her, you will have to go through us."

With that the oldest of the four turned and said, menacingly, "If you're here when we come back tonight, bitch, you and all these fuckers are dead. You've been warned." Just at that moment Edward, having heard the disruption from upstairs, came down and stood behind the unexpected visitors. The intruders turned and left.

"What was all that about?" Edward quizzed.

"I have no idea," I shrugged, "but they sounded very serious." And to this day I still have no idea what they wanted or why?

After that, the sailors who had been there dispersed quickly, some saying that they had to go back to Cerberus, others heading back into town. It was understandable. I didn't expect them to fight my battles for me. But who were those Aboriginal guys? And then a light bulb switched on in my head.

I had remembered the girls telling me that my Aboriginal friend had moved back into Jack's house shortly after I left and was living with him. Obviously, after Charlie had found me, Jack had sent her brothers around to do his dirty work. Oh no, if she only knew what he really felt about her. He was utilizing her and her brothers to punish me for leaving him.

That night the girls came and went. Edward asked what I wanted to do and I told him that I wanted to stay and be there when they came back. I didn't have much, but I didn't want to come home and find it all smashed up. This was my world. Besides, the door was still loose on its hinges. Edward had tried to fix it the best way he could, but without the correct tools it was useless trying. So we sat and waited and waited. Ten o'clock came and we both agreed that they were not coming, so we left. As I walked to Edward's car, I noticed Charlie was parked down the road.

God, doesn't he have anything better to do than to sit by the side of the road every single night and just watch me or follow me? Pervert!

We got into Edward's car and drove off. Instead of heading into town, we visited a friend who lived on the other side of town. I was too upset to go out and not very good company after what had happened that morning. Edward understood and stayed by my side. We had a good night and after an hour or so, they were able to cheer me up and make me smile. At about one o'clock in the morning we headed home.

As we neared the house I could see red and blue flashing lights. I turned and said to Edward, "There must be an accident or a fire down there."

As we got closer, I grabbed his arm and screamed. My house was on fire! The mongrels had burned down my house. Everything I had in the world, everything that I had ever worked for, was gone. It wasn't much, but I was back to square one again.

We parked the car and as we walked over to where the fire brigade was, we saw Charlie's car drive off. I hung my head, sat in the gutter, and cried. Edward found a police officer and asked what had happened. Apparently someone had reported seeing four men running from the house just before the fire. The fire had started in the front bedroom above the shop and had quickly caught hold. They wanted to question the young woman who lived there. Edward brought them over to me and they asked me a lot of questions. I told them what had happened that day and why I thought it had happened. Then the police officer advised me to turn around, walk away, and never come back—but I couldn't. He didn't even ask my name. The only mementoes I had of my children were in that house, in my bedroom, and I had to get them. I couldn't leave without Tammy and Jason's name badges.

We walked back to Edward's car and returned to my friend's house. I was a broken young woman, an empty shell. I had nothing left inside. I just couldn't see any point in going on. After the fire brigade left the next morning, we returned. Edward and I rummaged through the remains of the shop and the upper bedroom, and then I saw it in the rubble—Tammy's name badge. I pulled it out of the ashes and collapsed onto the burnt wood and articles that were strewn around me. I was covered in soot and looked a mess. I continued to look for Jason's name badge, but nothing. Just then I saw Edward heading out of the rubble and towards the street with an extremely angry face. I tried to line up which direction he was heading in, and then I saw it. Charlie's car.

Charlie's car was very distinctive. You couldn't hide it very well. It was a station wagon and was painted purple and white. It stood out like a sore thumb.

Edward started to run through the traffic towards Charlie's car, but Charlie saw him coming and took off quickly. Edward didn't have a chance of catching him. He yelled after the car, "Yeah that'd be right, you gutless wonder. Run, fuck you, run!"

Edward came back and put his arms around me and said, "That's it, I can't leave you here. You're coming to Sydney with me."

This took me by surprise as we'd never discussed me going with him. My relationships with the sailors usually ended when they left to travel to Sydney to meet their ship for the next part of their journey. They moved on, I never heard from them again, and I moved onto someone new.

I was glad to go. I was hoping this meant that our relationship was going to develop into something more. By the end of the week, we were on our way to Sydney. Edward had his first posting to HMAS Torrens and had to be on board the next morning, so it was going to be a non-stop drive from Melbourne to Sydney on the old Hume Highway.

The Hume was hairy at the best of times with its twists and turns. It was a killer highway, literally. So many people had lost their lives on it. We dropped in to say goodbye to Mom. She knew it was for the best after what had happened, and she made me promise to stay in touch and wished us a safe trip. As we reached the outskirts of Melbourne, I turned back to look at the skyline. I didn't want to forget it. My children lived there. I had only been out of Victoria once in my entire life to go to Cobar for my brother's wedding. So I was off on an adventure.

At one point the car broke down and the three guys we had with us had to get out and push to get it started again while I steered. Besides that, all in all, it was a pretty uneventful trip, but one that had to be taken for the sake of my future—and for my life. For the second time, Jack had almost succeeded in killing me.

Sydney was big. The cars bustled past faster and faster. The Sydney Harbor Bridge was amazing. And the ocean—in the middle of town! Unheard of. Turns out it's called a harbor. There were trains on the bridge and so much traffic it was rather scary. There was so much to see and explore—the Sydney Opera House had just been built and was still sparkling new. I was buzzing now at the thought of living in this big, exciting city with Edward.

But first, where to live was the major pressing issue. We dropped the guys off and then Edward turned to me and asked me where he could drop me off. My mouth fell open. *What the…*

"Edward, I have nowhere to go and nobody to go to," I said.

I had relatives in Sydney, but they didn't know me, and even if they did, they wouldn't want me around. Then I thought about my father. I had Edward stop at a telephone box and I rang any Forster I found in the phone book that lived in Parramatta. Yes, it turned out to be an aunty. I explained to her that I had just arrived in Sydney and was trying to find my father. She told me that she had no idea where he was, but she wished me well and said we'd have to catch up some time. (I was to find out later that she had told me a big fat lie.) I returned to the car with my shoulders slumped and told Edward it was hopeless.

"Okay," he said, "you'll sleep in the car tonight and we'll find somewhere for you to live tomorrow."

The car? Scenes of Jack flashed through my head.

"No, I won't!" I yelled at him. I had a little bit of money, so I made him take me to a caravan park. Early the next morning I bought a paper and looked in the real estate adverts. I didn't have a lot of money, so I needed something in my budget, and there it was: "Single room with semi-detached kitchen, shared bathroom, $20 a week."

I walked to the phone and rang the number on the advert. A lady told me I could come and have a look at it that day, so we did. It was at the back of a double-story terrace home in North Sydney, close to transport and shops. There was a kitchenette, pretty much like I had been brought up with at Mom's, and a separate bedroom with a double bed and a single bed. Both had lime green chenille bedspreads. Much like those back at the convent. There was a wardrobe and a set of drawers, a very small television, and a table with two chairs in the kitchen. It had pots, pans, cutlery, a dinner set, and towels—everything I needed to start again. More than I could hope for. I looked at Edward with such excitement, and then she asked if I was working. I looked to the floor and was just about to say no when Edward said he was working in the Navy and he would be responsible for the rent. My stomach tumbled and I looked at him with gratitude. With that she took our details and handed over the keys.

All I had were the clothes on my back—what I had walked out of the house with on the night of the fire—plus Tammy's name badge. Edward took me to the local shops and bought me a couple of new things to wear so that I could look for a job. I was passing the grocery store, Woolworths, on the way back to the flatette and there in the window was a job sign for a check-out operator. I knew I could do that, so I went in immediately and enquired. They asked me to come the next day for an interview, which I did, and I got the job. I always seemed to land on my feet.

Now I had a new life with someone who cared, a new house, and a new job. And I could be sure that creepy man Charlie would never find me. The world was my oyster. Edward and I had a great time. When he was off the ship, he was at my place and showing me what love could be like. He treated me well and he never hit me. Even so, I could feel something was not quite right.

I wrote to my mother often and told her how well I was doing. I was now paying my own way. Edward had not contributed to the household for some time. I found out he hadn't paid the rent when the landlady came knocking, asking for back rent. When I asked him, he said he'd forgotten. I told him it was fine and I would pay it from now on.

One night he walked in with some alcohol and asked if I wanted a drink. I said yes as I hadn't had a drink for a while. His drinking became a nightly event and more and more I could feel him pulling away from me. I usually never drank at home, so after that first night I didn't join in. But each night, out would come the bottle and he would drink until he fell asleep. He was not like Jack; he was very different. But three or four glasses of Bundaberg Rum and he would be sleeping like a baby.

I, however, resumed my usual position as if I were a robot. I would sit there and wait for him to wake up and tell me that I could go to bed. He questioned my motives for doing that. So over time I became easier with the fact that even if he was having a drink at home, I could go to bed if I was tired.

I know that I am not the easiest to get along with, but I have never been high maintenance, clingy, or needy. But if he wanted someone who adored him, that was me. If he wanted someone to put him on a pedestal, that was also me. I adored the man-boy ... then the crunch came.

Edward had gone home a couple of times to visit his parents—by himself.

He told me he was going home again that weekend to see them. I asked him when I was going to meet them. He back peddled on the question.

"Why?" I asked again. "Why don't you want to introduce me?"

He explained, reluctantly. "Mom and Dad don't want to meet you; they don't like you."

"But they've never met me. Why don't they like me? Why are they judging me?" I felt sick inside because I could see the beginning of the end. I knew his parents wielded great influence over him.

"Because you've been married and had children," he said. There it was. I hated that I was being judged because of the fact that I had been with Jack and had children. But I never felt sorry, not for one moment, that the two beautiful children who I grieved for every day were a part of my life, a part of me, and they always would be. Bugger his parents anyway; who needed them.

He came home the next night and told me that he had arranged with his parents for me to go with him after all. Great! I was so excited that they were going to give me a chance. We met up with his twin brother in Goulburn, who informed me in no uncertain terms that if I made his mother sick, he would come after me. I hadn't known until then that Edward's mother suffered from a severe immune system disorder, and if she went near someone with any kind of illness, she could easily catch it and it could kill her. I was very careful while I was there to keep my distance. They were nice enough to me, but their attitude was still very cool.

Edward was clearly a Mommy's boy. While we sat in the lounge watching television that night, he sat between her legs and she played with his hair. It was lovely to see that someone loved him as much as I did. I just wished I could make them understand how much that was. Edward's father had words with me before we left to return to Sydney. He basically told me that they didn't like me and never would, and they would do everything in their power to make Edward walk away from me.

I was very quiet on the trip back home to Sydney. I knew they were right. I wasn't any good for Edward; he deserved better. He was a good guy and deserved someone without so much baggage. We talked once we were home and he dedicated his love to me again. He told me that he didn't care what his parents said or did, he wasn't going anywhere. I wanted to believe him, but I'd been let down by so many in my life. My instinct was to protect myself from what may come, due to his closeness to his parents, and so I started to build the protection wall.

One week-end a few weeks later, I called the ship to talk to Edward as he told me he was on duty. But one of his mates told me that he went off the ship on the Friday to meet his parents and wouldn't be back until Monday morning. Apparently, his parents were visiting Sydney from Goulburn and were staying in a hotel.

Tears welled in my eyes. This was how it was going to be. Deceit and lies. Not a good foundation for a solid relationship! When he came home on the Monday night, I approached him about his absence from both me and the ship. He eventually told me that his parents had been up for the weekend and they wanted family time alone with him and his brother. These family meetings became a regular event, with me sitting at home alone while Edward was out with his family.

One such night, there was a knock on the door.

"Surprise!" came a shout from a very excited Leah on the other side of the door. I rushed to open the door and saw Sharon there also, standing right behind her with a big smile on her face.

"What are you doing here?" I screamed at them both.

"We came to see you."

Wow! I was so excited.

"Where's the fucker?" Sharon asked. (That was her nickname for Edward.)

"Out with his family," I replied.

"What without you?" came the shocked response.

I shrugged. "Yeah, they don't like me."

"Oh well, fuck 'em. Let's go out. We didn't come here to sit around," Leah said excitedly. It turned out that Sharon had fallen in love with a cook—Cookie—from another ship and had followed him to Sydney. While we got ready to go out, I tried to think where we could go. Sharon told me that she was meeting Cookie at the Texas Tavern in Kings Cross, nicknamed TT's.

Made up to the hilt, ready for anything and looking for fun, we boarded the train for Kings Cross.

34

Chance Number 2

∽

"… I remember … waking up at home in bed with a total stranger."

We finally found the Texas Tavern after passing through the kaleidoscope of life that is the bizarre but wonderful Cross: the ladies of the night, the guys looking at us like we were prize meat, the bikies who hung around the corner of Macleay Street just meters from the fountain. Then all the gorgeous looking trannies whom I would eventually come to understand and even love. Why hadn't Edward told me about this exciting place? Surely he would have known?

We followed the music and ended up downstairs in the disco. The colored lights flashed around everywhere. There were sailors all over the place. On the dance stage there was a mock-up silver space rocket, which was where the DJ sat, pumping out his boppy music. His job was to keep the patrons dancing and drinking. I would later find out his name was Jim. Sharon recognized someone in the distance and we started pushing through the crowd, heading for the table where he sat. Everyone at the table slid over to make room for us. I was in heaven. It had been so long since the discos in Melbourne and the fun that we used to have. My feet were moving and I just wanted to be on the dance floor, "shaking that thing".

After a few drinks and several requests to dance, I was up and away. I was having a great time, while Sharon was catching up with Cookie. Leah joined me and my dance partner on the dance floor. As I spun around to *Knock on*

Wood by Amy Stewart, I noticed a very familiar face entering the room with a girl on each arm, followed by another familiar face also with a girl on each arm. Edward! Edward wasn't out with his parents. He was out with his mate, who I was to notice always managed to have a multitude of girls around him and hanging off him. I was also later to find out, but not soon enough, that even though Edward's friend was a full-time serving member of the R.A.N., he was also a Kings Cross pimp who worked his girls hard. The girls on Edward's arm were prostitutes. Nice!

I left the dance floor, went back to the table, and told Sharon I was going to go home. I didn't dare tell her what I had seen because I knew she would make a scene and I just wanted to go.

"C'mon," she said. "Stay, don't go. I want to stay."

I said, "Stay, I'll go on my own."

"No, I'll go with you then." But even though she offered to come with me, I could see the look in her eyes and knew that she really wanted to be with her man. So I sat down.

I was grim faced and wanting to kill the one I could see in the distance, feeling the girls up, groping their butts as they stood there lapping up all the attention. It was only when I saw him stoop to kiss one of them that I had to go over and tap him on the shoulder. I don't know how many shades of red he turned, but I didn't say a thing. I just turned around and walked back to where Sharon was. I knew he was now feeling very uncomfortable, but he didn't make any attempt to move out of the situation to work things out with me.

I stood up and found the best-looking sailor in the house, walked over to him, and plopped myself down on his knee. It turned out that his name was Robert—my nickname for him was to be Mr. Roberts. He just threw his arms around me and pulled me closer.

"Hi," he said, "this is my friend, Shane."

Shane turned around and I almost had a seizure. I had gone out with Shane for about three weeks in Melbourne. It turned out we were better suited to being friends than anything else. He made a beeline for me and gave me the biggest hug. Mr. Roberts pulled me closer, saying I was his. I liked the way this made me feel. I liked Mr. Roberts. He was cuddly and I hadn't really experienced cuddly. Shane was chatting away, Mr. Roberts was cuddling me, and Sharon was in my face.

"Are you at it again?" she yelled, putting her hands on her hips. I pointed towards the bar where Edward stood with one of the prostitutes firmly wrapped around him.

"Fucker," she said. "I knew he was no good." She made a beeline for him.

Oh dear! I immediately said goodbye to Mr. Roberts and told him to reserve his knee for another time. I quickly moved to protect Edward from a fate worse than death—Sharon! Sharon was in Edward's face for a good five minutes, telling him what a lowlife fucker he was and how she was disgusted with him and so on. She warned him not to come home that night as he wasn't welcome, and if he did, she would have to do something drastic to him. I never went back near him—for both our sakes.

At the end of the night, the guys put us in a taxi and we headed back to my place. Sometime around 4 a.m. in the morning there was a knock at the door; it was Edward.

"I've forgotten my key. Let me in," he said.

"Fuck off!" Sharon shouted at the door. "Go back to your prostitutes, fool."

"Sharon!" I snapped. "Edward lives here."

"Well, he fuck'n shouldn't. He'd be out on his arse if he were mine," she snapped back.

I let him in. I wasn't talking to him, so I just put myself to bed and felt it was better dealt with in the morning when my head was clearer.

After this night the girls and I had a nightly ritual. Leah had moved in with me and Sharon frequently visited. So each day after I finished work, we would get ready to go out and disappear over to the Cross, to TT's. Every night it was the same crowd. We all knew each other. It was fantastic. I had never been so happy. If Edward felt like joining us, he was welcome to. But a lot of the time we went by ourselves, especially when he was on duty. I didn't think he would lie to me again because I had almost kicked his backside out that door. Besides, he had nowhere to hide with his prostitutes now.

Sharon and Leah met up with sisters who frequented TT's, and Mary-

CHANCE NUMBER 2

Jane from Melbourne moved up as well. We almost had all the girls we had hung around with down in Melbourne now up in Sydney—it was fantastic. Have I already said that? I had started a migration.

I was totally committed to Edward, one hundred per cent, except for the fact that I sat on Mr. Robert's knee every time I saw him, which I didn't consider playing up. Mr. Roberts and I were building up our little friendship. Like I said, he was cuddly and I loved his cuddles—I'd never had cuddles my whole life. He used to snuffle around my neck and that made me go all tingly. I didn't know that he actually really liked me. At a later date I would find that out. I wouldn't have thought I had a chance with him anyway. To me he was just Mr. Roberts.

I had befriended a lot of guys on Edward's ship. In fact, they seemed to like me and not him. Some said he was a gob, others told him for some reason that a ship was a lonely place, and also that there was nowhere to run at sea. He wasn't popular, but when he came home to me, he was everything to me! Until …!

One of the guys from the ship told me that when Edward was supposed to be on duty he wasn't. He was still riding around with the other guy, the pimp, and his girls! Edward had told me that I was only to call the ship at certain times to talk to him because I was getting him into trouble with the Chief. Well, that had been a set-up. The times he gave me to call were when he would go back to the ship to take my call and then leave again. So I went straight to the phone and called the ship to ask if he was there—and he wasn't. They told me where I could find him—across the road at the other hotel, the Chevron, better known as the "Shit-fight". Edward had told me I was never to go there because only whores went there and he didn't want me getting a bad name. Yeah, right! I walked across the road to the disco and there he was, in the corner with his mate and the harem, having a ball.

So I went back to TT's and I had a ball too. That was the night I kissed Mr. Roberts and he kissed me right back. But I felt ashamed of myself. I was so upset that I said I had to leave and I just went. A few days later, HMAS Torrens sailed for Asia and Edward went with it on a six-month tour. I received a few letters from Edward while he was gone, but I received a lot more from his mates.

I heard what he was up to while he was on tour from his mates' letters. I couldn't see any reason to sit around and wait for him to come back. One night after we'd come home from TT's, I heard a knock on my door. It was about 2 a.m. and we had been asleep. Two slightly inebriated sailors, giggling like little girls, stood on my doorstep—Shane and Mr. Roberts. I ushered them in so as not to wake the neighbors; I didn't need to be kicked out. We grabbed our dressing gowns and headed to the kitchen.

I welcomed Mr. Roberts' presence; in fact, I honestly had encouraged it. I knew what I was doing, and when Leah paired off with Shane, I took that as my cue to pair off with Mr. Roberts. After an hour or so, Mr. Roberts and I had done what I had promised I would never do. My relationship with Edward was now defunct. I loved the spirit and energy of Mr. Roberts, and I loved his need and desire for me. It felt primal. At the end of the night, though, we agreed that we should just stay friends and that this would go no further than us.

It never happened again. So it was back to sitting on his knee at TT's. How could I forget him though? I had desired him for so long and obviously the appeal had been shared, but my misplaced loyalty to Edward stood in the way of any possible future for us. So I did my best to forget Mr. Roberts "in that way".

Over the following weeks, I was kept up to date with all of Edward's antics through his mates. I received quite a few letters from different guys advising me of his latest beanie boy and street girl, and also a tattoo that he got which he neglected to tell me about in his own letter. I couldn't take anymore, so I went to TT's and blew myself totally away. I drank until I was numb and then some more. All I can remember is standing at the pinball machine, and the next minute I just fell backwards, like a reverse planking episode. The only thing I remember after that was waking up at home in bed with a total stranger.

Don't worry! Here was chance two!

I pulled the sheet up over my head and quickly checked that I was dressed. *Well, that's a relief.* I turned and looked in his direction. He had his eyes open.

"Hi," he smiled at me.

"Did we do anything here last night?" I asked warily, wagging my finger between him and me.

"No, I just brought you home and you kept calling me Edward and wouldn't let me leave. So I slept here. I hope you don't mind, but I'm fully dressed." He pulled the blankets back. "See!" he said. Yes, he was fully dressed in motor bike leathers and jacket. He introduced himself to me as Michael.

"Um, how did I get home?" I couldn't remember.

Apparently, when I passed out, nobody knew what to do with me. They knew where I lived but didn't know how to get me home. Michael put me into a taxi and took me home, totally unconscious. He found the key in my bag and let himself in and put me to bed. Oh my God! I had never, ever, gotten to that state before. I was deteriorating.

Michael said, "You could probably use something to eat," and he jumped up and scavenged around my kitchen, bringing back toast and tea. I sat in bed, amused at his antics. He was quite a likeable guy. No man had *ever* offered me breakfast in bed before, and I wasn't going to knock it back. He asked what I was up to that day and I told him, "Nothing." With that we became engaged in a deep conversation about anything and everything. I told him about Edward and why I had drunk myself into oblivion the night before. He told me that Edward didn't deserve me.

We got along like a house on fire and talked all day. We returned to TT's later where he bought me dinner before we headed downstairs to the disco. He only drank one drink and sat on water the rest of the night, as he intended to drive me home on his motorbike. It felt nice to have my arms around his waist and the wind in my hair. Sharon and Leah hadn't been around for a few nights, so I tasted a little freedom from Sharon's scowls about my behavior. It appeared that they had swapped TT's for the Chevron across the road.

Michael was a sailor, although he was on a different ship. He kept mostly to himself. He seemed like a very private person; I liked that. He was not boisterous or loud like some other sailors I had known. He was charming and polite, not my usual type or the kind I would normally be physically attracted to. He was small in stature, like Jack, which was usually a bit of a turn-off for me; but not with Michael. He had dark hair, cut navy style but longer on top, and his face had a distinctively European look to it. There was obviously something about him that attracted me, and when he pulled me towards him and kissed me, I kissed him right back eagerly. I wanted him and I wanted him bad. There was just something about him. We left TT's shortly after that to head home.

I was sure word would spread straight back to Edward as HMAS Hobart was setting sail the next day and would meet up with the Torrens later in the week. I was expecting an abusive letter any day as word travels fast in Navy circles. But to my surprise, nobody told Edward what had happened at all. I didn't care if they did. I was angry at him anyway, so angry that if he had been there, he would have been well and truly dumped. Playing up on me with beanie boys, really!

I had always been a sucker, constantly taking abuse from someone, always being used, always waiting and doing the right thing. Well, no more. No more Mrs. Nice guy, and when Michael shyly made advances towards me later that night, I didn't resist. We had sex—no, we made love—and it was incredible. It was like the Sydney fireworks on New Year's Eve. I cried. He was tender, loving, patient, careful, and attentive, making sure that I was fulfilled before he was. Yes, I had my very first orgasm.

I was twenty-two years old, had been married, and had two children, had lived in a steady relationship with a guy for two years and had a massive amount of sex in different forms from all different types of guys, and now I was a sobbing wreck with this gorgeous man, who was treating me with such respect, passion, and dignity. Michael had finally shown me what sex was all about—what it *should* be all about. Wow! I finally knew what I had been missing out on for a long time, and I was going to find it extremely difficult to go back to what I was used to.

Well, we spent the next two months together. I couldn't get enough of him. He was there every night after work, often taking me out to either TT's or just out somewhere for dinner. He was always the gentleman, attentive, and passionate. I loved it, and I loved him. One night we went to a North Sydney hotel for dinner. The juke box was playing music in the background. Someone had requested *Three Times a Lady*, by The Commodores. Michael took my hand and started to sing it to me, loudly, so everybody could hear. I was embarrassed, but the whole room went silent and just listened. When it was over, he received applause from every person in the room. He stood up and took a bow, and we left shortly afterwards.

Michael never gave me any reason to suspect that his intentions with me were anything less than honest and good. I had fallen head over heels in love with the guy. There was only one problem—the elephant in the room—Edward. Before I had met Michael, I had paid for my airfare to travel to Melbourne to meet Edward's ship on its return. It was also for me to go home and see my family. I explained to Michael that I was in a dilemma. Edward had no idea that I was with Michael and he expected me to be on that dock when his ship pulled in. I thought that to not be there would have been disrespectful and upsetting for him. I am many things but I have never been the bitch. I just couldn't do that, even though he had hurt me.

I was confused about my feelings for Edward. He had rescued me when I needed rescuing, and for that I was grateful. I needed time to figure out what I wanted. Thankfully, sweet Michael understood and told me that if I had to go, I should go. He wanted to give me breathing space to make a decision without feeling pressured. But he gave me one condition—he wanted an answer before the ship pulled in. He told me to go and be with my family and that if I decided it was him that I wanted to be with, I should call him and let him know. If I decided that it wasn't him and I wanted to stay with Edward, I still should ring him and he would be packed up and gone before I got back. And I would never see him again.

We spent what might be our last night together at home. It was depressing. We were both sad and my heart was breaking, just in case I decided against Michael for Edward. Why would I do such a stupid thing as that?

I took the plane to Melbourne and it wasn't long before I was at Mom's house. It was the day before the ship was due to arrive. I had been weighing up all the pros and cons of my situation. I was never terribly good at making decisions. I always made decisions based on what was best for everyone else, instead of what was in my heart. So, as I lifted the phone to call Michael, my heart was heavy. He didn't give me a chance to explain my decision. He just said, "I'll be gone when you get back. Thank you for letting me know," and he hung up the phone.

I sat there and tears cascaded down my face. I didn't think that they would ever stop. Chance number two, gone! If he had only been more forceful with me, I would have been his.

The next day I was at the pier when the ship came in, like the dutiful girlfriend I was. I sat and waited on the dock for Edward to come off the ship. I was going to come clean with him. Then I noticed his parents in the crowd. *You have to be kidding me. He could have let me know.* He came off the ship and made a beeline for them, half acknowledging me on his way through. He hugged his mother and father, and as they all turned to start walking away together, he quickly ran back over to me and said, "Wait at the Graham for me," and he was gone. No hug or cuddle, no happy to see you—he just turned and went.

The Graham was a hotel in Melbourne City. It was a well-known haunt for sailors. I jumped on a tram and cried all the way into the city. I realized what a stupid decision I had made, but it was too late. When I got to the city, I tried to call Michael again at my flat, but there was no answer. He was gone. What a fool I had been. When I got to the Graham, I bumped into the rest of the girls who hadn't yet moved to Sydney—Amber, Marianne, Katherine, and Jolene. They were happy to see me, except for Jolene who always gave off an air that she was better than I was. She asked in a snide voice, "So you still with that goofy looking guy that you used to hang around with?"

"Edward?" I asked, my eyebrows raised.

She said, "Yeah, that's him, tall, dark hair."

I turned and saw Edward coming down the stairs. "You mean him?"

Her mouth dropped open and she said, "Fuck'n hell, he is fuck'n gorgeous."

Edward had been in the tropics for six months. Other than the fact he was tanned, he stood six foot four inches high and had dark hair and green eyes. He had a gorgeous smile and a pleasant manner. Yep, he was a real lady whore and loved the attention of the opposite sex. He would just flash those pearly whites and their hearts would melt. Edward was no longer the goofy looking guy I had left Melbourne with. He was now handsome, well-built, and stylish.

We sat and had a few drinks and spent a few hours together, discussing what I had been told about him and what I had done in response. He was actually quite condemning of my actions but not his own. That upset me. But before he left to return to his parents, we decided to give it another go. I didn't see him again while I was in Melbourne and I left a few days later.

I returned to Sydney, to the flatette where I had been so happy with Michael. It felt so empty now and I was miserable. I just wanted to see him again. I was confused and discouraged. I couldn't understand the feelings that I had for him and how I could just let him go. He had made me feel amazing just by smiling at me. I had felt like I was the only person in the world to him. I rang him on the ship and asked him to come and see me, half expecting him to tell me to piss off. He was genuinely happy that I had called. As soon as he finished work he came right over—dependable, understanding, loving Michael.

We took one look at each other and it took seconds to end up in each other's arms. Now I think he may have thought that I had changed my mind, and in fact I had, but my mouth just couldn't say it. Several hours later, after talking about our situation, Michael left. This time he said that we could never do this again. He didn't like sneaking around. He wanted me, but he wanted all of me, not just the part of me that Edward didn't want. I understood his position and respected his decision to walk away, but I felt like a part of my heart went with him that day.

Several days later, Edward's ship pulled into Garden Island and I received a call from him stating that he was on duty. As usual I didn't trust him, so I rang the ship half an hour later—no Edward. Why was I continuing to put up with this? I had the perfect man in the wings and I wanted Edward? *Why*? Because of some self-disdain that I had. I was so angry and frustrated with myself. Who could understand my reasoning? I stayed away from the Cross and everyone else for a little while. Leah came in search of me, asking me to come out. I refused. I knew if I went out I would see Michael and I knew who I would come home with.

I talked it through with Leah and she told me that it was better the devil you know, and so it was to be Edward. I wasn't capable of directing my own life. I didn't feel in control at all; in fact, I felt lost and confused, like a little girl who couldn't decide what doll she wanted to play with. The only problem was that these dolls were human beings and they both had feelings and emotions.

A few weeks later there was another knock at my door. I opened it to find Amber, Marianne, and Katherine standing there. They had come to Sydney on the train and wanted to stay with me. I told them that I was happy for them to stay for a little while, but they would need to get their own rooms if they were staying long term as my place was just not big enough for us all. They were satisfied with that. It turned out there were spare rooms in the same boarding house and they happily occupied them. It was only a matter of weeks and Jolene arrived as well. Edward was in his element. He loved being surrounded by girls and the attention it got him. At least he finally came home every night.

The girls were at our place every night when we were not over at TT's. It was great to have them around. However, more and more I found Edward taking more notice of Jolene than he should have been. If the truth be known, she was leading him on, with the full intention of taking him, just because she could. I came in one night to find Edward in the bedroom with Jolene tied up on the bed. She was laughing her head off and he was on top of her tickling her. I asked them what was going on, but before he could answer I walked out.

I walked for hours in the cold night wondering what I had done. Reality struck and I realized for the first time I had made the wrong decision. I knew I just couldn't do this anymore and I fully intended to let Michael know the next day. The next morning I rang Michael's ship. I spoke to him and at lunchtime he came to see me. I told him to bring his motorcycle into the house, for the specific purpose of not spiking the girls' curiosity as to who I had inside with me. Then I pulled the blinds so they couldn't see in either. We started to talk and sparks were flying between us. So the talk ended and instead we ended up having sex. I later wished we had talked first. It would have given me more time to say what I really felt. When we were finished, and before I could say another word, the girls started to bang at the door and the windows, yelling out that they knew I had someone there and if I didn't open the door, they would tell Edward.

This made Michael very angry as he had said before he didn't want to sneak round. He stood up abruptly and said, "I can't do this anymore. Don't call me again." He grabbed his stuff, opened the door, and pushed the motorbike out, straight through the girls. If the girls hadn't arrived when they did, I would have told him that I was leaving Edward and I was his. It was too late. The damage had been done. He thought I was still just sneaking around behind Edward's back.

I told Edward when he came home that I wanted him to pack his things and leave. He couldn't understand what he had done. I told him that I didn't love him anymore; I hadn't loved him for a long time.

"You can do better than me, Edward," I explained. Then I saw him glance at Jolene. Ah! I realized he was already doing someone. Yes, despite having seen her tied up on our bed before, I had been in denial that something was going on, but not anymore ... All hell broke loose. Edward escaped back to the ship, so he said. Then Jolene and I finally had it out; sparks were flying. I told her not to come near me again. Then she left and went out also—I can only imagine where.

I called Michael's ship the next day, but he wouldn't take my calls. They told me he had asked for them to pass on a message to me, and the message was to not call him again. I went to TT's in the hope of seeing him, but he never showed up again. I had really blown it.

I met another girl at work, Yvette. Eventually she introduced me to her sister Jacqueline. We got along like a house on fire, and it wasn't long before I was dragging them out to TT's also. After having lost my chance with Michael, Edward and I got back together—old habits die hard—but our relationship was strained, hanging on by a thread. Jolene and I had patched things up a bit, at least superficially—I still didn't trust her as far as I could throw her. I knew why she was in Sydney and I wasn't about to allow her to have her way. I don't know why I was holding on so desperately. I should have let her have him. She actually deserved him, I thought that I needed him, though. I believe that is what kept me holding on so hard.

Jacqueline and Yvette fitted into the group well. We all frequented TT's and had a ball. It was coming into Christmas and Edward told me that he was going home to his parents' house for Christmas. Strangely enough Jolene went home for Christmas that year too. Edward headed off a few days before Christmas and did not leave me with a cent, despite knowing I had recently lost my job and had no money. The girls had no money either, or if they did, they wouldn't have told me.

By Christmas day there was no food in the house. We scraped together about one dollar and twenty cents between us. We knew it wouldn't get us anything, so we decided instead to go to the telephone box and make reverse charge calls home. Amber went first and then Katherine and Marianne. Then it came my turn.

My family was gathered at my sister's place and she accepted the reverse charges but asked that I never do it again. I told her it was only because it was Christmas and, yes, I wouldn't do it again. She had no idea that I hadn't eaten for nearly two days and that my Christmas meals consisted of water only. I listened as they told me what they were having for Christmas lunch. My salivary glands were working overtime, imagining what it would taste like. I just wanted to scream, "Stop!" They all sounded so cheerful and happy. I said Merry Christmas to everyone and hung up. I had tears in my eyes as I turned to the girls who were all the same. We were hungry!

On the way home Katherine had to go to the loo, so we stopped at the service station. As we walked past the cashier area, we saw the attendant eating his heated-up Christmas lunch. We all stopped and just stared at the meal. The guy stood up, looked at us, and asked, "Are you girls hungry?" We all just shook our heads.

"Here, take it," he said, handing the plate of food to us. Nobody hesitated. We all grabbed at the food and scoffed it down quicker than a pack of dogs. We thanked him very much for his kindness and left. We were totally embarrassed that we had to stoop so low to survive, but what the girls didn't know was that it wasn't the first time in my life I had gone hungry. I had eaten from rubbish bins before to survive, so this was at least one level above that.

That night we decided enough was enough. We dressed and hitchhiked to Kings Cross to be where we always felt happiest and looked after: TT's.

The guys were great. They bought us meals and drinks and even gave us our taxi fare home. What a night. There are a lot of people who have nowhere to go on Christmas Eve, but that night we had each other. We were like a family. We were the family we were having while we were not having a family. Some of the guys from HMAS Torrens were there. That is the night that Yvette met Glen, and he was really into her—such a lovely guy who was going to be there for us all in the near future, when we were really going to need it.

35

AUSTRALIA DAY WEEKEND 1979

"I saw my maternal grandmother standing on the front of the truck ... She was reaching her hand out to me, beckoning me to go with her. She smiled and waited patiently. I didn't feel the pain anymore."

I HIT TT's DANCE FLOOR like there was no tomorrow. As it was the Australia Day long weekend Edward was going home to his parents' house—again! *God, I feel like I'd do anything to change my life.* I had lost my job due to my own stupidity. I had a boyfriend I wasn't sure I could count on, and most of all I missed my children. I grieved for them every day. The wounds were still raw.

As I danced, and the alcohol swam around in my head, nobody could have guessed the thoughts churning around in my mind. They were telling a different story to what my dancing body may have been saying to the world ... *I need to go home. I need to see the kids.*

"Hey, Bev!" I heard Amber's voice shouting at me above the music. "Do you want to come to Melbourne with me?"

"What? Go to Melbourne?" It was as if I had put the idea into Amber's head. I nodded eagerly and then we asked Yvette if she wanted to come too.

"How are we going to get there?" she asked.

"I've lined up a lift down there for us, but we'll have to hitchhike back," Amber piped up. She had paid some guy ten dollars to drive us to Melbourne.

"Is that safe?" Yvette asked. She was referring to travelling alone with this guy plus the hitchhiking.

I said, "Yeah, if we go as a group. All we have to worry about is getting raped, and that won't happen if there is more than one of us." So she agreed to come with us.

"Great. That's settled," I said.

We went straight home, threw a few things together, and then jumped in the guy's car when he came to pick us all up.

The trip was a straight run through with no dramas. He dropped Yvette and me to my front door in Thornbury, and then Amber to her front door in Box Hill. Mom was really glad to see us but was worried about us hitchhiking back to Sydney.

We rested up for a while, but I couldn't wait to see the kids. When I went to Jack's house to see if I could visit with the children, Yvette came with me. Jack was quite surprised to see me standing at the door and asked me in. He looked different, but I had no doubt in my mind that he hadn't changed a bit. I kept a very keen eye on his every movement, ready to run at a moment's notice. He was really nice to Yvette. Butter wouldn't have melted in his sickly sweet mouth. He agreed to allow me a day with the kids and told me to come again the next day and he would have them there for me.

I was so excited that I was finally going to see my babies; it was the first time in two years. I woke early and at the agreed time we headed down to Jack's place. The kids were there as promised and, surprisingly, he allowed me to take them alone.

Jason ran to me with arms outstretched. "Mommy, Mommy!" he yelled.

Tammy stood back, a little more reserved, but eventually she mimicked Jason. She had been much younger when I left and I don't think she knew who I was.

We took the kids to the park, let them visit with my mom, and just spent quality time with them. The day went so fast. Towards the end, Tammy, who had been so shy at first, was like a koala wrapped around my leg; so much so that she didn't want to return to her dad. I had to peel her off. Jason cried as I walked away. I should have stayed away. It broke my heart all over again to see them, and then to say goodbye and walk away for a third time. God only knows what it did to them.

Jack wanted me to stay there the night so that the kids could wake up with me there the next morning, but I didn't trust him. I knew once he had me in his grasp, I would be his prisoner again. I was now a little stronger emotionally and kept Yvette close, just in case.

"No Jack, that won't be a good idea. It will only upset the kids more," I said, as I backed out the door. As I walked away I cried like a baby. My heart, my feet, every part of me, was heavy. Every step felt like I was walking with concrete boots on. I couldn't believe I had to go through this feeling all over again; it was like a dagger had pierced my heart. It is just the worst feeling; nobody should ever have to experience it.

Our time in Melbourne went too fast and before long I was giving my mother a kiss on the cheek and walking out the front gate. She told us to be careful on the treacherous Hume Highway, even though she travelled regularly up and down it with Uncle Geoff in his semi-trailer. She had said he was too busy to help us out and that we shouldn't ask for a lift back to Sydney with him.

Mom yelled advice as we walked out the door and down the sideway. "You ring me as soon as you get back, won't you? I'm so worried about you. Let me know you got there in one piece. Stay safe and don't get in with idiots! There are a lot of cowboys on that highway."

We had arranged to all meet at the station. Amber came by train from Box Hill and then we travelled together to Keon Park where we walked the short distance to the Hume Highway. Before long we were on the highway and picked up by our first car. He dropped us off at Seymour and then we were picked up by another car who took us to the Shepparton turn-off.

We were then picked up by a group of airmen from the Wagga Wagga Air Force Base, which was a remarkable experience. We hadn't really had anything to do with airmen until that day. We had met a soldier here and there but had mostly dealt with sailors.

They acted differently to sailors; in fact, they were probably more gentlemen-like in their mannerisms. They told us that they were going to Wagga Wagga, but it wouldn't take us far out of our way and plenty of trucks went through Wagga, so we'd easily get a lift to the highway again. We felt at home with these guys.

We trusted the Defense Force, so we jumped in. As promised they delivered us to the front gates of the Air Force base, where we jumped out and continued on our journey.

Dusk was falling and we were getting tired and hungry. None of us had any money, so we couldn't buy anything to eat. I heard the roar of a truck and ran to the side of the road where I put my thumb out. The truck came to a halt and the truck that had been trailing him also stopped. My first thought was trouble, but the truck driver jumped out and asked, "How many of you are there?"

"Three," I piped up.

He walked the distance to the cab of the second truck and spoke briefly with the other driver. Then he returned to his truck, opened the passenger door, and swung his young son down into his arms. He carried him up to the other truck, tucked him in, and shut the door.

The truck pulled away from the side of the road and took off into the night. He pointed to the passenger's side door and said, "Well, I can't leave you here in the dark. It's too dangerous."

I thought it was so nice of him, moving his own child out for us. I clambered up and sat beside him. Yvette climbed in beside me and Amber sat next to the window. We were still worried about rape, and if it was going to happen to anyone, I felt it should happen to me, which is why I chose to sit next to the driver. The other two girls were younger than me and I felt I had to protect them at all costs. But the driver, who introduced himself as Frank, made us feel comfortable, saying that he liked the extra company as it was a long drive. He couldn't believe that we were left by the side of the road in the dark.

We roared along the highway, finally turning off onto the Hume and heading towards Sydney. Frank was quiet for a long while. Yvette rested her head back and her eyes were closed. Amber had her window down with her head resting on her hand, while her elbow rested on the window rim, half in the window, the other half out. She was enjoying the wind blowing through her hair.

It was warm in the cab of the truck as it was a summer's night. I just sat and watched the road ahead. I attempted several times to strike up a conversation with Frank, but it was hard over the roar of the engines. After a while I noticed his eyes were fixated on the white line on the road. He was concentrating.

We thundered along the highway with not a care in the world. The gentle rocking of the cab on the roadway was making me weary and slowly a feeling of calm came over me. We came up over a rise and headed down into a notorious section of road on the old Hume Highway called "Sylvia's Cutting". The truck started to gather momentum as it went down the hill. The sound of its gathering speed drew me out of my calm state and I was suddenly on alert. Something ahead grabbed my attention—red, blue, and yellow flashing lights in the gully below.

"Frank!" I yelled because he was not slowing down; in fact, the truck was still gathering momentum. I don't think he could hear me over the roar of the engine. "FRAAANK! I think there's been an accident down there," I yelled, as loud as I could. He still just stared straight ahead. I had no idea at the time but he was in a state called "white line fever", or "highway hypnosis". He was tired and his mind was probably miles away, though he still had his hands gripped firmly on the wheel and his eyes fixated on the road ahead. I started to panic, overwhelmed by a sense of urgency that had escaped me until that moment. I leant over and hit Frank on the chest as hard as I could and screamed over and over, "FRANK, STOP. FRANK STOP!"

But it was too late.

Only sixty meters from the back of the other truck Frank came back to reality and slammed on all his brakes. The truck whined and groaned like a wounded animal. The air brakes were so loud. I will never forget the sound of those brakes; that sound is forever etched into my soul.

I instinctively reached across and tried to grab Amber to pull her head in the window because I knew she had fallen asleep with her head on her hand. Instead, my arm grabbed Yvette and I pulled her in behind me. We hit the back end of a stationary semi-trailer, which was stopped in the center of the carriageway, with such force I was thrown through the windscreen, smashing my head into the tail gate of the truck we had hit.

Yvette's head smashed into the back of my head full force, propelling me forward even harder. Immediately, I was thrown back into the cab and pinned down by the legs as the steel ridge from the trailer of the truck we had hit smashed through the front end of our prime mover. As the truck continued forward, the front of the cabover (flat nosed) prime mover vacuum sealed Yvette, Amber, and I, entombing us in torn, crumpled, and bent steel. To get us out they would literally have to peel the front of the truck off us a like opening a can of sardines.

The truck was then propelled backwards down the highway and upwards, becoming airborne for almost a full sixty meters before coming to rest back down on the road. The trailer on our truck was loaded with potatoes and they scattered everywhere.

Then, as quickly as it had begun, the prime mover started to slow down. It groaned to a halt, and the CB radio that had been on the roof swung down and smashed me in the front of the head. We found ourselves lying backwards in the cabin with our heads hanging downwards towards the roadway. I was staring up at the stars. People came from everywhere.

"I've killed them, I've killed them all!" Frank had jumped out of the cab just before impact and I could hear him saying this over and over with such despair in his voice. He must have been so relieved later on, though, that his son hadn't been in the truck with us. I'm not sure if the little guy would have survived.

The whole accident seemed to happen in slow motion—which is why I can remember everything in such detail. While it was happening, there was no pain, no feeling. It was like my brain had switched all of that off to save my sanity. But when everything became quiet and I was sitting in that truck looking up at the stars, the pain arrived with a fury. My senses caught up with what had happened and pain seared through my body from the tip of my toes to the top of my head. Blood from my head injury poured into my eyes.

The pain. *Oh my God.* It was unbearable.

"Yvette, Amber!" I yelled, over and over ... No answer. *Oh no, they're dead!* Neither of them moved ...

Then the next minute Yvette grabbed my left arm from under the steel and started pulling it, crying, "Oh no, the pain ... Ow ... It's really hurting ..." She whimpered.

She was crying, I was crying. *This was NOT supposed to happen. Rape, a possibility but not an accident. You can't be hurt in a truck* I thought. It had not crossed our minds; I thought we were so safe once Frank had picked us up.

"It will be okay, Yvette, it will be okay ... Amber, Amber. Are you okay, Amber?" ... No answer. I tried to pull my arm away from Yvette because she was pulling on it so hard, shaking it up and down with every wave of pain that reeled through her body. My arm was so sore and every time she pulled it, pain tore through my body.

I struggled to free myself, but from the chest down I couldn't move. I've heard about a mental strength that you can acquire in times of extreme trauma. I guess I experienced it that night as I then put my right arm up and pushed really hard. I felt the front end of the prime mover move, relieving the crushing feeling on my chest, allowing me to breathe. Until then my breathing had been laborious and shallow. It may very well have saved our lives, as I would later find out that people can die from crush injuries when they are released from being crushed for a period of time.

A truckie named Ken Cunningham jumped up into the driver's side of the cabin with us and asked if we were alright. I just looked at him. I can't remember Yvette saying anything and Amber definitely didn't speak. He grabbed my right hand and held it tight, assuring me that I was going to be okay and that they were working to get us out.

I asked him weakly, "Is an ambulance coming? I'm really sore."

"Yes, love. One will be here real soon. It's just over the horizon."

In fact, it was on its way but was having problems getting to us because it was the end of a public holiday long weekend and the highway had banked up on both sides of the accident. The police in Gundagai had heard the boom from the impact in the quiet of the night and had jumped in their police cars and headed out of town in both directions, trying to find us. An ambulance was waiting to be told where to go. Nothing was happening; there was no movement. I could hear a lot of things going on next to Amber but nothing around Yvette and me. I asked if Amber was okay.

"Yeah," said Ken, "she'll be right, mate. Don't you worry." I relaxed, knowing that she was going to be okay. And then I realized I needed to go to the toilet.

"I need to go to the toilet. Can I hop out and go? I promise I'll get back in."

Ken replied gently, "No, you'll need to just go where you are."

It took me a while before it finally got the better of me and I had to pee where I sat. Ken kept wiping what I thought were tears from my face. I later found out it was blood that was pouring down from the wound in my head.

All of a sudden I saw my maternal grandmother standing on the front of the truck. She had passed away only a few years before. She was reaching her hand out to me, beckoning me to go with her. She smiled and waited patiently. I didn't feel the pain anymore. I released my hand from Ken's and I turned to him saying quietly, "I'm sorry, but I have to go now. Nanna has come for me." As I reached out towards her and shut my eyes, Ken's palm suddenly came hard and fast across my face. I couldn't see Nanna anymore.

I looked at him, tears welling in my eyes again. "Why did you hit me? Why did you hurt me? Aren't I hurt enough?"

He said apologetically, "You can't fall asleep, love."

I found out later that he had kept me alive. If I had shut my eyes, I could have died as I was in shock. I had lost a lot of blood and was ripe for the grim reaper. I have Ken to thank for giving me my life back. That's the only time in my life I've been grateful for a smack in the face.

I kept asking for the ambulance and each time I did, Ken told me it was just over the hill. That must have been one bloody big hill. Time seemed to have stood still. Just over the hill might as well have been fifty kilometers away, and it probably was. I kept hearing guys telling Ken he was doing a good job. Someone asked him if he wanted to be relieved, but he said, "No, these are my babies in here now."

I saw red and blue flashing lights. They were a little bit different to the white flashes that I had been seeing from holiday makers, who had been unbelievably walking up to the accident to take happy snaps to show the folks back home.

There was a lot of discussion at the front of the truck then some guys jumped up on the front, sending pain searing through my legs. They fed a rope through the front of the truck and used another truck to pull the front end of the prime mover off us. Every time they pulled, I screamed as a burning pain shot through my left leg. I wanted to kill them! I squirmed in my seat as much as I could, to try to distance myself from these men who were trying to rescue me.

I looked to my left and Amber was gone. They had her. I hoped it was only a matter of time before I was out of there also. More pulling, more pain and then Yvette was gone. I was not aware that they were also worried about the petrol tank of the truck and were watching that for leaks.

It won't be long now, I kept reassuring myself. Then more pulling, and with each slight movement forward, I screamed harder and louder as the pain burned through my leg. Every sense in my body was alive and adrenalin was shooting through it. Then Ken yelled, "Stop! The gear stick is in her leg." Thankfully they stopped. A police officer and a truckie climbed in with a small handsaw that someone had found in their truck and they cut the end of the gear stick, releasing my leg from the truck's hold. The gear stick had pierced through the lower part of my knee and had been sitting just below the knee cap. When they had pulled the front of the truck forward, the gear stick had travelled further and further up the inside of my leg, until finally it had exited just above the knee. No wonder it bloody hurt. Once the gear stick was cut clear, they continued to pull and I continued to yell. Something still wasn't right.

My foot was burning; it felt like it was burning off. I heard one of the truck drivers shout from outside the truck, "Quick, pull faster; her foot's on the radiator."

But it wasn't the radiator that was burning me; that had long cooled. The skin had already been burnt by the radiator just after impact and had now stuck to it. Now my foot was being slowly and painfully peeled off the pipe by the truck shifting every time they pulled on the rope. This sent a burning sensation through my foot as it was released. He moved my foot off the radiator and they continued to work.

Two hours and forty-five minutes since the accident, I thought I was finally going to be released from my tomb, but no. I was still sitting there. The front of the truck was off me, and for the first time through the entire ordeal I felt that nothing was right with the world. Something was wrong. I couldn't feel my legs anymore and wasn't sure if I still had them. I actually felt like I was never going to escape. I cried again, not a loud cry, but a whimpering sound like an injured animal.

I could hear the whispered discussions from the passenger side of the truck where they had taken Amber and Yvette from. Then an ambulance officer jumped up into what was left of the crumpled, wrecked cabin and said, "We all think that you don't have the guts to get out of the truck by yourself."

I looked at him strangely. *Why is he talking to me like that?* I looked at him and said, "You're probably right. I can't even feel my legs, so I don't think I can walk."

He turned and looked at two truck drivers who were gathered by the side of the truck. One of them turned to the other and said loudly, so that I could hear, "Gutless, I tell ya. Bloody women, boo hoo," as he rubbed his eyes and mocked me. "Can't do anything for themselves," he continued. That made me angry; they hadn't said these things to Amber and Yvette. Why were they being so mean to me?

I still sat there. Then the ambulance officer said to me while patting the seat beside me, "If you can't put your legs up here then I'm afraid we'll just have to leave you there." Well, that was all he had to bloody say! If they were trying to make me angry, they now succeeded. I put my right arm on the side of the seat and pushed myself around, swinging my battered, bleeding legs towards him and the seat. My left foot just hung, lame, unstable, as if it had no bones in it. It looked weird, and when my brain finally made sense of it, I realized it was backwards.

Everything after that happened so fast. The two truckies who had been "making fun of me" grabbed my legs. Ken climbed over the middle to support my head, and before I knew it, I was laying on the gravel by the side of the road. I was blinded by flashes and the police were asking people to back off and give the ambulance officer room to work. Bloody tourists.

"Where's Amber, where's Yvette?" I kept asking.

"In the ambulance," was the reply.

I could barely see in the back of the ambulance; however, Amber and Yvette were both there and being attended to. I felt a tearing on my skin as the ambulance officer and a couple of the truckies put a lump of wood, which had been a white mile post on the side of the highway, between my legs and started to secure all of them together with rope, the same rope they had used to pull the truck off us. I had a bandage wrapped around my head and one around my arm. Then with a one, two, three, I was hoisted off the ground and onto a hammock of sorts, which was to be hooked to the underside of the ambulance roof.

I couldn't see Amber or Yvette as they put me into the ambulance. They hooked the hammock securely to the roof and then the back doors were quietly shut—we were off. I could hear the siren of a police car off in the distance. The ambulance officer was in the back with us and another police officer who was in contact by radio with the pilot police car ahead drove the ambulance. The pilot was clearing the way and relaying any pot holes and bumps back to the driver of our ambulance. Back then they only had one ambulance officer in country areas, so the police were depended upon to help in exceptional circumstances.

We didn't seem to be going very fast and I found myself mesmerized by the red flashing light I could see so clearly above my head through the small hole in the ambulance roof. But there was no siren. That gave me a sense of relief; that meant that there were no serious injuries. We were all okay. The ambulance continued ever so slowly on its journey, sometimes coming to a near stop on certain parts of the road. I remember thinking that I wished they would go a bit faster. I just wanted to stop the pain. There was a lot of chatter between the police car ahead and the ambulance, but I couldn't make out what they were saying most of the time. Come to think of it, I don't remember any of the conversation in the ambulance. Thank heavens they didn't rock the ambulance around too much. I was in horrible pain.

Finally, the ambulance came to a stop and the rear doors flew open. There were people everywhere. Amber was slid out on her stretcher first and then Yvette. I waited for my turn, but it didn't come. I laid there repeating, "Hello?"... No response. I was alone.

I laid there for what seemed like forever. I think a good ten minutes went by. Then the police officer, ambulance officer, a male nurse, and a female nurse came out and lifted me down from my hanging position and put me onto a trolley. They started to wheel me down the corridor. As they did, a young nurse was running past in the opposite direction. She was crying. As she went past I asked, "Are you okay?" She just looked at me, put her hand over her mouth, and vomited. She ran off crying.

The nurse who was wheeling me looked down from above and said, "And you're asking people if *they're* okay, wow."

I was wheeled into casualty. I had never seen so much blood. The doctors and nurses were covered in it. It was on the floor around the trolleys and on the material dividers that were pulled back between the beds. Now I knew why the young nurse was not feeling well; it made me feel nauseous too. I had people at me, cutting my clothes off: first the scissors slid up one leg then the other. Up the front of my chest and down my arm. Snip went the bra strap, snip on the other side then snip on either side of the underpants. I looked to my left and saw Amber. She was laying there just staring at me, eyes fixed. I stared back at her, but there was no recognition. People were talking at me, all at once. "Can you feel this? Can you feel that?" But all I could concentrate on was the nurse trying to put a line in Amber's neck.

"Leave her alone," I yelled as she groaned in pain. And then I just whimpered. "Leave her alone, please."

Then they pulled the curtain. I tried to raise my head to see Yvette, but she was over in the corner with another team of people working on her.

What's happening? The room was spinning, the pain intense. Then I saw them wheel Amber out of the room on her way to x-ray. Her head was severely injured on the side that had been hanging out the window. There was blood everywhere. As I scanned her body, I screamed. Her arm was missing! *Her arm, where is her arm?*

"What happened to her arm?" I screamed at the nurses. "What happened to it? What did you do with it?" I was trying to get up off the table to go to her.

The male nurse pushed me back down and said, "They haven't found it yet. There's a chance they might though." They continued to buzz around me. That made no sense to me ... 'may find it'? *What did that mean? Why did they take it off her in the first place?* Nothing was making sense.

"What year is it? ... Who are you? ... Where do you live?" The questions kept coming and coming. "Who are the other girls? What are their names? Where do they live?" I answered as many questions as I could before it was my turn to go to x-ray.

The x-ray guy threw me around the table like a floppy doll. He didn't seem to care if I was in pain or that he was causing more pain. So far they had not given me anything for pain relief. I remember him saying to the other person who was in x-ray with him, "Two broken legs, left and right, tibia and fibula, crushed left foot, no solid tarsals or metatarsals can be seen. Smashed left humerus and compound fracture to the forearm with some serious breakages. It doesn't look good; she might lose that. And a small hairline fracture to the skull." Not necessarily in that order.

I remember waking some time through the night. I was in intensive care and Amber was beside me. She was sleeping and looked peaceful now. I had a big bowl under my left arm with about half an inch to an inch of blood in it, maybe more; the memory is a bit jumbled. I looked over and saw a bottle of water on my cupboard and I tried to reach with my good arm. My fingertips could just touch it, but as I slowly rolled it towards myself it fell to the ground. A nurse came running. "No, you can't have that; let me get you a clean bowl," she said.

I must have fallen back to sleep because morning came and I awoke to see an older woman with a funny hat on staring at me. "We're just taking you to theatre now."

For three days I lay unconscious, but the sound of familiar heavy footsteps that I had heard many times before brought me out of it and into the here and now. Clip, clop, clip, clop. My mother's footsteps were heading down the corridor towards the room.

I opened my eyes and saw her coming up the hallway. I reached my good arm out to her and found myself crying out like a little girl, "Mommy, Mommy, Mommy."

She moved faster towards me and grabbed me by the shoulders. Looking me straight in the eyes, she scolded, "I was so worried about you. I told you I didn't like you hitchhiking."

"Mom, where are Amber and Yvette? Are they okay" I asked.

"I don't know; I just got here. Robyn drove me up. Why didn't you tell the police who you were? They only found me last night. I heard about the accident on the news and I waited for the police to knock on the door, but when no one contacted me I didn't think it was you," she explained. Mom looked at me with such worry in her eyes. I had never seen her show such concern and love for me in my life. The accident was almost worth it!

She said, "I have to do this, I'm sorry, love," and she pulled back my sheets. She collapsed into the chair. "Oh my God, thank God," she breathed out. "I was told that you had lost both your legs."

Word about the accident had apparently travelled to TT's pretty fast. Glen from HMAS Torrens had taken leave and was at the hospital in Wagga Wagga the next morning. They asked him if he knew who I was and he advised them that I was going out with one of the sailors on his ship. While in Sydney I had been using Edward's surname, so any identity in my bag only led them back to my small flatette in Sydney.

Glen gave them Edward's surname and they contacted the ship and found out that Edward was at home with his parents. They rang his home and his father took the call. He thanked them for letting him know and hung up without giving them any details on me. Edward's story was that after the call to his parents' home, they locked him in his bedroom as they did not want him to go to the hospital in Wagga Wagga. They did not want him around me. Edward had to go back to the ship, so they couldn't keep him locked up forever. When he got away two days later, he called the hospital to ask about us and told them who I was. He also told them where he thought my mother lived. The police took it from there and found Mom.

Edward never came to the hospital, not even the following weekend when he could have. Glen didn't leave the hospital, and shortly afterwards Amber's boyfriend also arrived. The only one who didn't show was Edward. His excuse—his father had warned him not to come, or else. Or else what? He was a grown man.

Amber's mother burst into the room shortly after my mom arrived. She had heard I was awake. I'm not sure what I expected, but it wasn't the very personal attack I received—Amber's mother blaming me for forcing her daughter to hitchhike back to Sydney and for taking her spending money that they had given her.

The verbal assault was too much—the anger in her voice and the hostility. I looked from her to Mom, "What money? We didn't have any money," I quietly voiced.

"Yeah after *you* spent it all," was the reply.

Mom asked her to leave the room and to leave me alone. But she was not leaving until she got some answers ... answers I couldn't give her. Apparently, Amber had been given her train fare home to Sydney and had chosen to hide it away, probably to spend at TT's later. She had told her mother that we spent it, at my insistence. I hated that I was always the one blamed for everybody else's issues.

I suggested that she speak with Yvette because I knew Yvette would back up my story. I couldn't believe that Amber had money the whole time and didn't tell us. I wouldn't have expected her to spend it, but just to know she had it in case of an emergency would have made me feel better. It was a big thing to have money in our circle. We were standing by the side of a dark highway, hungry, and she didn't even have to be there. Mom copped it later as well, in the dining room when they went to eat. My reception from Yvette's mother was slightly warmer. She was accompanied by her other daughter, who asked me what happened. I presume she was able to explain it to her mother.

None of these mothers shared with me how their daughters, my friends, were doing. It was Jacqueline who had to tell me the injuries incurred by the others. Yvette had massive leg injuries, bad enough that she almost lost her leg. She had been placed in traction to help the muscle in her leg to reattach, as it had been ripped from her calf during the accident. She would require numerous surgeries in her future to fix her injuries, but if the muscle didn't reattach properly, she could still lose her leg. Other than that she was in shock but was going to be okay.

I learned that Amber had a massive head trauma, which is why the ambulance had driven so slowly to avoid bumps and hadn't used a siren. But she was now awake. Her left arm had been severed on impact and they were not able to reattach it as it was found under the last bag of potatoes cleared from the highway the next day. The man who found it had cried. He looked at her perfectly manicured nails and said, "You can tell she is a good girl."

She also had both legs broken above the knees and was in traction. She would require extensive rehabilitation but was doing okay under the circumstances. She was struggling badly with the idea that she had lost her arm.

I couldn't look at Jacqueline. Everyone had blamed me for the accident and for the fact that the girls had been hurt. I wanted to curl up in a ball and die. My mood went from being happy to see my family to being depressed pretty fast. I blamed myself. Even though Amber had money and didn't even need to be there with us, I still blamed myself—everyone else did so why not?

"Bev, you can lead a horse to water, but you can't make it drink," said Mom. She was my only supporter. "You didn't do this. These girls came of their own free will; you didn't force them into that truck. This is not your fault."

I said, "I just wanted to come home."

Then Mom put it all into perspective for me. "You're all still alive. That's all that counts. Injuries will heal—you're alive." she said

Both my legs were broken just above the ankles and my left foot was totally crushed. They were not sure if it would heal but had done their best placing pins in each tarsal, metatarsal, and the phalanges to keep them together.

My second toe on my left foot was too badly damaged, so they just pinned it to the third toe rather than cutting it off. It couldn't be repaired; the bone was shattered. Now it has a mind of its own.

Both legs were in plaster from toes to upper thigh, just below the pubis. My left arm, which had borne the brunt of the impact as we smashed into the back-end tailgate of the other semi, was smashed to bits. It had been fractured in many places, with a compound fracture where the bone had pierced through the skin.

The elbow tip had been chipped off and lost in the impact. They had pinned it in the hope that it would take but had prepared me that if it didn't, I may still lose it. There were a lot of fractures and they had to piece it all together like a jigsaw puzzle.

The arm was plastered from my hand up to and encompassing my shoulder. When Yvette had been holding my arm during the accident, she had been holding the bone that was sticking out of the skin on my left arm.

My head was fine, although there was a very small hairline fracture at the front and cuts where I had been thrown through the windscreen. Massive amounts of windscreen glass had embedded itself into my skull. Considering my head had smashed through that windscreen and into the steel bars holding the load on the back of the other truck, I'd say I have a tough noggin! My face was fine. Other than shock, as well as multiple surgeries in the future and rehab, I was going to be okay too.

The truck that we had hit had lost his front right-hand steering tire. He couldn't continue up the hill without it and there was nowhere for him to pull off the road to safety. Frank had come down the hill at full speed with the idea of not having to crawl up the hill in front of him. If Frank had been more alert, we could have avoided the truck and no accident would have occurred.

However, fate saw to it that our futures would be very different to our pasts. Sylvia's Cutting was a notorious black spot. There were so many accidents and deaths there over the years and Recar set up the Australian Truck Drivers' Memorial in Tarcutta to honor those who died in this spot. Usually the cars ended up as wrecks. Some were just pushed over the side and dropped into the gully to lay there and rust in a make-shift automobile graveyard.

When I returned to the site of the accident just recently, thirty-two years later, it sure looked different to what I remembered. I realized how close we came to death that night on the highway. After many years of holding in the shock of the accident, I broke down, shaking from what I was looking at.

To this very day thoughts of the accident always bring to mind the words to a song called, *500 Miles* by Bobby Bare.

Mom stayed long enough to arrange for me to be moved by air ambulance back to Melbourne as soon as I was well enough to travel. I was transferred almost two weeks later. After everything had died down and our parents had left to return home, the nurses wheeled Yvette's and my beds to each other so that we could see each other and say hello. Neither of us saw Amber; she didn't want to see us.

The day came for us to be taken home. Yvette and I were both taken to the airport in separate ambulances. She was loaded onto the Westpac Rescue Helicopter while I was loaded into the Royal Flying Doctor Air Ambulance. We waved goodbye to each other on the tarmac. Yvette was heading to Sydney and I was returning to Melbourne to be nearer to Mom. Amber had already been flown to Melbourne and was settled into her hospital.

I was met by an ambulance in Melbourne and taken to PANCH hospital, my home away from home. I spent six months in that hospital and Mom came every day. She would sit with me for hours. No, she wasn't drunk. I believe she may still have drank at night, but not through the day, not when she was with me. Mom had changed from when I was a child. Our relationship was slowly starting to heal.

Edward's ship, the HMAS Torrens, pulled into Melbourne during that time and apparently he went with Jolene to visit Amber. I didn't even know that they were in town until Glen turned up at PANCH.

He asked, "Has Edward been in to see you yet?"

"I didn't even know you guys were here!" I replied in surprise. I hadn't heard from Edward in a very long time.

"He'll be here tomorrow night; I'll make sure of it," Glen said as he bid me farewell.

I cried all night. Glen went back to the ship and ripped into Edward. Edward rang the hospital, but the nurses wouldn't let him talk to me; I was too hurt.

The next day I prepared for Edward's visit. I did my hair and put on a little bit of makeup; as good as I could anyway. If he came, I would be pleased to see him, though a part of me expected that Glen wouldn't be able to get him to come. But there was one problem. I had been having trouble with my bowels from being bedridden. My legs had had to be re-broken because they had not been set correctly in Wagga, so I was back to square one and I was not able to get up out of bed to use the regular toilet. So, let's just say that things had backed up a little.

The nurse, Gwenda, kept coming in to advise me that she wanted to give me a suppository—"Medical comes before visitors, no matter who they are," she said with a smirk on her face.

But I kept refusing because I was expecting Edward any time. Six o'clock in the evening came and went and no Edward. Seven o'clock, nothing! Eight o'clock came and went—nobody. I had hoped that he would come; I hadn't seen him for a very long time. But now my hopes dropped.

Gwenda came in and said, "Can't wait any longer; bend over." Very upmarket! But I loved Gwenda's sense of humor.

Ten minutes later I'm sitting on a bed pan, the curtains pulled around my bed, and a head pokes through the curtains. Holy hell—or holy shit might be more apt—he came!

"Get out!" I screamed.

The nurse came running. She asked if Edward and Glen could wait outside and explained to them that I had just been given a suppository and could be a little while. She also pointed out that it was after visiting hours, but as it was a special visit she would allow it.

When they came back in, Glen explained that they were late because Edward had visited Amber first. That prompted me to ask Edward who I was to him.

He mumbled, "It might be better if we break up." With that he left.

I sat there dumbfounded. I wanted to cry, but no tears came and instead a massive lump grew in my throat.

Glen said, "Don't worry. You're better off without him anyway. He's been screwing anything that moves while you've been in hospital, especially a chick called Jolene. I'll see you tomorrow night."

Glen hurried out the door after Edward to share the taxi back to the ship. Glen annoyed most people, but he had been nothing but kind to me. I appreciated him greatly. It seems he was the most genuine person in my life at that time, besides Mom.

I was stunned; the tears now came and wouldn't stop. The nurse sat and held my hand most of the evening. Edward tried to call several times to see if I was alright, but the nurses abused him. They had become quite good friends with me, since I had been there so long, and they were disgusted that he had treated me so badly. They understood how I felt and how long I had waited to see him. I had kept my picture of him beside the bed and I would never fall asleep without saying goodnight to him. He broke my heart. They told him over the phone that I was fine and sitting up in bed, laughing at a comedy on television. They thought it was reasonable to treat him with the contempt he deserved. I didn't hear from him again until after my release.

⁌

Six months after the accident, I was finally released from the hospital. Mom begged me to stay in Melbourne where she could help me. It's strange, but even though I had longed to hear those words from her during the time I spent in the convent, and even though she had been sitting with me nearly every day these past six months, I felt a pull to go to Sydney. Unfinished business, perhaps?

I explained to her that, other than her, there was nothing left for me in Melbourne. The children were a major pull, but I was not ready to open a door for Jack to walk straight back into my life. I had made my life in Sydney and Leah had agreed to let me stay with her and look after me there—she was a great friend. Mom felt sad but understood. Besides, I didn't want Charlie parked outside my house every day and tracking my every move.

Departure day arrived. My legs were still in plaster, and would be for some time, and my arm was now fixed, although the pin holding it together was still firmly in place. So it was strong enough that I could use crutches to get around. It was going to be hard, but it was necessary. I was a woman on a mission and determined to prove that I could stand on my own two feet, literally.

Mom helped me to go to Box Hill to see Amber before I left for the airport. I told her how sorry I was and that I wished I could turn back the clock. She said she was happy to see me, but I found her to be a little cool. She had since told her Mom about the money, owning up that I hadn't known, so I was off the hook with that. Blaming me for the accident though would never go away; it would always be my fault that they were hurt. I saw that she had flowers and cards everywhere—so many. Her bed area looked so pretty, with all the colors hanging over and around her. At the head of her bed, on her bench, everywhere. I had received two cards. They had sat by the side of my bed my entire stay in hospital.

Again I felt sad. Was I jealous? Sure. I didn't understand why nobody liked me enough to really care. I wasn't a bad person. I just didn't fit—I never did. She showed me pictures of the visitors that she had received and the beautiful flowers that they had given her. Edward's were particularly nice…

36

Chance Number 3

> "My eyes went straight to him like a moth to a flame, as if there was a golden thread linking my heart to his—something I had never experienced before."

I WAS WINGING MY WAY to Sydney, firmly wedged between the seats in first class. *First class!* Because I couldn't bend my legs, they had to put me up the front of the plane and across two seats. I reached Sydney and Leah was there to greet me at the airport. Shortly before my accident I had moved to a new boarding house in Neutral Bay, and when they found out about the accident they had moved all of my stuff into storage. Leah had picked it up for me and put it all away in the room I would occupy at her and her boyfriend Stephen's house. Leah had moved in with Stephen, her love from Melbourne. It was terrific that he agreed to have me there, but why wouldn't he? He idolized Leah and anything she wanted she got. I was what she wanted at this moment.

One of the first things I did when I got to Sydney was rush to Yvette's bedside—well, hobble as fast as I could. I was mobile but still required a lot of help because I couldn't bend my legs at all—the plaster made sure of that. I was shocked when I saw the state of her leg. I cried inside but kept a brave face so as not to upset her.

Amazingly, her area was also adorned with many cards and flowers. Not as many as Amber but still a considerable amount. She told me that Jacqueline had flown to Melbourne to visit Amber in hospital. Another surprise for me! I felt disappointed that Jacqueline hadn't visited me too.

Other than my one visit from Edward and two from Glen, Mom had been my only regular visitor. Other family members had only visited once during the six months I was in hospital.

Yvette looked well and was really happy to see me. She hadn't been out of bed yet and was suffering all the symptoms of being bedridden that I knew so well. We talked all about it for a long time, and then when I left it was with an unplanned "bang"!

My plaster slipped on the hospital floor as I was leaving and I knocked her vase of flowers down into the back of her television. This sent smoke pouring into the air as the water hit the electronics. I was so clumsy in my plasters. She understood though. I knew it would probably cost her money and I offered to pay for it, but she said not to worry. She was just really happy to see me.

Afterwards, Leah and I sat and talked. I told her what was happening with Edward and Jolene. I felt sad and finally gave in to my feelings, blubbering all over the place. I took short, sharp breaths as I sobbed.

Leah wanted to kill Edward. She was pissed at him for what he had done, and even more pissed off at Jolene. After I calmed down, I gave her an update on Amber and told her I hoped to visit Yvette again the next day.

Leah said, "I know what will cheer you up. Let's go to TT's."

It didn't take much to convince me. I needed to get back out and live, plaster or no plaster! I had been locked away in a hospital bed for just over six months. So she helped me to dress. I put on some makeup, did my hair, and we jumped into a taxi and headed to Kings Cross. She had called Stephen to let him know. He was getting off the ship a little later and told her he would join us there.

The taxi pulled up outside TT's. While Leah paid, I struggled up the few stairs at the front of the building. I could hear the music pumping from the disco downstairs. Oh, downstairs! I hadn't thought about that. Nobody had taught me to do stairs on crutches in this toe-to-hip plaster. All they did was make sure I could hold myself upright and walk in a fashion, with the crutches and two very ugly, large, brown boots.

Leah caught up with me and said, "Hang on." She ran downstairs and returned with our favorite doorman/bouncer. He stood about six foot five inches and was built like a brick dunny. He came up to me, bent down, and gave me a kiss on the cheek.

"Welcome back," he said before he scooped me up in his arms and carried me down the stairs. Now, I liked that sort of treatment!

As I got to the bottom of the stairs with Leah carrying my crutches, the music stopped and Jim the DJ said over the microphone, "Welcome back to one of our favorite girls. We're glad you're alive. We thought we had lost you." He started playing *I'm Alive* by Electric Light Orchestra. Everyone in the whole disco stopped, looked my way, and applauded.

I felt like a celebrity and Leah had a smile glued across her face. It wasn't long before everyone was offering to buy me a drink. As far as I knew HMAS Torrens was at sea and I wasn't likely to see Edward, so I was relaxed. I didn't feel like being upset, not tonight.

A really cute guy attached himself to me, a bit of a knight in shining armor. Everywhere I went he cleared the way. He really looked after me. I danced the night away on the dance floor with my crutches to songs like *Dancing Queen* by Abba. I felt fabulous, free, and the happiest I had felt in a very long time. I tired rather quickly—probably just a little bit too much too soon. I didn't realize at first that the faces I was seeing around me were familiar. Too familiar!

After what seemed a really long night, my knight in shining armor carried me upstairs to a waiting taxi. When he went to jump in with me and Leah, one of the guys going past said, "That's Edward's girl, mate. I wouldn't be going anywhere with her."

He looked at me and I turned and said, "I'm not Edward's girl. He hasn't been my boyfriend for months."

My knight turned to the guy and said, "Ah well, mate. I'll take my chances against big bad Edward," and he jumped in beside me and asked, "Where to?" Leah gave the taxi driver the address.

My knight, Derrick, stayed for a coffee and was just about to take his leave when the phone rang.

Leah said, "Who would be calling at this time of the night?"

I said, "I'll give you two guesses."

She didn't need any—it was Edward. The Cross is like a jungle vine; it has no secrets. It didn't take much to work out the conversation by just listening to Leah from my side of the call.

Leah said, "Edward, don't call here again. She doesn't want to talk to you. Yeah, he's here, so what? She'll fuck whoever she likes, Edward. You've got nothing to do with it anymore. Oh, fuck off," and she hung up.

The phone rang again and Derrick said, "Do you mind?" as he pointed to the phone. He was a true gentleman, really polite and friendly. He was nice, definitely someone I'd like to keep around.

Leah swept her arm in the air, rolled her eyes, and said, "Be my guest."

Derrick took the phone. "Hello. Yeah, I'm him. Why? ... Yeah, we're just about to jump into bed, mate. Can you call back tomorrow? She's tired ... Mate, you can't tell her what to do. You're nothing to her now."

My heart was tearing in two. I felt so sorry for Edward having to hear all of this.

Derrick continued, "Mate ... Edward ... Do not tell me who I can fuck ... if I want to fuck her I will, with her permission of course and there is nothing you can do about it," and he hung up.

The phone rang again. Stephen picked it up and hung it up immediately, then left it off the hook.

Derrick turned to me and said, "Oh well, I hope that helps. Have you got a pen? I'll give you my number." Yes, he was a sailor too—and on another ship, thank heavens! He continued, "I will understand if you don't call me, but I hope you do. I'm going to go now. I hope he doesn't come around, bothering you. Let me know if you need me and I'll come back." I thanked him and he left.

I sat down on the bean bag with help from Leah and Stephen. I had to jam my feet up against theirs, hold onto their hands, and just fall straight back, depending on them not to drop me. Leah covered me up with a blanket and we started to watch television. I thanked them again for helping me. Knock, knock, knock on the door.

"What the hell," Leah said.

Stephen opened the door, and who was standing there but Edward. I ripped into him. I told him he no longer had any rights where I was concerned; he'd blown that chance. I asked him where Jolene was and why he wasn't crawling into her pants. Apparently, they were not officially a couple and she was in Melbourne. He asked if he could talk to me, privately.

Stephen looked at me as if to say, "Do you want me to get rid of him?" He was ready to throw him out on his backside. But I agreed to talk to him.

We went into my bedroom and sat on the bed. He tried to touch me and I pushed him away.

"Don't bother," I said. My skin crawled at his touch. For once he hadn't been drinking; however, after several hours of begging me to take him back he threw up anyway. I felt truly sorry for him, but I still said, "No." It was nearly four o'clock in the morning now and he was still begging. He had thrown up several times. I was so tired that I gave in and finally agreed to take him back. He was the doting boyfriend for about three weeks. Then Jolene was back in town and Edward started acting weird again.

Meanwhile, I had told Leah that I really didn't want to be a burden on her and Stephen anymore, as they were just starting out. I could feel the tension between them; taking me on had been a huge responsibility. So I spoke to the manager at my old boarding house and they gave me a room straight away. I moved back and felt a degree of flexibility and privacy that I hadn't had for a while. I know Leah did her best to look after me, and I was extremely grateful for her help. But I realized that I liked my own company and I missed that. I had had six long months in hospital to soul search and make some major decisions about my life and what I wanted in my future. Sydney didn't really fit the criteria anymore.

I believe that a great thing happened to me at that time. My life came to a dramatic and sudden stop, which allowed me to take stock of the direction I was heading. Old habits die hard and it takes a lot to physically and emotionally remove yourself from the path that is easy and to divert yourself onto virgin ground. I remembered that I didn't want to be on the road I was travelling anymore. I was ready for more; I was ready to change my life for the better. I needed to start making the changes that I had deliberated over for the six months I was in hospital. Edward no longer fitted into those plans, or so I thought…

I have no idea why I caved in—again—though he was very convincing that things would change, that I would be his eternal love. I suppose I gave in to what was familiar; it was just easier. Edward came over several nights later. He hadn't helped me move my stuff; he just turned up for a bit of rough and tumble and then went missing again for days. The girls at the boarding house told me to get rid of him. They said he wasn't really interested in me; he had been flirting with them as well. I knew that he flirted; it was one of his things. I just hadn't realized that it was so obvious to everyone else. I suppose I had blinkers on.

After a month or two I finally decided to call it quits. He came over one night and I told him. "It's over, Edward. Enough is enough. You're not emotionally available to me. You're only here for yourself. I want you to take your stuff and go." The song by Abba, *One of Us*, plays in my mind when I think of this time.

So I packed up anything that belonged to him and pushed him and his stuff out the door. He sat on the other side of the door, knocking gently and slowly. He told me that he wasn't going to leave and that he wasn't ready to end it. I ignored him.

After an hour or so he said, "The last ferry just left. So how am I supposed to get back to the ship now?"

I said, "Stop expecting me to continually solve all your problems. Swim … ship ahoy sailor boy."

I heard laughter coming from upstairs; the girls had been listening.

While he was sitting on the other side of the door crying, I was mourning what could have been. My heart was breaking, but soon a smile found its way across my face as I thought of the absurdity of it all. I shuffled around busily packing my own belongings; I had decided to go home to Melbourne.

The next day I called Mom to ask if I could come home to her. She said that she had been expecting me and the bungalow was empty. "Come home, I'll look after you."

I had one last night out before I left and met up with a guy who was just gorgeous, but it was too late for me to start anything new with him. The next morning as we cuddled up together in my single bed we talked about ourselves. It turned out his surname was very familiar and when I asked if he had a brother, he said, "Yes."

After further discussion it turned out that Mr. Roberts had a secret—a big brother who was also in the Navy. We both laughed and decided that our relationship could not go any further, although he had said he wouldn't mind if it did. I gave him my address in Melbourne and told him to look me up if he ever pulled into port down there.

We corresponded for a while and saw each other again once only, but on a platonic basis. In fact, a lot of the guys and I corresponded together, especially my friends on HMAS Torrens.

With the help of another male friend, I made my way to the airport the next day. As I settled into my seat on the plane, awaiting take-off, I stared out the window. Melancholy set in. I felt indecision about what I was doing, leaving behind all the friends that I had made over time … All the good times and bad times flashed through my mind. But now it was time to say goodbye to the Defense Force guys I had met and hello to a normal life. Yeah, you got it in one—you thought I was going to say, *Leaving on a Jet Plane* by Peter, Paul, and Mary. Well, it does fit, but no, it's a song called *Fly Away* by John Denver.

When I look back now, it's rather funny because the Defense Force had been in my blood for a very long time. I was after all a Defense Force brat. If I was to change the way my life was heading, and it was time to do so, I had to wave goodbye to that life—the life of partying, boozing, and clubbing—and all the craziness involved with it. I had not yet hit rock bottom, but I was a fast learner and I knew that if I stayed I would. I had to go and create something normal. I couldn't go back to the one night stands and the "what ifs". What if he is the right one for me … what if?

I knew Edward would not follow me to Melbourne. He was not that committed; was he ever? However, in fairness to Edward, he was young and he had actually helped me through a pretty rough patch in my life. I am grateful that he was there for that. We touched down at Tullamarine Airport and after a short taxi drive I arrived at Mom's front gate. The taxi driver helped me in and Mom and I sat and talked for a long time—for the first time, adult to adult. My tears flowed steady and freely for the first time in front of my mom. It was something very different for me. She was sad for me, sad that it hadn't worked out with Edward. But Mom's way of saying you need to get over it was, "There are plenty more fish in the sea." I just couldn't see that at the time. My heart wanted to go back, but to what? There comes a time when you just have to let go; it was my time now.

My days were taken up with appointments at the hospital and rehabilitation, mostly for my arm because my legs were still in plaster. I had gone back to seeing my social worker because I was doing it tough emotionally, and other than that I stayed in the bungalow and just listened to music and wrote letters. I was haunted by the bungalow; however, it was my only refuge. It seemed that I had made some pretty good friends while I lived in Sydney, and at least four guys from Edward's ship kept in touch with me regularly by mail. I had a couple of other guys from different ships writing to me as well. I didn't mind writing to them all; it kept me busy. After all, what else did I have to do? Just learn the words to *Cool for Cats* by Squeeze? Which of course I did. Honestly, would I not? Only someone who knows me could understand why I would do that.

My letters also kept them up to date with a little bit of news while they were away. I was a lifeline from home for many of them. HMAS Torrens had sailed for a six-month tour and the guys enjoyed receiving my letters. I never wrote to Edward. I had permanently erased him from my life. He did write to me once and asked where his letter was, explaining to me that it was embarrassing hearing all my news from the other guys on his ship. It went unanswered.

Somewhere around this time, an application that I had put in to join the Navy was actioned. I had been sent an appointment date for testing. Mom helped me go to the testing center. It was a long day. First came the testing for Maths and English and so on. Then if you passed that, you were sent to the psych and then onto the medical. I went through all the phases. The only problem I struck was when the doctor doing the medical asked me to squat.

He had his back turned to me when he said, "Now squat." I could have quite easily ignored him and not said anything, but I just said, "I can't."

He turned and looked over his glasses at me. "Have you got something wrong with your knees?"

I looked down at my legs and said, "Um, no, I'm in plaster from my toes to my hips."

"Oh," he said. "Oh." He had thoroughly examined me on the table in his room before this. It made me wonder how thorough these medicals actually were.

I received a letter a few weeks later to tell me that I was "temporarily medically unfit" for duty and that I would need to undergo further medical checks once my condition had improved. Other than that everything was okay, and depending on the outcome of my future medical, I could be enlisted in the Navy. Well, there was something I could look forward to in the future. A career in the Navy, and boy would I give them hell.

※

The big day came. Today they were removing the plaster from my legs. Mom and I headed off to the hospital. I was scared; I hadn't seen my legs since the day of the accident. I knew there had been a lot of cuts and injuries to them, and after seeing Amber and Yvette's legs, I didn't know what to expect. Actually, I was more than scared; I was terrified. My head was spinning with questions. *Will they be mended enough? What if I stand up and my legs break again?*

The plaster was cut away from my legs with a small handsaw. I was petrified that they would cut me and I had to keep asking for a break. But eventually they cut the entire length of both plasters and were ready to remove them.

The doctor came into the room to stay with us, and when the plasters were peeled back off my legs, I gasped. The plaster had been on for nearly seven months and it stank inside. The stench made me feel ill. They were a sorry sight as the muscles in my legs were wasted, but they explained that my muscle system would restore with physiotherapy. It wasn't as bad as it could have been. Because I had been walking around on crutches for some time, some muscle structure had stayed intact.

The hair on my legs was about an inch long and jet black. They advised me not to shave it off as it would grow back worse. They said it would fall off in a short period of time by itself. I certainly bloody hoped so!

The scarring on my legs was not too bad. There was a fair bit of scabbing;

however, they were dry scabs that had fallen off over time and were just stuck on my leg from where the cuts and wounds had healed. (Yeah, I know, yuck) Any stitches had been removed when they did the surgery to re-break my legs all those months ago, and the pins in my foot had been removed at the same time. The only pin I still had was the one in my arm.

Using my crutches, I stood on my legs for the first time without plaster to support me, and I can tell you it was one of the scariest things I have ever had to do. It is amazing the scenarios your mind can conjure up. It took a lot of coaxing to trust that my legs would not fold under me and break in half again. They wanted me to try and use walking sticks instead of crutches to help build muscle, but all I could think of was old ladies. I must admit I am sometimes vain and I wasn't ready for that yet. They assured me it was the best thing that I would do for myself, so I took them home—and my crutches.

After weeks of rehabilitation, learning to walk again, and physiotherapy to strengthen and gain mobility back in my limbs, I was starting to feel a lot better. Initially, my knees wouldn't bend as they had been kept straight for so long, and the pain was excruciating when I tried to move them. It was something that had to be done, though, if I was ever to return to normal.

One Saturday afternoon, Mom came down to get me from the bungalow. She said, "You have a call."

"Who from?" I asked. I grabbed my crutches and followed her down to the house. My friend Debra, who I hadn't heard from for a very long time, was on the other end of the phone.

"Do you want to come out tonight?" she asked. I thought about it for a moment—the fact that my legs were still not good, crutches, nothing to wear, so I answered "No." It was not a hard decision.

"Pleeeaaassseeee," came the whining response. How could I resist her?

"Okay," I said. That was not a hard decision either.

"Good. I'll come and pick you up at six o'clock," and with that she hung up the phone.

I had a shower, put on some makeup, and did my hair. I threw on a dress I'd had for a while and went and sat in Mom's kitchen to wait for her arrival. While I waited, I picked up my Horoscope Almanac and turned to the date—August 3, 1979. I sat and read it with a smile on my face, and then I looked at Mom who was eyeing me with curiosity.

I said, "As if anyone would want me like this; this must be Debra's lucky night."

My horoscope said verbatim: *"You will play the go-between for two people who will fall deeply in love, or you will meet the love of your life, the person who will make all your cherished dreams and wishes come true."*

Mom just laughed.

Debra arrived and Mom waved us goodbye at the back door. We boarded a tram and went into the city. First stop was the Graham Hotel, where we had a drink. Before long the hotel was full of navy guys. I was screaming inside. I really didn't want to be pulled back into this life again. And then a bunch of guys arrived that I had known forever; they were off HMAS Tobruk. It had arrived in town that day.

We sat in a booth with them and had plenty to drink. It really didn't take long for me to get tipsy. I hadn't drunk any alcohol for quite some time. Debra jumped up and said, "Come on, I want to go dance."

"Where are we going?" I asked.

"There is a nightclub in St Kilda; we'll go there."

We jumped in a taxi and headed for Mickeys Disco along the beach at St. Kilda. Before long we arrived at the front door. I struggled out of the car with my crutches and bag while Debra fixed up the fare. I stood at the door to the nightclub, looking inside. The music was thumping, there were people everywhere. This disco was so much bigger than Texas Tavern in Sydney.

Then I saw him.

I looked across the room, and when I say across the room, it was about seventy meters from where I stood in the doorway to where he was seated. My eyes went straight to him like a moth to a flame, as if there was a golden thread linking my heart to his—something I had never experienced before. He sat quietly amongst his rowdy mates, just looking around. I grabbed Debra's arm and for a moment felt slightly off balance.

"Are you okay?" she asked.

"Yes," I responded, "there he is."

"Who?" she yelled over the music.

"Him," I pointed, "the guy I'm going to marry."

"Who is he?" she looked at me with a quizzical look on her face.

"I don't know," I said. "I just know that he's the man I am going to marry."

"How are you going to marry him if you don't know him?"

I said, "Well, best I go meet him then."

"But, Bev, there's nowhere to sit."

"Watch this," I said determinedly. Without hesitation I walked over to where he sat with his mates, with Debra in tow. I sat at the table beside them, even though it had a "Reserved" sign. I knew I would already know him by the time we were asked to move by the bouncers, and that is exactly what happened. By the time the bouncer finally came over and said, "This table is reserved, you'll have to move," I had already struck up a conversation with the guys on his table.

The guys said in chorus, "Come and join us."

So we did. He, my future husband, my soon to be love of my life, the be all and end all of my universe, had said hello to me once, and any words other than that had to be pried from his lips. He was a shy boy! To date I had not really met one of those.

I slid in beside him and felt my whole body tingle as my leg touched his. He looked at me also. Did he feel it too? The table was lively; everyone was talking. My man was introduced to me as Shaun. He looked very young, about nineteen or so. When he stood, he was about six foot three inches and had very dark brown hair, cut in a serviceman's short back and sides.

Was he Navy? I didn't think so; there was a different type of air to this guy. He had reflective, happy, brown eyes that shone when he smiled, and his smile extended all the way from his lips to his eyes—a genuine smile from an unmistakably warm-hearted, gentle man. He wasn't fat and he wasn't skinny. He was well built with a muscular frame and obviously worked out. On his chin was a cute cleft—my mother had once told me that only strong men had clefts in their chin. I was captivated by him. I think I stared at him all night.

I had one dance, on crutches, with this man of my dreams, which he had asked for. While I was on the dance floor, he protected me from the bumps and jabs of other people around me. But still he didn't say anything to me. He just smiled with a goofy sort of shy smile. I was beginning to think that he didn't like me, but I still had no doubt that I would marry him.

Later that evening, we found out that they were all Army guys. Well, I did want a change. Most of them were pretty noisy, except for my listener. Shaun sat drinking water all night, taking in the conversation. I just sat there taking him in. When I asked why he wasn't drinking, he told me he was driving. He didn't elaborate.

Closing time arrived and we had to leave. We went for a quick walk to the beach, which was next to the night club. I love the beach and still do, but I couldn't walk in the sand with my crutches, so Shaun swept me up in his arms and carried me to the footpath. I quite obviously was not picking up his signals.

The night was over and I hadn't even gotten a number or contact for him to try and see him again. He had made no passes at me, to give me any indication that he was interested in me. None that I recognized anyway. I was used to guys coming onto me a lot stronger. I was waiting for any type of request to go out again. Someone suggested that we all get a hotel for the night so Shaun didn't have to drive Debra and me home first before they headed back to Puckapunyal. It was unanimously agreed that we would do just that. It wasn't the first time I had stayed overnight in a hotel with Defense Force guys; in fact, Debra and I were pretty used to it. It was just something that was normally accepted and done. But Army! Oh well, the old saying was "where the Army goes the pong goes". I was changing that to "where my love goes I go".

We all piled into a dingy motel and spread ourselves around the three beds to sleep. Shaun chose the big bed and before I could open my mouth, Debra jumped in it, as did one more guy. I was disappointed but still knew that he was mine. I ended up sharing a bed with one of the other guys, much to my dismay. I spent most of the night fighting him off.

The next morning Shaun drove us to Debra's house before taking the guys back to camp. He still hadn't said a thing all night, and even on the very long trip to Debra's house he sat silent. I sat in the front between Paul and Shaun, with the gear stick between my legs. This was way out of character for me as I was petrified of driving anywhere with anybody after the accident, and definitely didn't like being near a gear stick. But here I sat, with my heart in my throat, in the middle of a car where there was no seat, only the middle to balance on, because I was in love with the man at the wheel and wanted him that badly that I was willing to put my life at risk to get him. Besides, there was not enough room in the back seat.

Even though he didn't talk, every time he had to change the gearshift, he would playfully grab my leg and smile at me—that gorgeous goofy smile—sending electricity into *every* part of my body. That made it all worthwhile.

When we reached Debra's house, everyone piled out of the car to let Debra and I out. I hesitated. I looked him straight in the eyes, trying to muster all the courage I had inside to ask him to come back.

Instead, he put his hand on my leg and said, "Will you go out with me tonight?" I was later to learn that those words had taken all his courage to get out.

I hopped away on my crutches, feeling like Cinderella in glass slippers who had just had the most enchanted evening of her life, and I just knew it wasn't going to end there. I knew he was my chance number three. Thinking back to that night reminds me of an extremely old song, called *Some Enchanted Evening* from the movie *South Pacific*, which I might add, would be my second favorite movie after *The Wizard of Oz*.

37

My Prince

✤

"He stood there tall and proud, his love for me on display for all to see."

WE ARRANGED TO MEET at the London Hotel in the city. Shaun didn't know where it was but said that he would find it. Debra argued with me all day that Shaun wanted to be with her. She said that he had made advances towards her in bed the night before. By the time we got to the London, she was adamant that he was hers. I settled it quite amicably once and for all. The London Hotel had booths to sit in with a table and long chairs on either side. I told her that if she sat on one side of the booth and I on the other, then surely the one he sat next to was the one he wanted. She agreed. Besides, I wasn't actually sure he would show up.

Shaun and his mate walked in right on time; Shaun has always been punctual. It was not hard to recognize them. That same tumble in my stomach occurred as Shaun's and my eyes met. I smiled. He smiled. And then he slid into the booth beside me. I kicked Debra under the table, making her yelp. She didn't seem awfully happy, but all's fair in love and war, and he was mine after all. I had seen him first.

He put his arm around the back of me and sent my senses into overload. Every part of me tingled with electricity. He asked what I would like to drink and then promptly went to the bar and bought it for me.

A few of the Navy guys had started to mingle around us; they wanted to know what "Pongos" were doing in their pub. How did they know? I told

Shaun to let me handle it and I advised them in no uncertain terms that they were there with us and that we would be leaving soon. You should never put Army and Navy at the same drinking hole, unless of course you are willing to sprinkle in a few Airmen for them all to fight. They wanted to know why we were with Army guys, as if they had any right to ask; they assumed we were Navy property. The air was thickening.

I quickly finished my drink and said, "Come on, let's get out of here." I didn't know where we were going to go, just anywhere but there.

As we were walking out the Navy guys were yelling down the stairs after us, "You know you're making a huge mistake. They're not as good as us. Where the Army goes the pong goes."

I turned and shouted back, "Where this Army goes, so do these girls. Bye guys." And I gave them all a cheerful wave as we walked out.

Shaun helped me down the stairs on my crutches and took my bag so that I wasn't so burdened down. We made our way to the car and he suggested that we go to the boozer at Watsonia Army camp and play a little pool. I was all for it, but asked if he would mind dropping me off at home first to change as I hadn't been home and I knew Mom would be worried. He didn't mind.

I hopped inside on my crutches, knocked on Mom's door and said to her when she opened it, "It was me, Mom. I found him."

"Who?"

"The guy from the book. You know; the one who is going to make all my dreams come true."

She laughed.

I said in a more serious voice, "No, Mom. I have met the most amazing guy. He doesn't drink, doesn't smoke, doesn't swear, and doesn't hang out with bad women."

Again she laughed and said, "So what's he doing with you?"

I saw the irony and laughed as well. "I have to go change. He's waiting for me in the car." And I quickly left.

We arrived at Watsonia Army Camp and as Shaun drove towards the front gate, the guard stepped back and saluted.

"Why is he saluting you? Don't they just salute officers?" I asked. I was confused. I figured that somehow I had managed to pick up an officer.

"Yeah," Shaun responded, "the sticker I have on my car is from Puckapunyal and must indicate an officer here at Watsonia."

We had a great night at the boozer and were entertained by all the guys that came out of the woodwork when they heard there were girls there. When the boozer closed, several of them asked Shaun if he could give them a lift into town. Shaun said he didn't mind so long as none of them sat in the front as that was my seat and he didn't want my legs hurt. He had gone from one very quiet guy to one very protective guy in a very short time. Debra hadn't hooked up with anyone in particular but had more than a few takers at this stage. They all piled into the back seat. There were eight of them, including Debra, and there were some pretty funny noises coming from that back seat during the journey.

As we headed towards the front gate with *Ring My Bell* by Anita Ward blaring from the car stereo, arms and legs hanging out of every window of the car, the guard at the gate again stepped back and saluted, and we drove out laughing. It was the stupid look on his face that set us off. We drove down the street singing to the song at the top of our voices. What a night! That was the most fun I had had in years.

Again we clambered into a motel for the night. That time Shaun claimed a single bed and invited me into it with him. I snuggled into him, listening to the giggles and bumps coming from around the room once the light went out. Debra had finally hooked up with one of the guys and I didn't want to know what she was doing. A sliver of moonlight shone through the window, catching Shaun's eyes as he laid there staring at me in the dark. I was totally infatuated by this man. He pulled me right into him and our lips met for the first time. How to describe that very moment ... His lips were soft, sensual, hungry. And when he kissed me, he kissed me passionately, taking me to the very edge of ecstasy. I had *never* been kissed with so much fervor, *ever*, in my entire life. My face flushed with excitement and expectation.

After refusing Shaun's advances, for about two hours, he quieted down. I felt like I had been in a wrestling match with an octopus. Eventually, I fell asleep with my head on his chest, listening to the steady beat of his heart. The last thing I wanted to do was have him think badly of me, which is why I wouldn't give in to his advances. Well, not straight away anyway. This relationship was going to be different. This was going to be "my forever". I knew for sure this was my chance number three, and everybody knows that chance number three is lucky. I had no idea at the time that I was to be his first real sexual encounter. When I woke the next morning, everyone except Shaun and I, were up and ready to leave the room to hunt down breakfast. We just lay there, waiting for them to leave. My heart was racing with anticipation at where this liaison was heading next.

The door shut behind the last one and Shaun looked at me with his gorgeous, puppy dog eyes. He nuzzled into my neck and kissed me. Well, that was it for me; I was gone. I figured I'd held out long enough. My tummy was tumbling and parts of me I had forgotten existed were lighting up like neon signs. He didn't even have to ask—I was his. He was very gentle with me and exuded love and passion. His desperation was such a turn on. We made love, and then we made love again. I couldn't get enough of him and it was obvious he felt the same. There was just something about our union, something magical.

Some of the others returned, but not before we had showered and dressed. Then we all left. Shaun took me home to get changed. I knocked on Mom's door and introduced him.

"Hello, Mrs. Forster," Shaun said.

"Ooh," came Mom's reply, her eyebrows raised as she looked him over with approval. Then he reached out and shook her hand gently but firmly. "Call me Joy," she crooned.

I told Mom that we were just going to the bungalow so I could get changed and then we were off again. Shaun was already walking off in the direction of the bungalow that I had pointed to.

"Don't come home again if you lose this one," Mom whispered with a smile on her face. She had only just met Shaun, but it certainly wasn't hard to be won over by his sexy voice, gentle nature, amazing smile, glittering eyes, and his tall, handsome stature. I believe that Mom was just happy to see me happy, finally.

The following weekend Shaun arrived to pick me up and take me out. This was our second date, but really only day three of our relationship. The bungalow door was open to let in some air. I looked up and saw one hell of a sexy soldier walking up the path towards my bungalow. He still had his uniform on as he had driven straight from work. He walked in the door, bent down, put his arms around me, and kissed me. I nearly stopped breathing, it was so good. Then he handed me his pay packet and asked if I could sort it out for him. We sat and worked out a budget.

Later that night we went to visit my brother, who was ex-Army. Shaun and Danny got along like a house on fire. I guess with my brother's approval of him, Shaun's fate was sealed. We ended up staying over for the night. As we lay together on the lounge room floor, where we were sleeping for the night, Shaun rolled onto his left side and cupped his cheek with my hand. He gazed at me with those enchanting eyes and said, "I love you. Will you marry me?" Yes, that's right. Day three ... and he had asked me to marry him.

"What?" I choked. "No, we've only just met. You don't even know me properly. You can't make that type of decision yet," I scolded. I had found out that he was only eighteen; I was twenty-two.

After all that I had been through leading up to this moment, and still had to go through in my future, I needed to make sure that the man I married was aware of what was involved with taking me on. He looked so disappointed, so I added, "But when we know each other better, yes, I will marry you, if you still want me. But I will let you know when *I'm* ready." That made him happy and before long he was sound asleep.

At that point I was quite complicated, suffering with what would be later diagnosed as PTSD (Post Traumatic Stress Disorder), as a result of the accident and from the many years of being bashed by Jack and abused as a child. Nightmares kept me awake at night and I would pace the bungalow, often going without sleep for days. I had very low self-esteem and often degraded myself verbally, putting myself down for silly little mistakes that I made. The clincher was the fact that I had been told I could no longer have any children. Shaun couldn't have understood these things. He had never had to deal with them at such a young age. He assured me many times over in the following weeks, months, and years that he was not going to walk out and abandon me because of them. His nature was such that you just believed him and felt safe and secure when he gave his word.

The next night he took me to meet his mother, Mary—Mom G. She was amazing; she was still quite young and had survived so much in her life already. She had been one of the first open heart surgery patients in Australia and also survived a massive stroke that saw her lose most of her verbal and motor skills, including the ability to talk and walk. She was lucky to have survived at all. Nevertheless, she still maintained a sense of humor and used it on us while we were visiting. After being there with her for some time that night, Shaun and I bedded down together on her lounge room floor to stay overnight. Sometime during the night, Mom G. came and stole our clothes, or the ones I wasn't wearing at the time, and *all* of Shaun's were gone. The next morning she thought it was funny to torment him, asking him to jump up and cook breakfast for her. Shaun was learning to be an Army cook at the time, although Mom G. had already taught him to cook well before he enlisted. Then she tried to pull the blankets off him. She was a scoundrel. He shocked her by jumping up out of bed stark naked and asking her where the toaster was. She told him where his clothes were amid her barrels of laughter. It was actually lovely to watch; the trust and love between them was very obvious. I felt so lucky and hoped that maybe in time Mom G. would impart some of that love to me also.

I spent many hours with her after this night, helping her to learn to talk again by using flash cards she had been given for rehabilitation. I would often travel the distance by train to her house to help her during the day while Shaun was at the Army base doing his course. They say if you meet a prince, he was raised by a queen. He certainly was! Queen Mary. Sadly Mom G. died very young and never got to see the outcome of our union. I'm sure that she would be very proud of her son, and me.

Eventually, though, Shaun's mother returned to her daughter's care in Tasmania. I certainly had enjoyed my time with her. Shaun and I had been living at my mother's house in the bungalow, sharing a single bed that sank in the middle. It had its perks, sleep not being one of them. Mom G. offered her flat to us—lock, stock, and barrel. We accepted gratefully and moved in the next day. Life was great. Now I was the homemaker again. Shaun spent his weeks in Seymour at the base and every night I would sit and write copious amounts of love to him in letters that I sent to him every day in the post. Now, most normal people would write maybe one or two pages; mine tallied six to ten pages a night. I did say that I had a sleeping problem. On weekends, Shaun would arrive promptly when he could, and we would spend our weekends going out to nightclubs with our friends, making love, sleeping, and eating.

About six weeks after we moved into the flat together, I started to feel ill. I was throwing up in the morning and feeling queasy most of the day. I went to the hospital to find out what might be wrong and I was told that I was about two months pregnant. I was so happy but at the same time so very apprehensive and scared that Shaun would feel trapped like Jack had. I was already pretty sure that the doctors would not allow me to have the baby, as had happened in the past. My worst fears were confirmed. I was not allowed to have the baby. We had tried the pill, but it always sent my blood pressure soaring, probably because of my underlying kidney disease. They had inserted an IUD, which had to be removed because it had perforated my uterine wall. So the only form of birth control that was safe for me at that time was condoms, which we did not use.

I waited for Shaun to come home, and then with a heavy heart I sat him down and told him the news. He was genuinely upset, not because I was pregnant but because all of this had made me sad.

"It doesn't matter if you can't have children; I'm okay with that. I love you. It's you I want, not a baby."

I was totally overcome by his understanding and love. For such a young man he had wisdom far beyond his years. He was always honest and caring with me. Shaun attended the hospital with me and sat in the waiting room while the procedure was done to terminate the baby. When I came out of theatre crying, Shaun cried with me. Together we sat solemnly in my room as it was an overnight stay. He held my hand and assured me that he still loved me, more than anything, and he wasn't going anywhere. My stars had been right that first night. They had said that I would find the love of my life, and I had.

Everything was wonderful, until after a few weeks I realized that during our nightly phone calls, Shaun was quite distant, even cool. When he came home that weekend, he called me into the bedroom. I could tell that something was not quite right. He isn't good at hiding secrets from me. He sat with his back up against the wall and I sat on the end of the bed.

"What's up?" I asked. I knew what was coming, but even so I couldn't prepare myself for it. I didn't want to believe it was even possible that this could be happening.

"I've been thinking," he said slowly. "I think we should break up." He couldn't look me in the eyes; his head hung low. Then he went into a whole spiel of reasoning as to why.

I countered every argument.

"I am young and I'd love to travel."—"Why can't we travel together? I'd like to travel too."

"I have hobbies that I'd like to pursue."—"Then pursue them. I'd love to come along and watch you do them."

For each argument I came back at him. He was ripping my heart out of my chest. I could see it in his hands, slowly dying with each word he spoke. I finally broke down, totally inconsolable. At least he never mentioned my inability to have a baby.

Tears were raining down my cheeks, and every second the lump in my throat got bigger and I started to gulp for air. After a few hours of talking like this we mutually agreed to end our relationship. I knew someone had put him up to this; we had been so happy. I had my suspicions, even though at the time he would not divulge who it had been.

Sharon had arrived in Melbourne to meet Cookie's ship. She had asked us to meet her at the London Hotel that evening to catch up; she had never met Shaun. He agreed that he would still come with me that night, but the following day he would help me to pack and return to Mom's place.

I dressed and put on the least amount of makeup that I could get away with. It was very obvious I had been crying. I didn't feel like going out and makeup and clothes were not going to fix the way I looked. We boarded the train to the city, sitting away from each other. I just wanted him to hold me and I needed him to touch me, but he remained indifferent. He was resolved that we were over. In fact, I think it was probably one of the hardest things he had ever had to do. We remained quiet for the entire journey; there was nothing more to say.

We arrived at the London and slid into a booth while we waited for Sharon and Cookie to arrive. In fact, it was the same booth that we had sat in not so long ago when it was me he chose to be with. Sailors were mulling around. Some who knew me came over and said hello. Sharon walked in the door with a couple of other people, one of them Cookie. They slid into the booth with us and we all introduced ourselves. The boys found they had a lot in common.

The others were laughing and having fun, but Shaun and I really were affecting the mood.

After about twenty minutes, Sharon turned and said, "For fuck's sake, guys. Smile. What the fuck is wrong with you both? Anyone would think your cat just died."

I was just about to answer her when Mr. Robert's brother recognized me. He came bounding over to the booth, leaned over the back of it, putting his head between mine and Shaun's, and planted a kiss firmly on my cheek.

"How the hell are you? Are you here by yourself?" he asked.

I was just about to respond yes, because that's how it felt, when Shaun slid his arm around my shoulder and said, "No, she isn't."

Shaun then turned to me and said, "I was wrong, you're mine and I can't live without you. I've been really miserable; can you please forgive me?"

"Yes, of course I will," I eagerly replied, grabbing his hand. How could I not? He was the love of my life.

After this I found out from Shaun that a few weeks after the termination, one of the older biddies who lived in the flats, who had been friends with Mom G., had had a chat with Shaun over a cup of tea. She talked to him about our relationship, telling him that he was too young to be tied down to someone as old as me, who already had children and couldn't have anymore. She also told him that he was young and still had a whole lot of life in front of him, which would be far better off spent with no one to tie him down. She convinced him that he wouldn't be able to travel or have any hobbies, and also that his mother had told her she didn't like me. Shaun had gone back to Puckapunyal with a heavy heart and a lot of thinking to do, which he had not shared with me. After this, we promised to always share our thoughts with each other and that nobody else would ever come between us.

Not long afterwards we moved out of the flat and into an Army unit. Shaun wanted us away from certain influences that were there, so he had our relationship recognized as de-facto and we were then entitled to all that goes along with it. As Shaun had been financially supporting me, it only stood to reason that we were a couple. He applied for an Army unit and within the week we were given the keys to a unit in South Yarra, near Chapel Street.

The day we were moving out of the flat, we heard a cat fight in the vacant block next door. I looked over the fence to see a little kitten caught between two fighting adult cats. I became very distressed by it. Still today I can't cope when animals, or people, are being hurt.

My knight in shining armor jumped the fence and chased after the kitten, which by then was running from him. Shaun only returned to the flat once he had the little one in his hands. It had run into a small hole in the fence and every time he tried to pull it out, it attacked his hand. Shaun had scratches all over him and this dangerous little monster was hissing and spitting all over the place. It was actually quite comical. We took it with us, later finding out that it was a girl, whom we named Pussycat.

For the first week Pussycat lived under the heater in the unit. If anyone went near her, she would rear up and spit at them. Shaun was scared of her, and for a little while she had us both bluffed. We left milk and food, trying to coax her out, but she wouldn't have a bar of it. Eventually, worried about her health, I went to the heater, put my hand in, and pulled her straight out. She hissed at me but didn't scratch me, and then she settled into my arms. She was very weak, but with tender, loving care, I nursed Pussycat back to health and she became a very devoted pet. And yes, she and Shaun became great friends too.

One day I received a phone call from Jack. I didn't know how he had got my phone number, but he asked if I would like to see the kids. He promised to bring them over the following weekend. I don't know why the change of heart, but I gratefully accepted his offer.

Shaun was a natural with them and they loved him. He played tiggy with them and kicked a football with Jason. It was a totally wonderful day. He interacted with them far more than Jack, and they loved it. Shaun got to meet and talk to Jack that day. They had lunch with us and for a little while it actually looked like Jack had cleaned himself up a bit. He looked happy and healthy, nothing like I had explained to Shaun. My daughter was to be baptized and Jack wanted to know if we would like to come; it was the following week. We went, but we were treated quite coldly at the church by both Jack's mother and him, so we decided that we would call it a day at the church, and even though there was an after party, we went home.

We lived in the unit at South Yarra for just on two years. We made many friends in the other units, some who are still in our lives now. We never found that type of community in any other place we were sent. The units were unique and so were the people. It was fun; there was always something going on. We would all move from one unit to the next during the day, having cups of coffee, talking, and enjoying each other's company.

I was still not working as I was in rehabilitation, learning to walk again and having much-needed rectifying surgeries on my left foot and arm. I still spent a fair bit of time in plaster, with Shaun having to care for me as well as work full-time, shift-work. He cooked, washed, ironed, and doted on me. Then there were the other operations that I also had to go through, and there were many.

One of my friends had a baby daughter who I idolized. I loved her then and still love her now, as if she was one of my own. I would often steal her away in her pram and take her for long walks to give her Mom a break. That was the closeness we shared at that time. I enjoyed my time with Mandy as I still missed my own babies very much.

We had a lot of trouble around us in the units, but for us it was one in, all in. The units were surrounded by public housing commission and those units were in turn occupied by new Australians. We came under attack often as they didn't like us. You would be sitting there, quietly minding your own business and having dinner, and a rock would fly through the window. As you were running down the stairwell to find the culprit, you'd put out the call and everyone would join you in the hunt.

The community around us was great; we had many friends, support, and a whole lot of love. But my underlying self-esteem problems were certainly putting a huge, unnecessary strain on Shaun and our relationship. I had trouble believing that someone so gorgeous in nature could love me. So I continually pushed him away by putting myself down.

I often called myself names like "fat" and "slut", and then I would suspect and accuse him of playing up on me. I had issues with the fact that he was younger than me and feared he would run off with someone more his own age, like Edward had. I had been hurt so many times in my life it was just truly hard to believe that someone had come along who was more than totally faithful to me. I became possessive of him, wanting to control him and everything he did, when in fact I had no reason whatsoever to doubt him, or his love for me. Shaun was mature enough to cope with my low times and sensible enough to help guide me back to normality.

One night we were in the kitchen. I was hovering around behind him while he cooked dinner. Suddenly his arm shot up and I was filled with terror. My stomach seemed to lurch up into my mouth and I couldn't breathe. I immediately threw myself onto the floor and curled up into a little ball in the corner with my hands over my head—an instant ducking reaction I had become very good at during my time with Jack. I was crying and shaking with fear. Shaun, quite shocked, bent down and gently helped me up from the floor, wrapping his arms around me.

"What's wrong?" he asked.

"I ... thought ... you ... were ... going ... to ... hit me," I stammered between sobs.

"I was just reaching up to get something down from the cupboard ... I would never hit you."

There were issues around Jack and the children that we had to face, or more to the point, the lack of seeing the children. Jack was now punishing me for being with someone else, so he withheld the children from seeing me. I'm sure he only allowed the children that one day with me to torment me even further by withholding them at a later date. I could only see them at Jack's mother's convenience, and that was once in a two-year period. I had to give up any chance of gaining custody through the courts as I was told on numerous occasions that it didn't matter how or why I left, I was classed as a deserting mother. Therefore, no court in the land would look at my case, or help. We literally spent thousands of dollars and continually got the same answer. At one stage, we even sold all of our furniture, except the bed, to pay for solicitors.

But still, Shaun was always there for me. He put up with my eccentricities where it came to housework, with non-stop scrubbing and cleaning until everything was regulation standard (convent standards). He would salute the linen closet as he walked past, in deference to the perfectly aligned piles of expertly folded linen. He even put up with the clutter I was gathering around myself. I had a driving need to have things because I had always been denied so much. Shaun is very anti-clutter.

Apart from all of this, we shared a magical two years together weathering all. We had moved in with each other only four nights after we met. Many had said it wouldn't last, but we did last—we prevailed. He was there for me in every way. He took me and cared for me as I was. He never expected me to change; he built me up with love, understanding, and patience. He allowed me to be who I was, warts and all, without putting me down as Jack had done for years. We never argued, not once. We talked a lot, often passionately about things that we disagreed about, but not once did we ever argue or raise our voices, separate, or hit out at each other. I told Shaun very early in the relationship that if he ever hit me, even just once, I was gone. I have only ever seen him angry enough to hit out once. Thank God he wasn't angry with me.

One night Shaun and I went out to Menzies Tavern, which was a well-known night club in Melbourne at the time. We were with friends, and of course our friends were friends with people we were no longer friends with. So when we arrived this night, we followed our friends through the crowd to a table where everyone was seated. As I squeezed through to get to the vacant seats at the end, with Shaun holding my hand, I was shocked to see Jolene and Edward seated at the table. *Interesting*, I thought.

She spotted me, staring at me with a stupid Cheshire cat grin on her face. She greeted me with an attitude, not realizing that I was actually with Shaun. She flashed her ring finger in front of me, on which was a brand new sparkling diamond ring that she had received from Edward. Mine lay at the bottom of Port Phillip Bay where I'd thrown it at him on his return from Singapore. I leant forward and gently took her ring finger in my hand, then

I leant into her and said, "Beautiful ring, Jolene, but sloppy seconds aren't my style."

I smiled and continued walking, holding Shaun's hand up in the process. She shot daggers at me the entire night as I sat there quite happy with my man doting on me. Edward was hardly seen anywhere near her all night. He was too busy chatting to other women; nothing had changed, just the fiancé. I was so very happy at that moment. She may have got what she was after, but she was not really happy. She made several attempts to strike up a conversation with Shaun that night, only to be ignored. Shaun knew who she was and did not want to cause me any angst by talking to her. That is just the way he thinks. Personally, I wouldn't have cared; I knew that he was mine. I trusted him enough to know that she didn't have a hope in hell of taking him from me.

※

Shortly after this, the big day arrived. Shaun had asked me again several times during that two year period to marry him. Each time I told him that I would let him know when the time was right to be married, when I believed and felt safe enough. He had proven himself to me many times over, and finally, I had no doubt in my mind that he would never leave me. April 7, 1981, almost two years after we first met, I said it as he walked in the door from work.

"Yes, I will marry you."

He was over the moon. He picked me up and threw me in the air, while trying not to break me. He was so excited that he wanted to be married straight away. But I pulled the reins in because I knew there was so much to prepare. I figured we'd need at least a month! A month? Yep, I hadn't organized a wedding before and I really had no idea how much there was to do. And one month is only four weeks!

I was finally going to have my white wedding in a church, with a fantastic reception and the love of my life by my side. Now, at first this was much to the dismay of Mom, who told me if I married in white, she would not attend.

"Mom, the color of the dress doesn't matter. This is the *best* thing that has ever happened to me in my life, and I want the day to be perfect. And that means you being there too." She agreed to come. I wanted Tammy and Jason to be page boy and flower girl, but Jack wouldn't allow it.

The one month lead up to the wedding was very intense. I had to arrange not only a church wedding but the annulment of my marriage to Jack through the archdiocese. Even though I was legally divorced from him by then, it was a requirement of the church that the same marriage be annulled before I could marry Shaun in the church. And being a Catholic I wanted my forever marriage in a church; it meant the world to me. The paperwork only came through from the archdiocese, after much harping, the night before the wedding!

The wedding dress, bridesmaids' apparel, and flower girl and page boy outfits all had to be found and altered. We had to organize floral bouquets and flowers for button holes as well as choose and make the floral table decorations for the reception center. Finding a reception center that wasn't already booked was a nightmare. We couldn't get the cars or photographer or so many other things we wanted because of the short lead time. However, the invitations were already printed and the date was set, so we just had to do it. Shaun and I made our own wedding cake, so that took a bit of pressure off us.

I also took it upon myself to arrange a nine-week honeymoon to the United States, Canada, and back to Australia through Hawaii, taking in Disneyland, Las Vegas, Niagara Falls, and so on. Visas were required. Shaun's went through okay, but I had committed and was charged with a small crime while living in Sydney, and of course Miss Honest put it on her visa application, so that held things up. That also only came through the day before the wedding, and we were due to fly out of Melbourne on the Sunday morning after the wedding. And then, even after that, they only gave me a single entry visa, which meant we were going to have to leave our tour and travel across Canada on a Greyhound bus to get to the embassy for another visa so that I could continue with the tour and get home.

All in all it was quite stressful, though I thought I had handled it well, right up until the night before the wedding when we received the bridesmaids' dresses from the store. They had been individually tailored by Katies, who used to do that back then. I had requested that a protective cover be placed inside both of the chiffon sleeves of Amber's dress, to cover the many scars left from where she had lost her arm in the accident. It had been her only concern with the dress. Shaun had picked them up from the store and brought them home with him, but when we examined them we found that Katies had put the covers into the wrong dress! I had a meltdown ... but got over it and got onto solving it. I don't know how many people we called, but 'that shop' opened very late on a Friday night and those dresses were fixed.

On Saturday, the ninth of May, 1981, I awoke to my wedding day.

I excitedly looked out the window and saw looming grey, wintery-looking clouds. *Bummer.* My unit was full of people—Mom, Mom G., sister, sister-in-law, brother, nieces, nephews, bridesmaids—all of them wanting a part of me. "Can you help me with my makeup?" "Can you do this up for me?" "Where did you put this?" I felt overwhelmed. *Geez, isn't this the bride's day? Aren't they my 'maids' for the day to look after me?* When I was at the hairdressers, I even had to make my way back in a taxi alone because everyone else had all gone and left me there.

The grey skies turned to snow, and then sleet made it difficult to walk. This was totally out of character for Melbourne, right? Nevertheless, if it could happen, it would happen to me and it would happen on my wedding day. It was freezing and my dress was an autumn dress.

When I arrived home, Mom shuffled me to the bathroom. She could see how stressed I had become. She filled the bath and made me get in. Mom sat by the side of the bath on the floor and washed my back, talking to me about enjoying the day and not letting everyone and everything get to me. I was frustrated and infuriated with some. I cried. I felt torn from pillar to post and the last thing I felt I could do was to relax and enjoy the day.

When I finished my bath, I went next door to my neighbor's place. The look on my face told them I needed somewhere to hide. They offered to make me a cup of coffee and give me some reprieve for a few moments, but then the photographer arrived. They helped me to get ready. Photos were taken and my little tomboy niece, who had been told not to run down the stairs on the way to the cars, ran and tripped, falling a few stairs down to the balcony. I was sad for her. She had grazed her leg and was quite upset, but she picked herself up and kept going. Tonka tough that one!

I reached the front door of the church where my brother put his arm out for me to hold. Danny was walking me down the aisle as my father hadn't responded to his wedding invitation. Even though I felt rather hurt by him refusing to come, I think I would have preferred Danny to do it anyway. He was the man in the family, not my father.

The music started. *Whiter Shade of Pale* by Procul Harum. It was played beautifully by the church organist, and together Danny and I made our way, knees shaking, towards the altar.

Danny turned to me and said, "You know only one of us is coming out of this the same, don't you?"

As I walked down the aisle, I could see my prince ahead. All the stress and troubles of the day just dissolved. He stood there tall and proud, his love for me on display for all to see. I was melting, my heart was pounding. He took my breath away and I just couldn't wait to be on his arm, as his wife. My heart started doing flip flops and my knees weakened just a little bit more. I found myself perspiring and depending on my brother to hold me up.

I wondered what Shaun was thinking as he stood there smiling, with that crazy, cute smile that he has. He was looking down the aisle towards me. *Does he like what he sees?* I wondered. He looked so handsome, so noble in his Army uniform, as did the groomsmen. Our best man was not in the Army so we blended him in with a green velvet suit. The brass from the buckle on Shaun's belt was shined so highly to military standard that it glinted when it captured the lights from the altar. We walked further up the aisle and I noticed the creases on Shaun's pants where they met his knees were shaking, as were the tips of his fingers.

He is as nervous as I am, but not for the same reason. I was the bride and I think it is a natural state for a bride to be nervous on her wedding day. Shaun was not a public speaker back then and we had an audience; he was petrified.

I walked past my mother and she smiled and reached over to hold my hand. I grabbed her hand briefly and she squeezed mine, but I continued the march forward, getting closer and closer to the moment when I would be the wife of the gorgeous man waiting for me at the altar. We reached Shaun and my brother passed my hand to him.

"Good luck," Danny whispered. Then he took a seat next to Mom. Shaun put his arm around me and immediately started to fiddle with the back of my dress, something he still does today when he is uncertain of a situation.

He bent down and whispered in my ear, "You look absolutely gorgeous. I love you and thank God you came." As he took my hand in his, electricity tore through my body. My stomach was tumbling and my heart was pounding, but this time it was pounding with love. I felt like it would burst out of my chest. *Yes, I love this man and I am ready to be devoted to him for the rest of my life.* I had never been more certain of anything in my life.

When we looked into each other's eyes while the priest was talking about the love that we shared for each other, Shaun cried. I cried. I could see the waves of love radiating from him the entire time he said his vows. His heart was on his sleeve and open to receive me as his wife. His mother passed a tissue up to the altar so that he could wipe his eyes—I still have that tissue.

The old saying goes, "Happy is the bride who is rained upon." Well, it rained, hailed, sleeted, and snowed in Melbourne that day and I couldn't have been happier—and nothing has changed. My wedding was beautiful. When we walked out of the church to be pelted with confetti, the only ray of sunshine that had come out all day shone straight on us. It was just like a sign from God and was captured by the photographer's camera so that ray of sunshine could be kept in our lives forever. Shaun would not stop kissing me, no matter what I did or what the photographer said. Every time the photographer went to take a photo, Shaun would kiss me. Eventually, the photographer just gave up and we have a lovely wedding album filled with pictures of Shaun kissing me.

We had our reception in the middle of the Fitzroy Gardens in The Pavilion Reception Centre, a glasshouse. It was beautiful. We had great fun with our family and friends.

It was time for the bridal waltz, our first dance as husband and wife. Shaun held me tightly and looked down into my eyes. A smile spread across his face as he whispered, "I love you. You look so beautiful and you're all mine." We danced to Elvis Presley's *The Wonder of You*.

All the words to that particular song were very special; it was a song that was very meaningful for both of us. I looked up into his loving face and cried as he spun me around the floor. We invited our bridesmaids to join us with the groomsmen who were all in Army uniform and then played another appropriate song called *Soldier Boy* by The Shirelles.

Our dream wedding was followed by our dream honeymoon overseas, the first of many overseas journeys we would take together. See, people can be wrong. Shaun treated me, and still continues to treat me, like a queen. To me, he is and always will be my king. I would do anything for him. I love him.

∽

When we returned from our honeymoon, Amber invited us to her twenty-first birthday party. Edward and Jolene were there. Edward approached me to congratulate me on my marriage, while Jolene was shooting daggers in my direction again. I believe that she even tried to make me jealous at one stage, but all I felt for her was pity. Before Edward could reach me, Shaun was by my side with his arm around me, claiming me as his. Edward put his hand out to shake Shaun's hand and said, "The best man won. Do you mind if I kiss the bride?"

Shaun stepped in front of me and said, "Over my dead body." Edward backed off and walked away. God, that felt good.

It wasn't long before the Army posted us away from Melbourne, and two years later our little man Daniel was born, followed in very quick succession, twelve months later, by his younger brother Ashley. This was after having found a doctor who boo-hoo'd the old idea that a woman couldn't have multiple caesareans and agreed that I could have more babies. I had tried and failed with so many pregnancies we were beginning to think that it would never happen. And then it did—twice. Daniel and Ashley were both wanted and loved when they arrived, and always will be. Two more beautiful children; I really felt so very blessed. When I thought of those that I had to leave behind, Tammy and Jason, my heart always remained heavy. Things would change in the future, but for now I still legally could not have them with me. Every time I thought of the unborn babies that were taken from me, I grieved for them, and I still do. But I eventually learned the best thing was to continue to tell myself, that, for whatever reason, God wanted them to come back home to Him. It is the only thing that keeps me from going insane, to this day.

My pregnancy with Daniel was complicated by a gall bladder attack at eight months' gestation. They had to operate to remove my gall bladder as I was turning jaundiced and it was required to save both our lives. Ashley's pregnancy was totally effortless, although he was born four weeks premature. They were both delivered by caesarean section, with Shaun in attendance by the same doctor who recently delivered both of Daniel's children. My granddaughters!

Shaun is and always has been a devoted and loving husband and father. He would walk the floor at night with the boys when they teethed; he would get up in the middle of the night for feeds to let me rest. My sons adore him. He is their role model and much, much more. He was the miracle that I had waited and searched so hard to find. Finally, thank goodness, that miracle found me. There is a song called *To Sir With Love* by Lulu. It is the story of a male school teacher who patiently, lovingly, and respectfully takes students from a very rough London school and teaches them to respect and love themselves, and to have pride in who they are. Shaun is my "Sir". So honey, this book is for you, with all my love. Thank you. Thank you for believing in me.

18	Penitents	162
19	Double Trouble	169
20	The Great Escape	175
21	Goodness, Gracious Me	183
22	Weddings, Frogs & Toads	194
23	Changes in the Convent	207
24	The Three Stooges	213
25	Jealous Guy and Sweet Sixteen	220
26	Going Home to No Home	230
27	Jack	242
28	Homeless	253
29	My Rollercoaster Pregnancy	265
30	Motherhood & Memories	282
31	To Die or Not To Die	299
32	The Last Straw	313
33	Hello Sailor	325
34	Chance Number 2	344
35	Australia Day Weekend 1979	358
36	Chance Number 3	379
37	My Prince	393

Epilogue   413
About the Author   417
Good Shepherd Children International   419

Contents

Acknowledgements 9
My "Why" 11
Prologue 19

1 Daddy's Little Girl 21
2 Childhood Antics 28
3 The Confrontation 39
4 Changes 45
5 Runaway 55
6 P.S. Bubby, I Love You 65
7 On the Road Again 71
8 The Loss of Innocence 79
9 Groomed 91
10 Mislaid Innocence 106
11 Jingle Bells 114
12 Blah Blah Blah 118
13 Expelled 126
14 R.I.P. Saturday, 27 September 1969 131
15 The Not So Good Shepherd Orphanage 140
16 The Daily Grind 148
17 School Days 155

Epilogue

Over the years, I often sat and thought about Tammy and Jason in quieter moments and continued to guide my love to them on the wings of angels. I could not have known that they were being abused in the worse way possible. That was the last thought that had crossed my mind when I first left them with Jack, thinking it would be only temporary. For many years I believed them to be safe, until it became obvious they weren't. But that's another story… And not mine to share.

Over the years my efforts to maintain contact with them were thwarted at every turn. Every letter and card was returned unopened, every gift returned as well. Later on as they grew, all phone calls were monitored and their efforts to talk to me were guided by what they had to say, forced by the adults in their lives who should have been more mature. I knew that the words were not what they wanted to say. But, as it turns out, if you throw enough mud at somebody, some of it always has to stick. I would do anything to be able to go back and make it different for them, but until you live through this, you have no idea what the future holds. Quite simply you cannot live a life of regrets.

My relationship with my daughter Tammy has been strained now for nearly three years, but we are making tentative steps towards healing our relationship. My daughter is happily married and has four beautiful children.

My eldest son Jason has not had a good life. Fighting demons of mental illness combined with illegal street drugs has seen him homeless and living on the streets for many years. It seems that schizophrenia is hereditary.

My other two sons have grown beautifully—the product of a loving, stable family home and a father with good genetics! Both of them have flourished and have terrific careers. They survived and blossomed even through some very difficult circumstances with their older siblings. Daniel has married and has a beautiful wife Rebecca, who has given me two beautiful granddaughters, Angelina and Scarlett.

At age twenty-eight I was diagnosed with a terminal illness—Polycystic Kidney Disease or ADPKD. It is genetic. I am now in end stage renal failure and don't know how much longer my kidneys will hold out. They have done well so far and I hope that they continue to do well. I want to be around for a very long time. They have, though, overshadowed my entire life, and I have shielded myself from doing many things I would have liked to do because of them.

After twenty long years of Defense Force living, twenty-eight interstate moves in that time, many jobs, schools, and challenges, I'm happy to say that Shaun's and my relationship survived and thrived. This year Shaun and I celebrated our thirty-second wedding anniversary and nearly thirty-five years of living together. In that time we have never had one fight as we discuss everything. Sometimes these discussions may get a little loud, but we never fight.

He has been my rock, my savior, my knight in shining armor, my hero, and the love of my life. I would be lost without him. I do not need him to complete me, although having him around helps, so he says. We are so very lost without each other. He has taught me that I am an independent woman, who chooses to love him and keep him around.

Third time was a charm.

Together we have helped each other to grow. We still do, and neither of us regrets one minute of our lives together, even with the challenges that we have faced, and we have had many.

We re-affirmed our vows to each other on our twenty-fifth wedding anniversary, and I can honestly say that I love him a little more every day. If

EPILOGUE

you had told me thirty-five years ago that I was going to love him even more than I did then, I wouldn't have believed it. I stood in front of my gorgeous husband, family, and friends that day and said these words to him:

> *"Shaun, you have been more to me than a husband. You are the love of my life; you are every breath that I take, my soul mate, and my twin soul. Our lives are so entwined now that sometimes it is hard to know where mine ends and yours starts. We are so alike in so many things, yet so different, and that is what makes our marriage work so well. You have always loved and respected me, even though it has been rough sometimes. A lot of men in your position would have dropped the bundle many times over with me, but your kindness and patience has persisted and got us through."*

But marriage is more than just two people. Marriages are a combination of two people, their children, their closest family members, and the nearest and dearest of friends that enter that circle of love. Shaun and I have been very blessed to have all of the above. We are a very close knit family, having moved around Australia for twenty years in our marriage. Only having ourselves to depend on has brought us together. Along the way we have managed to make some very dear friends, who we just wouldn't be able to live without. So thank you, from the very bottom of my heart. A song by Elvis says it all ... *Memories*.

So that is my story. As you can see, there have been a lot of ups and downs over the years, but there was always hope. I'm not a millionaire. I haven't performed miracles. I can't even say that I am well known, but I have survived and thrived. I just want everyone going through similar circumstances to know that so long as you never give up hope, or never give in, you can do it too. You can survive, and thrive. You just have to believe in yourself; believe that you are strong enough to get through it. Be brave; take one step at a time. There is always a silver lining.

I hope that you too can find your person in shining armor, just like I did. I was very lucky that Cupid was around that night, but I firmly believe that enchanted evening, so long ago, was meant to be. My horoscope had given a hint of what was waiting for me. Would I have found him without that hint? I don't know.

There is so much more to my story … thirty-five years of it, but I have to end it somewhere. Thank you for sharing my journey. I hope that I have been able to take you on a journey of hope. Like I said at the start, I do not wish for you to think of me as the victim; I am far from it. I have had some tough times, but who hasn't? No, this story is much more than that. It is a testimony of hope. *My gift to you and a gift to myself.*

A wise man once said, *"When you come to the last page, close the book."* Very wise words indeed. I look forward to an amazing future and all that it will bring. The book is now closed.

About the Author

Sandi Gamble is the first-time author of *Broken: An Extraordinary Story of Survival by One of Australia's Forgotten Children.* Sandi was born Beverley Forster and grew up in Melbourne, Victoria, Australia. She was brought up in a very turbulent time in Australia's history at the end of the Second World War when many families were being torn apart by the problems facing the returning veterans, and as such she became part of a generation of forgotten children, better known as Forgotten Australians. There are recurring themes in the lives of many of the 500,000 Forgotten Australians: placement in institutionalized state and Church homes, neglect, disconnection, loss of identity, sexual and emotional abuse, self-harm, and dysfunctional relationships, to name a few. Sandi managed to overcome the many such obstacles from her childhood and went on to become a woman of substance, one who always reaches out to help others.

Throughout her professional life, Sandi has worked in various Australian Government departments in Customer Service and Training. She is a qualified NLP Life Coach and is currently studying to be a counselor so that she might be of service to other Forgotten Australians who have not yet found their way out of the dark. Sandi's message is that life is not hopeless; there is always a silver lining that you can keep moving towards, leaving your past behind to create a better future. In writing her memoir, Sandi actually walked back to her past but as an important part of her personal healing journey. While her healing journey is far from over, she feels better equipped to cope with any issue that should arise in the future. She hopes and prays that her story can provide inspiration for those who remain burdened by their past and for those trying to understand loved ones whose past is impacting their life now.

Sandi's favorite quote, which is the mantra for her life, is as follows:

"You are not responsible for the negative programming you picked up in childhood. However, as an adult you are one hundred percent responsible for fixing it." Ken Keys Jnr.

Connect with Sandi:

Website: www.sandigamble.com
Facebook: https://www.facebook.com/AuthorSandiGamble

Good Shepherd Children International

Good Shepherd Children International is a privately owned site set up so that children, now adults, who had been kept in the care of the Good Shepherd could reconnect with their peers and heal. We do not have any nuns, auxiliarys or priests on the site. The site is owned and run by Sandi Gamble and is by invitation only.

To request an invitation please send your details including the convent that you were kept in and your email address to: sandi.gamble@bigpond.com

The site, as at the date of printing, has 84 members from all over Australia and one from Ireland. If you were kept in any Good Shepherd institution, this is your site: **http://goodshepherdgirls.ning.com**

Profound healing takes place when people open up and socialize with their peers.